A Dictionary of
Human Resource Ma

A Dictionary of

Human Resource Management

Edmund Heery

Mike Noon

OXFORD
UNIVERSITY PRESS

OXFORD
UNIVERSITY PRESS

Great Clarendon Street, Oxford OX2 6DP

Oxford University Press is a department of the University of Oxford.
It furthers the University's objective of excellence in research, scholarship,
and education by publishing worldwide in

Oxford New York

Auckland Cape Town Dar es Salaam Hong Kong Karachi
Kuala Lumpur Madrid Melbourne Mexico City Nairobi
New Delhi Shanghai Taipei Toronto
With offices in
Argentina Austria Brazil Chile Czech Republic France Greece
Guatemala Hungary Italy Japan South Korea Poland Portugal
Singapore Switzerland Thailand Turkey Ukraine Vietnam

Oxford is a registered trade mark of Oxford University Press
in the UK and in certain other countries

Published in the United States
by Oxford University Press Inc., New York

© Edmund Heery and Mike Noon, 2001

The moral rights of the authors have been asserted
Database right Oxford University Press (maker)

First published 2001

All rights reserved. No part of this publication may be reproduced,
stored in a retrieval system, or transmitted, in any form or by any means,
without the prior permission in writing of Oxford University Press,
or as expressly permitted by law, or under terms agreed with the appropriate
reprographics rights organization. Enquiries concerning reproduction
outside the scope of the above should be sent to the Rights Department,
Oxford University Press, at the address above

You must not circulate this book in any other binding or cover
and you must impose this same condition on any acquirer

British Library Cataloguing in Publication Data

Data available

Library of Congress Cataloging-in-Publication Data
A dictionary of human resource management /
  [compiled by] Edmund Heery and Mike Noon.
    p. cm.
  Includes bibliographical references.
  1. Personnel management—Dictionaries. I. Heery, Edmund. II. Noon, Mike.
HF5549.A23 D53 2001   658.3'003—dc21   2001021770

ISBN 0–19–829618–5
ISBN 0–19–829619–3 (pbk.)

10 9 8

Typeset by Charon Tec Pvt. Ltd, Chennai, India
Printed in Great Britain on acid-free paper by
Antony Rowe Ltd., Chippenham, Wiltshire

To our parents

Irene and Mattie
    and
Audrey and Ken

Preface

'Something to do when it's too wet for train-spotting' was the response of one of our colleagues when he learnt we had begun work on a dictionary of human resource management. In fact, neither of us has ever been of the train-spotting persuasion though we admit that over the past twelve months we have become obsessive about collecting and defining HRM terms. A number of people have helped feed our obsession. First, and largely responsible for the exercise, are students at Cardiff and De Montfort universities who agreed it was a good idea and who market-tested the first definitions. It was their feedback that convinced us we were not becoming peculiar and that the dictionary would meet a real need of those studying HRM, industrial relations, and other degree courses that involve analysis of the employment relationship. Another source of reassurance has been David Musson, our editor at Oxford University Press, who backed the project from the outset and who has provided constructive criticism and support throughout. We would also like to convey our appreciation to the scores of authors whose work we have mined for terminology and meanings. Particularly useful sources included Derek Torrington and Laura Hall's textbook *Human Resource Management*, and similar volumes by Ian Beardwell and Len Holden, Karen Legge, Ashly Pinnington and Tony Edwards, Stephen Bach and Keith Sisson, Mick Marchington and Adrian Wilkinson, and Graham Hollinshead and his colleagues at the University of the West of England. Other invaluable sources were Michael Jefferson's *Principles of Employment Law*, *People Management* magazine, and the booklets, commentaries, and reports produced by ACAS, the Health and Safety Executive, and the Institute of Employment Rights. We decided early on not to include references in the dictionary entries and would like to acknowledge the debt we owe to the many scholars, journalists, and commentators whose work we have drawn upon to help compose the entries. Finally, thanks are due to Carolyn and Janet for trying to understand our obsession and to the Heery offspring for surrendering the PC on Sunday mornings. Now that the job is finished we are both going to try and get out more.

E.H.
M.N.

October 2000

Contents

Preface   vii

Introduction   x
   Why a Dictionary of HRM?   x
   Coverage   xii
   Themes   xv
   Types of Entry   xviii
   Using the Dictionary   xxii

The Dictionary   1

Appendix 1: Classification of Key Terms   415

Appendix 2: Abbreviations and Acronyms   435

Introduction

Why a Dictionary of HRM?

Human resource management (HRM) is an expanding field of business education and academic research that is served by a growing body of literature. In the UK alone there are two academic journals devoted to the field of HRM—the *Human Resource Management Journal* and the *International Journal of Human Resource Management*—and several others that cover its subject matter. There are also some high-quality textbooks that summarize theory and research and describe current management practice for students (e.g. Bach and Sisson 2000; Beardwell and Holden 1997; Legge 1995; Marchington and Wilkinson 1996; Pinnington and Edwards 2000; Torrington and Hall 1998). Nowhere, however, is there a concise guide to the many theoretical and technical terms that are used by academic researchers and commentators and those practising in the field of HRM. The aim of this dictionary is to rectify this deficiency by providing concise, easily comprehensible definitions of HRM terms.

A dictionary is needed because the language of HRM can be obscure and difficult for those new to the field, particularly for those who are not native English speakers. Partly this is because HRM has its fair share of pretension, cliché, and euphemism: we have entries for 'downsizing', 'dumb-sizing', 'rightsizing', and 'upsizing'. It is also due to management fashion and the transient jargon promoted by consultants: we have entries for 'stick to the knitting', 'management by walking about', 'tough love', 'walk the talk', and 'business process re-engineering'. The prime, and perfectly legitimate, reason, however, is that any field of academic enquiry and professional practice requires a technical language to provide exactness and express its particular ideas, issues, and concerns. While we have taken pleasure in puncturing pretension, therefore, our main purpose has been to provide clear, unfussy definitions of the many technical and theoretical terms that a person studying or practising HRM is likely to encounter. From 'absenteeism' to 'zero-hours contracts', 'vertical segregation' to 'continuous professional development', 'expectancy theory' to 'personality tests', we have tried to make the language of HRM transparent.

The dictionary has been written mainly with student readers in mind and is designed as a supplement to any of the main HRM textbooks currently available. We have written for the novice exposed to the language of HRM for the first time, either on a specialist course or within a general business and management programme that includes elements of HRM. In our experience even the most basic textbooks assume some prior knowledge and can use language that students find difficult. The dictionary is offered as a support in this kind of situation. If students encounter puzzling references to 'mediation', 'mission statement', 'model employer', 'moments of truth', 'monopsony wage', 'Myers–Briggs type indicator', or 'mystery shopper' then it can solve the puzzle and allow learning to proceed.

We hope that it will also benefit other readers. University teachers on HRM, industrial relations, work sociology, employment law, occupational psychology, and other courses should find it a useful aid. We know from our daily work that teachers of HRM are continually defining terms, clarifying concepts, describing techniques, and explaining theories to students in their lectures, seminars, and tutorials. The dictionary should help with all these activities. Practitioners may also find it useful. While a single volume of this kind cannot match the detailed handbooks on employment law and other aspects of HRM that managers and trade union officers use, it may serve as a first port of call in dealing with an issue. We have covered a substantial portion of UK and European employment legislation and there are entries dealing with all the key HR processes that are regulated by law, including discipline, dismissal, equal opportunities, trade union recognition, transfer of undertakings, and working time. Practitioners may also find the dictionary helpful in decoding the mass of information they receive from the business media, government agencies, management consultants, and their own professional organizations. The dictionary is topical and covers issues, policies, and techniques that have currency in the real world of HRM. Thus, there are entries on 'e-recruitment', 'work–life balance', 'managing diversity', 'competence-' and 'team-based pay', and 'stakeholder pensions'. For those who have to keep abreast of the latest developments in HRM the dictionary should provide a rich source.

Coverage

HRM has no single accepted definition itself and in our entry for 'human resource management' we have listed ten current uses of the term. Setting complexity aside, however, it can be said that the academic field of HRM tends to be defined in two competing ways (Noon 1992: 16–18). On the one hand it is defined in terms of a particular approach or historical phase in the management of employees (Storey 1995). HRM, on this view, has supplanted traditional personnel management and is distinguished by the integration of human resource policies with wider business strategy and the adoption of sophisticated management techniques, targeted at individual employees, that result in flexibility, high commitment, high performance, and quality (Guest 1987; Poole and Warner 1998*b*). On the other hand, HRM can be defined more loosely as the study of a particular field of management activity, which implies no particular approach. Thus, Sisson (1990: 1) in his introduction to the first edition of the *Human Resource Management Journal* defined the subject matter of HRM as pertaining 'to the policies, procedures and processes involved in the management of people in work organizations'.

It is this second, looser, definition that has guided the compilation of the dictionary. Terms that relate to the first, specific, usage have been included and there is a series of entries that describe the contours of 'high commitment management' (e.g. strategic integration, internal fit, organizational commitment, functional flexibility, responsible autonomy, teamworking, Total Quality Management). But we have defined our terrain broadly and included words that extend far beyond this narrow definition. The unglamorous but worthy lexicon of traditional personnel management is thoroughly represented (e.g. recruitment, selection, training, job analysis, job evaluation, payment system, redundancy, and retirement). So too is the retro language of rediscovered industrial relations and there is broad coverage of trade unions and collective bargaining, reflecting the recent revival of collective institutions, at least in the United Kingdom.

In mainland Europe, collectivism never experienced the shock that it felt in Britain in the 1980s, and in Germany, France, Ireland, Italy, Sweden, and the Netherlands, there is less of a sense of system transformation than in the UK. What has occurred in Europe, however, has been the movement towards economic and political integration with the development of European social policy in its wake. Despite the weakness of many measures adopted and the continuing disappointment of many progressive pro-Europeans, EU social policy now casts a long and lengthening shadow over the field of HRM (Taylor 1998: 299–301). This is reflected in the content of the dictionary. The institutions and processes of the European Union are covered (e.g. European Court of Justice, directive, negotiation track, qualified majority voting, UNICE) as are the main themes in its social policy (e.g. Acquired Rights Directive, collective redundancy, European works council, National Action Plan, parental leave, Part-Time Workers Directive). In addition, we have included terms that relate to the practice of HRM in the separate member states of the EU, reflecting the growing integration of national economies and interest in learning from different traditions. Thus, we have entries for 'codetermination', 'works council', 'worker director', 'extension procedure', 'social pact', 'social partner', and similar terms that have crossed the English Channel and now form part of the language of HRM in the UK.

HRM is a field of study (and management practice) and not an integrated discipline, like psychology or economics. As a consequence, its boundaries are fuzzy and encompass a range of academic disciplines which have competing assumptions and methods but share an interest in the employment relationship. These characteristics are reflected in the content of the dictionary. Fuzziness can be seen in the inclusion of terms that extend beyond the management of employees narrowly conceived. Thus, we have included terms that refer to the organizations of employees themselves and the expression of employee voice through trade unions and other representative bodies (e.g. trade union, shop steward, full-time officer, closed shop, staff association, professional association). There is also extensive coverage of the actions of states and supranational bodies, like the International Labour Organization, that become involved in regulating management action (e.g. corporatism, employment law, Equal Opportunities Commission, international labour standards, regime shopping, tripartite regulation, voluntarism). Finally, coverage of management has been extended upwards away from the employment relationship to embrace wider issues of business organization (e.g. boundaryless organization, decentralization, diversification, extended organization, M-form, modular organization) and business strategy (e.g. balanced scorecard, cost minimization, first-order strategy, quality enhancement, resource-based view, short-termism, sustained competitive advantage, table stakes). We felt inclusion of the latter type of term was particularly important given the emphasis in recent writing on 'integration' and 'fit'; that is, the deliberate linking of human resource policy to wider developments in business management (e.g. Lawler 1990; Tyson 1995).

The dictionary also contains terms drawn from a variety of academic disciplines. Psychology is probably the major contributor, reflecting its practical application in the fields of recruitment, selection, training, and reward. We have entries for the major psychological theories that inform HRM research (e.g. attribution theory, equity theory, ERG theory, reinforcement theory) and the central concepts of work psychology (e.g. dual commitment, intrinsic reward, job satisfaction, leadership, self-efficacy). Other significant contributions are taken from organizational behaviour (e.g. contingency theory, goal displacement, organizational culture, role conflict), sociology (e.g. effort bargain, emotional labour, flexible specialization, protective practice, social movement theory), and economics (human capital theory, internal labour market, monopoly wage, transaction costs). Employment law is also very well represented, while other disciplines, such as political science, have provided occasional entries. As HRM has matured as a field of study it has begun to produce its own theoretical equipment and agenda for research, for example on the link between HR practice and business performance (Godard and Delaney 2000; Whitfield and Poole 1997). But it continues to be shaped by the established social science disciplines and the content of the dictionary reflects this.

Themes

In compiling the dictionary we have divided the field of HRM into sections or themes. Entries are presented conventionally from A to Z but they were collected under thirteen headings. These are as follows:

1. *Employee resourcing.* The first group of entries covers the processes of obtaining a workforce and releasing employees when they are no longer needed or wish to move on. It includes definitions of the full range of recruitment and selection techniques used by employers (e.g. assessment centre, interview, job description, psychometric test) plus more general terms, reflecting different approaches to the management of human resource 'flow' through the organization (e.g. casualization, human resource planning, meritocratic organization).

2. *Work organization and working time.* Entries under this heading cover the organization of work and working time, including new developments associated with employers' search for flexibility in the use and deployment of labour. Specific features of work organization and working time are included (e.g. annual-hours contracts, just-in-time) together with general terms that relate to broad trends in the way in which work is organized (e.g. lean production). Current developments in work organization are fully covered (e.g. hot-desking, mass customization, teleworking).

3. *Employee development.* This group of entries covers the techniques and processes through which employees acquire skills and competencies. Terms relate to deliberately managed training and development activities (e.g. outward bound courses, training needs analysis) and to less structured, informal processes through which workers learn (e.g. learning climate, workplace learning). There is also coverage of recent government initiatives to promote training and raise skill levels across the working population (e.g. Investors in People, Modern Apprenticeship, University for Industry).

4. *Employee reward.* This is the longest group of entries, reflecting the extensive technical language that has been developed to manage the process of remuneration. All aspects of reward management are covered, including the setting of pay rates, payment systems, payment structures, and workplace benefits (e.g. pay determination,

performance-related pay, pay spine, occupational pension). In addition to the techniques of remuneration, entries cover underlying economic and psychological theories that have been developed to interpret the process of reward in employing organizations.

5. *Employee involvement and participation.* Entries under this heading relate to the techniques developed by employers to communicate with and involve their employees in aspects of business decision-making. As such, they describe the management agenda for worker participation. This has been an expanding element within HRM and entries cover the full list of employee involvement techniques that have been applied in recent years (e.g. kaizen, quality circles, team briefing). There are also entries on financial participation and profit-sharing, aspects of reward that are intended to foster employee identification with the employer.

6. *Conflict and control in employment.* Entries collected under this heading cover the generation, expression, regulation, and control of conflict within the employment relationship. They include terms that relate to the open expression of conflict through the institutions of collective industrial relations (e.g. arbitration, overtime ban, strike, work-to-rule). Also included, however, are less visible types of conflict (e.g. fiddles, restriction of output, sabotage) and the procedures and techniques that employers use to ensure management control of work and workers (e.g. consumer reports, disciplinary procedure, surveillance).

7. *Discrimination and equality.* This is another long list of entries, reflecting the continued elaboration of the equality agenda in European and domestic employment law and in management practice. Entries cover all aspects of discrimination and equality at work in the fields of sex, race, disability, age, and sexual orientation. Legal concepts and terminology are fully covered (e.g. direct discrimination, equal value, positive action), together with management and trade union initiatives to promote equal treatment (e.g. contract compliance, equal pay audit, equality bargaining, mainstreaming, Opportunity 2000).

8. *Health, safety, and welfare.* An extremely important, though little researched, area of HRM is that which concerns health and safety and employee welfare. Entries have been included that cover the main elements of health and safety law and processes of inspection and

enforcement (e.g. duty of care, Health and Safety Executive, noise at work, risk assessment, vibration). Also covered are current initiatives in the field of employee welfare, such as stress management and the provision of health education at the place of work.

9. *Management roles, techniques, and strategies.* While the first eight categories cover different aspects of the process of management, the ninth category covers management itself. Entries under this heading include those which describe different management functions and roles and the organizations of managers and employers (e.g. champion of change, Chartered Institute of Personnel and Development, employers' association, line manager, personnel management, re-engineering tsar). Also included are generic management techniques, such as SWOT and PEST analysis, and terms used to analyse different aspects of management strategy (e.g. second-order strategy, macho management, polycentric management, portfolio planning, synergy).

10. *Employee representation.* Terms included under this heading relate to another of the primary 'actors' in the employment relationship. The majority refer to trade unions, the primary representative organizations of employees, and include definitions of union types (e.g. business unionism, closed union, craft union, open union), union roles (e.g. activist, convenor, general secretary, organizer), and aspects of union organization and behaviour (e.g. union democracy, union density, union renewal). Other definitions included in this category refer to alternative systems of worker representation, such as those based on works councils or non-union staff and professional associations.

11. *Collective bargaining.* Entries in this category describe the institutions of collective industrial relations. They include a range of terms that relate to the central activity of collective bargaining (e.g. bargaining unit, enterprise bargaining, industry bargaining, joint regulation), plus terms that cover other aspects of the collective relationship between employers and trade unions (e.g. certification, disclosure of information, labour–management partnership, union voice).

12. *National and international regulation of employment.* The third main actor in the employment relationship is the state and its agencies. This category covers government regulation of the employment relationship through law and other mechanisms at both national and

supranational levels. Many entries relate to the institutions and policies of the British state (e.g. Advisory, Conciliation, and Arbitration Service, employee assistance programme, Low Pay Commission) but there is also extensive coverage of international regulatory bodies, including the European Union and the International Labour Organization. The trend towards globalization and resulting pressure for closer regulation of international labour markets is reflected in the inclusion of terms relating to the formulation of international labour standards (e.g. corporate codes of conduct, freedom of association, Declaration of Philadelphia). While many entries refer to specific institutions and policies, others under this heading describe broad patterns of state intervention in the employment relationship (e.g. counter-mobilization, juridification, social partnership, statutory regulation, union exclusion).

13. *Concepts and theories used to study HRM.* The final category includes social science concepts and theories that are used to study or analyse HRM. Most of these terms have a general relevance to the study of the employment relationship and are not restricted to particular aspects of management. They include broad theoretical and ideological currents (e.g. behaviourism, Marxism, syndicalism), more specific theories or bodies of theory (e.g. attribution theory, labour process theory, regulation theory), and key theoretical and methodological concepts (e.g. determinism, market failure, path dependent, perverse effect).

To assist readers in identifying linkages between entries, in Appendix 1 we have grouped all definitions into these thirteen categories. The intention is to allow the easy identification of associated terms so that a reader interested in the areas of 'employee development' or 'employee representation', for example, can find a cluster of definitions with a common theme.

Types of Entry

While entries can be classified in terms of their subject matter, and the aspect of HRM with which they deal, they can also be classified in terms of the type of word or term defined. HRM is an applied academic field and we were conscious from the outset that the dictionary must include relatively abstract theoretical and conceptual terms drawn from the core social sciences, plus descriptive terms relating to the specific techniques and, often mundane, practice of human resource management. Both kinds of term have been included in the dictionary. In fact, we feel that that there are five main types of terms defined in the dictionary.

The first type includes theoretical terms. At one extreme we have concise definitions of general theories of society, social change, and human behaviour that inform the analysis of HRM. For example, there are several definitions that express the idea that we are witnessing a fundamental change in the way in which work is organized and experienced with important consequences for the management of people in employing organizations. These terms are often prefixed with the word 'post-' and include 'post-Fordism', 'post-industrial society', and 'postmodernism' (Crouch 1999: 39–43). At the other extreme are the tightly framed theories favoured by economists and psychologists, which consist of specific hypotheses that rest on clearly articulated theoretical assumptions. Examples of these 'middle-range' theories within the dictionary include 'efficiency wage' and 'principal–agent' from economics and 'needs theory' and 'Herzberg's two-factor theory' from psychology. Another type of theoretical, or perhaps more accurately ideological, term that has been included is those that express a particular, broad perspective on HRM. Thus, there are entries for the main 'frames of reference' (which is itself defined) identified by industrial relations researchers, such as 'pluralism' and 'unitarism'. These are based on competing interpretations of the scope for conflict and co-operation within the employment relationship. Essentially, pluralists assert that the existence of conflicting interests between workers and managers generates a need for independent trade union representation, while unitarists emphasize the scope for co-operation and tend to deny that independent representation is necessary (Heery 1993).

The second type of term overlaps with the first and includes key theoretical concepts. These are terms with a more specific meaning that have been developed within a particular body of theoretical knowledge or, alternatively, within a prescriptive framework designed to guide management action. As such, they constitute the building blocks or constituent elements of theories and models of HRM. We have definitions for all the main concepts that have been employed in the continuing debate about the meaning, causes, and effects of human resource management, including 'soft HRM', 'hard HRM', 'bleak house', 'competency', 'empowerment', 'functional flexibility', 'high commitment management', and 'competitive advantage'. We have also included concepts from alternative theoretical traditions and perspectives. In industrial relations theory, for instance, a central claim has been that employer and trade union behaviour is powerfully determined by the structure of collective bargaining (Clegg 1976; Sisson 1987). Accordingly, we have entries for the main dimensions of bargaining structure, such as 'bargaining coverage', 'bargaining level', and 'bargaining scope'. Also covered by this heading are entries that describe central concepts in employment law. There are entries that refer to legal concepts in the common law of contract (e.g. express term, implied term, wrongful dismissal), in UK statute law (e.g. reasonableness, redundancy, unfair dismissal), in the law of the European Union (e.g. derogation, subsidiarity), and in international law (e.g. child labour, social clause).

The next category of definition is more concrete and includes terms that describe management and other processes that affect the employment relationship. Many of these terms have a specific meaning within particular theories of HRM but they also have a general currency and are used widely in common management parlance. They describe the activities that arise at each stage of the employment relationship, from the employee joining to his or her leaving the organization. Thus, there are entries for 'recruitment', 'selection', 'induction', 'appraisal', 'training', 'employee involvement', 'reward management', 'promotion', 'discipline', 'dismissal', and 'retirement'. There are also entries that address the processes of collective industrial relations (e.g. collective bargaining, joint consultation) and the ways in which the state intervenes in and regulates the employment relationship (e.g. employment law, dispute resolution, social partnership).

Yet more specific are entries that describe particular techniques or tools for practising human resource management. This is probably the largest group of entries within the dictionary. It embraces different methods of recruitment and selection (e.g. blacklisting, contingent work, critical incident job analysis, expatriation, in-tray exercise), different approaches to employee development (e.g. action learning, apprenticeship, career management, continuous learning, mentoring), techniques of appraisal (e.g. behaviourally anchored rating scales, peer appraisal, self-appraisal, 360-degree feedback, 540-degree feedback) and different types of collective agreement between employers and trade unions (e.g. concession bargaining, facilities agreement, pattern bargaining, productivity bargaining). There are also entries for different forms of work organization and different approaches to corporate strategy, reflecting the coverage of issues that extend beyond the management of employees narrowly conceived. A final group of entries that belong under this category are those that describe particular HR policy initiatives launched by business or by government. Examples include 'Baldridge Award', 'Management Charter Initiative', 'Race for Opportunity', 'Social Charter', and 'Welfare-to-Work'.

The fifth type of entry covers roles and institutions. Many of these describe different types of manager and management functions. Thus, there are entries for all the different roles assumed by HR specialists that have been identified by management theorists, including 'adviser', 'architect model', 'changemaker', 'clerk of works', 'contracts manager', 'handmaiden', 'internal consultant', 'management consultant', 'management guru', and 'regulator'. There are also entries for different forms of management and employer organization that are both general (e.g. confederation, pay club) and specific (e.g. Chartered Institute of Personnel and Development, Confederation of British Industry). In addition, and reflecting the broad scope of the dictionary, there are entries for non-management roles and institutions. Different representative positions in trade unions are described, as are different types of trade union, and we have included definitions of key labour organizations, including the Trades Union Congress and European Trade Union Confederation. Governmental institutions are also well represented. For the UK, there are entries that describe the activities of several important agencies that regulate or support the process of human resource management. These include the Commission for Racial Equality, the Disability Rights Commission, the Health and Safety Executive, JobCentres, the Office of Manpower Economics, and xxii *Introduction*

Pay Review Bodies. These are supplemented by entries for international institutions whose activities impinge with increasing significance on the work of HR managers in the UK and other countries. Examples of this type of entry include the Council of Europe, the European Court of Justice, the European Foundation for Quality Management, and the European Industrial Relations Observatory.

Using the Dictionary

The dictionary has been designed for ease of use. Entries are listed alphabetically and take two main forms. The first and largest group consists of full entries, where the term is accompanied by a definition. The second group comprises words that are not accompanied by a definition but which refer the reader to another entry. This is usually because these words are synonyms for other terms that have been fully defined. Examples of both types of entry are shown in Fig. 1.

Fig. 1. Specimen Entries

high commitment management (HCM) is an approach to the management of people that emphasizes the need to develop organizational commitment among the employees, on the assumption that this will lead to positive outcomes such as lower labour turnover, better motivation, and improved performance. The importance of increasing commitment has been recognized in various approaches to people management (for example, theory Y (see **theory X and theory Y**), **high trust**, **responsible autonomy**, and **employee involvement**) but was popularized in the 1980s by management theorist Richard Walton, whose **normative approach** advocates that organizations move from a strategy of 'control' to a strategy of 'commitment' in the management of employees. This reflects a concern amongst commentators at that time (particularly in the USA) that traditional methods (see **Fordism**) were no longer an appropriate means of organizing and managing people. This seemed particularly pertinent given that US organizations were faced with increasing competition from Japan and other countries in South-East

Asia, all of which had a different approach to management (see **theory Z**; **Japanization**) that seemed to be delivering good results in terms of productivity, profitability, and market share. More recently, HCM is being used as a general term that embraces a diverse range of human resource practices and techniques (sometimes labelled high commitment practices—HCPs) designed to improve the overall performance of the organization through generating commitment amongst the workforce. An alternative term, high involvement management, is used by some commentators. [See **high performance work practices**; **empowerment**; **soft HRM**.]

high commitment practice (HCP) see high commitment management

high involvement management see high commitment management

intrinsic reward A reward that is integral to work and which is obtained by performing work tasks. Examples of intrinsic rewards include **job satisfaction**, challenge, autonomy, pride in work, and a sense of achievement. [See **extrinsic reward**; **reward**.]

Japanization is the term used to describe changes in western industry that involve the adoption of techniques of managing and organizing production that were developed by Japanese-owned companies in Japan. In particular it centres on the use of production techniques such as **just-in-time** that require particular forms of external buyer–supplier relations and internal work organization, such as **teamworking** and **kaizen**. The term has been criticized for: (1) assuming that there is one 'Japanese way of managing' when in Japan there is a diverse range of strategies; (2) obscuring the viewpoint that the techniques are new methods of management control that have more to do with the conflict between management (capital) and employees (labour) than with that between nations; (3) overstating the extent of change and failing to acknowledge developments in the West, such as **Total Quality Management** or **functional flexibility**, that share similarities with the supposed Japanese model. Whilst accepting some of these criticisms, the main proponents of Japanization, organization theorists Nick Oliver and Barry Wilkinson, argue that the term remains an appropriate shorthand to describe the changes in UK industries that depend on ideas of organizing and managing transferred from Japan.

kaizen or continuous improvement is a concept that encourages employees and managers to look constantly for ways of making changes to any system or process that will improve performance. This idea stems from Japanese production systems, in particular those of the motor giants such as Toyota. Once an improvement has been suggested, it is evaluated and, if found to be of benefit, standardized across the operations. Critics sometimes argue that such a system is exploitative, since it captures the ideas of shopfloor employees, adopts them across the organization, and leads to performance improvements, but does not reward those who came up with the idea in the first place. Defenders of the system argue that employees experience the **intrinsic reward** of seeing their ideas put into practice and getting recognition from management—which in some cases might lead to more favourable appraisals or one-off bonuses.

normative approach A set of guidelines that state how things ought to be done. Therefore a normative theory or model typically tells us how various concepts or ideas should be linked together in order to produce certain desirable outcomes. A normative theory or model is not based on **empirical evidence**, but is a set of ideas that have been theoretically derived through a process of logical thinking.

Full entries are of variable length (compare high commitment management and intrinsic reward in Fig. 1), reflecting the variable complexity of terms being defined. They aim to give clear, readily understandable definitions of the meaning or meanings of HRM terms. In many cases they also provide some contextual background, provide illustrative examples, and, when a theory or concept is controversial, list some of the main criticisms. This relatively generous approach to definition is illustrated by the definitions of 'high commitment management', 'Japanization', and 'kaizen' in Fig. 1. We hope that it has resulted in a text that is more readable and a more useful guide than would have been the case if definitions had not been expanded. Although there are short, single-line entries where this is appropriate, we have tried to pitch many of the definitions midway between the extremely concise entries typically found in specialist dictionaries and the full-blown exposition of terms, complete with references, found in encyclopedias (cf. Black 1997; Poole and

Warner 1998a). We should also confess that we have not been shy of expressing opinions and, while much of the text is dispassionate, our own preferences, or 'normative approach', occasionally shine through.

Entries that are not accompanied by a definition are illustrated in Fig. 1 by 'high commitment practice' and 'high involvement management'. The latter of these terms is effectively a synonym for 'high commitment management', while a definition of the former is incorporated in the entry for 'high commitment management'. Other examples of terms without definitions include 'cost leadership', which is synonymous with 'cost minimization', 'culture', which is covered by 'organizational culture', and 'customer service questionnaires', which is embraced by 'consumer reports'. The inclusion of entries of this kind reflects the fact that the HRM vocabulary is marked by a multitude of parallel terms with identical or very similar meanings. By referring the reader to another, full definition, however, we hope to aid understanding of terms that are not themselves defined.

Fig. 1 also illustrates the cross-referencing of entries. Where an entry has a word or phrase in bold type this means that it is defined elsewhere in the dictionary. The entry for 'high commitment management', therefore, is linked to those for 'theory X and theory Y', 'high trust', 'responsible autonomy', 'employee involvement', 'normative approach', 'Fordism', 'theory Z', 'Japanization', and so on. The purpose of this cross-referencing is to allow readers to identify a cluster of terms dealing with a common theme, highlight the connections that can be made between discrete areas of HRM, and allow the ready movement between more abstract, conceptual entries and those that describe concrete practice. All three types of linkage can be seen in the five full entries in Fig. 1. Thus, there are two, associated entries (high commitment management and Japanization) that refer to recent developments in the design of work systems. The latter of these is then linked to a particular employee involvement technique (kaizen), which in turn is linked to the field of reward management via a cross-reference to 'intrinsic reward'. The relatively concrete definition of 'high commitment management', moreover, is linked to the more abstract 'normative approach' which describes a particular approach to theorizing within the field of HRM.

To aid further appreciation of the links between entries, Appendix 1 has been compiled. As we have explained, this consists of alphabetical lists of all entries under the thirteen thematic headings set out above. These lists present the theoretical and technical vocabulary for each of the main elements of HRM: employee resourcing, employee involvement, reward management, collective industrial relations, and so on. They are designed to highlight the natural clusters amongst entries and provide a second means whereby readers can find definitions of associated terms.

In addition, Appendix 2 consists of an extensive alphabetical listing of abbreviations and acronyms that appear in HRM texts. There are more than 500 entries that include the names of employers' organizations and trade unions, government agencies and programmes, major pieces of legislation and legal shorthand, management techniques and academic journals. The list is international in scope and includes the names of the main business and labour organizations from North America, Australia, Japan, and the European Union, complete with translation into English where this is appropriate. Acronyms that refer to entries in the main body of the dictionary are entered in bold type. The purpose of the list is to enable readers to check the full name of the many sets of initials that can confuse, but which liberally sprinkle the business press and academic literature on human resource management.

References

Bach, S., and Sisson, K. (2000), *Personnel Management: A Comprehensive Guide to Theory and Practice*. Oxford: Blackwell.

Beardwell, I., and Holden, L. (1997), *Human Resource Management: A Contemporary Perspective*, 2nd edn. London: Pitman Publishing.

Black, J. (1997), *Oxford Dictionary of Economics*. Oxford: Oxford University Press.

Clegg, H. A. (1976), *Trade Unionism under Collective Bargaining: A Theory Based on Comparisons of Six Countries*. Oxford: Basil Blackwell.

Crouch, C. (1999), *Social Change in Western Europe*. Oxford: Oxford University Press.

Godard, J., and Delaney, J. (2000), 'Reflections on the "High Performance" Paradigm's Implications for Industrial Relations as a Field', *Industrial and Labor Relations Review*, 53/3: 482–502.

Guest, D. (1987), 'Human Resource Management and Industrial Relations', *Journal of Management Studies*, 24/5: 503–21.

Heery, E. (1993), 'Industrial Relations and the Customer', *Industrial Relations Journal*, 24/4: 284–95.

Lawler III, E. E. (1990), *Strategic Pay: Aligning Organizational Strategies and Pay Systems*. San Francisco: Jossey-Bass Publishers.

Legge, K. (1995), *Human Resource Management: Rhetorics and Realities*. Basingstoke: Macmillan.

Marchington, M., and Wilkinson, A. (1996), *Core Personnel and Development*. London: Institute of Personnel and Development.

Noon, M. (1992), 'HRM: A Map, Model or Theory?', in P. Blyton and P. Turnbull (eds.), *Reassessing Human Resource Management*. London: Sage Publications.

Pinnington, A., and Edwards, T. (2000), *Introduction to Human Resource Management*. Oxford: Oxford University Press.

Poole, M., and Warner, M. (eds.) (1998a), *The IEBM Handbook of Human Resource Management*. London: Thomson Learning.

——, and —— (1998b), 'Introducing Human Resource Management', in M. Poole and M. Warner (eds.), *The IEBM Handbook of Human Resource Management*. London: Thomson Learning.

Sisson, K. (1987), *The Management of Collective Bargaining*. Oxford: Blackwell.

—— (1990), 'Introducing the *Human Resource Management Journal*', *Human Resource Management Journal*, 1/1: 1–11.

Storey, J. (1995), 'Human Resource Management: Still Marching on or Marching out', in J. Storey (ed.), *Human Resource Management: A Critical Text*. London: Routledge.

Taylor, R. (1998), 'Annual Review Article 1997', *British Journal of Industrial Relations*, 36/2: 293–311.

Torrington, D., and Hall, L. (1998), *Human Resource Management*, 4th edn. London: Prentice Hall.

Tyson, S. (1995), *Human Resource Strategy: Towards a General Theory of Human Resource Management*. London: Pitman Publishing.

Whitfield, K., and Poole, M. (1997), 'Organizing Employment for High Performance: Theories, Evidence and Policy', *Organization Studies*, 18/5: 745–64.

A

ability to pay is the principle that pay rates and pay increases should be set with primary regard to the financial performance of the individual employing organization. Ability to pay can be contrasted with other principles of **pay determination**, such as the **rate for the job** and **comparability**, which seek to establish a link between pay rates within the firm and those outside. According to some, the principle of ability to pay has exercised increasing influence over pay determination as a result of the decline of trade unions and **collective bargaining**.

absenteeism is the practice of regularly failing to turn up for work. Employees are contractually obliged to be available for work during specified hours, and failure to do so without legitimate reasons (for example, ill health) can result in **dismissal**. Therefore, the level of absenteeism is monitored closely by most organizations in order to identify employees who are in breach of their contracts of employment. If absenteeism persists, then it is good practice to provide counselling before moving on to any disciplinary procedures. It might be the case, for example, that absence is due to personal or family problems that the employee needs to address, and that given guidance and support a solution can be found. In some circumstances, absenteeism might be a symptom of problems at work—for example, stress, inability to cope, work overload—which counselling might be able to identify. Given the general tendency for employers to expect greater commitment (see **organizational commitment**) from their employees, absenteeism is increasingly likely to be viewed as a sign of low commitment and an inappropriate attitude. [See also **presenteeism**.]

ACAS see **Advisory, Conciliation, and Arbitration Service**

accreditation for prior learning (APL) occurs when students taking vocational qualifications are exempted from part of the programme of tuition because they can demonstrate they have already attained the level of competence required, either through taking another formal qualification or through their work and personal experience. APL is an important component of competency-based vocational education (see **National Vocational Qualifications**), where the emphasis is on the outputs of the programme (i.e. developing and demonstrating competencies) rather than the inputs (i.e. a period of time spent studying for a formal qualification).

Acquired Rights Directive see **Transfer of Undertakings (Protection of Employment) Regulations**

acquisition see **takeover**

action learning is a method of **management development** based on the completion of practical assignments and problem-solving tasks within business, which become the basis for reflection and learning.

action short of a strike Forms of **industrial action** that impose pressure on an employer through actions that fall short of a withdrawal of labour. These might include an **overtime ban**, **go-slow**, or **work-to-rule**. In the UK, 'cut price' industrial action of this kind has been estimated to be twice as common as striking.

action short of dismissal see **detriment**

activist A trade union member who is active either at workplace level or within the union's system of internal government. Union activists frequently assume a representative position, such as **shop steward** or branch officer, though occupancy of a formal office is not a condition of activism.

additional voluntary contributions (AVCs) are optional, extra payments made by an employee into an **occupational pension** fund to enhance the level of accrued benefits. AVCs attract tax relief and are a cost-efficient means of saving for retirement.

adhocracy is a term coined by management theorist Henry Mintzberg to describe an organization that is operating in a complex and dynamic competitive environment and consequently has very little formal structure. Typically such organizations will be highly technical in terms of their core business and will be composed of specialists and professionals. Adhocracy can be contrasted with **bureaucracy**. [See also **virtual organization**.]

adjourning is the fifth stage of the five-stage model of group development (see **stages of group development**).

adoption leave is a period of paid time off work that a man or woman is allowed to take on adopting a child. Adoption leave is not widespread—there is no legal provision in many countries. However, progressive organizations recognize that the adjustment of a parent to a new child is as important for adoptive parents as it is for birth parents.

adviser A role that can be adopted by a manager who is primarily responsible for personnel/human resources. Advisers act as internal consultants to other managers by providing strategic direction on the management of human resources. This strategic focus means they are less concerned with day-to-day personnel issues, and have passed on responsibility for this to line managers (see **devolution**). The term 'adviser' was coined by management theorist John Storey to describe one of four potential styles of managing human resources (the others being **changemaker**, **handmaiden**, and **regulator**).

Advisory, Conciliation, and Arbitration Service (ACAS) ACAS was created in the UK in the 1970s as part of the then Labour government's reform of industrial relations and is an independent statutory body charged with improving industrial relations and providing services for the resolution of collective and individual industrial **disputes**. ACAS is a tripartite institution whose council consists of an independent chair and representatives of business, labour, and academia, and whose workforce consists of civil servants specializing in industrial relations advice and dispute resolution.

Under the Employment Relations Act 1999, ACAS is charged with a general duty 'to promote the improvement of industrial relations', but its original mission to promote **collective bargaining** was withdrawn by the Conservative government in 1993. The main functions of ACAS are (1) to provide facilities for **conciliation**, **mediation**, **arbitration**, and enquiry in collective disputes; (2) to provide a free advisory service on industrial relations and human resource management; (3) to publish codes of practice on aspects of industrial relations; (4) to provide conciliation in individual employment disputes before they enter the **Employment Tribunal** system. Recent developments in ACAS's role include the broadening of its field of competence as the volume of individual employment law has increased, the introduction of arbitration as a means of resolving individual disputes, and the provision of extensively used telephone helplines on employment law and **personnel management**. In addition, ACAS has expanded its advisory work and developed a method of consultancy, based on **joint working parties**, that organizations can use to improve aspects of their industrial relations. ACAS publishes an annual report which describes its activities and includes a summary of developments on the UK employment scene.

affective commitment occurs when an employee stays with a particular organization because he or she shares its values and objectives, and feels a sense of loyalty. [See **organizational commitment**.]

affirmative action is the term used in the USA to describe initiatives designed to promote **equal opportunity** and redress the existing disadvantage experienced by some groups. It is a combination of both **positive action** and **positive discrimination**, backed up by affirmative action laws that developed out of the civil rights movements of the 1960s.

ageism is the practice of discriminating against someone on the basis of their age. It is based on the belief that age determines ability and level of performance, and that by categorizing people according to age it is possible to identify those most suited to particular roles and tasks within an organization. Typically, ageism is used to describe situations where older people are discriminated against in favour of younger people. However, the term equally applies to discrimination against younger people. [See **equal opportunity**.]

agency labour is labour that is provided by a private recruitment bureau or **employment agency**. The traditional function of such labour (**temps**) has been to cover for absence or provide additional support for short periods. There has been a movement in recent years, however, towards the supply of agency labour on a longer-term basis, known as **insourcing**. Agency labour has grown rapidly since the early 1990s and partly for this reason there have been a number of initiatives to regulate the industry and protect its workers. In 1997 the **International Labour Organization** passed a new Convention (No. 181) and Recommendation (No. 188) on Private Employment Agencies and a European **directive** on agency labour is pending. Partly in anticipation of the latter the UK government issued new regulations for the private recruitment industry in 2000, the key feature of which is to clarify the **employment status** of agency labour. In most cases agency workers are to be treated as employees of the supplying agency and therefore are entitled to the legal protection conferred by employee status.

agency theory see **principal–agent**

AIDS policy is developed to deal with the situation when employees develop acquired immune deficiency syndrome (AIDS). It is recommended officially that organizations develop such a policy. The main elements of an AIDS policy include: information about AIDS and how it is contracted; reassurance for those with the disease that they will be treated no differently from others with a serious illness; a procedure for dealing with those who refuse to work with AIDS sufferers (including disciplinary action); and steps to minimize the risk of infection for those administering first aid.

alcohol policy A company policy that regulates the consumption of alcohol by employees and in many cases states that the use of alcohol during work time, even when entertaining, is prohibited.

Alcohol policies also typically set out penalties for improper use or unauthorized drinking and may provide counselling and support for employees who are diagnosed as suffering from alcoholism.

All-Employee Share Plan An Inland Revenue-approved **employee share ownership** scheme that was established in the UK in 2000. Under the plan employers establish a trust which purchases shares and distributes them to all qualifying employees. 'Free' shares may simply be allocated to employees, though it is permissible to link shares to employee performance. Under another arrangement employees can purchase a 'matching' or 'partnership' share for each free share that is allocated. To encourage take-up of the scheme there are various tax benefits for both employers and employees. For example, employees who keep their shares in a plan for five years pay no income tax or National Insurance Contributions on those shares. [See **Save-As-You-Earn share option scheme**.]

all-out strike A **strike** that embraces all workers involved in a dispute and that will continue for 'as long as it takes' to secure a settlement. All-out strikes can be contrasted with **selective strikes** that involve only a proportion of the workforce and protest strikes that may last for only a day or two.

analyser A type of firm identified by Raymond Miles and Charles Snow in their typology of 'strategic types'. Analyser firms tend to avoid excessive risks but excel in the delivery of new products and services. Typically they will concentrate on a limited range of products and technologies and seek to outperform other companies on the basis of **quality enhancement**. [See **defender**; **prospector**; **reactor**.]

annual-hours contracts are contracts of employment where the total hours to be worked in a twelve-month period are specified, rather than the weekly hours. This provides employers with the flexibility to devise a shift system to ensure continuous operations. Traditionally annualized hours were adopted in the manufacturing sector, but increasingly it is a popular system for organizing work time in the service sector, especially where twenty-four-hour, seven-day-week services are provided.

annual leave or paid holiday entitlement has long been an important employee **benefit**, enjoyed by most UK employees. Until recently, however, there was no statutory entitlement to annual leave and many temporary and part-time employees were denied paid holiday. The adoption of the **Working Time Directive** by the European Union has changed this situation and under the working time regulations there is an entitlement to four weeks' paid leave for all employees who satisfy a three-month service requirement. This provision brings the UK in line with most other European countries, where there is a long tradition of statutory entitlement to paid annual leave.

application form A form completed by job applicants which provides the information on which initial **selection** decisions are based. Forms should be realistic and appropriate to the level of job to be filled and should ideally be piloted to ensure they can be readily understood and completed. Detailed personal information that is not relevant to the job should not be sought. Where information is requested for gender and ethnic monitoring it should be kept separate and used only for this purpose. Increasingly, application forms are designed in order to collect information relating to the main competencies required for a particular work role.

appraisal is the process of evaluating the performance and assessing the development/training needs of an employee. In other words, there are two sides to appraisal: (1) the judgmental side, where actual performance is compared against performance targets and feedback (positive and negative) is given; (2) the developmental side, where the needs of the individual are evaluated in terms of the training required to improve skill and knowledge in line with future performance objectives. The overall balance will vary from organization to organization, or even between different departments within the same organization. In some circumstances an appraisal is also used to determine the pay increase an employee will receive; thus, a favourable appraisal means a higher reward whereas a poor appraisal leads to no pay increase. The problem with linking an appraisal to a pay award is that it inhibits honesty and openness—employees are unlikely to point out the problems they have had, their shortcomings, and their training needs if they think this will have a negative effect on their pay. Therefore, the judgmental side tends to dominate, and the employee might become overly defensive. This is a problem because an appraisal is meant to be of mutual benefit to the employee and employer. Both parties gain because the appraisal is supposed to be a formal, well-structured, frank discussion of what the employee can offer and what support he or she needs from the organization, and what the organization expects and what it is prepared to give. But if the employee is feeling defensive, the frankness of the discussion will be compromised. Problems also occur if the appraisal is poorly structured—often through a lack of preparation by the appraiser—or if it is not treated seriously by one or both of the parties involved. When undertaken properly, the appraisal system involves a considerable amount of time and effort from managers, so, not surprisingly, there are management cynics in every workplace who view appraisal as an unnecessary bureaucratic exercise which takes them away from their 'real' work. Similarly there are cynical employees who view appraisal as an unnecessary hoop they have to jump through every year, because it makes no difference to how they undertake their work or the opportunities they are given. [See **self-appraisal**; **peer appraisal**; **360-degree feedback**; **attribution theory**.]

appraisal portfolio The set of techniques used to evaluate the performance of an employee. The portfolio may vary between departments within an organization, and in some circumstances the portfolio for each employee may vary within a department. While this might be acceptable to the employee—particularly if the employee has an influence in nominating the assessment techniques being used—it raises problems for comparability, fairness, and equal opportunities.

appraisal-related pay is the term preferred by ACAS to describe **merit pay** systems which link earnings to the results of an individual performance **appraisal**. ACAS has identified two main forms of appraisal-related pay. The first is 'performance-against-objectives', in which the award of a salary increase or bonus is dependent on the employee attaining a series of **SMART** objectives. The second is 'rating', in which employees are rated by a line manager on a series of work-related competencies. Under both systems employees are allocated to one of a limited number of overall performance categories which determine the level of reward they receive.

appraiser The person responsible for undertaking an **appraisal** of an employee (the appraisee). The appraiser is often the employee's line manager, since he or she is thought to have the best knowledge of the employee's performance, attitude, and competency. Whilst the line manager may be the best placed to be the appraiser, he or she does not necessarily have the appropriate skills to undertake an appraisal interview, so in some organizations the appraiser is a specialist from the personnel department.

apprenticeship is a fixed period of training in which a skill or craft is learned, and where a contract is signed by the employer which protects the apprentice from being fired prior to the completion of the training. Nowadays, apprenticeships are rare and trainees are more likely to have training agreements that specify the type of training they will receive and the standards they must achieve. In the UK, the standards are frequently based on specifications set out in National Vocational Qualifications, which means the successful trainee gets a nationally recognized training certificate.

Approved Code of Practice (ACOP) Issued by the **Health and Safety Executive** under the **health and safety regulations**, ACOPs are designed to provide detailed guidance to employers on how to comply with health and safety law. Like other statutory **codes of practice** they are not legally binding, but a failure to comply with the code may be used as evidence against an employer by a court of law.

approved profit-sharing (APS) see profit-sharing

arbitration is a means of resolving **industrial conflict** through the involvement of a third party, an arbitrator, who recommends a solution to the dispute. In most cases the decision of the arbitrator is binding on the parties to the dispute, hence 'binding arbitration'. In the UK arbitration services are mainly provided by ACAS and arbitration is used to resolve both collective and individual disputes at work. Arbitration is an important means of avoiding the outbreak of or resolving strikes and other forms of industrial conflict.

architect model of personnel management. One of three types of managers identified by management theorists Shaun Tyson and Alan Fell (the other types being **clerk of works** and **contracts manager**). The 'architect' is characterized as a type of personnel manager who is strategically involved in the business, with an important role in ensuring that employment policies are appropriate to the wider business strategy. They are creative and innovative in devising policy.

Article 6 agreement An agreement setting up a **European works council** or equivalent information and consultation procedure that has been negotiated through a **Special Negotiating Body**.

Article 13 agreement A voluntary agreement between a multinational company operating in Europe and its workforce to establish an information and consultation procedure on transnational issues; that is, a **European works council**. Companies with an agreement of this kind in place are exempt from the requirements of the European Works Council Directive 1994 under Article 13, provided they negotiated the voluntary agreement before 22 September 1996. It has been estimated that there are approximately 400 of these voluntary agreements in large European companies, most of which were signed in the two years immediately prior to the 1996 deadline. The advantage to companies of concluding this kind of agreement in advance of the directive was that it gave maximum scope to develop an information and consultation procedure suited to the structure and traditions of the firm. [See **subsidiarity**.]

articulation is a term used in academic **industrial relations** to refer to the integration of **trade union** activity or **collective bargaining** at industry and local levels of the **industrial relations system**.

For example, bargaining could be described as articulated if **framework agreements** negotiated at industry level contain opening clauses that allow further negotiations on specific topics at enterprise level.

assessment centre A selection technique typically used for appointments to posts that will involve considerable investment in future career development. For example, many employers recruit graduates onto management training schemes and their methods of selection often include an assessment centre. Although time-consuming and costly, assessment centres are deemed to be appropriate because they allow candidates to be assessed over several days using a range of tests and simulation exercises. This produces a more rounded view of the candidates, potentially leading to better-quality selection decisions. Critics argue that assessors rarely use all the dimensions tested in the assessment centre when making their final decisions, and although assessment centres score high on reliability, they often rate poorly in terms of predictive validity.

associate is the preferred description for an employee in a growing number of companies, particularly those that are seeking to generate **organizational commitment** among the workforce.

at-risk pay is that proportion of remuneration which is contingent on a measure of employee, workgroup, or organizational performance and which has to be 're-earned' in each pay period. At-risk pay is also known as **variable pay** and there has been a shift in the management of pay in recent years towards reliance on this kind of reward. Companies have been advised by pay consultants to reduce the proportion of consolidated base salary within total remuneration and expand that which is at risk, in order to maximize management control over worker behaviour. Examples of at-risk pay include annual profit-share, **sales commission**, and performance bonuses which take the form of a one-off non-consolidated cash payment.

attendance bonus A **bonus** payment that is dependent on employees attaining an attendance target during the period over which the bonus is calculated. For example, payment of the bonus could be dependent on full attendance or on sickness absence remaining below a set number of days within a monthly or quarterly period. Essentially these bonuses penalize workers for sickness absence and there is some evidence that their use has increased in recent years as employers have initiated more exacting procedures for the management of **absenteeism**. They are indicative of a shift towards a more contractual employment relationship in which employers more tightly specify levels of performance and standards of behaviour and tie these explicitly to remuneration.

attendance record The official log of an employee's presence at work. The record will note holiday entitlements and keep a track of days off sick, late attendance, and non-attendance. The record might reveal patterns of absence that can be investigated—for example the employee who is late for work every Thursday during the soccer season when the local team has a Wednesday evening fixture. Attendance records are sometimes used by employers when making decisions about **redundancy**.

attended time is the time the worker actually spends at the workplace in any single period. [See **basic working time**; **real working time**; **working time**.]

attitude survey A tool used by management to assess the opinions and morale of the staff. Normally it takes the form of an anonymous self-completion questionnaire that asks employees to rate various aspects of the organization on satisfaction scales. The questionnaire might also include some open-ended questions where respondents are invited to write their own comments. Data from the questionnaire are analysed to produce an overall profile of attitudes amongst the workforce. If respondents are asked to provide details of their job, department, age, length of service, etc. it is also possible to produce attitude profiles for sub-groups within the organization.

attribution theory explains how people evaluate the behaviour of others. All behaviour is considered to be determined by either internal or external factors. Internal factors are within your own control—in other words, you have chosen to behave in a particular way. External factors fall outside your control, so your behaviour is limited or determined by influences outside your control. This means that behaviour at work, for example performance or absenteeism, is attributed to internal or external influences, and this leads to positive or negative impressions of an individual. For example, if a **line manager** considers an employee's poor performance to be due to internal factors (such as laziness or lack of care) he or she is likely to be dealt with more harshly than if the poor performance is considered the result of external factors (such as poor-quality raw materials or technical problems). Interestingly, research has revealed how biased people tend to be in their judgment of others. We have a tendency to attribute the success of other people to external factors and our own success to internal factors. Similarly, we tend to attribute the failure of others to internal factors and our own failings to external factors. Knowledge of attribution theory and awareness of these attribution errors can be useful to managers in the **appraisal** process when they assess their employees' performance and when they ask their subordinates to undertake **self-appraisal** and **peer appraisal**.

atypical work is any pattern of work that does not follow the traditional male norm of full-time, permanent employment with a single employer. It includes **agency labour**, **part-time** work, **casual work**, **temporary contracts**, **self-employment**, **homeworking**, and **zero-hours contracts**. There is evidence that at least some forms of atypical work are growing and this has elicited two responses from commentators and policy-makers. On the one hand, atypical work has been welcomed as evidence of labour market **flexibility** and a means of securing **work–life balance**. On the other hand, it has been seen as evidence of declining **security of employment** and a movement towards a more insecure labour market, in which employees are at risk of exploitation. The policy of the European Union towards atypical work has been informed by both perspectives: non-traditional work is encouraged but it must also be regulated to ensure it is undertaken voluntarily and does not lead to a degradation of employment standards. To ensure the latter, a number of **directives** have been adopted in recent years that deal with part-time work, work to a fixed-term contract, and agency work. Broadly, these directives seek to prevent the abuse of atypical work (e.g. employment on a succession of fixed-term contracts) and ensure equal treatment (see **equal opportunity**) for atypical workers with workers on traditional contracts in the same employment. [See **contingent work**; **non-standard work**.]

automatically unfair Under UK employment law there are a number of reasons for dismissal that are 'automatically unfair' and dismissal for these reasons would result in an **Employment Tribunal** finding in favour of the dismissed employee. The situations when dismissal is automatically unfair include: (1) dismissal for membership or non-membership of a trade union; (2) seeking the **National Minimum Wage**; (3) pregnancy or childbirth; (4) asserting a statutory right; (5) **whistle-blowing**; (6) seeking to be represented in a company procedure; (7) activities undertaken as a health and **safety representative** or as an employee-nominated trustee of a pension fund. There is no qualifying period for protection from **unfair dismissal** for reasons that are automatically unfair. [See **fair reasons for dismissal**.]

autonomous workgroup (AWG) A form of work organization that emerged in the 1960s based on the theory that improvements in performance can be attained if employees are highly motivated and fully involved in the direction and control of their work. The autonomous workgroup organized its own work rota, methods, division of labour, etc., but was accountable for achieving certain production targets—in other words, the group had responsibility and authority for organizing the work, although the overall process was controlled by management through the output and quality targets. In some respects the autonomous workgroup is a forerunner to the contemporary concept of **self-managed team**.

autonomy at work is the extent to which employees are allowed to work independent of close supervision and to use their own discretion in undertaking their work. High autonomy means that employees are likely to be able to alter the pace of their work, how they perform the tasks, and the quality and quantity of their output. Low autonomy is when employees have no control over these aspects of their work. This low autonomy/low discretion is typically a feature of **scientific management** and production line work (see **Fordism**). In contrast, high autonomy/high discretion is typically a feature of professional and managerial work. [See also **responsible autonomy**.]

B

back pay is payment in arrears to make up for past under- or nonpayment of wages.

balanced scorecard A technique for measuring organizational success and identifying areas for improvement and action. The idea of the balanced scorecard came from management theorists Robert Kaplan and David Norton, who recognized that organizations often focused too much on financial criteria for **performance management**, thereby neglecting other features that help to deliver competitive advantage. Their solution was to devise a method by which managers can translate their vision into clear measures of success through balancing the financial perspective with three other, equally important perspectives: the customer, the internal processes, and innovation and learning. Each perspective requires the managers to identify different factors that are critical to success, and to devise key performance measures for these factors. The resultant 'balanced scorecard' will be a template for the organization to evaluate its overall performance and identify areas of strength and weakness. Of course, the measures on the scorecard will differ from organization to organization, but the principle of 'balance' across these measures will be the same.

Baldridge Award A prestigious US award for success in **Total Quality Management** that was established to celebrate good practice and diffuse techniques of quality management through American business. [See **European Foundation for Quality Management**.]

band see **pay range**

bargained constitutional is a **management style** that is said to characterize much of the unionized segment of the British economy. Its central characteristic is tolerance of collective organization amongst employees but reliance on detailed collective agreements and procedures to regulate trade union activity. Management's purpose, therefore, is to ensure that unions do not acquire 'excessive' power or restrict the right to manage outside the narrow field of terms and conditions of employment.

bargained corporatism see **corporatism**

bargaining see **workplace bargaining**

bargaining coverage is the proportion of the workforce that is covered by **collective bargaining**. It is important to note that bargaining coverage is not the same as **union density** and that in most countries a higher proportion of workers are covered by collective bargaining than are trade union members. Indeed, in countries with centralized systems of bargaining, like France and Germany, the majority of employees have at least an element of their pay and conditions determined through bargaining, while only a minority are members of trade unions. In these countries many employees become **free riders** by accepting the benefits of union membership without actually joining. In the UK, just over a third of workers have their pay determined through collective bargaining and bargaining coverage has declined markedly since the mid-1970s, when more than 70 per cent of workers were covered by collective pay-setting institutions. [See **bargaining level**; **bargaining structure**.]

bargaining group See **bargaining unit**

bargaining level The point or level in the economy at which **collective bargaining** takes place between employers and trade unions. Within a national economy there are a number of potential bargaining levels; bargaining may take place at the national level, at the industry or sectoral level, and at the enterprise and workplace levels. Within the European Union there is also scope for bargaining at supranational level, through the negotiation of **framework**

agreements, which cover all member states. While one particular level of bargaining may predominate, it is common for bargaining to take place at different levels within a national economy. For example, basic terms and conditions of employment may be negotiated at industry level with local supplements negotiated at the workplace. In some countries, such as Sweden and Germany, bargaining is relatively centralized and multi-employer agreements negotiated at higher levels are the most important. In other countries, such as the UK and the USA, in contrast, bargaining is relatively decentralized and concentrated at the enterprise and workplace levels. The international trend is for lower levels of bargaining at enterprise, workplace, and business unit to become more important. The level of bargaining is an important component of bargaining structure and can have a significant influence on patterns of trade union behaviour and bargaining outcomes. Where bargaining is concentrated at enterprise level, for instance, unions tend to rely heavily on local activists, adopt more decentralized patterns of organization, and engage in relatively frequent strike activity involving small numbers of workers. The economic consequences of decentralized **enterprise bargaining** include a relatively high level of income inequality and a relatively wide union **wage-gap**.

bargaining scope refers to the range of employment issues that are the subject of **collective bargaining** between employers and trade unions. Where unions are strong, the scope of bargaining may be broad and encompass aspects of work organization, training and development, and business strategy as well as pay and conditions of employment. Where unions are weak, in contrast, bargaining scope is likely to be narrow and restricted to basic terms and conditions, such as rates of pay, hours of work, and **annual leave**. Evidence for the UK suggests that the scope of bargaining has narrowed in recent years and, indeed, in many unionized workplaces there is evidence that rates of pay are no longer the subject of negotiations with trade union representatives.

bargaining structure refers to the pattern of **collective bargaining** within a national economy. It has a number of dimensions including **bargaining level, bargaining coverage,** and **bargaining scope**; that is, the point in the economy at which bargaining takes place, the proportion of workers covered, and the range of issues that are the subject of bargaining. In addition, some commentators refer to the depth of bargaining, meaning the extent to which bargaining is an ongoing process with unions becoming involved in the implementation and revision of collective agreements. Within **industrial relations** theory it has been argued that bargaining structure exerts an important influence over the behaviour of trade unions and employers and shapes the pattern of **industrial conflict**.

bargaining unit A bargaining unit or group is a set of employees who are recognized for **collective bargaining** by an employer and have their terms of employment set through the same **collective agreement**. A bargaining unit might comprise all or a proportion of employees within a particular industry, enterprise, establishment, or occupation. The decentralization of collective bargaining, however, means that most bargaining units are made up of employees in the same class of employment within a particular enterprise or workplace; for example, production operatives within a manufacturing company, or supervisory, clerical, and technical grades within a business unit of an insurance firm. The UK's statutory **recognition** procedure confers recognition on workers within a designated bargaining unit. Where there is a dispute between an employer and an employee over the extent of the unit (i.e. over which workers should be included) this can be referred to the **Central Arbitration Committee** (CAC) for adjudication. In making its decision the CAC must take into account a number of factors including the views of the employer and trade union, the need to avoid excessive fragmentation of bargaining, and the compatibility of the unit with 'effective management'.

base pay Base or basic pay is the rate of pay for a job or grade in an organization, to which can be added various supplements, **benefits**, bonuses, and allowances. Base pay, therefore, is the core element of **remuneration** that reflects, at least notionally, the market value for a particular type of labour. Advocates of the

new pay assert that base pay should be kept to a relatively low level, in order that employees become dependent on **variable pay**, which is contingent on performance, to make up their earnings.

basic pay see **base pay**

basic working time is the number of weekly or annual hours set out in the employee's **contract of employment** or in a **collective agreement** between a trade union and an employer. **Attended time** and **real working time** may be substantially higher than basic working time as a result of **overtime** working.

batting average effect is a change in a statistical indicator that arises because of a change in the population of cases and not because of change within cases. For example, average **union density** might fall within an economy because firms with high union membership close down and are replaced with firms that have low membership, and not because membership is falling within workplaces. Similarly, labour **productivity** might rise in a period of recession, not because of improvements in the use of labour within companies, but because low-productivity firms close down, causing the average productivity figure to rise.

Battle of Seattle The violent protests by environmental and labour activists that erupted at the meeting of the World Trade Organization in Seattle in 1999. The protests attracted worldwide publicity and linked the issues of global regulation of labour standards and trade liberalization in the political agenda.

beauty contest The competitive bidding undertaken by trade unions attempting to secure **recognition** from an employer. Beauty contests involve unions presenting rival recognition packages to an employer in the hope that they will be chosen to represent workers at a new facility or previously non-union enterprise. As the pejorative term suggests, the employer chooses the 'most attractive' union—usually the one with the terms of recognition that are the most favourable to the employer. The process is also criticized for being undemocratic because it involves unions concluding recognition agreements without reference to the views of their existing or prospective members. [See **single-union agreement**; **sweetheart deal**.]

behavioural event interview is an alternative term for **situational interview**.

behaviourally anchored rating scales (BARS) A technique for evaluating the performance of an employee which can be used as part of the appraisal process. The technique involves: (1) breaking down a particular job into its key tasks (performance dimensions); (2) identifying a range of possible behaviours that can be displayed by an employee in undertaking each task; (3) placing these behaviours on a scale ranging from ineffective performance to excellent performance; (4) assessing the jobholder (employee) against these scales for each of the tasks. As a consequence, a profile of job performance is created for each employee covering the various aspects of his or her work. Typically the process of devising the performance dimensions involves jobholders themselves, and this gives greater authenticity to the rating scales. [See **behavioural observation scales (BOS)**.]

behavioural observation scales (BOS) A technique for evaluating the performance of an employee which can be used as part of the appraisal process. Like **behaviourally anchored rating scales** the BOS technique involves a process of identifying the key tasks for a particular job, but the difference is that employees are evaluated according to how frequently they exhibit the required behaviour for effective performance. The scores for each of these observed behaviours can then be totalled to produce an overall performance score. In such instances the various measures of behaviour are normally weighted to reflect the relative importance of the measure to the overall job.

behaviour-based competencies see **competency**

behaviourism is a body of psychological theory that is concerned with identifying the conditions that stimulate patterns of human behaviour. In its extreme form it makes no inferences about the internal mental processes that underlie behaviour but assumes that human beings react to positive and negative stimuli in their external environment. [See **reinforcement theory**.]

Belbin's team roles Management consultant Meredith Belbin developed the idea that for a team to function effectively it needs key roles to be performed by team members—each role contributing a specific skill or behavioural dimension to the team dynamics. The 1993 version of Belbin's framework identifies nine roles, and although there is not space to detail them, the list that follows provides a brief overview of the principal strengths each role brings to the team and the associated key skills each offers. (1) Plant—brings creativity, offers problem-solving skills. (2) Resource investigator—brings enthusiasm, offers communication skills. (3) Co-ordinator—brings maturity, offers delegation and decision-making skills. (4) Shaper—brings dynamism, offers drive and action skills. (5) Monitor-evaluator—brings sober judgment, offers evaluative skills. (6) Teamworker—brings co-operation, offers social skills. (7) Implementer—brings reliability, offers practical skills. (8) Completer—brings conscientiousness, offers finishing skills. (9) Specialist—brings dedication, offers scarce skills/knowledge. Some commentators have pointed out that Belbin's framework has only limited application in work settings because of practical considerations: (*a*) team members are often chosen by function rather than other qualities, and (*b*) the team might have fewer than nine members.

beliefs are propositions that individuals hold about work, organizations, society, etc. Beliefs are a person's understanding of how things are. Therefore, when referring to **organization culture**, beliefs help to sustain a common understanding of why and how the organization exists in its present form.

benchmarking is the technique of comparing organizations in order to identify 'best practice'. Managers might benchmark their organization in order to assess how it is performing, to identify areas for improvement, and to look for new ideas. The purpose is to identify best practice and to transfer all or part of this to one's own organization. Invariably the transfer process involves adapting the ideas and techniques to industry-specific or organizational-specific circumstances. In theory, any aspects of the organization's operation can be benchmarked, including human resource policies and practices (training methods, equal opportunities policies, remuneration packages, etc.), providing they can be measured in a consistent manner across all organizations being compared.

benefits Employee benefits or 'fringe benefits' form part of **remuneration** and consist of a broad range of special payments or benefits in kind. Some of the most frequent and valuable benefits to employees are occupational **sick pay**, **maternity pay**, and **pensions**; **company cars** and membership of sports and health clubs; access to education and opportunities for personal development; staff discounts and benefits in kind which reflect the employer's line of business, such as lower mortgage rates for bank employees. An important function of benefits is to provide for employee security in the event of disruption to regular earnings, while in other cases benefits may confer status or serve as an aid to recruitment and retention. Many core benefits, such as health care, sick pay, and maternity pay, reflect and enhance statutory provision. They may also reflect a **management style** that stresses the employer's obligation to 'care for' employees. Indeed, benefits like company canteens, housing, welfare, and recreational services originate from a tradition of **paternalism**. Over time, however, benefits may come to be viewed as entitlements and legally have been classified as elements of remuneration. They are also frequently the subject of **collective bargaining** and benefit provision in both the UK and the United States is typically more generous in unionized companies. Current trends in benefits include a movement to benefit flexibility (see **flexible benefits**), where employees are given an element of choice over the particular benefits they receive, and the provision of 'family-friendly' benefits, such as special leave arrangements to cope with child- and elder-care.

big hat, no cattle is a pejorative description of the HR function that emerged in the USA in the 1980s when interest in HRM was growing. It expresses the view that, despite the claim of advocates of HRM that the HR function contributes to the strategic management of companies, in reality it remains marginal and excluded from critical business decisions.

binding arbitration see **arbitration**

biodata A technique used in the **selection** process. Biodata are pieces of information that can be objectively categorized (for example, qualifications, years of relevant experience, positions of responsibility). Particular weightings are given to the various categories according to their importance and so each candidate will get a 'score' based on his or her biodata. This can be an effective sifting mechanism in order to reduce the pool of applicants to a smaller number (i.e. shortlisting). It is only possible to use the biodata technique where the same information is available for all candidates; therefore, some organizations ask applicants to fill in biodata questionnaires rather than relying on information from **application forms** or **curricula vitae** (résumés).

black hole A **non-union workplace** that is also characterized by an absence of sophisticated or developmental HRM.

blacking is a form of secondary **industrial action** in which workers refuse to handle materials, products, or equipment because they originate either from a company engaged in a dispute with its own workforce or from a country with a poor record of labour and human rights. [See **secondary action**.]

blackleg is a traditional dialect term for a **strike-breaker**.

blacklisting is the practice of recording the names of known trade union **activists** by employers, employment agencies, and business organizations. The purpose of blacklisting is to allow the vetting of job applications and to exclude union militants from employment. Under the Employment Relations Act 1999, blacklisting has become unlawful and those who believe they have been discriminated against in this way have been given the right to complain to an **Employment Tribunal**. There is also provision for a **trade union** to bring a case on behalf of members who have suffered blacklisting.

bleak house is a label given to the non-union segment of the economy, or at least that element of it characterized by harsh hire-and-fire employment practices. The term highlights the fact that union-based systems of **participation** have not given way to **direct participation** or **employee involvement** in many cases, but to **unilateral regulation** of the **employment relationship** by managers.

block vote The aggregated votes of trade union members that are cast on their behalf by elected representatives or delegates. Criticism of union reliance on the block vote has led to greater reliance on **postal balloting** by trade unions, even when this is not a requirement in law.

body language is the set of non-verbal signals a person transmits through their posture, eye contact, gestures, and facial expressions. A huge amount of information is transmitted and some psychologists suggest that training in interpreting body language is an essential skill for managers to have in any interview situation. For example, it is suggested that when a person is lying or is withholding information they may use certain hand gestures, such as concealing their mouth, or may blink for slightly longer than normal. However, it is important to note that there are significant cultural differences in the use of body language. For instance, maintaining eye contact when you are being asked a question is considered polite in some cultures but rude in others. These cultural differences mean that an over-reliance on body language could lead to a misjudgment of the person and accusations of racial **discrimination**.

body work is work in which the physical appearance and sexuality of the worker is integral to the tasks performed. Work of this kind is very common in the service sector where employees interact directly with customers. For example, female flight attendants in the airline industry may be required to maintain a strict weight–height ratio to ensure they are attractive to male passengers. [See **emotional labour**.]

bona fide occupational qualification (BFOC) The US equivalent of a **genuine occupational qualification** (GOQ) in the UK. It allows discrimination on the basis of sex, age, religion, or national origin in certain circumstances where the job requires that characteristic. Under US law, race can never be a BFOC, which contrasts with the GOQ in the UK.

bonus A payment that is made in addition to the basic **wage** or **salary** and which, in most cases, is linked to the achievement of a performance target or behavioural standard of some kind. The defining feature of bonuses is that they are supplementary payments, usually in cash, which are not consolidated into the basic salary or wage; that is, they have to be re-earned afresh in each bonus period by the employee. Bonuses are a constitutive element in a wide range of payment systems and may form part of **profit-sharing**, **merit pay**, **sales incentive**, and other performance-related systems of remuneration. Reliance on bonuses has increased in recent years as a result of the interest in **variable pay**.

boundaryless organization An organization where there has been a concerted effort by managers to break down (1) the internal barriers that separate different levels in the hierarchy, different functions, and different departments, and (2) the external barriers between the organization and its suppliers, customers, and even its competitors. Initiatives towards becoming boundaryless include greater **flexibility**, **cross-functional teams**, **delayering**, and **empowerment**.

bounded rationality occurs when there are limits to the information available to decision-makers that prevent them making 'informed', rational decisions.

brainstorming is a problem-solving technique for generating ideas. In small groups, people shout out ideas which are written onto a board or flipchart. The idea does not have to be justified and no one is allowed to comment or otherwise pass judgment, no matter how bizarre or impractical the idea might seem. The process continues until the supply of ideas runs out within the time limit set, and then the group begins discussing and evaluating the ideas.

branch The basic unit of trade union organization in most UK unions, equivalent to the union 'local' in North America. Union branches may be based upon a particular workplace or enterprise or cover a particular geographical area such as a town or district. Branches elect their own officers (e.g. secretary, chair, women's officer, membership secretary, and treasurer), who in an enterprise or workplace branch will become the main workplace union representatives. Territorial branches, in contrast, may be rather distant from workplace trade unionism, though they may accredit **shop stewards** and act as advisers or negotiators on behalf of workplaces. Branches can vary tremendously in size, vitality, and functions, depending on union traditions. In some unions they may enjoy considerable autonomy and may even appoint or elect their own paid, full-time officers. The trend in recent years has been to establish workplace branches in order to connect the formal system of **union government** more directly to the needs of employees at their place of work. As the basic unit of trade union organization, branches elect delegates and representatives to higher-level union committees.

breadwinner The main wage earner in a household. Traditionally this was considered to be the man, but increasingly women are becoming the primary earners and households are relying on dual or multiple earners (multiple breadwinners) to provide the standard of living they need (or want).

Bridlington principles are the rules initially formulated by the UK **Trades Union Congress** in the 1930s to regulate inter-union competition for members and **recognition** from employers.

briefing groups see **team briefing**

British disease In the 1970s the British disease was defined narrowly in terms of strike proneness and as a more general malaise, the symptoms of which were strong unions, **restrictive practices**, low productivity, and poor relative economic performance. In fact, the British workforce has never been unusually **strike prone**, and while strike activity was high in the 1970s this reflected an international trend. Many believe that the British disease was cured by Prime Minister Margaret Thatcher in the 1980s through her government's programme of anti-trade union law. Today strike activity is at an all-time low but other symptoms of the disease, such as relatively low productivity and poor manufacturing performance, persist. This suggests that trade unions have been blamed excessively for the UK's poor relative economic performance. [See **Winter of Discontent**.]

broad-banding is the replacement of a graded **pay structure** comprised of multiple short grades with a small number of broad pay 'bands', usually four or five in total. These broad bands provide extensive scope to reward performance, skill level, and market value and are associated with a switch to a more individualized system of **reward management** in which there is emphasis on **paying the person** as opposed to the job. Broad-banding is associated with the **delayering** of organizations and the introduction of a flatter organizational structure in which there is emphasis on teamworking and **functional flexibility**. Within a flat organization (see **flat/tall structure**) there is less scope to reward employees through promotion through successive grades, and broad-banding provides an alternative mechanism for continuing **salary progression**. As such, it can support **continuing professional development** in high-skill jobs and alleviate the problem of skilled or professional workers seeking managerial promotions in order to secure higher earnings. Broad-banding is also advocated as a way of promoting **lateral career** development in which employees move across occupational boundaries at the same organizational level but receive salary progression for doing so. Finally, broad-banding is associated with the movement towards greater line management responsibility for personnel decisions, as line managers typically exercise discretion over the placement of individuals within the band. [See **grade**.]

brownfield site An industrialized area of a city. The term is used to differentiate the traditional industrial areas from the **greenfield sites** outside cities.

bullying see **workplace bullying**

bundles theorists argue that there is a set of human resource practices that, when combined together, produce a positive effect on organizational performance/productivity. For instance, it might be argued that when teamworking, performance-related pay, empowerment, and competency-based systems of appraisal and training are configured, there is an overall improvement in measures of organizational effectiveness such as increased productivity, lower employee turnover, and better financial performance (see **high performance work practices**). Importantly, some very ambitious claims have been made for these 'bundles' with some researchers asserting that a particular bundle will improve any organization, irrespective of its particular circumstances. This approach means that bundles theorists reject the importance of **external fit**. Instead, they emphasize the value of ensuring an appropriate **internal fit**. However, the various bundles researchers do not agree on what constitutes the best bundle of practices that organizations should adopt. But the most scathing criticism of the bundles approach is that it tends to lead to the conclusion that there is one best way of managing people (the right bundle) when in practice there may be a variety of approaches that could produce positive effects.

bureaucracy An organization's formal rules and procedures are usually referred to as its bureaucracy. It is common for the term bureaucracy to be used as a criticism of an organization. For example, employees will sometimes complain that the organization is 'too bureaucratic', meaning that they feel too constrained and lack **autonomy**. In this sense bureaucracy is seen as undesirable and to be avoided, but in practice all organizations have some form of bureaucracy, and so it is more accurate to refer to the 'extent of bureaucracy'. The original meaning of the term comes from sociologist Max Weber, who defined it as consisting of five components: (1) clearly defined duties and responsibilities of all organization members; (2) a hierarchy of positions showing lines of authority; (3) written rules and procedures; (4) **meritocratic organization** appointments; (5) rational decision-making.

bureaucratization is the process of increasing the amount of formal rules and procedures in an organization. [See **bureaucracy**.]

burnout is when an employee no longer has anything to offer the organization because he or she has reached a stage of physical and/or emotional exhaustion. Burnout is usually the result of overworking, high pressure, tight deadlines, and unrealistic organizational demands on the individual. It is often preceded by symptoms of stress.

business case The justification of progressive HR policies, such as **equal opportunities**, employee **participation**, and union **recognition**, in terms of their contribution to business performance. Arguments of this kind are very common in the HRM literature. However, critics of the business case claim that it provides only a narrow justification for improving employment conditions and that reform can be justified on the grounds of social justice or employee welfare even when there is no discernible benefit, or even a cost, to employers.

business ethics is the application of ethical reasoning to the situation of business organizations, including their role as employers. It is a growing field of academic research and teaching in university business schools and may also inform management practice, via **mission statements**, **corporate codes of conduct**, social auditing, and the codes of practice of management and **employers' associations**. Within the field of business ethics there is a range of competing positions that are grounded in different schools of moral philosophy. These positions include **deontology**, **utilitarianism**, and justice-based theories of ethics (see **distributive justice**;

procedural justice). Essentially, these positions consist of arguments for identifying ethical or desirable management practice. Action (i.e. HR policy) may be considered desirable because it treats employees as ends-in-themselves with rights to dignity, privacy, and respect (deontology); because it promotes the greatest good of the greatest number (utilitarianism); or because it satisfies the tests of procedural and distributive justice (justice-based theory).

business lifecycle refers to the stages through which a company will pass during its period in existence. The main stages are usually identified as business start-up, early growth, maturity, and decline. The literature on **strategic integration** of HRM and business strategy suggests that different sets of HR policy and practice are appropriate to each of these stages of development.

business process re-engineering (BPR) is the technique of analysing the current operations and systems within an organization in order to identify and eliminate anything that does not add value. Whilst there are various forms of BPR, there are a common set of key components: moving from a function-focused to a process-focused approach; restructuring to achieve cross-functional integration (see **delayering**; **downsizing**); introducing incremental change; developing full use of information technology; examining all work activities (including management); adopting the customer's perspective of the organization; and allocating ownership for all processes. Advocates of BPR encourage managers to think the unthinkable, forget about the organization's history, and start from a blank sheet of paper. Importantly the focus of the 're-engineering' activity is the process, not the people—and in this sense BPR is distinct from **culture change programmes**. Indeed, this has led some critics to argue that BPR is dangerous because it fails to take sufficient account of the human dimension. The main proponents of BPR are management consultants Michael Hammer, James Champy, and Thomas Davenport.

business unionism is a description often given to the dominant form of trade unionism in the United States, which refers to the concentration of trade unions on a narrow, economistic agenda pursued through collective wage bargaining. In the words of Samuel Gompers, an early American union leader, the objective of business unionism is 'More'; that is, the improvement in the price of labour for unionized employees within a, largely accepted, capitalist economy. Business unionism is often counter-posed to welfare or **social movement unionism**, in which the objectives of trade unionism are couched broadly in terms of the pursuit of social change and methods that encompass political and community action. For much of the post-war period American unions were politically conservative and focused primarily on **collective bargaining**. They have always maintained a link with the Democratic Party, however, and the trade union movement in the USA has encompassed many diverse and many radical elements that extend well beyond narrow business unionism.

C

ca'canny is a traditional dialect term for **restriction of output**.

cafeteria benefits A form of **flexible benefits** which provides maximum choice to employees in determining the form of their remuneration package. Cafeteria benefits provide 'across-benefit' flexibility, in that the employee can choose which particular **benefits** to receive up to a predetermined value. Despite the attractiveness of this option, cafeteria benefits remain relatively rare owing to their administrative complexity.

captive audience meeting A compulsory meeting of employees arranged by an employer in response to a trade union organizing campaign. The purpose of the meeting is to dissuade workers from joining the union or voting in its favour in a **certification** or **recognition** ballot. [See **union busting**.]

career The series of jobs that a person has throughout his or her working life. Traditionally, a career was considered to be a progression from lower to higher levels in the organization, and/or from junior to senior status in one's occupation or profession. Increasingly, these ideas of career progression along a **career path** or up a **career ladder** are being replaced with new concepts such as the **portfolio career** and **lateral career moves**. [See also **career anchors; career management**.]

career anchors are those aspects of working life we value and which help us to define our skills and our worth. They develop in the early years of our careers when we begin to recognize our own abilities and the aspects of work that we enjoy most. Career anchors help to guide choices about job changes. They constitute a source of stability across a person's working life, even though later on we might find ourselves increasingly dissatisfied with our job. The term was coined by organizational theorist Edgar Schein, who has identified eight career anchors: technical or functional competence, managerial competence, security, creativity, autonomy and independence, service or dedication to a cause, challenge, and balanced lifestyle.

career block A career block occurs when a person cannot progress any further in an organization because there is an absence of new opportunities. The block is not the fault of the employee, but due to the organization. For example, a career block might occur if the organization has **delayered** so there are fewer promotion opportunities; alternatively a career block might be experienced by a woman who is faced with **discrimination** from senior managers who refuse to promote her. When employees experience a career block it usually means they have to leave to get promotion, although increasingly organizations are encouraging talented employees to take **lateral career moves**.

career ladder is a common metaphor used to describe how a career can be depicted as a series of steps up the organizational hierarchy. However, the notion of the career ladder is becoming less relevant because contemporary organizations are adopting flatter structures with fewer levels in the hierarchy—or, in terms of the metaphor, fewer rungs on the ladder. Instead, some organizations are encouraging **lateral career moves**, rather than upward moves, and so a more appropriate concept is the **portfolio career**.

career management is the process through which the aspirations and abilities of employees are assessed, and their personal development is planned and guided, in line with the opportunities available in the organization. It involves a range of techniques, such as **mentoring, training, appraisal,** and **competency** assessment (see also **career track/path; career anchors**). For the organization, career management allows talent to be identified and employees to be placed in jobs where their skills can be used effectively. In particular, it provides the opportunity for **management succession planning**.

career path see **career track**

career plateau This occurs when the upward **career track** of an employee has flattened out. This is because the person is deemed by managers to have reached his or her full potential and cannot be promoted further in the organization.

career portfolio see **portfolio career**

career track or career path A metaphor to describe the progress an individual makes through an organization. Typically it implies promotion through the hierarchy, although increasingly organizations are recognizing the importance of **lateral career moves**, particularly through wider use of project management. Employees who are fast-tracking through the organization are on schemes that allow them to progress more rapidly than normal—for example, graduates joining the police force are often on fast tracks to plain clothes ranks. Such schemes can be problematic because those on the fast track are often not in any particular role long enough to gain a full breadth of experience and may not see the full consequences of their actions. Moreover, there can also be resentment and poor motivation amongst those employees who have not been selected for the fast track.

cascade communication is a process of passing information down from the top of the organization, through all the levels in the hierarchy. It is based on the principle that, at each level, managers are responsible for briefing their subordinates, who in turn pass the information on by briefing their subordinates (see **team briefing**), and so on until the information gets to the bottom of the hierarchy. The supposed benefit of this method is that it involves managers more directly in the communication process, thereby forcing them to take ownership of the information and to present it in a way that is meaningful and justifiable to their subordinates. The people on the receiving end of the message at each stage are more likely to listen because there is less power difference between them and the sender (their line manager) than there would be if the communication were a 'message from the top'. [See **direct communication**.]

cash in hand Although many employees get paid in cash (rather than through a bank account), 'cash in hand' refers to a cash payment that has not been taxed and does not include any deductions for National Insurance etc. Most cash in hand payments are illegal because they are not declared to the government Inland Revenue Department.

casualization is the process of increasing the **numerical flexibility** of the workforce by putting people on short-term and temporary contractual arrangements which allows the use of labour to be matched more closely to fluctuations in demand.

casual work is employment that is offered on a short-term basis, for a fixed period of time or until a particular task has been completed. Sometimes the term is used to refer to work that is paid on a **cash in hand** basis. [See **casualization**.]

Central Arbitration Committee (CAC) The CAC was created by the Employment Relations Act 1975 in the UK and is the latest in a series of standing national arbitration bodies which dates back to the early years of the twentieth century. On its foundation the CAC consisted of an independent chair and deputy chair with two panels of side members representing employers and trade unions. Its function was to provide a range of **arbitration** services, but these were whittled away by successive Conservative governments until by the mid-1990s the CAC was restricted to providing voluntary arbitration in **trade disputes** and adjudicating in disputes over **disclosure of information** for the purpose of collective bargaining. From being a relatively marginal body within British industrial relations, however, the CAC has recently assumed a much more significant role. The Employment Relations Act 1999 charges the CAC with determining applications for statutory trade union **recognition** and has endowed the CAC with considerable powers for interpreting and applying the regulations governing statutory recognition. To enable the CAC to fulfil this task there have been additional appointments made under a new procedure; persons appointed must have experience of industrial relations and include those with experience of representing employers and employees, and appointments must be ratified by the Secretary of State after consultation. Within the statutory recognition procedure, cases are considered by a panel of three members of the CAC, consisting of the chair or deputy chair plus a representative each of employers and employees.

centralization is the process of concentrating power and control at a single location within the business. Personnel departments tend to be centralized in most organizations for two main reasons. First, centralization provides consistency of policy and practice across the whole organization—particularly important to ensure equal opportunity and fair treatment, the breach of which might give rise to legal action. Second, it is cost effective since it saves the duplication of resources.

ceremonies (in relation to organizational culture) are extravagant, occasional events designed to celebrate the achievements of the organization and its members, and reinforce the **values** and **beliefs**.

certification is the legal process in North America through which a trade union is 'certified' as the bargaining agent for a group of employees. As such, certification is equivalent to legal **recognition** of a trade union in the UK. In the United States certification is overseen by the National Labor Relations Board (NLRB) and usually involves a process of election, in which the union must prove a clear majority in favour of union representation. In Canada, the primary mechanism used is a 'show of cards', that is, the union simply has to demonstrate to the regulatory authority that it has the majority of the workforce in membership. The latter procedure reduces the opportunity for the employer to campaign against certification (see **captive audience meeting**) and partly for this reason unions are more successful in Canada in certification campaigns. In both countries there is a procedure for decertifying a union under certain conditions, thus ending the collective relationship between the workforce and employer.

Certification Officer (CO) The Certification Officer (in the UK) was created by the Employment Protection Act in February 1976 to certify and regulate the internal activities of independent **trade unions** and **employers' associations**. The Certification Officer maintains a list of trade unions and employers' associations, inspects their internal accounts, and oversees the processes of merger and transfer of engagements. The Officer also determines the independence of trade unions from employers. Under the Employment Relations Act 1999 the Certification Officer has been given a new set of powers to hear and adjudicate in cases where members complain about union breaches of their own rules and trade union law. The Certification Officer publishes an annual report that contains information on trade union numbers, mergers, membership, political funds, and finances.

champion of change is a temporary role given to a manager which entails taking responsibility for a particular change initiative or a programme of change within an organization. Typically, the champion must get commitment to the change from other managers, rally support and enthusiasm from employees, ensure that resources are allocated and used effectively, and monitor the total process.

changemaker A role that can be adopted by a manager who is primarily responsible for personnel/human resources. Changemakers are focused on the broader business objectives and concern themselves with ways that the management of human resources can contribute to achieving these objectives. They are interventionary in the sense that their main concern is with devising policies and processes that integrate day-to-day personnel issues with all other aspects of the business. This includes the **devolution** of people management to line managers. The term 'changemaker' was coined by management theorist John Storey to describe one of four potential styles of managing human resources (the others being **adviser**, **handmaiden**, and **regulator**).

chapel is the traditional name for a workplace trade union organization in the printing industry. A chapel is the equivalent of a workplace trade union **branch** for printers, journalists, and other trades within the print and media sector. The lead representative within a chapel is known as the 'Father' or 'Mother of the Chapel'.

chargehand is a traditional term for the lead 'hand' or worker within a workgroup who has minor responsibility for **supervision**.

charisma is a quality possessed by some individuals that encourages others to listen and follow. Charismatic leaders tend to be self-confident, visionary, and change oriented, often with eccentric or unusual behaviour.

Chartered Institute of Personnel and Development (CIPD)

The professional association for personnel/human resource practitioners in the UK. It offers advice and support to its members as well as promoting good practice and providing the accreditation for professional training courses and qualifications in personnel management. However, unlike other professions, such as accountancy, personnel/HR specialists are not obliged to become members of the CIPD, or to take professional qualifications. Nevertheless, most of the leading firms insist on CIPD membership and qualifications for their personnel staff. The CIPD has over 100,000 members. It was formerly titled the Institute of Personnel Management (IPM) but merged with the Institute of Training and Development in 1994 and became the Institute of Personnel and Development (IPD). The IPD was awarded a Royal Charter on 1 July 2000 and formally changed its name. The award of the Charter symbolizes the increasing stature of the IPD and is likely to increase both its potential to attract personnel professionals into membership and the weight that is given to its opinion in public policy discussion of employment issues.

check-off is the deduction of union subscriptions from wages by the employer. Check-off has been relied upon heavily by unions in the UK as a means of collecting membership income, and the provision of check-off facilities has been one of the main supports to trade unionism granted by employers. The practice has been criticized for making unions dependent on employers and minimizing direct contact with members who retain their membership through inertia and become mere 'paper trade unionists'. The practice of check-off was attacked by the Conservative government in the 1990s and legislation was introduced requiring that employees renew their consent every three years. This law has been withdrawn, but it prompted trade unions to rely more heavily on direct debit as a means of gathering subscriptions.

child labour refers to any economic activity performed by a person under the age of 15. However, the 'child labour' that generates most concern is that which prevents effective school attendance and which is performed under conditions hazardous to the physical and mental health of the child. The term does not usually refer to light work after school or young people helping out in a family business. Across the globe it is estimated that there are more than 120 million children engaged in full-time work, the vast majority of whom live in developing countries. Exploitative child labour is a major target of campaigners for **international labour standards**, and in 1999 the **International Labour Organization** agreed on a treaty for the eradication of the worst forms, defined as slavery, forced labour, child prostitution and pornography, drug trafficking, and work that harms children's health, safety, and morals.

chiseller An employee who, although competent at his or her tasks, underperforms and is carried by his or her work colleagues. Unsurprisingly, chiselling is frowned upon by other employees and chisellers are persuaded or coerced into improving their performance by co-workers. Chiselling can be a particular problem when employees work in **teams** and receive **team-based pay**.

Citizens' Advice Bureau (CAB) A local office of the National Association of Citizens' Advice Bureaux (NACAB), a voluntary organization that exists to provide free advice to UK citizens on a range of consumer, tax, and other problems. Increasingly, CABs provide advice on employment issues and may act as mediators between employees who have a grievance and their employers.

Increasing resort to CABs by employees is indicative of the continuing need for employment advice and representation despite the decline of trade unions.

clerk of works model of personnel management. One of three types of managers identified by management theorists Shaun Tyson and Alan Fell (the other types being **architect** and **contracts manager**). The 'clerk of works' is characterized as a type of personnel manager concerned with employee issues on a day-to-day basis and dealing with routine employment administration. They have no strategic involvement in the business and employment policies tend to be ad hoc and short term. They are responsive to the demands of **line managers**, where formal authority lies.

clocking on/in is the act of registering attendance at work. An employee will clock on by inserting a time card into a machine that records the arrival time, and will clock off/out at the end of their shift. The data are used to produce **attendance records** for employees and calculate hours of work for the payroll department. Although clocking on is usually associated with blue-collar work, many white-collar workers are expected to fill in timesheets, or be sitting at their desks by a certain time in the morning. Generally, however, white-collar work has been less rigid in terms of hours of attendance. [See **flexitime**.]

closed shop A situation where employment is conditional on trade union membership. Equivalent terms in North America are the 'union shop' and 'compulsory unionism'. In the UK historically there were two forms of closed shop: the pre-entry closed shop operated by **craft unions**, which required workers to be members of the union before they could be offered employment, and the post-entry closed shop in which an offer of employment was conditional on joining a recognized trade union. The former had its origins in unilateral attempts by craft unions to regulate the supply of skilled labour, while the latter was subject to **joint regulation** and originated in attempts by employers and unions to formalize workplace industrial relations in the 1970s. The Conservative reform of industrial relations law in the 1980s led to both forms of closed shop becoming unlawful and individuals now have a right in law to seek compensation from an **Employment Tribunal** if they are denied employment because they are not union members. The legal position in the UK today, as in the rest of Europe, essentially supports the right of employees to join or not to join a trade union, though informally the closed shop survives in certain industries.

closed union A trade union with a narrowly defined **job territory**, which restricts its membership to workers within a particular enterprise, industry, or occupation. In the UK, for example, the National Association of Head Teachers is a closed union in two senses. It restricts its membership to the field of education and, within that field, confines itself to representing head teachers and their deputies. Another form of closed union is an **enterprise union**; that is, one that restricts its membership to workers in a single employing organization. [See **open union**.]

coaching is a regular series of training or development sessions where an experienced employee with considerable expertise guides a novice. Since coaching takes place on a one-to-one basis it provides a more intense training and learning experience customized to the specific needs of the individual. It is also a more formal and regulated method of passing on expertise through on-the-job training than the inadequate practice of **sitting-with-Nellie**. This means the coaches have to be specially selected and 'trained to train', so that they can pass on their skills and knowledge effectively.

code of practice Under UK law the **Advisory, Conciliation, and Arbitration Service**, the **Commission for Racial Equality**, the **Disability Rights Commission**, and the **Equal Opportunities Commission** have the right to issue statutory codes of practice, subject to the approval of Parliament and the appropriate Secretary of State. Codes have been issued dealing with **disciplinary procedure**, **disclosure of information**, time off for trade union duties and activities, **equal opportunity policy**, and **equal pay**.

Their function is to disseminate models of good practice. Breach of a code is not itself unlawful but the **Central Arbitration Committee** or an **Employment Tribunal** can take a breach into account when judging an issue. Codes of practice, therefore, constitute a form of 'soft law'. [See **Approved Code of Practice**.]

codetermination is the legal principle that decisions within the enterprise must be taken with the approval of the workforce. In Germany **works councils** have a legal right to codetermine a number of issues, such as the arrangements for **annual leave**, changes in **payment systems**, and workplace **discipline**. Effectively, the law endows the works council with a right of veto in these and other areas, such that managers have to secure its agreement before introducing change. Codetermination is also used to refer to the system of **worker directors** that exists in Germany.

coercive comparison see **leapfrogging**; **whipsawing**

cognitive tests see **psychological tests**

collective agreement A written or oral agreement between an employer and trade union that is the product of **collective bargaining** and allows for the **joint regulation** of the employment relationship. Collective agreements can specify the **substantive rules** that govern the terms and conditions of employment and can also determine **procedural rules** governing the behaviour and interaction of managers, workers, and trade unions. In many countries collective agreements are legal contracts and can be enforced in law. In the UK, however, they have the status of 'gentlemen's agreements' and are not legally binding, though they are typically incorporated within the **contracts of employment** of individual employees.

collective bargaining is the process through which **trade unions** and employers negotiate collective agreements that set the rates of pay and terms and conditions of employment of workers. Collective bargaining is a process of **joint regulation** and can be differentiated from **unilateral regulation** of employment by employers or unions and **legal regulation** through the state.

In the UK, though not in other countries, the collective agreements to which it gives rise do not in themselves constitute legal contracts, though they may be incorporated in the **contracts of employment** of individual employees. There is also a tradition of relatively informal collective bargaining in the UK, particularly at workplace level, in which agreements take a minimal form or are not written down at all. Industrial relations researchers have identified a number of dimensions of collective bargaining which collectively are known as **bargaining structure**. The main elements of bargaining structure are coverage (the percentage of employees affected directly by agreements), level (bargaining can be conducted at multi-employer, single-employer, international, national, sectoral, regional, and local levels), scope (the range of topics covered), and depth (the extent to which agreements are jointly implemented and reviewed). In the UK in recent years, the trend has been towards reduced coverage, bargaining at lower levels, diminished scope, and less depth. In less than twenty years bargaining coverage has declined from more than two-thirds to about one-third of the workforce, multi-employer bargaining has collapsed in many sectors, and the scope of bargaining has been narrowed to basic terms and conditions of employment. Managers have also assumed greater control over the implementation of agreements. All these developments are a manifestation of the decline of trade unions. A further distinction which has been drawn is between **integrative bargaining** and **distributive bargaining**. The former is characterized by joint problem-solving and an attempt to identify solutions in bargaining that are beneficial to both sides. The latter is more adversarial and takes a **zero-sum** form in which gains secured by one side involve losses for the other. [See **bargaining level**; **bargaining unit**.]

collective conciliation see **conciliation**

collective employment law is that branch of **employment law** that regulates the activities and behaviour of **trade unions, works councils,** and **employers' associations** and the pattern of interaction between the two sides of industry. It is concerned with issues such as the rights of workers to collective **consultation** and **codetermination**, the freedom of trade unions to organize, internal **union government**, trade union **recognition**, **collective bargaining**, and **strikes**, **lockouts**, and other forms of **industrial action**. In the UK there have been major changes in collective employment law over the past two decades. These have included the requirement placed on unions by the Conservative governments of the 1980s and 1990s to rely on **postal balloting** and the narrowing of trade union **immunity**. More recently, under the Labour government, there has been the introduction of a statutory recognition procedure and the extension of **European works council** legislation to the UK.

collective labour law see **collective employment law**

collective laissez-faire is a description of the traditional system of **voluntarism** in British industrial relations. It refers to the arrangement whereby state intervention in employment relations was kept to a minimum on the assumption that the collective institutions of **trade unions** and **employers' associations** would regulate the labour market through **collective bargaining**.

collective redundancy occurs when an employer makes twenty or more employees redundant at one establishment over a period of ninety days or less. In the event of a collective redundancy in the UK, there is a legal requirement to notify the Department of Trade and Industry and engage in **redundancy consultation** with representatives of the workforce. These legal obligations stem from the EU directive on collective redundancies of 1975.

collectivism see **individualism**

combine committee A form of trade union organization which brings together workplace representatives from all the separate establishments within a multi-site enterprise. For example, the combine committee in a large manufacturing company would consist of delegates from each plant who would elect the committee's senior representatives. In the UK in the 1970s, combine committees were an important feature of industrial relations and were often viewed as rival organizations to 'official' trade unionism. They continue to exist but are now much less prominent and influential, reflecting the general decline in workplace trade unionism in the intervening period.

Commission for Racial Equality (CRE) A statutory body established under the UK's Race Relations Act 1976. It has four main responsibilities: to monitor the implementation of the Race Relations Act; to give advice to employers on reviewing their human resource practices with regard to race/ethnicity; to give advice to complainants; and to investigate organizations breaching the legislation.

commitment see **organizational commitment**

common rule The principle or device of the common rule was identified by social reformers Sidney and Beatrice Webb as a key value of trade unions. It refers to the pursuit of standardized terms and conditions of employment for union members which guarantee uniform treatment by the employer. Unions may be committed to the common rule because it is intrinsically fair, prevents favouritism and victimization, and provides shared interests through which collective organization and activity can be developed.

comp-and-ben see **compensation**

company car A vehicle offered to an employee as part of a remuneration package. Company cars may be used by their recipients on company business but they are also available for private use and are an important feature of **remuneration** for managers and professionals in the UK. Company cars have become less tax efficient in recent years but they remain an attractive **benefit** because the burden of maintenance and replacement is assumed by the employer. In addition, a company car is a potent badge of status and its value and power are an indicator of career success in many occupations. [See **tax efficiency**.]

company council A popular term for a consultative committee, in which elected representatives of employees meet managers to discuss aspects of HRM and business policy. A key feature of company councils in the UK is that, although trade unions may have representatives on the council, they have no monopoly of representation and union and non-union representatives sit down together. [See **single-union agreement**.]

company discount A benefit provided for many employees in retail and other service sector organizations. Company discounts allow employees to purchase goods from their employer at a reduced rate.

company loan A loan offered to an employee by an employer as part of a remuneration package. Company loans may be interest free, as is the case with loans for the purchase of annual season tickets for rail travel to work. More substantial loans are likely to incur interest, but at a lower rate than that offered by commercial suppliers. [See **benefits**.]

Company Share Option Plan (CSOP) An Inland Revenue-approved **share option** scheme that is discretionary; in other words, the company can select the employees and directors it wishes to reward. In most cases, CSOPs are restricted to senior managers and are used as a means of overcoming **principal–agent** problems in the reward of executives. [See **executive pay**.]

company union A union established and funded by an employer in order to pre-empt unionization by an external and independent **trade union**. **Staff associations** are sometimes accused of being company unions as there may be a question mark over their degree of independence from management. Company unions can be distinguished from **enterprise unions**, which are fully independent but which confine their membership to employees of a particular company.

comparability is the principle that rates of pay and rates of pay increase should match those elsewhere in other enterprises, industries, or occupations. Comparability is an important touchstone in wage negotiations, and public sector trade unions, in particular, endeavour to maintain the relative value of their members' earnings through comparison with general movements in earnings across the economy. [See **ability to pay**.]

comparable worth is the term used in North America to refer to the concept of **equal pay** for work of **equal value**.

comparative industrial relations involves the comparative study of the **industrial relations systems** of two or more countries in order to identify and explain patterns of **convergence** and **divergence**. [See **industrial relations**.]

comparator A named person in the same or associated employment who is cited by an individual making a claim for **equal pay** or **equal opportunity** before an **Employment Tribunal**. A woman taking an equal pay case, for instance, might cite one or several men at her place of work who are receiving higher pay for work of **equal value**. In this situation the presence of a 'token male' earning the same amount as the woman does not preclude comparison with other men who are paid more. Under equal pay legislation and the regulations on equal treatment for part-time work, a comparator must be an actual person, though under sex and race discrimination law it is possible to use a hypothetical comparator. There has been criticism of the requirement that comparators must be drawn from the same employment because job segregation means that it is difficult for women taking equal pay cases to find a male comparator doing similar work or work of equal value.

compensation is payment for work which 'compensates' the employee for the 'disutility' of labour. The rather negative connotation associated with the term has led some personnel specialists to replace it with **reward** or **reward management**, more upbeat alternatives. 'Compensation' and 'compensation and benefits'—'comp-and-ben'—are also used to refer to the specialist activity involved in administering and managing remuneration systems and to the specialist group of managers who have responsibility for this area. This latter usage is particularly common in North America.

competence-based pay A payment system that relates **salary progression** or a cash **bonus** to the display of 'competencies' by individual employees. Systems originate in the identification of competency, understood as the key attributes and behaviours of employees that underlie good performance in a particular organization or job. Competency might include: team management or membership; priority setting or personal organization; **networking**; customer service orientation; staff and personal development; change orientation; performance management; and communicating information. Individual employees can be rated against a list of this kind through an appraisal procedure and allocated an overall competency assessment. This assessment can then be used to determine the award of bonuses or progression through a **pay range** or **salary matrix**. Interest in competence-based pay has risen as a result of the wider use of competency frameworks within human resource management. Its supporters claim that it can reinforce key patterns of behaviour and so raise business performance but, like any system of **appraisal-related pay**, competence-based pay can be costly to design and administer and is vulnerable to charges of subjectivity and bias. [See **merit pay**.]

competency A competency-based approach to managing people focuses on the skills and talents needed to be able to perform a particular task to a certain standard. The assessment of competencies is useful for various aspects of the management of human resources: setting standards of performance that can be expected from employees and appraising them against such standards; assessing the training and development needs of individual employees; and identifying the skills, abilities, and characteristics needed when recruiting and selecting new employees. The issue of a competency-based approach has become popular in the management literature, but the problem is that different writers define the term in their own distinct ways. And, to complicate matters further, some authors argue there are distinct differences between the meanings of competence and competency, or competences and competencies. The important point is not to get worried about the language, but to recognize that the general approach taken by most commentators is to break competency down into two categories: behaviour based or work based. Behaviour-based competencies are personal characteristics/attributes that contribute to effective job performance (for example, interpersonal skills, attitudes, motivation). Work-based competencies are specific skills and abilities required to perform the job to a specific standard (for example, the use of spreadsheet software, fluency in spoken Japanese, management of a budget). A focus on competency not only allows for the development of employees, it also provides a new means of rewarding people; thus there has been a growing interest in systems of **competence-based pay**.

competitive advantage occurs when an organization is implementing a strategy that has not been adopted by its current or potential competitors. 'Sustained competitive advantage' occurs when these current or potential competitors are unable to copy the firm's strategy. In other words, whereas competitive advantage might be temporary, sustained competitive advantage is permanent. [See **resource-based view**.]

competitive strategy is the strategy adopted by a company to secure **competitive advantage** under particular industry conditions. It is common to distinguish generic types of competitive strategy, such as those resting on **cost minimization, quality enhancement**, and product innovation. The assumption is that firms can or must respond to competition by choosing strategies that enable them to gain an advantage within their chosen product market. That is, by producing goods and services more cheaply than competitors, by producing more reliable and better-quality products, or by being innovative and successful at bringing new products to market. It is commonly recommended that **human resource strategy** should be developed to support competitive strategy, with techniques and policies being selected that will generate employee attitudes and behaviour which are congruent with a particular route to competitive advantage.

component wage job A job that provides a wage that contributes to household income but which is insufficient to maintain a household. Many part-time, seasonal, and casual jobs provide only component wages.

compressed working week A pattern of **working time** that is becoming increasingly common and which involves the reallocation of work time into fewer and longer blocks during the week. The total length of work time remains unchanged, but each shift or period at work is lengthened. Typically, working time is reorganized so that the same basic hours are worked in four and a half days a week, or nine days out of ten in a fortnight. [See **temporal flexibility**.]

compulsory competitive tendering (CCT) is a requirement for public sector organizations to allow private sector firms to bid for the delivery of services (such as catering, cleaning, security, transport) in competition with any internal provision by the organization itself. The policy was developed by the UK Conservative government of the 1980s, and the intention was to introduce 'market relationships' into the public sector on the assumption that this would drive down cost and improve efficiency, whilst ensuring quality through contractual obligations. CCT led to the transfer of many public sector jobs to the private sector and to cuts in pay and conditions of employment for many public sector manual workers, who found they could only win tenders by accepting an inferior employment package. The compulsion to tender has been relaxed under the Labour government elected in 1997, but the practice of competitive tendering and the transfer of service delivery to the private and voluntary sectors has continued. [See **marketization**; **transfer of undertaking**.]

compulsory redundancy occurs when employees are selected for redundancy against their will. Where compulsory redundancies are used, a number of selection criteria may be applied to decide who will lose their job. These include **last-in-first-out** and selection on the basis of skills or qualifications, standard of work performance or aptitude for the work, and attendance or disciplinary record. To avoid complaint to an **Employment Tribunal** it is important that selection criteria are applied in a consistent and objective way and that employees are not selected for an unfair reason, such as trade union activity or disability.

compulsory unionism see **closed shop**

computer-assisted instruction (CAI) is a training technique where the individual is guided by a computer program through the information to be learned. The method is flexible because trainees can progress at their own speed, skip material they are already familiar with, and undertake the training at their own convenience. The programs provide tests and assessment at each stage and provide immediate feedback to the trainee.

computer-mediated brainstorming is based on the same method as conventional **brainstorming** but uses computer software to channel the ideas from group members dispersed at computer terminals. This has a number of advantages: ideas can be generated simultaneously and independently; ideas remain anonymous; contributors might feel less intimidated; and contributors do not have to be in the same physical location.

concertation is a pattern of industrial relations in which there is a broad accommodation between business and labour and the two sides co-operate to reach mutually acceptable solutions to common problems. Concertation is likely to be manifest in reliance on **integrative bargaining**, **joint consultation**, and the adoption of a **mutual gains** strategy by employers.

concession bargaining is a term originally coined in the USA to refer to **collective agreements** in which trade unions surrender improvements in pay and conditions that they have previously secured in order to promote firm competitiveness and protect employment. Concessions have included the surrender of inflation-plus wage formulae, acceptance of pay freezes and **two-tier wages**, which institute lower pay rates for new starters, and the withdrawal of work rules that inhibit **flexibility**. Concession bargaining is associated with recession and the intensification of competitive pressure on unionized companies and, according to some analysts, indicates the reduced capacity of unions to secure a wage mark-up for their members in a more open, competitive economy.

conciliation is a form of dispute resolution in which a third party, or conciliator, helps the parties find a mutually acceptable solution. In the UK the **Advisory, Conciliation, and Arbitration Service (ACAS)** provides two kinds of conciliation. Collective conciliation seeks to resolve industrial **disputes** between employers and trade unions and may be triggered by a request from either side or by a joint approach. In the mid-1990s ACAS dealt with about 1,300 requests for collective conciliation per year. Individual conciliation occurs when an ACAS officer seeks a settlement between an employer and an employee who has made a complaint to an **Employment Tribunal**. Thousands of claims are received each year and a great many are resolved through individual conciliation. The object is to provide a swifter, cheaper, and less acrimonious resolution of individual disputes. There has been some criticism of the process, however, on the grounds that compensation awarded to employees through conciliation tends to be less than that awarded by a full tribunal hearing. [See **arbitration**; **mediation**.]

concrete ceiling The seemingly impenetrable barrier that prevents the progression of members of ethnic minorities into senior management jobs. [See **glass ceiling**.]

confederation A central representative organization of either business or labour. A trade union confederation is a representative body whose members are individual **trade unions**, while an employers' confederation is a representative organization of **employers' associations**. In the UK the **Trades Union Congress** (TUC) is a confederation of this kind: its membership consists of 78 affiliated trade unions. The **Confederation of British Industry** (CBI) is an example of an employers' confederation, although it also has individual companies in membership. Confederations fulfil a number of functions for their members but their key role is to act as the voice of either business or labour in dealings with government and supra-governmental agencies, such as the European Commission. There are international labour and business confederations. On the labour side, for example, the **European Trade Union Confederation** (ETUC) has in membership 65 national trade union centres from 28 countries, while the International Confederation of Free Trade Unions (ICFTU) represents 213 centres from 143 countries.

Confederation of British Industry (CBI) Formed in the 1960s, the CBI is the main representative organization of business in the UK. Its membership consists of individual companies plus **employers' associations** and its primary function is to lobby government to ensure pro-business employment and other policies are pursued. The CBI has been successful in recent years in weakening some of the main employment legislation introduced by the Labour government (e.g. on trade union **recognition**) and has proved itself an effective lobbyist. Unlike its equivalents in other European countries, the CBI has no role in **collective bargaining** or the co-ordination of **pay determination**. Indeed, its policy has been to advocate the **decentralization of bargaining** in recent years. The CBI is a member of UNICE and has tended to take a tougher stance than many continental employers' bodies in the **social dialogue**. Generally, it is opposed to the further elaboration of European social and employment policy.

conflict resolution see **dispute resolution**

conformist innovation see **deviant innovation**

conglomerate An organization involved in multiple businesses. The businesses are very much independent from each other, with their own general managers and divisional boards setting business strategy.

consolidation is the incorporation of incentive or other supplementary earnings in the basic rate of pay. Consolidation effectively involves the withdrawal of a supplementary payment, perhaps because it has ceased to influence employee behaviour, with the earnings hitherto received being included in the basic rate. [See **base pay**.]

constitutional is a **management style** that recognizes trade unions and establishes formal procedures and **collective agreements** to control and regulate the employment relationship. [See also **bargained constitutional**.]

constructive dismissal (in the UK) is a **dismissal** that arises because the employer has breached the **contract of employment** and forced the employee to resign. Examples of situations that have been accepted by tribunals as amounting to constructive dismissal include giving an employee an unjustified warning, using foul and abusive language, failing to provide a safe system of work, and deliberately failing to pay wages. In cases of constructive dismissal the employee can seek remedy at an **Employment Tribunal** using the law on **unfair dismissal**.

consultant see **management consultant**

consultation occurs when managers seek the views of employees and take them into account when making decisions. The focus of consultation may be the individual employee but more usually managers consult with employee representatives. The latter may be trade union representatives, as occurs with traditional **joint consultation** in the UK, or they may be non-union representatives, including works councillors. Viewed as a form of worker **participation** in management, consultation is stronger than information-sharing but weaker than forms of joint decision-making such as **codetermination** and **collective bargaining**. Partly for this reason, trade unions are sometimes sceptical of the value of consultation. Consultation is also viewed with scepticism by some because it tends to concentrate on non-controversial and perhaps relatively unimportant issues, while more important questions to do with pay, hours of work, and other conditions of employment are the subject of collective bargaining. Under European law there is a requirement on employers to engage in consultation with workforce representatives on specific issues, including **health and safety**, **collective redundancy**, and **transfer of undertakings**. In other areas the law provides an incentive to consult, for example **working time**. In addition, in large multinational enterprises there is a general obligation to consult on aspects of business policy that affect workers in two or more member states of the European Union (see **European works council**). The European Commission has produced proposals to extend this general requirement to consult to all companies in the EU with fifty or more employees, but a **directive** giving effect to these proposals has yet to be adopted. In most member states, though not Ireland and the UK, an obligation of this kind already exists and managers are required to consult with **works councils** over a broad range of business decisions.

consultative is a **management style** that attempts to build constructive relationships with trade unions, and develop **dual commitment** amongst the employees. [See also **consultation**.]

consumer boycott The decision by customers not to buy particular goods and thereby demonstrate disapproval of a company's employment or environmental policy. Consumer boycotts have been organized by trade unions involved in industrial **disputes** and seeking **recognition** from employers in the United States. They have also been organized by advocacy and campaigning groups seeking to improve conditions for workers in supplier firms in developing countries.

consumer reports Information about employee performance that is gathered by managers from consumers and used to **discipline**, **reward**, or identify training and development needs amongst employees. Consumer reports can be obtained in a number of ways, though the most common are surveys of consumers (customer service questionnaires), customer complaints, and the employment of 'mystery' or 'bogus' shoppers to report directly on employee behaviour (see **mystery shopper**).

content theories of motivation see **motivation**

content validity see **validity**

contestation is a pattern of industrial relations in which neither employers nor trade unions recognize the legitimacy of the other side. As a consequence there is no stable accommodation between business and labour and there are recurrent bouts of intense conflict.

contingency theory suggests that the effectiveness of an organization is dependent upon managers taking into account various factors that can impact in a negative or positive manner on the organization—the main contingent factors being environment, technology, size, product diversity, and people employed. In fact, it is misleading to use the term contingency theory, since there are a number of contingency approaches, all of which differ in terms of the particular contingency they stress as being most influential. There is a further complication with the contingency approach. Some commentators tend to imply that the organization should adapt to its particular circumstances, others suggest that the organization, through its actions, can influence or change its circumstances. Whilst the contingency approach rejects the idea that there is 'one best way' of managing/organizing, it tends to suggest there is one most appropriate way for each particular set of circumstances (contingencies). This leads critics to argue that the contingency approach fails to explain how and why different organizations can achieve success even when they respond to the contingent factors in different ways.

contingent pay is pay that is linked to measures of individual, group, or company performance. Contingent pay is used as a means of incentivizing workers and promoting shared interests in higher output, productivity, customer satisfaction, and other indicators of business success. [See **at-risk pay**; **competence-based pay**; **performance-related pay**; **variable pay**.]

contingent work is work that is performed by workers with conditional or transitory employment arrangements, such as temporary, agency, and casual workers. Together, these form the **contingent workforce**. Contingent work arises because companies have a temporary need for a particular product, service, technology, or skill at a particular time and place.

contingent workforce That section of the workforce in non-permanent or **precarious employment**. The main groups who fall within this category include **agency labour**, casual workers, temporary workers, seasonal workers, workers with **fixed-term contracts**, **freelances**, subcontractors, and workers with **zero-hours contracts**. All these groups are characterized by their disposability when viewed from the perspective of the employer. Some definitions of the contingent workforce include those engaged in **part-time** work. However, although part-timers are more likely than full-timers to be engaged on a temporary contract, the vast majority are employed on permanent contracts and consider themselves permanent employees. [See **numerical flexibility**.]

continuance commitment occurs when an employee remains with a particular organization either because there are costs to leaving (loss of friends, loss of pension benefit, loss of familiar environment, etc.) that outweigh the benefits of taking a new job in a different organization, or because there is a lack of alternative employment opportunities. [See **organizational commitment**.]

continuous improvement see **kaizen**

continuous learning is the process through which employees and managers meet the challenge of perpetual change that faces many contemporary organizations in a highly competitive, turbulent environment. Knowledge and skills quickly become obsolete, so there is a requirement to update them constantly through training and development. Learning becomes an important feature of the organization, and contributes at the least to its competitive survival and, at best, to its **competitive advantage**. Continuous learning is a vital component of the **learning organization**. [See **lifelong learning**.]

continuous professional development is the concept that the members of a profession should commit themselves individually to improving their knowledge and understanding throughout their careers, and keeping up to date with all developments within their chosen professions. This also entails learning from their own experiences and making a conscious effort to identify deficiencies and weakness in order to redress these through formal training and development. [See **continuous learning**.]

contract at will see **employment at will**

contract compliance is an arrangement under which public sector agencies specify that a condition of the award of contracts to private companies is that they meet a number of employment standards, for example, that wages are equal to the rate set by **collective bargaining** for the industry or that the company has in place an **equal opportunity policy**. In the UK most forms of contract compliance are unlawful under competition legislation introduced by the Conservative government of the 1980s.

contract of employment An agreement that an employee will work for an employer in return for wages which comes into effect as soon as an offer of employment is accepted. The contract need not be written down to be legally valid but under the UK's Employment Rights Act 1996 most employees are entitled to a written statement of the main terms of the contract. This must be provided within two calendar months of starting work and must cover issues such as the rate of pay, the hours of work, holiday entitlement, **notice period**, disciplinary rules, and any **collective agreements** that affect terms and conditions. Employment contracts consist of **express terms** that have been explicitly agreed and **implied terms** that have not been the subject of agreement, but nevertheless are enforceable in law. Statutory employment rights override contracts and an express term cannot generally be used to waive employment rights. Contracts can be changed in a number of ways, though the general principle is that both sides have to agree to an alteration in the contract. This might be done through a verbal or written agreement, through collective bargaining, through a clause that allows for subsequent variation to occur, or simply by the employee accepting a changed working situation. A contract can be ended by the employer or employee, normally by giving the required notice of termination. But if the employer fails to give notice the employee may be able to take a case for damages to a court for **wrongful dismissal**. Employees also have statutory protection against **unfair dismissal**. Not all workers in employment have a contract of employment; **self-employed** workers have a contract for services. In establishing whether a contract of employment exists, the courts have developed four tests. These consider whether the worker is controlled by the employer, is integrated into the employing organization, is economically dependent on the employer, and whether there is mutuality of obligation as demonstrated by long-lasting or regular employment and the right of the worker to refuse work. [See **employment status; written particulars.**]

contracts manager model of personnel management. One of three types of managers identified by management theorists Shaun Tyson and Alan Fell (the other types being **architect** and **clerk of works**). The 'contracts manager' is characterized as a type of personnel manager who is an expert negotiator, maintaining order and regulating the employment relationship through systems based on formal polices and procedures. Although not strategically involved in the organization, he or she provides important support for line managers by offering professional expertise.

controlled autonomy describes a situation where members of a workgroup are obliged to meet performance targets due to peer pressure, rather than due to external management control. Some commentators argue that it is an example of how employees can be duped by managers into self-exploitation.

convenor 'Convenor of shop stewards' is the title frequently given to the principal representative within a workplace trade union organization. Convenors are typically elected by the members of a **shop steward** committee and occupy the lead role in relations with management. Although less common than in the past, it is still established practice for large employers to support the position of convenor through the provision of paid time off work and office and other facilities. [See **facilities agreement**.]

convergence is the idea that national employment systems will converge on a common pattern as a result of shared technological development, common exposure to the global economy, or the emergence of supranational institutions like the European Union, concerned to harmonize employment conditions across member states. [See **divergence**.]

cooling-off period A period of delay before the commencement of **strike** action that is ordered by a court to prolong the search for settlement to an industrial **dispute**. Under US labour law the President can order an eighty-day delay to the start of industrial action if the latter threatens the national interest.

co-ordinated bargaining A property of national systems of **collective bargaining** that ensures wage negotiators co-ordinate their activities and take into account the combined impact of their bargaining on the national economy. Co-ordination can be achieved through a number of mechanisms including the centralization of the bargaining system, the acceptance of standard-setting agreements in lead industries or firms, or the activities of central union and business **confederations**. According to labour economists, the effects of co-ordination tend to be lower **pay dispersion** across the economy and less inflationary pressure, which in turn allows a higher level of employment. Critics of the British system of collective bargaining contend that it is insufficiently co-ordinated, with the result that wage inequality, inflation, and unemployment are higher than they otherwise might be. [See **bargaining level**; **pattern bargaining**; **shunto**.]

core competencies are key activities and skills present within an organization that provide the source of its **competitive advantage**. They constitute those activities that the organization performs well and which have developed through a process of **organizational learning**. The core competencies are central components of the organization around which strategy can be developed. They can vary enormously from organization to organization; for example, they could include technical expertise in a particular process; customer service; capacity to innovate; communication methods; data handling. However, not all activities that an organization excels at or which managers are proud of should be considered core competencies. The main advocates of the importance of core competencies

(Coimbatore Krishna Prahalad and Gary Hamal) suggest that for any organizational resource to be labelled a 'core competence' it must satisfy three criteria: (1) offer access to a number of markets; (2) be seen as valuable by customers; and (3) be difficult for competitors to copy.

core employees are those who undertake value-adding activities considered by management to be vital to the success of the organization. The term is normally used in connection with the **flexible firm model**.

corporate anorexia is a condition where the organization has slimmed itself through **downsizing** to such an extent that its survival is threatened. It has become weak and unable to take new opportunities through a loss of skills and a demoralized workforce.

corporate clan A metaphor used to evoke the image of a community of like-minded individuals working together within the organization for mutual gain, and sharing the same values and beliefs.

corporate code of conduct A set of desirable labour standards or employment practices that are adopted by corporations to regulate management practice in supplier companies, particularly those based in developing countries. Codes have been adopted increasingly by large companies in response to pressures from trade unions, campaigners, and consumers and heightened public awareness of the question of **international labour standards**. The main components of codes include prohibitions on **child labour**, forced labour, discrimination on the grounds of sex, religion, and race, and reliance on inhumane disciplinary sanctions. They also typically include clauses on **health and safety**, fair wages, and **working time**, and in some instances guarantee **freedom of association** and **collective bargaining**. Codes are often based on the conventions of the **International Labour Organization** and are enforced through systems of monitoring of management practice in supplier firms.

corporate culture see **organizational culture**

corporate governance refers to the control and organization of private corporations. It is an issue of relevance to human resource management for two reasons. First, it is argued with increasing frequency that national systems of corporate governance shape the pattern of **employment relations** within the economy. In the UK, for instance, the system of corporate governance emphasizes accountability to shareholders and there is an active market for corporate control that encourages firms to seek a high return on investment. These features of corporate governance, in turn, are said to encourage **short-termism** and an opportunist or adversarial approach to workforce management (see **downsizing**; **redundancy**). Second, in the countries of continental Europe systems exist that allow for worker participation in company management through **works councils** and **worker directors**. In the light of this experience it is suggested that the system of corporate governance in the UK should be changed to introduce similar arrangements and allow a wider range of **stakeholders** to influence company management.

corporate killing is a new criminal offence proposed by the UK government in 2000 to replace the previous crime of involuntary manslaughter. It emerged from concern at the inability of the courts to prosecute successfully companies whose negligence had contributed to the deaths of workers, consumers, and members of the public. Under the law corporations can be held responsible where 'conduct in causing death fell below what could reasonably be expected'. The penalties include unlimited fines and a requirement to correct the cause of any accident. In addition, any individual who can be shown to have had some influence on the circumstances in which a management failure led to a person's death will be disqualified from acting in a management role. Individual managers may also be liable for prosecution for the other new offences of reckless killing and killing by gross carelessness.

corporatism is a system of political economy in which organized economic interests become involved in public policy-making and national economic management. Within a corporatist system the central **confederations** of business and labour become engaged in discussions with government over economic and social policy and may conclude broad agreements or **social pacts** over issues such as wage inflation, training policy, taxation, and welfare expenditure. Business and labour organizations, additionally, may become responsible for the implementation of policy, such that trade unions have to ensure that wage bargaining does not generate inflation and employers are required to meet national training targets. Corporatism is often associated with the emergence of tripartite public institutions in which business and labour are represented alongside government. [See **social partnership; tripartism**.]

corrective principle The corrective principle underlies many contemporary disciplinary and dismissal procedures. It is based on the belief that **discipline** within employing organizations should not be purely punitive but should seek to amend and correct ill-disciplined behaviour. It is for this reason that many procedures consist of a number of stages, beginning with oral and written warnings before proceeding to more serious action, such as suspension or **dismissal**. The object is to provide an opportunity for the employee to improve his or her behaviour. The corrective principle also gives rise to reliance on training and other forms of intervention to assist the employee in overcoming problems and improving performance. [See **disciplinary procedure**.]

cost leadership see cost minimization

cost minimization is a **competitive strategy** that is based on producing goods and services more cheaply than competitor firms. According to many commentators, cost minimization is the dominant strategy within UK business and is also a primary objective of resource-constrained public services. Critics claim that it encourages the employment of low-wage and low-skilled labour and promotes adversarial, low-trust employment relations as companies seek continually to reduce **headcount** and hold down labour costs.

cost of living award (COLA) An increase in pay to match an increase in the cost of living and so maintain the real value of earnings in the face of inflation. Cost of living awards have been a particularly noteworthy feature of North American **collective**

bargaining, where agreements may specify a cost of living increase plus an additional amount to provide for an increase in real earnings. This separation of the components of a pay increase is less common in the UK but matching the percentage increase in the rate of inflation is a basic objective of most union wage negotiators.

Council of Europe An intergovernmental body established in 1949 which should not be confused with the European Union. Its aim is to achieve greater unity among its member states through agreement on common action, which includes the sphere of labour standards. To this end, the Council of Europe enacted a Social Charter in 1961 that guarantees nineteen fundamental social and economic rights, including the right to work, the right to organize, the right to bargain collectively, and the right to protection and assistance for migrant workers and their families. The Charter also establishes a supervisory system of national reports submitted every two years for examination by a committee of independent experts. The Council of Europe adopted the **European Convention on Human Rights and Fundamental Freedoms** in 1950, which was transposed into UK law through the Human Rights Act 1998. Although not dealing directly with employment issues it is anticipated that the latter will impinge significantly on UK **employment law** in the coming decade. [See **international labour standards**; **Social Charter**.]

counselling is the provision of supportive and confidential advice to employees to help them overcome problems and cope with work- or home-based crises. It may be offered by trained counsellors within a company welfare service or by specialist outside agencies. The kinds of situation in which employers offer counselling include **redundancy**, **harassment**, **stress management**, and in dealing with health problems, such as alcoholism or drug abuse. [See **occupational health care**.]

counter-mobilization is action taken by governments and employers in response to collective mobilization of workers through trade unions. Counter-mobilization by the state might involve the passage of anti-trade union and anti-strike laws, as occurred under the British Conservative governments of the 1980s and 1990s. Counter-mobilization by employers might consist of strike-breaking, the victimization of trade union activists, and other attempts to weaken or marginalize trade unions.

craft union A **trade union** that organizes the members of a skilled manual occupation, such as boilermakers, compositors, electricians, engineers, or woodworkers. The primary method of craft unions has been control of labour supply through the **apprenticeship** system and the pre-entry **closed shop**, which in the nineteenth century provided the basis for the unilateral setting of wages and conditions. In the UK craft unions have traditionally been highly democratic in their internal government but elitist and exclusionary with regard to the less skilled. Technical change has eroded the basis of craft unionism in most industries and craft unions today have largely disappeared or been absorbed within larger unions that recruit across occupational boundaries.

critical incident job analysis is an approach to **job analysis** that identifies key situations or events in the job which must be dealt with effectively by a competent jobholder. These critical incidents can then inform the writing of a **job description** and **person specification** and can be used to frame questions to be asked in a **situational interview**.

cross-functional team A group of employees who are from the same level in the organizational hierarchy but who all have specialist skills to offer. They are brought together as a team to accomplish a specific task and are then disbanded. A cross-functional team is therefore temporary and project focused.

culture see **organizational culture**

culture change programmes are processes and systems designed to transform the attitudes and behaviour of employees and elicit their commitment to the values that senior management deem important to the success of the organization. [See **culture management; organizational culture**.]

culture management is the technique of attempting to influence the attitudes and behaviour of employees through manipulating the symbolic context in which they work. It is an attempt to get employees to share the same set of beliefs and values as the senior managers in the organization. The purpose is to improve organizational performance by harnessing the commitment, loyalty, dedication, and co-operation of all employees. Culture management is based on the assumption that an **organizational culture** can be created and manipulated in line with wider business strategy. It also assumes that a **strong culture** is preferable to a **weak culture**.

culture mapping is a technique for identifying the mismatch between existing employment practices and **management style** and the values that are embraced in an organization's **mission statement**.

culture shock is the surprise and disorientation a person can experience when placed in a situation where the dominant beliefs, values, and norms are radically different from those held by the person. Typically culture shock is experienced when people visit a different country, but it can also be used to describe the confusion, concern, and feelings of being an 'outsider' that are experienced when a person moves from one organization to another, or one social group to another. Through familiarization and **socialization**, the culture shock can gradually subside. Alternatively if the person finds him- or herself unable to adjust to or accept the new culture, he or she might choose to leave at the first opportunity.

curriculum vitae (CV) or résumé. A record of achievement— a personal history detailing education, qualifications, previous work experience and achievements, and current job responsibilities. A CV needs to be a concise, yet informative, summary of career achievements. The contemporary approach to constructing a CV is to detail work experience in reverse chronological order, thereby starting with the current job and listing responsibilities and achievements in clear bullet point format. There are numerous companies that now offer 'professional CV services'—in other words, for a fee, they will design and print your CV so that it (supposedly) stands more chance of being read by prospective employers.

custom and practice consists of informal work rules that grow up over time and come to be accepted and taken for granted by workers and managers. Many customary rules originate in concessions granted by lower-level managers and form part of an exchange in which managers secure co-operation in return for concessions on timekeeping, work-pace, and the operation of payment systems. They may come to be regarded as constraints and **restrictive practices** by managers, however, and the restructuring of business in recent years has led to an attack on many customary work rules.

customer care is the idea that service organizations and their workers should be highly responsive to the needs of customers and deliver quality service as a means of cultivating customer loyalty and guaranteeing repeat business. As such, it is a concept that is related to **Total Quality Management**. Customer care programmes can have important consequences for both work design and training policy within organizations. For example, employees may be trained in customer interaction or coached in 'scripts' that have to be spoken when dealing with customers. There may also be an element of **job redesign** as employees are given wider discretion to deal with customer complaints and requirements.

customer-facing jobs require employees to have direct contact with customers. [See also **internal customer**.]

customer service questionnaires see **consumer reports**

cybersquatting is the act of registering the name of an organization as a web address and then attempting to sell the address to the organization concerned for a sum of money greater than the registration fee, thereby making a profit.

cycles of control is a thesis developed by industrial relations theorist Harvey Ramsay to account for the rise and fall of employer interest in worker **participation**. Ramsay argued that employers turned to participation when their authority was threatened in periods of full employment and labour **militancy**. In periods of unemployment and labour quiescence, however, they resorted to non-participative styles of management.

D

data protection Under UK and European law employees have a number of rights with regard to personal data held by their employers. These rights are currently set out in the Data Protection Act 1998, which implements the EU Directive on the Protection of Personal Data 1995. Under the provisions of the Act, employees have a right to receive a copy of their personal files on request, whether held in an electronic or paper-based system, and to demand that any inaccuracies be corrected or removed. They also have the right to be told whether and for what reason personal information relating to them is being processed, the nature of the data, and the people to whom the information may be disclosed. [See **surveillance**.]

deadwood is a term sometimes used to describe managers and professionals who are deemed to be ineffective. The word implies that although they were once useful, they no longer serve any purpose and need to be cut out of the organization. To be described as deadwood is a term of abuse. Terms with a similar meaning are 'past his or her sell-by date' and 'hit the buffers'.

decentralization occurs when power and control cease to be concentrated in a single location and instead are dispersed throughout the organization. A decentralized organization might set up cost centres or profit centres, and allow these to run as autonomous units—indeed they are often described as **strategic business units** (SBUs). Such units are free to make their own decisions over their particular operations, although they remain accountable to senior management. There might be very good commercial reasons for decentralizing: to allow different parts of the organization to adapt their operations to meet the needs of their customers and respond to their competitive environment. Often the personnel department in an organization is centralized to provide consistency across the whole of the organization. However, the process of **devolution** has meant that there is a tendency to decentralize some personnel activities. The problem is that this might lead to an inconsistency of approach across the organization and perceptions of inequity.

decentralization of bargaining The decentralization of collective bargaining has been a notable trend in British industrial relations and in the industrial relations of many other countries in recent years. It involves two main changes in the level of bargaining: a movement from national or industry-level bargaining towards bargaining at the enterprise and a movement within the enterprise towards bargaining at business unit or establishment level. In the past, trade unions have exerted pressure for bargaining decentralization in order to secure higher rates of pay in profitable companies. More recently, however, the pace has been set by employers, who have advocated decentralization in order to secure flexibility, tie labour costs to performance, and reflect a broader **decentralization** of operational management to cost and profit centres. [See **bargaining level**.]

Declaration of Philadelphia The Declaration of Philadelphia is a statement of aims adopted by the **International Labour Organization** in 1944 and embodies basic principles of economic justice. It declares the following: that labour is not a commodity; that freedom of expression and of association are essential to progress; that poverty anywhere constitutes a danger to prosperity everywhere; and that all human beings, irrespective of race, creed, or sex, have the right to pursue both their material well-being and their spiritual development in conditions of freedom and dignity, of economic security and equal opportunity. The Declaration continues to provide a focus for campaigners for **international labour standards**.

deductions from wages are amounts deducted from an employee's gross wage by the employer before payment. Under UK legislation deductions are lawful if they are authorized by statute (e.g. tax and National Insurance), notified in writing to the employee (e.g. payment of union subscriptions or repayment of a **company loan**), or authorized by contract (e.g. contributions to an occupational pension scheme). Employees can recover unlawful deductions by taking a case under the Wages Act 1986 to an **Employment Tribunal**. The Act contains special provision to regulate the deductions for loss and breakages for those in retail employment, including shop assistants, insurance agents, and bus drivers. Employers are entitled to recover losses but deductions must not exceed 10 per cent of gross wages on any single pay day.

defender A type of firm identified by Raymond Miles and Charles Snow in their typology of 'strategic types'. It is a mature firm in a mature industry that seeks to protect its market position through efficient production, strong control mechanisms, continuity, and reliability. [See **analyser; prospector; reactor**.]

deferred pay Under European equality law, an **occupational pension** is defined as deferred pay. In other words, it forms part of remuneration and represents payment for labour but is withheld until the point of retirement in order to provide for security in old age or because of medical incapacity. The inclusion of pensions in pay is important because it establishes the legal principle that there should be equal treatment within **pension** schemes for men and women doing similar work or work of **equal value**.

defined benefit pension see **final salary pension scheme**

defined contributions pension see **money purchase pension scheme**

degeneration The degeneration or decay of a **payment system** occurs when earnings cease to be based on a formal measure of work. The degeneration of a time-based payment system (in which pay is based on time spent at work) would be manifest in workers taking longer breaks or finishing shifts before the set time, so that the link between payment and time spent working becomes attenuated. Degeneration can also occur in incentive-based payment systems. This occurs if bonuses and other performance payments are made to employees regardless of output or where, over a period of time, employees receive increasing earnings for the same level of output. Degeneration can arise because of slack systems of management control or because employees possess bargaining power, due to their position in the system of production, or due to their skills being in short supply. According to some commentators, the degeneration of **payment by results** is an inevitable feature of all schemes and requires the periodic overhaul and replacement of payment systems.

degradation of work is a thesis that suggests there is a progressive deterioration in the content of work within capitalist societies. This degradation increasingly affects clerical, professional, and managerial labour, as well as manual workers, and is manifest in the **deskilling** of jobs and the introduction of new management controls over work and workers. The thesis is adopted by commentators whose perspective stems from **labour process theory**. Critics of the thesis contend either that the dominant trend in work is towards **upskilling** or that there is a variable pattern of change across the economy. [See **scientific management; surveillance; work intensification**.]

dejobbing means reducing the number of jobs in the organization through the combined processes of increasing **functional flexibility**, **delayering** the hierarchy, and **downsizing** the workforce.

delayering is the process of removing levels in the hierarchy. The purpose is to give the organization a flatter structure and thereby push decision-making down to lower managerial levels. The assumption is that this will produce quicker decision-making by managers who are closer to their customers and more in touch with their competitive environment. The reasoning behind delayering lies in the belief that as organizations grow they become cumbersome, bureaucratic, and inflexible. Moreover they can be stultified by rules and procedures, slow decision-making processes, and a lack of creativity. The solution is to flatten the structure (delayer) to streamline the operations and increase flexibility and responsiveness (to customers and competitors). Rarely does delayering occur in isolation—it is normally associated with other management initiatives, such as **Total Quality Management, business process re-engineering**, or continuous improvement (see **kaizen**). Delayering has important consequences for managers because not only does it invariably lead to some job losses (see **downsizing**), it also increases the workload and responsibilities of lower-level managers. Even if it is accepted that some of the activities of middle management add little or no value and can be eliminated or contracted out, there are inevitably many aspects that will be passed down the hierarchy, which leads some commentators to suggest that many contemporary managers are now seriously overworked, although they may also be better paid.

Delphi technique A method of group problem-solving that is designed to produce a decision based on expert consensus. The technique prevents the experts from meeting face to face to arrive at decisions. Rather, each expert provides potential solutions to particular problems in isolation by completing specifically designed questionnaires on paper or, more recently, via computer. The results of the questionnaire are compiled centrally and sent back to the experts. They are asked again for their solutions and opinions, and again the results are compiled centrally before being returned to the experts. The process continues in this manner until consensus is reached—which is presumed to be the optimum solution. Although a somewhat time-consuming technique, the use of computer networks can considerably speed up the process. [See also **brainstorming; nominal group technique**.]

demarcation is the technique of defining the boundaries between jobs and thereby establishing the tasks and responsibilities of different employees. Demarcation lines were particularly important in establishing different grades of work and setting pay levels. Traditionally employees would only undertake tasks within these demarcated boundaries and this system of clearly defined and segmented jobs was particularly appropriate for Fordist production techniques. Contemporary organizations have moved away from demarcation towards **functional flexibility**, which is seen by management as a more suitable way of organizing work to meet customer needs in an increasingly changing and intense competitive environment. For trade unions, demarcation provided a logical structure around which to organize representation of employees and bargain for terms and conditions. The removal of demarcation has meant that trade unions have had to restructure and rethink their methods of organizing and representing employees.

demarcation dispute An industrial **dispute** over the right of an occupation to undertake a particular class of work. For example, in manufacturing a demarcation dispute might arise over who should undertake routine maintenance of machinery—skilled fitters or semi-skilled machine operatives. Demarcation disputes historically have been a feature of craft labour markets where competing **craft unions** have tried to preserve the entitlement of their members to undertake certain types of work. They have become less common with the decline of traditional manufacturing and the movement towards **multi-skilling** and **functional flexibility** in industry. The issues of demarcation and the possibility of dispute continue, however, in areas of professional work, where there is often intense interprofessional rivalry over the allocation of tasks, for example between doctors and nurses over responsibility for primary care.

demographics are characteristics such as sex, age, race/ethnic group, marital status, or educational background that can be collected to provide statistical profiles of a population. Therefore, within a workplace it is possible to collect and compile demographic information in order to gain a profile of the workforce. Such a profile is useful for **human resource planning**, **equal opportunities**, and **human resource development**.

demotion is the act of moving employees down the organizational hierarchy, reducing their responsibilities and status, and lowering their remuneration. Demotion might arise as a result of incompetence or negligence by the employee, and thereby constitutes a form of punishment. Alternatively, demotion might arise through no fault of the employee. For example, when an organization undertakes **delayering** there are managers who must accept a lower-status position, with fewer responsibilities (even if they do not suffer a reduction in pay), or else leave the organization. Demotion is the opposite of **promotion**.

demotivation is a loss of the motivation to work by employees. Demotivation may be manifest in poor timekeeping, failing performance, a lack of due diligence, and declining engagement with work tasks. It might arise for any number of reasons, though management action is often the source of demotivation. If employees believe they have been unfairly treated, if good work performance has failed to attract recognition or reward, or if targets and incentives are too demanding, then demotivation may result. It may also be the product of a **management style** that relies on **negative reinforcement** and thereby erodes workers' sense of **self-efficacy**. [See **equity theory; motivation; job stress**.]

deontology is the ethical principle of duty or dutiful behaviour. Within the sphere of HRM it asserts that policies towards employees, such as equal and fair treatment or acceptance of **freedom of association**, should be adopted because they are right in themselves and not because they promote improvements in business performance. [See **business case; business ethics; utilitarianism**.]

derecognition is the termination of union **recognition** by an employer. Derecognition amounts to the employer ceasing to accept a **trade union** as the authorized representative of its members within the enterprise. However, derecognition is not a clear issue and it is important to distinguish between full and partial derecognition. Under the former all contact between the union and employer will come to an end while under the latter elements of union recognition will be retained. Partial derecognition may involve the withdrawal of union rights for certain categories of employee (e.g. manager), for certain issues (e.g. pay determination), and for certain processes (e.g. collective bargaining). There was an increase in derecognition in the UK from the mid-1980s until the election of New Labour in 1997. Prominent examples included News International, British Coal, and the major oil companies. Under the Employment Relations Act 1999 there is a legal procedure through which derecognition can occur if it is requested by the workforce or if the employer can demonstrate a collapse of trade union organization.

deregulation Within the field of HRM deregulation refers to the weakening or removal of employment rules from the labour market, in order to give maximum scope to the forces of supply and demand to set wages and the level of employment. It is a policy advocated by free-market economists and neo-liberal politicians and is based on the conviction that the regulation of the labour market promotes inefficiency and generates **perverse effects**. Two kinds of employment regulation may be targeted by a policy of deregulation. First, statutory employment rights providing protections to individual workers may be abolished or weakened. The UK Conservative government of the 1980s and 1990s, for example, abolished the **wages councils** that set minimum rates of pay in low-wage industries and lengthened the **qualifying period** for protection from **unfair dismissal** from six months to two years. Second, **joint regulation** and **collective bargaining** may be targeted through legislation that weakens trade unions and makes it more difficult for them to secure **recognition** and bargain effectively with employers. Again, the Conservative government provides an example with its extensive reform of trade union law, which narrowed trade union **immunity** and made it much more difficult for unions to use the strike weapon.

derogation is a clause within a European **directive** that permits variable or flexible implementation provided certain conditions are met. For example, the **Working Time Directive** allows for the length of the average working week to be calculated over a longer period of time provided this is done with the agreement of the workforce.

deskilling is the process of reducing the skill content of jobs as a result of technical change or **job redesign**. The most influential theorist of deskilling is industrial sociologist Harry Braverman, whose 1974 book *Labor and Monopoly Capital* outlined a general tendency towards deskilling and the **degradation of work** within capitalist societies, under the conditions of increasingly competitive economic environments. His ideas launched an interest in studying the labour process (see **labour process theory**) and although his work has been widely criticized, his legacy remains important—not least in its fervent attack on Taylorism (see **scientific management**) and **Fordism**.

determinism (1) At the individual level, determinism means that people are not free to choose their own actions. They are constrained by external factors that are beyond their own control. True determinists would believe that all their behaviour is beyond their control, and that they are totally without free will. At the other extreme are those who believe they have total choice, with no external constraints. In reality, most people hold viewpoints that fall between these two extremes by accepting that whilst there are constraints on their actions, they also have some freedom of choice.

determinism (2) In the context of organization theory, determinism means that an organization is constrained by particular circumstances, thereby limiting management choice of action. The dominant determining factor can vary. For example, some theorists of determinism argue that environment is the most important factor that provides either opportunities or limitations for decision-makers in an organization. From this perspective, the extent to which the environment is stable or turbulent, or dynamic or static, will constrain managerial strategy. To take another example, technological determinists might argue that the way work can be organized is entirely dependent on the particular technology in use; they would reject the idea that it is possible to have different ways of working which are equally efficient for any given technology. In other words, determinists believe that managers are victims of their circumstances and have only limited choices when devising strategies or taking action. [See also **contingency theory**.]

detriment Employees have a statutory right in the UK not to be subjected to detriment, or action short of dismissal, on trade union grounds. The purpose of this law is to prevent unfavourable treatment by employers of those who join or become active in trade unions or who refuse to join a **trade union**. The Employment Relations Act 1999 contains an important clarification of the meaning of 'detriment' and states that it includes not just a positive act (such as denying promotion to union activists) but also an omission. This is an important change because it makes it difficult for employers effectively to bribe employees to surrender union membership or **collective bargaining** by offering more favourable conditions to those on **personal contracts**. Employees are also protected from detriment in relation to their role as safety representatives, trustees of pension funds, employee representatives, and if they exercise their rights under the Public Interest Disclosure Act 1998. An **Employment Tribunal** can award compensation for detriment and there is no maximum payment.

deviant innovation is a term coined by management theorist Karen Legge to describe an approach to personnel management that attempts to broaden the measures of organizational success from the conventional business and production values to include social values. In contrast, 'conformist innovation' is an approach that accepts the conventional success measures and seeks ways of managing people to meet these bottom-line objectives. Therefore, a personnel manager could be described as a deviant innovator if he or she uses new techniques and ideas for managing human resources that challenge conventional thinking and force other managers in the organization to view employees as assets. On the other hand, a personnel manager could be described as a conformist innovator if he or she is willing to adopt new tools and techniques only if they can be shown to improve the efficiency of managing people in line with the conventional management thinking that views employees as a cost.

devolution is the act of passing power, control, and responsibility from one part of the organization to another. Typically this means passing it down the hierarchy to lower levels, and in this way it is often associated with **decentralization**. An important contemporary development has been the devolution to line managers of some of the activities that have traditionally been the responsibility of the personnel department. For example, staff appraisal, grievance handling, discipline, and setting pay levels are being devolved to line managers in some organizations, thereby leaving the personnel specialists free to concentrate on the strategic aspects of managing people. Researchers disagree as to the extent of such devolution and point to the potential problems that can occur, such as work overload and the lack of specialist skill possessed by line managers.

differential The advantage in the rate of pay or earnings enjoyed by a higher-paid group of employees over a lower-paid group. Differentials are usually expressed as a percentage figure or, where the differential is very large, as a multiple of the lower rate of pay. Skilled manual workers, for instance, might enjoy a 30 per cent differential over unskilled manual workers, while the differential over other employees of senior executives might be equal to ten times the median salary within the organization. Differentials may be calculated within an organization or across an industrial sector or entire economy, and while they are usually calculated to examine differences between occupational groups, the concept can also be applied to differences between the sexes, ethnic groups, the able-bodied and disabled, and the more and less educated. From an organizational perspective, it is common to draw a distinction between internal and external differentials (note these may also be called internal and external relativities). An internal differential or relativity is the advantage in pay of an occupational group or grade compared with other occupations or grades within the organization. An external differential or relativity is the advantage in pay over members of the same group working for other organizations. In a large, profitable company, for instance, skilled workers will enjoy an internal differential over the unskilled but may also enjoy an external differential over skilled workers in smaller, less profitable companies. The trend in the UK and the United States has been for differentials to widen both within and between organizations in recent years, as part of the general movement towards greater inequality in the labour market. Within organizations the earnings of the better paid, and particularly senior managers, have tended to pull away from those of the lower paid, and within occupations there has also been a process of greater dispersion of earnings. [See **pay dispersion**.]

dignity at work policy A policy that is designed to eliminate harassment and bullying of employees and to ensure, in particular, that women workers, members of ethnic minorities, the disabled, and gays and lesbians are guaranteed respectful treatment by managers and co-workers.

Dilbert A key management figure to emerge from the pen of cartoonist Scott Adams, and the eponymous hero of the book *The Dilbert Principle* (Harper Business, 1996). It is essential reading for anyone who takes the process of management too seriously.

dilution is the use of less-skilled labour to undertake work traditionally performed by apprentice-trained craft workers. Dilution has often been fiercely resisted by skilled workers and their trade unions, who have seen it as a threat to jobs, earnings, and status. In the UK during the two World Wars dilution involved the use of women workers in munitions factories and other areas of traditionally male employment.

direct communication is the process whereby managers contact employees through various techniques such as **team briefing**, **cascade communication**, and newsletters. The main idea behind the concept is that managers are communicating without any intermediaries, such as the trade union representative. Direct communication is considered by some commentators to be one of the indicators of how managers are marginalizing the role of the trade unions.

direct control see **responsible autonomy**

direct discrimination and indirect discrimination are legal definitions of unlawful action under the terms of the anti-discrimination legislation in the UK. Direct discrimination occurs when the treatment of, or attitude towards, a person is less favourable because of their sex, race/ethnicity, or disability, and where there is no **genuine occupational qualification** that justifies the favourable treatment. Indirect discrimination occurs when an unjustifiable requirement or condition is applied equally but has the consequence of disadvantaging a larger proportion of one sex than the other, or a particular racial/ethnic group (it does not apply to disability). An unjustifiable requirement or condition means that justifications cannot be made on any grounds other than sex or race.

direct effect Provided they are unconditional and sufficiently precise, articles of the founding treaties of the European Union can have direct effect in the courts of member states. This means that individuals can enforce their rights under the treaties in a national court, even if there is no relevant domestic legislation. For example, cases have been taken to **Employment Tribunals** in the UK under Article 141 of the EC Treaty (formerly Article 119), which guarantees the right to **equal pay**. European **directives** can also have 'vertical direct effect' where the employee is employed in an 'emanation of the state', such as a local authority or privatized utility.

directive A European statute that is adopted by the Council of Ministers and which must be enacted by member states through a national Act of Parliament or an equivalent measure. Directives typically set out a framework of principles and legislative objectives, therefore, which is given greater detail as it is transposed into national law, regulations, or collective agreements. In the employment sphere there are important directives dealing with **health and safety, equal pay, equal opportunity, transfer of undertakings, collective redundancies, atypical work, working time,** and **European works councils**. Under European law, directives have vertical **direct effect**; that is they can provide the basis for a legal case against an 'emanation of the state' but not against a private individual or company. Action of the latter kind can only be initiated on the basis of national law giving effect to a directive. Under the **negotiation track**, agreed at Maastricht, the content of directives can be negotiated by the **social partners**.

direct participation is a system of worker participation in management decision-making that rests upon the direct involvement of individual employees. [See **employee involvement**; **indirect participation**.]

direct reports are the employees accountable to a particular **line manager**.

disability Arriving at a robust definition of disability is very difficult because different social groups have different views on what constitutes ability and disability. For instance, being short-sighted is not considered a disability in western societies where correction lenses (glasses or contact lenses) are readily available. However, in developing countries where the cost of correcting short-sightedness is beyond the economic means of the average person, it can be considered a disability. Consequently there is a range of physical and psychological differences between people that might in some circumstances be described as disability, yet not in others. Nevertheless, the legal definition of disability in the UK, identified by the Disability Discrimination Act 1995, is 'a physical or mental impairment that has a substantial and long term effect on a person's ability to carry out normal day to day activities'. [See **discrimination**.]

Disability Rights Commission (DRC) The DRC was established by the Labour government in 1999 and is the UK's third equality commission alongside the **Commission for Racial Equality** and the **Equal Opportunities Commission**. It discharges broadly the same functions and has equivalent powers with respect to the rights of the disabled as do the other commissions. The DRC is charged with reviewing the Disability Discrimination Act 1995 and recommending its amendment, has rights of investigation and enforcement of disability legislation, and is responsible for advising employers on how to secure equal treatment of disabled employees. It replaces an earlier and weaker body, the National Disability Council, established by the Conservatives in the 1990s.

disciplinary interview An interview to which an employee is called to reply to a complaint or charge under a formal **disciplinary procedure**. In most cases, the interview will proceed from a statement of the complaint, through the employee's response and cross-questioning, towards a summing up, which may result in the issuing of a disciplinary warning or penalty. The interview may include statements from witnesses and the representation of the employee by a co-worker or trade union official. Advice for employers on the conduct of disciplinary interviews is provided by the **Advisory, Conciliation, and Arbitration Service**.

disciplinary procedure A formal procedure that is established by managers to uphold disciplinary standards. Procedures frequently contain a statement of disciplinary policy and a listing of acceptable and unacceptable behaviour. In addition, they set out rules to be followed in dealing with cases of indiscipline, including a statement of the penalties attached to various forms or levels of misconduct. The **Advisory, Conciliation, and Arbitration Service code of practice** on discipline and **dismissal** recommends that procedures should be written down, should allow for the proper investigation of disciplinary cases, including the collection of evidence, and should allow for an employee defence through a representative, such as a trade union officer. The employee should also have a right of appeal. ACAS further recommends that, except in cases of **gross misconduct**, there should be no dismissal for a first disciplinary offence. Partly for this reason, most procedures embody the **corrective principle** and operate through a number of stages. This allows for employees to be warned about their conduct and allows them to change and improve, possibly after retraining or **counselling**. Formal disciplinary procedures exist in the vast majority of UK companies that employ more than twenty-five employees and their spread across the economy has been a notable feature of the **formalization** of workplace industrial relations since the 1960s.

discipline is the process of setting and enforcing acceptable standards of behaviour within the employing organization, in many cases through the medium of a formal **disciplinary procedure**. Disciplinary standards and the rigour of enforcement are highly variable across workplaces, reflecting differences in the economic position of enterprises, the status, gender, and bargaining power of workers, and the customs and traditions of different industries. Despite variation, however, a basic and nearly universal distinction is drawn between relatively minor forms of ill discipline and more serious offences, such as theft, fraud, and violence, which constitute **gross misconduct**. Offences of the first kind include problems with attendance, **absenteeism**, and performance and are likely to be addressed in the first instance through minor sanctions, while offences of the latter kind typically result in **dismissal**. Sociologists have noted that workplace discipline often takes the form of a 'negotiated order', in which there is a degree of flexibility and 'give and take' in the application of formal disciplinary rules. Forms of behaviour that contravene formal standards may be tolerated (e.g. early finishing) as a means of maintaining good working relationships. Notwithstanding this observation, however, there is evidence of a tightening of disciplinary standards in UK workplaces, which reflects the broader shift in the balance of workplace power towards employers since the early 1980s.

disciplined worker thesis A thesis about recent change in workplace relations based on two core propositions. The first is that there has been an intensification of work and a tightening of disciplinary standards associated with the introduction of **Total Quality Management**, **lean production**, and other new forms of work organization. The second, and counter-intuitive, proposition is that many workers view this change positively and welcome a work environment that is better managed and more challenging.

disclosure of information The requirement in law for employers to provide information to the representatives of recognized unions to allow them to engage in **collective bargaining**. The information to which unions are entitled can include data on pay rates and labour costs, business performance, staffing levels, conditions of service, and productivity. If a union feels that it has been denied access to bargaining information it can complain to the **Central Arbitration Committee** and, if the complaint is accepted, the employer can be required to provide the information. The obligation to disclose information for collective bargaining was imposed on employers in the Employment Protection Act 1975. The underlying rationale is that bargaining will be more effective and more likely to result in a mutually beneficial outcome if both sides are adequately informed. ACAS has produced a Code of Practice on the *Disclosure of Information to Trade Unions for Collective Bargaining Purposes*.

discrimination is the process of judging people according to particular criteria. For example, in the selection process for a teaching post, the appointment panel might discriminate in favour of a candidate who answers their questions clearly and concisely, and discriminate against a candidate who mutters and digresses from the point. However, when most people use the term discrimination they tend to mean *unfair* discrimination. The word is mainly used to denote that the criterion on which the discrimination has occurred is unjust. So it is likely that most people would not describe the example above as discrimination because they would consider the criteria the panel used (clarity, conciseness) as fair. However, if the criterion the appointment panel used to choose between candidates was gender or race, then most people would consider it unfair and recognize it as discrimination. [See **equal opportunity; direct discrimination; positive discrimination**.]

dismissal or 'the sack' in common parlance, occurs when an employer terminates the employment contract. In law, dismissal can occur in three ways. First, 'express', 'actual', or 'direct' dismissal occurs when the employer terminates the contract with or without notice to the employee. Second, dismissal can occur as a result of the non-renewal of a **fixed-term contract**. Third, there can be a **constructive dismissal** where the employer breaches the contract of employment, allowing the employee to leave employment without tendering his or her resignation. An employee who is dismissed is entitled to **written reasons for dismissal** and has two potential remedies. A case for **unfair dismissal** can be taken to an **Employment Tribunal** on the grounds that the dismissal was for an unfair reason or failed the test of **reasonableness**. Alternatively, a case for **wrongful dismissal** can be taken. Dismissal is a common occurrence in business but the rate of dismissal is significantly higher in small firms, in the private sector, and in companies where there is no trade union.

dismissal with notice is the final penalty for employee misconduct that falls short of **gross misconduct**. For example, if employees are persistently late, absent, or perform to a low standard and have failed to improve their conduct then dismissal with notice may occur as the final stage within a **disciplinary procedure**. Before leaving their employment, therefore, the employees will work their **notice period** or, as is more usual, will receive payment in lieu of notice. Minimum notice periods are set down in law.

dismissal without notice is immediate or summary dismissal and should only occur in the event of **gross misconduct** by the employee. The effect of gross misconduct is to destroy the employment contract and consequently the employer is entitled, lawfully, to dismiss without notice.

dispute An employment or industrial dispute is an expression of conflict between employers and employees. It can refer either to the issue that generates conflict or to the actions taken by those who are party to the conflict; for instance strikes are sometimes described as industrial disputes. Disputes can arise for a wide variety of reasons and assume a number of different forms. A basic division can be drawn, however, between individual disputes between employers and their employees and collective disputes that involve employers and trade unions. A major purpose of the **industrial relations system** is to allow the handling and resolution of employment disputes with minimum disruption to the economy and wider society. [See **dispute resolution; disputes procedure.**]

dispute resolution is the process of settling industrial disputes, which in many cases will involve the use of **third-party intervention** to conciliate, mediate, or arbitrate between the two sides. The provision of dispute resolution services is an important aspect of state intervention in employment relations. In the UK this function is currently discharged by the **Advisory, Conciliation, and Arbitration Service** (ACAS).

disputes procedure is an industrial relations procedure established to allow the resolution of industrial disputes without recourse to **industrial action**. Disputes procedures typically proceed through a series of stages and conclude with the involvement of a third party, such as ACAS, to provide **conciliation, mediation,** or **arbitration**.

distance learning is study for an educational or vocational qualification at home with learning materials provided by post, television, or increasingly, the internet (see **University for Industry**). Many vocational and management courses are delivered in this way.

distinctive competence is a term used in business strategy for the strengths that give an organization an advantage over its competitors.

distributive bargaining A zero-sum approach to **collective bargaining**, in which gains for one side are made at the expense of the other. Distributive bargaining may flourish in a situation of **low trust** and be associated with the threat and deployment of sanctions by employers and trade unions. It is often characteristic of wage negotiations, where gains for the union and its members are achieved directly at the expense of the employer. Advocates of the reform of collective bargaining suggest that distributive bargaining be replaced by integrative or **positive-sum** bargaining, in which the two sides co-operate to find mutually beneficial solutions to shared problems. [See **integrative bargaining**.]

distributive equity is the perception of fairness felt by an employee about his or her remuneration in relation to his or her effort and contribution to the organization, and compared with other employees. [See **equity theory**.]

distributive justice is the ethical principle of 'fair shares' commensurate to input, within either the individual enterprise or the wider economy. The principle might be given effect through a **gain-sharing** or **profit-sharing** plan that ensures employees are rewarded for contributing to improvements in enterprise performance. [See **business ethics; procedural justice**.]

divergence is the concept that national employment systems will remain distinctive and will not converge on a common pattern. The sources of divergence have been variously identified as national culture, the institutions of industrial relations, the strategies of ruling elites, and the structure of national economies. [See **convergence; path dependent**.]

diversification occurs when the managers of an organization make the strategic decision to expand their business by either (1) adding new, related operations and functions to their existing products/services, or (2) developing new products/services that bear no relation to their existing ones.

diversity see **managing diversity**

divestment occurs when a diversified corporation gets rid of one or more of its subsidiary businesses through sale, liquidation, or management buyout. The decision to divest may arise due to a lack of **synergy** between the subsidiary and the parent company.

divisionalization is the process through which an organization's structure is changed from being organized in functional departments (see **U-form**) to being configured around self-contained units based on specific product ranges or services, or geographical areas. The need for divisionalization frequently arises from organizational growth and **diversification**. [See **M-form**.]

division of labour is the extent to which jobs in an organization are subdivided into separate tasks. [See **scientific management; Fordism; job redesign**.]

domestic-incident leave is leave that is taken by employees to cope with domestic emergencies. Under the Employment Relations Act 1999 employees have an entitlement to take a reasonable amount of time off (which is unpaid) to deal with incidents involving dependants. Leave is limited to births, deaths, injuries, illnesses, the failure of arrangements for looking after dependants, and emergencies affecting a child at school or on a school trip. [See **parental leave; special leave**.]

Donovan Report The report of a Royal Commission into British industrial relations that was chaired by Lord Donovan in the 1960s. Its main recommendations were that the voluntarist tradition of **collective laissez-faire** should be maintained but that there should be a government-sponsored reform of workplace industrial relations. The key features of the latter were to be the professionalization of **personnel management**, the **formalization** of **enterprise bargaining**, and increased use of company industrial relations **procedures** to regulate conflict and reduce the number of **unconstitutional strikes**.

downsizing means getting rid of employees. It may occur through **redundancy** or **natural wastage**. Organizations have been downsizing to cut costs and streamline their operations in the face of increasing intensity of competition. As well as the obviously negative consequences for the victims of downsizing, there are wider implications for those who remain in the organization. There is the fear of 'who will it be next time' and the inevitable **work intensification** for those who are left. Particularly vulnerable to downsizing are managers, because it is an unavoidable consequence of **delayering**.

downward occupational mobility is a transition to lower-status and lower-paid employment. Movement of this kind is often typical of women who re-enter employment after a career break for childbirth. [See **demotion**.]

dress code A requirement that employees should wear certain forms of dress when attending work. For example, it may be expected that employees wear formal clothes (e.g. suits and ties) that are viewed as appropriate to a business environment. There has been a relaxation of dress codes in many organizations in recent years, however, with some companies instituting 'dressing down' days when employees are encouraged to come to work in casual clothes. The thinking behind this is that it promotes a more relaxed and productive work environment, conducive to **teamworking**. Dress codes can prove controversial and have been challenged in the courts when they discriminate against women as, for example, might occur when men wear trousers to work but women are forbidden to and are required to wear skirts.

dual burden refers to the involvement in paid employment of women while they continue to have prime responsibility for domestic labour and child- and elder-care. [See **sexual contract**.]

dual commitment is a term used to describe circumstances when an employee feels a divided loyalty between commitment to the organization and commitment to another group—usually a trade union or professional association. Some extreme commentators argue that if employees have dual commitment they can never be fully trusted to give 100 per cent to the organization. However, employees will always have multiple commitments to various institutions and people—for example, to family, friends, sports clubs, religious groups, community groups—and to expect total commitment to the organization is ludicrously unrealistic (see **greedy institution**). Besides, multiple commitments may reflect an appropriate balance between work, leisure, and social responsibilities. [See **organizational commitment**.]

dumb-sizing is a joke term to describe the process of getting rid of staff (**downsizing**) and then finding that the supposed efficiency gains through cost savings do not materialize.

duty of care Under the common law of contract employers in the UK owe a duty of care to their employees; that is, they are obliged to provide safe equipment, a safe workplace, and safe fellow employees. The latter means that dangerous practical jokers can be sacked. Recent cases have established that this duty of care extends to the realm of **job stress** and the obligation of the employer to ameliorate working conditions and practices that cause mental ill health.

E

early retirement occurs when employees retire from their job before the normal contractual age for retirement. It is often used as an alternative to **redundancy** because it allows people to leave work voluntarily and begin drawing an **occupational pension**. Early retirement can prove expensive, however, and with the progressive ageing of the workforce in the UK and other developed economies there is growing criticism of this method of workforce reduction.

earnings are the **remuneration** employees receive in return for work. Earnings might consist of a number of different elements, including the basic wage or salary and supplementary payments, such as shift or overtime pay, unsocial-hours payments, back pay, or payment for special duties and responsibilities. Earnings may be expressed as 'gross earnings', that is, the total amount earned before **income tax** and **National Insurance Contributions** are deducted, or as 'net earnings', the amount actually received in the pay packet or salary cheque once these and other contributions have been deducted. Net earnings are also commonly referred to as **take-home pay**. Under European law, employees are entitled to an itemized statement of their pay, which will set out earnings for each pay period (usually a week or month). [See **wage**.]

economic activity rate The proportion of the workforce that is either employed or registered officially as unemployed and seeking work.

economies of scale is a concept that describes a situation where an organization can increase its volume of production, but decrease the costs associated with each unit produced due to the standardization of both the goods being produced and the processes associated with their production. The advantages of economies of scale therefore push organizations towards becoming high-volume producers of standardized products and services, for **mass consumption** (see **Fordism**). However, more recently an additional effect of **economies of scope** has been noted by some commentators (see, for example, **flexible specialization**), which suggests that flexibility of production and service delivery is an increasingly important factor for organizations to consider.

economies of scope is a concept associated with the increasing availability of advanced technologies that allow for greater variation in the production of goods or services without incurring prohibitive costs. It means that organizations can take advantage of flexible methods of production or service delivery and thereby create a wider range of products or services to satisfy greater variation in customer demands, or offer a greater range to entice customers (thereby stimulating demand). Whereas **economies of scale** are associated with high-volume, standardized, mass production, economies of scope allow small-volume, flexible, batch production for niche markets. [See **flexible specialization; mass customization**.]

efficiency wage A concept developed within economics to explain why employers offer wages which seemingly are above the market-determined rate. Efficiency wage theory holds that employers offer high wages to reduce **labour turnover**, inhibit shirking and unobserved ill discipline, and create a sense of obligation (a 'gift relationship') in the employee, who responds with higher productivity. Efficiency wages may also generate a high volume of applications for vacancies, allowing the employer to select the best candidates. The ultimate result of these different mechanisms, according to the theory, is that high wages are self-financing as the employer gets more for paying more.

effort bargain The exchange of effort for **reward** which lies at the core of the **employment relationship**. This sociological concept captures the tacit or customary nature of the economic exchange within work and assumes that accepted norms regulate the worker's input. As such, it can guide the analysis of workplace conflict, which may arise when an established effort–reward ratio is disrupted through management action; for example, by managers seeking to raise effort levels without offering a pay increase in return. It can also be used to analyze change in the employment relationship, and arguably a feature of much work restructuring in recent years has been to shift the effort bargain in the employer's favour so that effort has increased disproportionately to reward. Finally, the process of 'effort bargaining' refers to attempts by workers to seek compensation in pay for any increase in effort.

e-cruitment see e-recruitment

e-learning is the acquisition of competencies, knowledge, and skills through electronic media, such as the internet or a company intranet. [See **computer-assisted instruction**; **on-line learning**; **University for Industry**.]

electronic cottages or telecottages are the premises where **telecottaging** is undertaken.

emotional labour is a concept developed by organizational sociologist Arlene Hochschild which describes the work performed by any service employee who is required, as part of his or her job, to display specific sets of emotions (both verbal and non-verbal) with the aim of inducing particular feelings and responses among those for whom the service is being provided. In this respect, employees are being required to control and use their own emotions in order to influence the emotional state of others. While some jobs (like nursing) have always had this dimension, it can be argued that emotional labour has become more widespread with the growth of the service sector and **customer-facing** jobs. Indeed, the term has become increasingly popular because of the emphasis on providing a quality service (see **Total Quality Management**) so that the customer or client is satisfied not only with the service provided, but also with the service encounter itself. [See **body work**; **customer care**.]

empirical evidence is information that has been derived through direct observation, experiments, or experience. Typically empirical evidence is generated in order to test theories. For example, in order to test the theoretical proposition that 'a happy worker is a productive worker', social scientists have examined whether there is a correlation between **job satisfaction** and individual performance, and have discovered that no direct relationship exists. Empirical evidence is therefore the basis of most academic research—although those researchers who focus solely on data are often criticized for being too empirically focused, and are labelled empiricists. [See **empiricism**.]

empiricism is a tendency to rely very heavily on data and to neglect theories and concepts. Empiricism is therefore an approach that rejects the idea that knowledge can be generated through abstract, logical reasoning alone. Instead it assumes that the basis of knowledge stems from direct observation, experiments, or experience.

empiricist Someone who stresses the importance of **empirical evidence** as the basis of all knowledge.

employability is the possession of marketable skills and attributes by an employee that are in demand from employers. The seeming decline of the **job for life** has led to increased interest in the concept of employability and, according to some, a 'new deal' is emerging in business, in which employers provide **training** and **employee development** opportunities to allow employees to maintain employability in return for commitment and effort. [See **psychological contract**.]

employee A worker who is hired under a **contract of employment**. [See **employment status**.]

employee assistance programme (EAP) A confidential personal **counselling** service funded by an employer. EAPs provide professional counsellors with whom individuals can discuss their work- and non-work-related problems, which may be emotional, financial, or legal or related to alcohol or drug misuse. [See **stress management**.]

employee development is the system of providing opportunities for employees within an organization to reach their full potential (through improving skill and **competency**), and become of greater value to the organization. Typically employment development incorporates three sets of activities: **training**, **management development**, and **career management**. The policies and techniques aimed at developing employees differ widely between organizations. Whilst many organizations claim that they value their employees, a good test of whether this is anything more than rhetoric is to assess the organization's employee development systems and budget. If employees truly are valued, then the organization will be willing to commit resources to them through employee development systems.

employee involvement (EI) is usually defined as those arrangements for worker **participation** that are designed by managers and instigated by employers. EI techniques include **direct communication**, **team briefing**, **suggestion schemes**, and **quality circles**. As this list suggests, EI initiatives are usually task based, leaving strategic business decisions securely in the hands of managers, and their adoption is motivated primarily by a desire to improve worker and business performance. These techniques are designed to encourage employees to identify with employer objectives and allow them to contribute directly to the improvement of business operations. There is evidence of an increase in the use of EI techniques in recent years, which is viewed by many as an indicator of employers adopting **soft HRM**.

employee participation see **participation**

employee relations is a common title for the industrial relations function within personnel management and is also sometimes used as an alternative label for the academic field of **industrial relations**. The term underlines the fact that industrial relations is not confined to the study of trade unions but embraces the broad pattern of employee management, including systems of **direct communication** and **employee involvement** that target the individual worker.

employee share ownership An arrangement whereby employees are granted shares in the company or given the opportunity to purchase them at a favourable price. Successive UK governments have advocated employee share ownership and there are a variety of tax incentives to encourage firms to introduce schemes and employees to participate in them. Schemes assume a number of different forms. Under one arrangement, employees join a **Save-As-You-Earn** (SAYE) scheme and use the proceeds to exercise a **share option**. Under another, a proportion of profits is allocated to a trust fund, which uses the money to purchase shares to be distributed amongst the workforce. Employee share ownership is advocated as a means of **financial participation** and as a route to securing **high trust** and co-operative relationships within industry. There is evidence that schemes are associated with improvements in business performance but research on employee responses suggests that they have only a modest impact on attitudes and behaviour. [See **All-Employee Share Plan; Company Share Option Plan; Enterprise Management Incentive; profit-sharing.**]

employee share/stock ownership plan (ESOP) see employee share ownership

employee voice is the process through which employees raise grievances and express needs and preferences at work, though it can also refer to the institutional mechanisms (e.g. **grievance procedure, open door policy, trade union, works council**) through which voice is heard. Voice is often contrasted with 'exit' as a response to discontent. 'Exit' means that workers leave an employing organization that is unresponsive to their needs and seek employment elsewhere, whereas 'voice' allows them to raise problems and have them addressed by the employing organization. This contrast points to one of the benefits of voice: it allows managers to design an employment system that accommodates the interests of workers and so reduces dissatisfaction and labour turnover. [See **exit-voice-loyalty; union voice.**]

employers' association A collective organization of employers, usually based upon a particular industry or industry segment. Prominent examples in the UK include the Engineering Employers'

Federation (EEF), the Newspaper Society, the Association of Colleges, the Producers' Alliance for Cinema and Television (PACT), the Chemical Industries Association (CIA), the Road Haulage Association (RHA), and the National Farmers' Union (NFU). Employers' associations are important actors within the **industrial relations system** of many countries and discharge a number of functions. In the past they were involved extensively in resisting unionization but today they engage in **collective bargaining** and processes of **dispute resolution** with trade unions. In addition, employers' associations lobby governments and provide a range of consultancy, research, and advisory services to their members. The latter activity has grown in importance in recent years as **industry bargaining** has declined in significance. Employers' associations continue to play a central role in industrial relations in many European countries, though there are indications of decline. These include reducing membership, non-membership amongst large, inward-investing companies, and tension between large and small firms, particularly over wages policy and relations with trade unions. Employers' associations are representative organizations and, in most cases, their activities are overseen by an elected council or conference. The commitment to democratic decision-making and accountability of trade unions, however, tends not to be as strong on the employers' side. Many employers' associations affiliate to **confederations** of business at national level (e.g. **Confederation of British Industry**) and European level (e.g. UNICE). [See **multi-employer bargaining**.]

employment is a term with two primary meanings. First, it is the state of being paid to work for someone else under a **contract of employment**. Second, it is the state of being gainfully occupied whether in an employed or **self-employed** capacity. Full employment occurs when everyone wishing to be gainfully occupied can find work.

employment agency A private **labour market intermediary** that provides **agency labour** to client organizations. Where an employment agency is used, therefore, a three-way employment relationship emerges involving the agency, the agency worker, and the client. Employment agencies have become more important labour market institutions across the developed world in recent years and the principal agencies, such as Manpower and Adecco SA, are major international employers in their own right. However, alongside these large, general suppliers of agency labour, there are many smaller companies that typically specialize in the supply of particular skills, such as acting, nursing, teaching, lorry-driving, or engineering. Recent developments in the activities of employment agencies have included 'relational contracting', in which the agency undertakes to provide all temporary labour for a large client company for a fixed period of time, and **insourcing**, where the agency manages agency labour at the client organization's work-site.

Employment Appeal Tribunal (EAT) A judicial body that hears appeals referred from **Employment Tribunals**. It consists of a lawyer chair (often a High Court judge) and two or four lay persons nominated by business and labour. As with Employment Tribunals, the lay persons can outvote the chair. In terms of precedence the EAT binds Employment Tribunals and is itself bound by decisions of the Court of Appeal and the House of Lords. The workload of the EAT has increased in recent years and it currently deals with more than 1,000 cases a year.

employment at will is the doctrine that employees can be hired and fired at will by the employer. Employment at will still prevails as a legal principle in the USA where non-union employees have very little protection from arbitrary dismissal. However, in the UK and other European countries, there are legal safeguards for employees to ensure that they are not dismissed unreasonably or without good cause. The law of **unfair dismissal** is particularly important in regulating the employer's behaviour in this regard.

employment law is the body of law that governs the sphere of employment relations. It consists of the legal rights and obligations of the various parties to the employment relationship (e.g. employers, workers, trade unions, employers' associations, and third parties) together with procedures for enforcing these rights and obligations. Enforcement is achieved through a compulsory mechanism provided by the state and rests on a number of legal sanctions that may be criminal (fines and imprisonment), or civil (e.g. an award of compensation), or administrative (e.g. withdrawal of a licence or subsidy by government). Employment law may be set out in statutes or in a comprehensive **labour code** or take the form of common law, that is, rules of law that are not based on legislation but on custom and usage and on judicial decisions. The common law of contract is a particularly important feature of employment law in the UK. Another distinction is between **individual employment law** and **collective employment law**, which regulate respectively the individual and collective aspects of the employment relationship. National systems of employment law differ markedly, with some countries relying heavily on statutory regulation while others have a tradition of common law. A further distinction can be drawn between states that rely heavily on **legal regulation** of employment and those with a tradition of **voluntarism**, characterized by greater reliance on **unilateral regulation** and **collective bargaining**. In addition to national systems of employment law there is a growing body of international law. This includes the **directives** and other legal instruments of the European Union, and **international labour standards** formulated by the **International Labour Organization** and other regulatory agencies. At both national and international levels employment law is a dynamic entity which is added to and extended through the passing of new legislation and case law; that is, clarifying or interpreting existing law in the light of changed circumstances and particular cases. Monitoring the development of employment law, ensuring compliance, and minimizing the risk of legal sanction are among the primary functions of specialist HR managers.

employment relations is an alternative and increasingly common label for the academic field of **industrial relations**. Unlike the latter term, it does not have a narrow association with trade unions and traditional manufacturing industry and so signals the fact that employment relations in non-union and service sector companies fall within the ambit of study. The continued use of the word 'relations', however, stresses the fact that the subject is not concerned solely with the practice of management but also embraces the interests and activities of employees, trade unions, and governments.

employment relationship The economic and social relationship between the buyers and sellers of labour. The term is used widely in the management and social sciences; it covers a broad range of relationships and is not restricted to a situation in which there is a formal **contract of employment**. It is legitimate therefore to refer to the employment relationship between **self-employed** workers and those who use their labour. The employment relationship has a number of dimensions. First, while it is in the first instance an economic exchange it can also form the basis of a social relationship, in which worker and employer accept mutual obligations and commitment (see **mutual gains**; **paternalism**). Second, it is both a market relationship, in which **labour power** or the capacity to work is exchanged for wages, and a work relationship, in which the employer uses that capacity in the process of production. Third, the employment relationship is indeterminate in the sense that the employer buys the worker's capacity to work but has no guarantee that the capacity will be used to perform productive labour. For this reason, employers must manage labour and either control or secure the co-operation of workers to ensure that labour power is transformed into useful work. Fourth, the employment relationship is often regarded as a relationship of subordination, as workers accept the authority and control of the employer within the employing organization. Fifth and finally, worker and employer bring different interests to the employment relationship, which in some cases provide for co-operation; e.g. workers want secure, well-paid employment and employers want high performance and this can result in a **productivity coalition**. In other cases, however, these competing interests lead to conflict, as when workers **strike** over the price of labour or engage in **restriction of output** because they value free time and autonomy and resent management control.

employment security see **security of employment**

employment status refers to the classification of workers according to whether they are employees, who are employed under a **contract of employment**, or independent or **self-employed** workers, who may work under a contract for services. This distinction is important in UK law because it determines the application of rights and obligations under legislation concerning employment protection, social security, and taxation.

Employment Tribunal (previously Industrial Tribunal) Employment Tribunals were established in the UK in the 1960s and are judicial bodies which hear and determine statutory employment claims. Essentially, they are specialist **labour courts** through which workers can enforce their statutory employment rights and obtain compensation and redress for breaches of these rights. Tribunals are composed of a lawyer chair plus two lay members or 'wingmen' [sic], representing business and labour. The jurisdiction of tribunals is extensive and has broadened considerably since they were first established. Currently they deal with more than fifty different statutory employment rights, including **unfair dismissal**, **discrimination** on the grounds of race, sex, and disability, **deductions from wages**, **equal pay**, breaches of contract, and **redundancy**. Employment Tribunals are meant to operate less formally than normal courts, though there is criticism of growing legalism within the system. This latter development is due partly to the fact that applicants who are legally represented have a substantially greater chance of winning their case. Appeals against tribunal judgments are generally allowed only on questions of law and are referred, in the first instance, to the **Employment Appeal Tribunal**.

empowerment is the process of passing on authority to make decisions to others in the organization. It requires all employees to take responsibility for the quality of their work, and act in the best interest of the customer. For example, supermarket employees might be empowered to take off display and put in the waste bin any product they would not buy themselves—thus they are using their discretion to make judgments about quality without having to check with their supervisor. Empowerment also allows decisions to be made at lower levels in the organization, thereby improving the responsiveness of the organization. It has become popular due to firms operating in a more intense competitive environment, where there is an emphasis on quality and getting close to the customer. Potentially, all employees can be empowered, although the type and extent of empowerment can vary considerably. For example, for employees in a fast food outlet empowerment may mean nothing more than being able to greet the customer in the way they choose. In contrast, an employee in a call centre for telephone banking may be empowered to make credit adjustments up to a certain level without seeking the guidance of the supervisor. Total empowerment rarely occurs since it would allow employees to influence all aspects of the business, such as decisions over investment, dividend levels, profit margins, and so forth. There are concerns amongst some commentators that empowerment is being used to disguise work intensification. It is argued that empowerment usually entails taking on more responsibility for more work but with no extra money. Furthermore, in many instances, case study research shows that empowered workers are subject to increasingly sophisticated systems of monitoring and control (see **surveillance**). Commentators have pointed out the irony of this: empowerment is about trusting employees by giving them more responsibility and autonomy over their work, yet managers are backing this up with control systems that suggest employees cannot be trusted. So critics of empowerment often argue that it is a term used to disguise the grim reality of **work intensification**, **job stress**, and exploitation.

enemy within A description of the National Union of Mineworkers in particular, and militant trade unionism in general, coined by the UK Prime Minister, Margaret Thatcher, during the miners' strike of 1984–5. Thatcher referred to the need to defeat the 'enemy within' and so bracketed the miners with the 'enemy without', General Galtieri and the Argentinian military forces, which had been defeated in the Falklands War. The description was indicative of the depth of antipathy amongst the Conservative Party towards trade unionism in the 1980s and expressed a belief that unions lacked legitimate purpose. [See **Winter of Discontent**.]

enterprise bargaining is collective bargaining between trade unions and the management of a single enterprise that results in collective agreements that cover all the separate employing establishments within the company. [See **workplace bargaining**.]

Enterprise Management Incentive (EMI) A share option scheme introduced by the UK government to help smaller companies recruit and retain high-calibre employees. Under the scheme a maximum of fifteen employees can be given tax-advantaged options over shares worth up to £100,000 at the time of grant. [See **employee share ownership; golden handcuff; golden handshake**.]

enterprise union A trade union whose membership is restricted to employees of a single enterprise. Enterprise unionism is the dominant form within Japan, though there are plentiful examples in the UK and **staff associations** generally take this form. It has also been argued that a system of de facto enterprise unionism has emerged in the UK as a result of the decline of multi-employer bargaining and its replacement with enterprise and **workplace bargaining**. According to this view, semi-autonomous workplace trade union organization within large general unions is equivalent to the enterprise unionism found in Japan. Supporters of enterprise unionism argue that it leads to a co-operative relationship between employer and union. However, critics claim that the dependence of the union on the individual employer leads to quiescence and ineffective representation. [See **company union**.]

entry shock is the mismatch between what newcomers expect the organization to be like before they join, and what they find it to be like after they have joined. The newcomer feels disappointment (or in some cases resentment) and the process of **socialization** becomes more difficult, or even impossible. Entry shock explains why some employees leave after a very short time—which is obviously costly for the organization since the recruitment process has to be repeated. This emphasizes the need for organizations to provide accurate information to candidates during the recruitment process—sometimes called **realistic job previews**.

environmental health officers employed by local authorities are responsible for **health and safety** inspection in certain kinds of premises. Local authority inspectors cover offices, shops, hotels, restaurants, warehouses, leisure facilities, and places of entertainment, while **health and safety inspectors** employed by the **Health and Safety Executive** cover other kinds of business.

equality bargaining A term that refers to the inclusion of **equal opportunities** and **equal pay** issues in the agenda for **collective bargaining** between trade unions and employers. Research indicates that equality bargaining is not a feature of many agreements and this has been explained in terms of the absence of women from negotiating roles and the conservatism of both management and trade union negotiators, who tend to confine bargaining to a narrow and customary range of issues. There are indications, however, of some unions seeking to promote equality bargaining in recent years.

Equal Opportunities Commission (EOC) A statutory body established under the UK's Sex Discrimination Act 1975. It has four main responsibilities: to monitor the implementation of sex discrimination legislation; to give advice to employers on reviewing their human resource practices with regard to gender; to give advice to complainants; and to investigate organizations breaching the legislation.

equal opportunity is the concept of ensuring fair treatment for all employees (or prospective employees) throughout the organization. It emphasizes the importance of judging people according to the qualities, skills, and competencies they possess, rather than prejudging them because of characteristics such as gender, race/ethnicity, disability, age, or sexuality. Advocates of equal opportunities stress that within an organization managers have a central role in ensuring fairness because they make key decisions at the critical junctures that fundamentally affect a person's career chances and quality of working life: recruitment, selection, promotion, appraisal, training/development, and reward. However, one of the main disagreements amongst advocates of equal opportunity is how to ensure it is put into practice. On one side are those people who argue that it is sufficient to ensure there are fair procedures in place so that there is *equal treatment* of all employees. On the other side are those people who say that fair procedures are not enough because they do nothing to remove the existing inequality within the workplace. People taking this latter point of view emphasize the importance of *equal outcomes*. For example, imagine a case of two employees (one a white man, the other an Asian woman) applying for promotion to supervisor. *Equal treatment advocates* would argue that the main concern is to ensure that the promotion procedures are fair, systematic, and open, and apply equally to both candidates. This would ensure that the candidates compete on equal terms, and the best one would get the promotion. In other words, to use a colloquialism, the candidates would be competing on 'a level playing field'. In contrast, *equal outcome advocates* would argue that ensuring fair procedures is not sufficient because it does not take account of the unfair disadvantage that either of the candidates might have because of prejudice in the past. The Asian woman might have had less opportunity to take responsibilities, and hence have a weaker CV, because of the prejudicial attitudes and actions of her current supervisor. Thus, equal outcome advocates would argue for existing disadvantage to be redressed through establishing **quotas** for disadvantaged groups to ensure they are represented in the various departments and in the organizational hierarchy. So, the Asian woman's competitive disadvantage because of past prejudice would be counterbalanced by the organization's obligation to strive towards a representative workforce—only then would the candidates have 'the level playing field'. To summarize: advocates of equal opportunity agree on the principle but differ on how to put it into practice. [See **managing diversity; equal opportunity policy**.]

equal opportunity monitoring is the technique of collecting and analysing data on the composition of the workforce (particularly with regard to gender, ethnicity, age, religion, and disability) during key organizational processes: recruitment, selection, appraisal, promotion, training, discipline, and dismissal. The data are analyzed to reveal whether particular groups are under- or over-represented, and organizational policy-makers can then decide upon what action (if any) to take to redress the balance. In other words, monitoring is concerned with gathering **demographic** information and using this to inform equal opportunity policy and action.

equal opportunity policy is the set of procedures an organization has established to ensure the fair treatment of employees. The policy should be set out clearly and published in an accessible form for all employees to see. Everyone within the organization is bound by the terms of the policy, and any breach can result in disciplinary procedures. Whilst having an equal opportunity policy is good practice, there is no legal obligation for an organization in the UK to have such a policy. [See **equal opportunity**.]

equal opportunity statement A public commitment to **equal opportunities** made by an organization. Many organizations will place statements on job advertisements, such as 'we are working towards equal opportunities'. Such statements are easy to make but much harder to put into practice, which means that they are often treated with scepticism by potential applicants. Some organizations also make statements about equal opportunities in their annual reports, reviewing the progress they have made in the previous year and outlining their intentions for the next year. [See **Opportunity 2000**.]

equal opportunity targets are the proportions of employees from different groups (women, ethnic minorities, disabled, etc.) at various levels in the hierarchy that the organization is aiming to attain in order to make it more representative of its customers/client base or the local community. These targets are seen as long-term goals that can be achieved through an awareness of equal opportunities and **positive action** initiatives that encourage disadvantaged groups to apply for jobs and undertake training and skills to help them compete for promotion opportunities. Equal opportunity targets should not be confused with **quotas**. Whereas quotas are legal requirements imposed on the organization, targets are voluntarily set by the organization.

equal outcomes see **equal opportunity**

equal pay The right in law for men and women to receive the same **remuneration** as a member of the opposite sex in the same employment who is engaged in similar work, work rated as equivalent under a common job evaluation procedure, or work which is of **equal value**. In the UK the right to equal pay is inscribed in the Equal Pay Act 1970, though the right to equal pay for work of equal value was only established in 1984 through an amendment. This amendment gave effect to the Equal Pay Directive of the European Community, which itself derived from Article 119 of the Treaty of Rome which enshrines the right to equal pay in European law. There is also an ILO Convention on Equal Pay, established in 1951. The right to equal pay establishes a right not just to the same basic wage but to all aspects of remuneration, including **benefits** in kind and **occupational pensions**. It is a complex area of law and an important feature in recent years has been the role of the European Court of Justice in refining and effectively extending the right to equal pay in a series of landmark judgments. Despite these changes, the law has been criticized for its excessive complexity and critics claim it is difficult to use and largely ineffective. Since its introduction there has been a narrowing of the gender pay-gap between men and women but annual hourly earnings of women in the UK are still only 80 per cent of those of men.

equal pay audit A systematic review of pay practice and outcomes undertaken to identify and eliminate sex **discrimination**. Potentially, an equal pay audit can embrace three types of review. First, a review of differences in pay and earnings of men and women, in order to identify prima facie discrimination. Such a review might consider differences in pay between men and women in the same grade, the distribution of the sexes across grades, and the proportion of earnings of each sex composed of incentive, merit, and other supplementary payments. Second, a review of **payment systems**, procedures, and practice that might contribute to unequal outcomes. For example, a review might examine the extent to which part-timers enjoy equal access to bonus and supplementary earnings or the extent to which decisions on pay are concentrated in the hands of male managers. Finally, the audit might extend beyond the area of pay to consider recruitment, promotion, training, and other aspects of HRM that impinge on the sphere of reward. The statutory Code of Practice on Equal Pay drawn up by the **Equal Opportunities Commission** recommends that an equal pay audit be carried out periodically by employers, and a number of trade unions have initiated audits of pay agreements to improve the relative earnings of their women members. Campaigners on equal pay frequently argue that a statutory duty should be placed on employers to carry out an equal pay audit. [See **equal pay; equality bargaining.**]

equal treatment see **equal opportunity**

equal value Jobs are of equal value or of **comparable worth** if they impose equivalent demands on jobholders, despite being dissimilar in content. Under European law women and men have an entitlement to **equal pay** if their job is of equal value to that of a member of the opposite sex in the same employment. This principle, of equal pay for work of equal value, was established in law through the Equal Pay Directive of 1975 which was subsequently transposed into UK law through a 1983 amendment to the Equal Pay Act 1970. The amendment was forced upon the then Conservative government by a decision of the European Court, which ruled that the UK had failed to implement the directive. The significance of the amendment lies in the fact that it allows a woman pursuing an equal pay case to select a male **comparator** in a different occupation who may belong to a different grade structure derived from a separate job evaluation exercise. This is important because of continuing occupational segregation and the tendency for jobs typically undertaken by men to be better paid. Since the change there has been a series of high-profile equal pay cases which have been based on the principle of equal value. As a result of these and other cases a number of organizations in public administration, finance, supermarket retail, and the utilities have altered grading and **job evaluation** procedures in order to incorporate the principle of equal pay for work of equal value. Despite these changes, women continue to be paid significantly less than men on average and the law has been widely criticized for being ineffective. Among the criticisms are that the complexity of the law and the special **Employment Tribunal** procedure which comes into play in equal value cases make it difficult for applicants to use. Many cases have dragged on for years and have been dependent on support from trade unions and the **Equal Opportunities Commission**. Critics have also attacked the provision for employers to defend equal value cases on the grounds that unequal pay is due to a 'material factor', such as market forces, which is not the factor of sex.

equity theory is a cognitive theory of **motivation** developed by J. Stacey Adams, which claims that employees will be motivated if they accept they are fairly treated in the workplace. By the same token, perceptions of inequitable treatment will lead to **demotivation**. The theory is founded on the insight that perceptions and feelings of fairness are based on the principle of comparison. In other words, employees evaluate their treatment in relation to a 'reference group'. Two kinds of comparison may be important for worker motivation. First, employees may compare their earnings with their level of effort and performance and increase their effort if they believe their rewards are excessive or reduce their effort if they regard them as niggardly. Second, employees will compare their own ratio of effort to reward with that of co-workers and act to raise or reduce effort if they believe their own treatment by management is out of line. The practical significance of the theory is that it points to the need for considerations of equity and fairness to be built into the management of reward systems and work allocation. [See **distributive equity**.]

e-recruitment (sometimes known as e-cruitment) is the recruitment of employees over the internet. Originally used mainly for technical and IT staff this form of recruitment has grown rapidly in recent years in line with growing use of the internet. It is used particularly for more junior or entry-level positions but all types of job can be and are advertised in this way. E-recruitment assumes a number of different forms. Many individual employers now advertise jobs on their own website and use internet recruitment as an alternative or supplement to external advertising. In addition, there are 'job boards' operated by specialist internet companies that act as **labour market intermediaries**, advertising vacancies on a website and holding details of those seeking work on file. Finally, there are internet directories that list job vacancies on company sites and allow free connection from the directory to the company website. E-recruitment consists in large part of advertising jobs through a new medium. It can involve more than this, however, and many companies perform initial screening of job applicants via internet questionnaires and even, controversially, apply **psychological tests** via the internet.

ERG theory This theory (devised by Chris Alderfer) is based on the assumption that people have three types of need: Existence, Relatedness, and Growth. Existence needs are concerned with physiological factors, which at work are expressed as concern over remuneration and working conditions. Relatedness needs are concerned with having meaningful interactions with other people—co-workers, managers, customers, etc. Growth needs are concerned with personal development, creativity, and feelings of achievement (see **self-actualization**). The message for managers is that policies and practices must be devised to help to satisfy these needs because this will result in fulfilled and motivated employees. Although very similar to **Maslow's hierarchy of needs**, ERG theory does not stipulate that the needs have to be met in a particular order. [See **needs theory**; **Herzberg's two-factor theory**.]

escalator of participation This expresses the view that systems of employee **participation** can be ranked in terms of the degree of decision-making power they bestow on employees. At the bottom of the escalator is the provision of information, followed by the exchange of communications between managers and workers. Next come **consultation** and **codetermination**, with workers' control, as might occur in a **workers' co-operative**, situated at the top.

essential service A public service that is essential for the maintenance of public health, safety, and order, such as the police, fire, or ambulance service. In many countries the essential nature of these services has been used to justify restrictions on the rights of their employees to join unions, engage in **collective bargaining**, and take **industrial action**. In the UK, for instance, police officers are denied the right to join a **trade union**, though the Police Federation serves as an equivalent, and cannot go on **strike**. As public services became more **strike prone** from the late 1960s there were repeated calls in the UK for a ban on strikes in essential services. Successive governments have drawn back from such action, though the regulations covering police officers have been extended to the prison service and the Conservative government under Margaret Thatcher imposed a ban on trade unions at the secret communications centre GCHQ (rescinded by the Labour government in 1997). [See **state of emergency**.]

ethnic groups see ethnicity

ethnicity is the concept of categorizing a person according to his or her ethnic group. An ethnic group has a shared history and a cultural tradition of its own. These features are usually identified through characteristics such as a common geographical origin, a common language, a common literature, and a common religion or belief system. Normally an ethnic group will be a minority within a larger community. Because an ethnic group is a cultural construct, it is constantly changing and developing, thereby creating its own identity and redefining itself. Therefore, the term ethnicity encompasses the dynamic nature of a social group, and is frequently used to replace the fixed and somewhat discredited concept of **race**.

ethnic monitoring see **equal opportunity monitoring**

ethnocentric management is an approach found in international firms where nationals from the parent country dominate the organization at home and abroad. In terms of decision-making, the subsidiaries have very little autonomy, and control resides in head office. This ethnocentric attitude stems from the belief that the **parent-country nationals** are best suited to run the business, irrespective of the local circumstances. [See **geocentric management; polycentric management; regiocentric management**.]

ethnocentrism is the tendency to view all issues from the perspective of one's own ethnic group and to fail to take into account the importance and value of different ethnic groups. In an organization, employment policies or practices that are ethnocentric are liable to have a discriminatory effect that disadvantages ethnic minorities. [See **stereotyping; discrimination**.]

European Centre of Enterprises with Public Participation (Centre Européen de l'Entreprise—CEEP) The European **confederation** of public enterprise employers. CEEP is one of the European **social partners**.

European Convention on Human Rights and Fundamental Freedoms (ECHR) The Convention was adopted by the **Council of Europe** in 1950. It was incorporated into UK law by the Human Rights Act 1998, which was fully implemented in October 2000, allowing human rights cases under the Convention to be heard in UK courts rather than at Strasbourg. The most relevant articles of the Convention for employment are Article 8, which guarantees privacy for someone's home life and correspondence (see **data protection; surveillance**), and Articles 10 and 11, which guarantee freedoms of expression, association, and assembly (see **freedom of association**). This applies to **trade union** membership and activities.

European Court of Justice (ECJ) The ECJ sits in Luxembourg and is a judicial body within the constitutional machinery of the European Union. It is composed of twelve judges, nominated by member states, who are supported by six advocates-general who review cases and provide a detailed submission and recommendations to the Court before final judgment. The task of the Court is to uphold, enforce, and interpret European law. It has primacy over national courts and acts as final court of appeal, dealing with cases that are referred to it by the UK House of Lords and its equivalents in other countries. In this capacity it has played an important role in interpreting and effectively extending European protective employment legislation in the fields of **equal pay** and **equal opportunity, transfer of undertakings,** and **collective redundancies.** The ECJ also hears **infringement proceedings**, initiated by the European Commission when a member state has failed to transpose a **directive** into national law. The ECJ must not be confused with the European Court of Human Rights based in Strasbourg.

European Foundation for Quality Management (EFQM)

A business foundation set up in 1988 to encourage organizations to adopt **Total Quality Management.** The foundation organizes the European Quality Awards, modelled on the **Baldridge Award** in the United States.

European Industrial Relations Observatory (EIRO)

An electronic information service on all aspects of **industrial relations** and **employment law** within the countries of the European Union. The service is provided by the European Foundation for the Improvement of Living and Working Conditions based in Dublin and is accessed via the internet. The EIRO's fully searchable website is at www.eiro.eurofound.ie

European Trade Union Confederation (ETUC)

An international trade union confederation which was founded in 1973 to provide a cohesive voice for the European trade union movement. The ETUC represents 65 national trade union centres from 28 countries, together with 14 industry federations. Its congress is held every four years and elects an Executive Committee and officers. The key function of the ETUC is to act as a **social partner** within the framework of the European Union, and among its main achievements are the negotiation of a series of framework agreements on **parental leave** and part-time and **atypical work**. These have been adopted as directives by the Council of Ministers under the 'negotiation' procedure of the European Union. The development of European social policy and the desire of the European Commission to promote **social dialogue** between the interests of business and labour have allowed the ETUC to assume a more prominent role. There is a continuing tension, however, between the ETUC and the major national **confederations** of labour, such as the German DGB, which are loath to concede vital decision-making powers to an international body.

European works council (EWC) A representative body of workers established for the purpose of information-sharing and consultation on transnational issues in multinational companies operating in Europe. Although there are examples of EWCs being established voluntarily, the majority have been created as a result of the European Works Council Directive of 1994. This required that EWCs be set up in companies operating in the member states of the European Economic Area (i.e. the member states of the EU plus Iceland, Liechtenstein, and Norway), provided they employed 1,000 employees with at least 150 in each of two countries. All companies above this size threshold are affected regardless of their country of origin; i.e. Japanese and American firms are covered as well as Dutch, French, and German. Initially the UK was excluded from coverage by the directive under its opt-out from the **Social Protocol**. Under the Labour government elected in 1997, the opt-out has been abandoned and the UK has implemented the directive through the Transnational Information and Consultation of Employees Regulations 1999. The main features of the directive are as follows: (1) multinational companies above the size threshold must establish information and consultation procedures (i.e. an EWC); (2) membership should be drawn from existing representatives at national level within the company; (3) a maximum of thirty representatives will constitute the EWC; (4) there will be an annual information and consultation meeting with central management; (5) extra meetings between management and a smaller select committee are possible where business restructuring impacts significantly on employee interests; (6) the remit of the committee is confined to transnational issues; (7) the substance of meetings will cover issues such as the enterprise's structure and financial situation, business plans and prospects, the level and trend in employment, and substantial changes in technology, location, and organization; and (8) the operating costs are to be met by the employer. These arrangements, however, constitute a fallback position and there is flexibility built into the provisions if certain conditions are met. For example, companies that had established voluntary arrangements before the final implementation date for the directive are exempt (see **Article 13 agreement**) and the directive allows for the creation of a **Special Negotiating Body**, drawn from existing representatives, that can negotiate a tailor-made procedure. The purpose of the directive is to extend the rights to **participation** in management that exist in most EU states at national level to the transnational level (see **works council**), reflecting the increasingly international scope of business activity. By 2000 more than 600 EWCs had been established and they now constitute an established element of the machinery of **industrial relations** in large European companies. Opinions vary, however, as to their significance. For some, they represent a major step towards the emergence of a truly European system of industrial relations: there is evidence of EWCs stimulating networks of trade union activity within large companies and, in a tiny minority of cases, they have successfully negotiated company-wide **framework agreements**. For others, however, EWCs are marginal and employer-dominated bodies that lack the crucial right to **codetermination** and exert little influence on business strategy. Elements of both interpretations may be right and it is likely that the role, activities, and significance of EWCs are highly variable, depending on management's orientation and level of support for the new institution and the extent to which worker representatives can draw upon the resources of external trade unions.

Eurosclerosis is the idea that European economies are rigid and sluggish and hence poor at generating employment because of an excess of labour market regulation and high **social charges**. [See **deregulation; neo-liberalism**.]

executive coaching is the development or strengthening of managerial competencies amongst executives through intensive dialogue with an independent consultant or senior colleague. [See **management development**.]

executive mentoring see **executive coaching**

executive pay The special arrangements that exist in private companies for managing the pay of executive directors. Executive pay typically consists of four main elements: basic pay, an incentive bonus scheme, a share option scheme, and an executive benefit package, the most distinctive element of which is a non-contributory pension. Particularly significant are the **bonus** and **share option** elements, which are designed to overcome a potential **principal–agent** problem and ensure directors act in accordance with the interests of shareholders. Bonus schemes may be short or long term, though long-term incentives (LTIs) have become popular as a means of retaining executives and ensuring the effective long-term management of company assets. Pre-tax profit, earnings per share, and other financial indices are the performance measures that are most frequently used within executive bonus schemes. Executives also frequently receive share options, the right to buy a block of shares on some future date at the share price when the option was granted. Executive pay has been a controversial subject in recent years as a result of the rapid growth of executive earnings, research findings that indicate limited connection between earnings and business performance, and the growth of income inequality. The differential that executives enjoy over other employees in the enterprise has grown enormously since the 1970s. In the UK the result has been a series of inquiries, including the reports of the Cadbury and Greenbury committees in the 1990s. These have recommended greater **transparency** and disclosure of executive pay and the use of **remuneration committees**, composed of non-executive directors, to determine the pay package. [See **fat cat**.]

executive search consultants (popularly known as headhunters) are specialists who find suitable people for senior jobs in organizations. They use contacts within the industry or profession to locate likely candidates and approach them directly on behalf of the client organization. Headhunters are expensive, often charging a fee of up to 50 per cent of the first year's salary.

exit costs are the financial and **transaction costs** incurred by a company when it closes down one of its sites and declares redundancies. Exit costs are likely to be higher in a country with relatively strict regulations governing **collective redundancy** that require extensive consultation with worker representatives and substantial redundancy payments. They are likely to be lower in countries with labour markets that are subject to relatively light regulation. What this means is that a **multinational corporation** that is seeking to reduce its capacity may opt to close down operations in more deregulated labour markets because it is easier and cheaper to do so. A state policy of **deregulation** to attract employment, therefore, may have the opposite, **perverse effect** as companies exit when they face a situation of excess capacity.

exit interviews are interviews undertaken with employees who have handed in their **resignation**. They can be useful for the employer because they provide a means of finding out why the employee is leaving which might be helpful in designing policies that can help to retain staff. For example, if a series of exit interviews revealed that high-performing employees were leaving because they felt there was greater job security elsewhere, it might lead the company to question whether they were using too many fixed-term contracts. Or if employees were leaving in order to get promotion it might lead the employer to review internal career opportunities, such as **lateral career moves**. Exit interviews can highlight particular problems—for example, poor working relationships, bad management skills, dissatisfaction with pay, communication problems—but there is no guarantee that leavers are being honest about the real reasons for quitting.

exit-voice-loyalty embraces the three possible responses to organizational discontent identified by the economist Albert Hirschman. Exit involves leaving the organization, voice involves expressing discontent within it in order to obtain the resolution of **grievances**, and loyalty involves tolerating grievances out of a sense of duty. [See **employee voice**.]

expatriate see **parent-country national**

expatriation is the process of sending managers to another country to run a subsidiary of a multinational organization. Before departure, the process should include an extensive period of training and preparation to ensure that the managers are familiar with cultural differences, and to reduce the likelihood of **culture shock**. [See **parent-country nationals**.]

expectancy theory is a theory of motivation that seeks to identify the conditions necessary for worker motivation to occur. Expectancy theory is rooted in cognitive psychology and is frequently classified as a 'process' theory of **motivation**. It originates in the work of Vroom, who identified three conditions for motivation to occur: valency, instrumentality, and expectancy. In basic terms what this means is that for a reward system to motivate employees it must offer rewards which are valued, and there must be a predictable link between the employee's input and the measure of performance and a further link between the performance measure and the reward available. The practical significance of the theory lies in the lessons that can be derived for the design of incentive systems. Thus, it may be important that these offer substantial incentive payments, make use of performance indicators which are fully under the employee's control, and operate in a transparent manner, such that a change in behaviour which leads to higher performance necessarily leads to higher rewards.

exposed sector That segment of the national economy that is vulnerable to international competition.

express term Part of the contract of employment that has been explicitly agreed by an employer and employee either in writing or orally. [See **implied term**.]

extended internal labour market The supply of employees outside the organization who have family or social ties with employees in the organization. Because of these connections, they have some knowledge of what it is like to work for the organization and therefore might more easily fit into the organizational culture than other potential employees in the **external labour market**.

extended organization An organization that does not produce goods or services directly, using its own employees, but rather relies upon **subcontracting** to perform its operations.

extension procedure A statutory procedure which allows a judge or government minister to extend the terms of a multi-employer **collective agreement** to employers who are not members of the signatory **employers' association**. Its purposes are to establish minimum terms and conditions, prevent undercutting by employers, and remove the incentive for companies to avoid trade unions. Extension procedures are an important feature of the labour markets of several European states, including Belgium, France, Germany, Greece, Italy, and the Netherlands. Equivalent legislation in the UK was abolished by the Conservative governments of the 1980s.

external consultant A person from outside the organization who offers independent, expert advice. [See **management consultant**.]

external fit is the process of ensuring that the human resource strategy conforms with the wider business strategy. The assumption is that a correct match between the two strategies will produce the optimum performance of employees in the organization. There are various matching models which prescribe how human resource strategy can be linked with business strategy. Whilst these models differ in terms of the policies they advocate, they are nearly all based on the assumption that HR strategy should be reactive to the overall business objectives and the stage of development of the organization—in others words, HR strategy can be devised by matching it to the existing business strategy. A variation of this approach comes from contingency theories that suggest that a range of factors must be taken into account when devising a HR strategy. It is not simply a case of matching HR to business strategy; other contextual variables must also be taken into account, in particular social, economic, political, legal, and technological issues.

externalization involves the **subcontracting** of activities previously performed inside the organization. It has been claimed that there is an increasing trend towards the externalization of HRM, with functions such as recruitment, selection, reward, and training being provided by external suppliers.

external labour market The supply of potential employees outside the organization. This can be local, regional, national, or international. [See **recruitment**.]

external recruitment see **recruitment**

extrinsic reward A reward that is obtained by performing work but which is separate from and not inherent to the work task. The most obvious extrinsic rewards are the pay and benefits that workers receive in return for work, though others might include promotion and improved job prospects. [See **incentive**; **intrinsic reward**; **reward**.]

Eysenck personality inventory (EPI) The pioneering **psychological test** developed by psychologist Hans Eysenck, which measures three dimensions: neuroticism–emotional stability; extroversion–introversion; and psychoticism–self-control.

F

face validity see **validity**

facilities agreement A collective agreement that provides **trade union** representatives with paid time off and other means of support for their role as employee representatives.

factor A characteristic of a set of jobs that is used in an analytical **job evaluation** scheme. Factors may include, skill, effort, decision-making, working conditions, and responsibility for people, finance, and equipment. Ideally, factors should be present in the jobs being evaluated to a greater or lesser degree, in order that individual jobs can be scored under each factor heading. The total scores across factors can then determine the sorting of jobs into a hierarchy and their division into a set of pay grades. Factors should be relevant, clearly defined, gender neutral, and cover the main features of the jobs subject to evaluation. Typically they are broken down into a number of 'factor levels', such that the factor skill will comprise definitions of high, low, and intermediate levels of skill. It is also common to weight factors, such that those that are more important to the employing organization carry a higher potential score. Skill, for instance, may be given a higher weight than working conditions. In choosing, defining, and weighting job factors it is essential that care is given to the question of discrimination, as gender bias in job evaluation schemes can perpetuate the underpayment of women and is contrary to **equal pay** law.

factory inspector see **health and safety inspector**

factory occupation see **sit-down strike**

fair reasons for dismissal To defend a claim for **unfair dismissal** an employer must be able to prove, in the first instance, that the dismissal was for a fair reason. The Employment Rights Act 1996 gives five reasons that can justify dismissal: (1) conduct, e.g. **absenteeism**, fighting, or theft; (2) capability or qualifications, including illness; (3) **redundancy**; (4) contravention of a statute, e.g. where a driver cannot work because of loss of licence; (5) some other substantial reason (SOSR), e.g. ending of a temporary contract, pressure from customers, or reorganization in the interests of efficiency. Even if the reason for dismissal is fair, the actual dismissal may still be adjudged unfair because the employer failed to act reasonably in the circumstances. [See **reasonableness**.]

false self-employment is where either the employer regards the individual as self-employed to avoid employment protection rights or the employee knowingly declares him- or herself self-employed for tax and National Insurance purposes. [See **employment status**.]

family-friendly policies are special policies adopted by the organization which are designed to be sensitive to the needs of family life. Such policies denote an approach that emphasizes the importance of encouraging employees to balance work and family commitment. Whilst many initiatives are aimed at women who choose or are obliged to work whilst also shouldering the main burden of childcare responsibilities, some initiatives are also designed to allow men to become more involved in family responsibilities. Specific policies include: allowing **flexitime**, providing paid **parental leave** beyond the legal minimum, **paternity leave**, career breaks, working from home, and paid leave for the care of elderly or sick relatives. [See **work–life balance**.]

family wage A wage that is sufficient to support a family, including a dependent spouse and children. The family wage was a traditional bargaining objective of male-dominated trade unions and found expression, before the introduction of **equal pay** legislation, in separate and higher rates of pay for male employees. The family wage is based on a male **breadwinner** model, in which it is assumed that men work and provide for a family, while women with children work as housewives. It can be contrasted with a component wage that is insufficient to run a household and which contributes to a total family income derived from two or more wage earners. [See **component wage job**.]

fast-tracking see **career track**

fat cat An abusive description of senior executives who receive large salaries and share options that purportedly are related to performance. The wide currency of the insult reflects public concern at rising income inequality and the extremely rapid rise in **executive pay** in recent years. In the UK, the term has been applied particularly to the senior executives of privatized utilities, many of whom have reaped large gains from the transfer to private ownership.

feminization is the increasing presence and influence of women in previously male-dominated occupations or institutions. Thus, one can talk about the feminization of the legal profession or the trade unions.

fiddles Workplace practices that involve fiddling expenses or customers, minor thefts of cash, produce, and equipment, and the manipulation of data on worker performance and timekeeping. Sociologists have analyzed practices of this kind in a range of occupations. Their research has indicated that 'fiddles' are often tolerated by managers provided they do not get out of hand and even though they are contrary to formal disciplinary standards. They can be interpreted either as a breakdown of management control of the workplace or as part of the 'give and take' upon which any working relationship depends.

final salary pension scheme A final salary pension scheme uses employees' length of service and final salary as the basis for calculating pension entitlement. A common arrangement in the UK is for an employee to accrue an entitlement of one-sixtieth of final pay with each year of service. Forty years' service in a one-sixtieth scheme will produce a **pension** of two-thirds of final pay, which is the maximum allowable under Inland Revenue rules. Final salary itself may be the salary on retirement, the average over the final three years of service, or the highest rate of pay during pensionable service. Many schemes allow employees to purchase extra years of pensionable service through **additional voluntary contributions** to compensate for service below a total of forty years. [See **occupational pension**.]

financial flexibility is the policy of adjusting employment costs in line with the demand for labour in the organization, and reflecting the supply of labour in the external labour market. In this sense, financial flexibility and **numerical flexibility** are closely associated—certain forms of numerical flexibility inevitably lead to greater financial flexibility for the employer. More generally, in terms of setting wage levels, financial flexibility means moving from uniform and standardized pay structures towards individualized pay systems. In particular it is associated with abandoning national pay frameworks that are negotiated with trade unions, and replacing them with either locally negotiated agreements or non-negotiated pay systems based on individual performance. Financial flexibility usually involves some sort of performance-based element to pay. [See **performance-related pay; merit pay; profit-related pay; profit-sharing**.]

financial participation is a term sometimes applied to **profit-sharing** and other arrangements that allow employees to share in the ownership and profits of the business. Financial participation therefore embraces employee share ownership, profit-sharing schemes, and worker co-operatives. Some regard the term as a misnomer, at least when applied to profit-sharing and share ownership schemes, because the ownership of a small proportion of company stock may provide for little or no participation by employees in the effective running of the business. [See **employee share ownership**.]

fired 'Being fired' or 'getting fired' are colloquial terms for **dismissal**.

firefighting is the metaphor used to describe how some managers are forced (or choose) to deal with problems as they occur rather than planning ahead and attempting to predict problems arising ('fire prevention'). Commentators argue that personnel managers are often forced into a firefighting role because they are expected to deal with employee problems, even though these problems often arise as a result of management decisions that are made without the involvement or advice of personnel specialists. This has led some commentators to argue that personnel specialists need to become more involved in the strategic decision-making processes of organizations, otherwise they will constantly be firefighting.

first-line manager A person at the bottom of the management hierarchy responsible for day-to-day operations in an organization. Traditionally this role was labelled **supervisor** or **foreman**, but increasingly the term first-line manager is being used. In part this reflects a change in the responsibilities of the role—he or she is expected to undertake a broader range of people management activities, such as appraisals and grievance handling, alongside operational activities. [See **line manager**.]

first-order strategy is a term coined by management theorists John Purcell and Bruce Ahlstrand in relation to **M-form** companies to refer to decisions concerning (1) the long-term direction of the firm (in other words, the enterprise's basic goals); and (2) the scope of the firm's activities (i.e. the range of markets and businesses served). [See **second-order strategy**; **third-order strategy**.]

five force framework An analytical tool developed by business strategist Michael Porter to show how a firm's competition is determined by five forces: existing competitors, threat of new entrants, threat of substitute products/services, bargaining power of buyers, and bargaining power of suppliers.

540-degree feedback is an extension of **360-degree feedback** whereby the feedback process goes beyond the organization to include customers and suppliers. However, the term is not widespread and some organizations include customer/client and supplier feedback whilst still calling the process '360-degree feedback'.

fixed-term contracts specify the period of time for which a person will be employed—in other words there is a date specifying when employment will terminate. For example, such contracts might be used where there is seasonal demand—such as fruit picking in the summer or delivering mail at Christmas.

Fixed-Term Contracts Directive The Fixed-Term Contracts Directive was adopted by the European Union in 1999 and implements a **framework agreement** negotiated by the European **social partners**. The purpose of the directive is to improve the quality of **fixed-term contract** work by ensuring the application of the principle of non-discrimination, and to establish a framework to prevent the abuse of such employment relations through the use of successive fixed-term contracts. [See **negotiation track**.]

flat/tall structure Organizations can be described as having flat or tall structures depending on the number of levels in the hierarchy, although there is no definitive number of levels that an organizational structure needs to have before it is deemed tall or flat. As organizations grow through employing more people, there is a tendency for the number of management levels to increase, and hence a taller structure emerges. Critics argue that, over time, this results in organizations possessing overly tall, cumbersome structures that inhibit flexibility. Consequently, a contemporary trend has been to **delayer** the hierarchy, resulting in a flatter structure.

flexibility is considered by management theorists to be a virtue of successful organizations. The assumption is that, in an increasingly competitive environment, only those organizations that can adapt quickly to changing conditions will be able to survive, let alone achieve competitive advantage. Critics argue that flexibility frequently benefits the employers but at a cost to employees, hence there is considerable scepticism amongst some commentators as to the 'virtues' of flexibility. The concept takes a variety of forms, so please refer to the specific headings for more precise definitions: **functional flexibility, numerical flexibility, temporal flexibility, financial flexibility.**

flexible benefits systems allow for a degree of employee choice over the form of **remuneration**. There are two main forms. Within-benefit flexibility allows the employee to take more of a particular benefit by surrendering cash rewards and vice versa. For example, an employee may opt to take more paid holiday, or a better company car, or a higher level of health insurance, though at the cost of reduced salary. Alternatively, benefits may be given up or taken in reduced form in order to receive more salary. The second form is across-benefit flexibility, which is also known as **cafeteria benefits**. Under schemes of this kind, employees are awarded either a sum of money or a number of points and can 'buy' benefits which suit their particular needs. An employee, therefore, could accept a lower-value **company car** and use the amount saved to buy additional **pension** or health cover. The use of flexible benefits has increased in recent years in both the UK and the United States for a number of reasons. Advocates emphasize the element of choice in these schemes and the fact that they can accommodate the needs of a more diverse and individualistic workforce. In addition, however, their use reflects the reduced **tax efficiency** of benefits, and particularly of company cars, which has led to the spread of cash-or-car options within company car schemes. Flexible benefits can also be used to enforce tighter control over benefit costs and this has been a major reason for their spread in the USA. A key feature in this regard is that schemes allow a proportion of the cost of expensive health care to be transferred to the employee. If total remuneration increases in line with inflation but health costs rise at a higher rate, then a higher percentage of the employee's total reward has to be allocated to maintain the value of the benefit. Despite the advantages to employers there are a number of constraints on the use of flexible systems and, in the UK, full-scale cafeteria plans remain rare. The latter can be complex and costly to administer and require a relatively sophisticated reward management function. They can also raise costs as the advantages of bulk purchase of benefits are diminished and as employees make maximum use of the suite of benefits on offer. [See **benefits**.]

flexible firm model A management technique for organizing the workplace using various forms of **flexibility** in order to optimize the use of human resources. Originally proposed by Jon Atkinson of the Institute of Manpower Studies, in 1986, it is based on the principle of segmenting the workforce into core and peripheral groups. The core group is composed of employees that are vital to the organization, functionally flexible, and difficult to replace (perhaps because of their skills, knowledge, or experience). The peripheral group is composed of employees who are numerically flexible because (1) their skills are in plentiful supply in the labour market, and so they can be easily replaced, or (2) they are only needed to complete particular tasks (irrespective of the scarcity or otherwise of their skills), or (3) they are only needed at peak times across the working day or week. From the employee perspective, it is better to be part of the core than the periphery since the former have greater job security, better remuneration and conditions of work, and better prospects. In addition to the core and periphery employees, the flexible firm model also identifies the importance of external workers—in particular, subcontracted workers who typically undertake activities such as cleaning and catering, which are not core to the business, although important to its running.

flexible specialization is a term coined by organization theorists Michael Piore and Charles Sabel in the early 1980s to describe craft-based, flexible, innovation-led, and customer-focused forms of work organization. In contrast to the standardized mass production of **Fordism**, flexible specialization emphasizes flexible production systems that can meet the demands for customized products in increasingly diversified markets. In particular, developments in microelectronic technology mean that machinery can be more easily used for cost-effective, small-batch production, whilst information-processing capabilities (particularly EPOS) allow production targets to be brought into line with sales data directly from the retail outlets. It is argued that such developments allow small and medium-sized firms to compete and thrive since economies of scale become less important. Critics argue that proponents of flexible specialization overstate the demise of mass markets, underestimate the influence of large firms, and overestimate the ability of small organizations to innovate. [See **neo-Fordism**; **post-Fordism**.]

flexing is the technique of adjusting the hours of staff to meet the fluctuating demands of the organization. [See **temporal flexibility**; **zero-hours contracts**.]

flexitime is a policy of allowing employees control over their hours of work providing that agreed 'core' hours are worked and that a contractually agreed total number of hours are worked in a given period (typically a week or a month). In practice, flexitime usually means that employees can vary their daily start and finish times to suit themselves.

flying pickets Pickets who are mobile and dispatched by their union to engage in secondary picketing away from their own place of work. In the UK, the use of flying pickets was a notable feature of the dispute tactics of the National Union of Mineworkers during its strikes of the 1970s and 1980s. [See **picketing**; **secondary action**.]

Fordism is a system of work organization based on the principles of **scientific management** but adapted to the mass production of standardized goods. Henry Ford developed the factory assembly line for the mass production of cars in the early twentieth century. His production system was characterized by several important features: linear work sequencing, an interdependence of tasks, a moving assembly line, the use and refinement of dedicated machinery, and specialized machine tools. The term Fordist is normally used to describe any work process with these features which produces standardized products. A key point to recognize is that Fordism is geared towards mass production, which depends upon mass consumption. Changes in patterns of consumption would therefore require changes in the work organization or else render Fordist production inappropriate. Some commentators have argued that such changes in consumption occurred towards the end of the twentieth century, and that now people are increasingly demanding specialized rather than standardized goods. They argue that instead of mass markets, there are niche markets, and that, to supply these markets, work must be organized in new ways which allow for greater flexibility. They label this new approach **post-Fordism**. Other commentators disagree and suggest that even though consumption patterns have changed, the traditional Fordist methods of work organization have simply been adapted to meet these changes—hence they use the term **neo-Fordism**.

foreman is the traditional, gendered term for a front-line manager or **supervisor**. In the nineteenth and early twentieth centuries the 'bowler-hatted foreman' was a powerful figure, directing work operations and responsible for the hire and fire of workers. Gradually, his power was reduced, from below by the unionization of workers in heavy industry, and from above by the growth of professional management.

formalization is the setting down of policies and practices in written documents. In the 1970s British workplace **industrial relations** underwent a major process of formalization as reliance on **custom and practice** to regulate the **employment relationship** gave way increasingly to reliance on written **procedures** and **collective agreements**.

forming is the first stage of the five-stage model of group development (see **stages of group development**).

4 Cs The four human resource outcomes in the Harvard version of HRM: commitment, competence, congruence, and cost-effectiveness.

frame of reference is a term used by **industrial relations** researchers to describe the main perspectives on the **employment relationship** within their field of study. Three primary frames of reference are usually identified: **unitarism**, **pluralism**, and radicalism. Each differs in its understanding of the relative interests of employers and employees. Unitarists generally believe employers and employees have common interests and consequently have little sympathy for independent representation of employee interests through trade unions. Pluralists, in contrast, identify opposing interests but believe these are capable of resolution through good industrial relations practice. On this view, trade unions play an important role in advancing the interests of employees and in regulating **industrial conflict**. The radical frame of reference (radicalism) also starts from an assumption of opposing interests but identifies little scope for accommodation within existing capit-alist societies. Militant trade unionism is required to defend worker interests, according to this viewpoint, but too often unions suffer **incorporation** and serve to reconcile workers to a set of economic relationships founded on exploitation.

framework agreement A collective agreement that sets out broad principles that apply across enterprises, the detailed application of which is fleshed out in further negotiations at company or workplace levels.

freedom of association has two dimensions: the right of citizens to combine freely and create associations and the collective liberty of these associations once formed. It is balanced by a right of dissociation; that is, to refrain from associating. The right of freedom of association is enshrined in a variety of international treaties. Examples are Article 20 of the Declaration of Human Rights 1948 and Article 11 of the **European Convention on Human Rights and Fundamental Freedoms**. The **International Labour Organization** also has conventions on freedom of association and the principle is upheld in both the Council of Europe Social Charter 1961 and the European Community **Social Charter** 1989. The Treaty of Amsterdam 1997, however, states that the European Union has no competence in matters concerning freedom of association, though this provision is currently under review. In the field of HRM the primary relevance of freedom of association is that it guarantees the right of workers to form and join **trade unions** and the right of trade unions themselves to operate freely without undue interference from the state or employers. Action against trade unionists or to undermine a trade union by an employer, therefore, can be viewed as contravening civil rights.

freelance or freelancer. Someone who works in a specialist activity but with no fixed employer. It is a name often given to **self-employed** journalists, technicians, actors, and musicians.

free rider Someone who accepts a benefit that is widely or publicly available (a public good) without paying for or contributing to its provision. An example would be a non-union member in a unionized company who accepts increases in wages negotiated by the union without paying union dues. The term is also sometimes applied to companies that use skilled labour without investing in training. [See **training levy**.]

friendly society An association of workers established before the development of the welfare state to provide mutual insurance in the event of unemployment, injury, sickness, or death. Many trade unions in the UK and other countries began life as friendly societies and many continue to offer insurance services of this kind to their members. [See **Ghent system**.]

fringe benefit see **benefits**

frontier of control A concept developed by Carter Goodrich in his path-breaking studies of management–worker relations after the First World War. It expresses the view that there is a ceaseless struggle for control in the workplace, with managers seeking to extend the frontier by securing new powers to organize and control labour and workers reacting and developing counter-strategies to win greater freedom from supervision. The concept assumes, therefore, that there is a basic conflict of interest between managers and employees and has been used most frequently by researchers from a pluralist or **labour process** tradition in studies of shopfloor bargaining and workplace trade unionism. For many, the frontier of control has shifted decisively in management's favour in the UK since the late 1970s, as more intensive competition and high unemployment have sapped the bargaining power of workers. [See **industrial conflict; restriction of output; restrictive practice; surveillance**.]

full-circle feedback see **360-degree feedback**

full-time officer (FTO) A paid employee of a **trade union** who is involved in the representation of union members. There are several thousand full-time officers in the UK and they play a key role in the **industrial relations system**, recruiting and organizing union members, representing individuals at tribunals and in company procedures, and conducting negotiations with employers. Full-time officers may be elected from the membership, but in most cases they are appointed and play a role in trade unions akin to that of the civil service; they provide expert support, skills, and knowledge and are formally subordinate to elected conferences, committees, and lay officers. In reality, FTOs play a central and often dominant role within unions. Their job titles are highly variable and their functions also can vary, with some specializing in recruitment and organizing, while others concentrate on **collective bargaining**. FTOs are organized hierarchically with the **general secretary** at the apex and district, regional, or divisional officers/organizers at the base. [See **organizer**; **union bureaucracy**.]

functional flexibility is the policy of training employees to increase their skills and abilities so they can undertake a greater range of tasks. It means that within a work area employees can vary the tasks they undertake to meet the particular business needs. Often functional flexibility is associated with **teamworking**. Functional flexibility also requires a reduction of the **demarcation** between tasks. [See **job redesign**.]

functional silos A term used within **business process re-engineering** (BPR) to denote areas within an organization where managers occupy a privileged position in terms of resources and influence, and where they use this for their own, self-interested, functionally oriented motives rather than for the wider benefit of the business. BPR recommends the removal of a function-focused approach and its replacement with a process-focused approach, thereby destroying the functional silos and encouraging cross-functional integration.

G

gagging clause A clause within a **contract of employment** that prevents the employee from releasing company information to outsiders, such as journalists, politicians, or trade union officers. Clauses of this kind have been inserted in the contracts of public service professionals, managers, and other employees to discourage **whistle-blowing**. Despite these clauses employees may have some protection if they do release information to outsiders under the terms of the Public Interest Disclosure Act 1998.

gain-sharing is a form of output-based **incentive** which operates at company or workplace level. There are a variety of forms, including the Scanlon and Rucker Plans and Improshare, but common to most is an attempt to link payment to a measure of value-added. Value-added is calculated by deducting labour costs and expenditure on raw materials, energy, and support services from the income derived from the sale of the finished product. If value-added increases above a target figure, then it is shared between workforce and company in accordance with a pre-set formula, which in most cases allocates between 40 and 50 per cent to the employees. The aim is to produce a group incentive which, unlike **profit-sharing**, more directly reflects the contribution of the workforce to business performance. Another significant feature of gain-sharing is that the reward element frequently operates alongside procedures for communication and involvement. Managers provide continual feedback on the achievement of value-added targets while employees provide recommendations for improving performance through **suggestion schemes** and small group activities. Two other noteworthy features of gain-sharing plans have been highlighted by researchers in the United States. First, their use is associated with the presence of **trade unions** and **union voice** may play an important part in establishing the strong element of reciprocity characteristic of these schemes. Second, and perhaps related, gain-sharing is associated with high levels of company performance and, although it is a system of payment found most often in traditional manufacturing, appears to be relatively effective.

garden leave If an employee resigns in order to take up a position with a competitor organization, his or her current employer might put the employee on 'garden leave'. Effectively this means the employee receives full pay but is required to stay away from the workplace until the period of notice has been served. Typically this can occur where the employee has access to commercially sensitive information that might be of use to the new employer. Alternatively, by mutual agreement, the employer and employee can waive the **notice period**, thereby freeing the employee from his or her contract and allowing employment with the new organization to begin immediately.

gatekeeper An individual who controls, and possibly restricts, the flow of information into, within, or between organizations.

gender-blind is a description applied to social theories that ignore issues of gender and assume that patterns of work, career, and management that apply to men, also apply to women.

gender contract see **sexual contract**

gender pay-gap The earnings difference between men and women. It is normally measured by comparing male and female average hourly earnings, though average weekly and average lifetime earnings are also used. Currently in the UK the average hourly rate of women's pay is about 80 per cent of average male pay. Importantly evidence of a gender pay-gap remains if one controls for education, experience, and other measures of **human capital**. [See **equal pay**.]

gender reassignment is a sex-change, and although this is a rare medical event, it is an issue that has been dealt with in sex discrimination law. In the UK in 1999 the Sex Discrimination Act (SDA) 1975 was amended to prohibit discrimination on the grounds of gender reassignment, following a judgment of the **European Court of Justice**. To avoid breaking the law employers with an employee planning to undergo gender reassignment should: (1) agree the point at which the employee will change his or her name, personal details, and social gender; (2) discuss the medical procedure and agree time off work for treatment; (3) agree the procedure for informing work colleagues; (4) develop a method for dealing with employees' reactions to the situation; (5) agree a **dress code**, if necessary, and the point at which the employee will begin to use single-sex facilities.

General Household Survey (GHS) A UK government survey that collects information on the labour force and patterns of family expenditure. Along with the **Labour Force Survey** it is a major tool of analysis for labour economists.

general secretary is the title of the principal trade union officer in most UK **trade unions**. The general secretary is a paid **full-time officer** who leads the union and is responsible for implementing its policy and managing its resources. The main public figures of the trade union movement are the general secretaries of the largest, most prominent unions. In virtually all cases, general secretaries are elected to their posts by a secret ballot of members. This is a requirement of legislation introduced by the Conservative government in the 1980s, which was designed to ensure the replacement of **militant** union leaders with moderates, purportedly more in tune with membership opinion. The effect, in most cases, has not been to change the political leanings of union leadership but to endow general secretaries with greater authority, by virtue of their electoral mandate.

general strike A **strike** that involves the entire trade union movement and seeks to paralyze the economy through a general withdrawal of labour. Because of the scale of action, a general strike necessarily raises questions of public order and governance and may be seen as a direct threat to the established social and political system. Partly for this reason, use of the general strike has been advocated by revolutionaries and syndicalists as a means of overthrowing capitalism. In the UK, there has been only one true general strike, called by the **Trades Union Congress** in 1926 in support of striking coal miners, although Ulster Unionists in Northern Ireland used the tactic in the 1970s to block constitutional reform. In other countries with politicized and radical trade union movements, general strikes are more common and are likely to occur in periods of political crisis. They have been called to hasten the end of an established political order, as happened in some of the former communist countries during the 1980s. They have also been called by trade unions seeking to rally support for a government of the left under threat of overthrow from the political right.

general union A trade union that organizes workers across occupational and industrial boundaries and which, as a consequence, has a highly diverse membership. General unions emerged in the UK in the late nineteenth century amongst unskilled and semi-skilled transport, factory, and utility workers. Since then general unionism has become the dominant form, not just in the UK, but in other countries as well, such as Germany, the Netherlands, and the USA. The largest unions in the UK, UNISON, T&G, AEEU, and GMB, are all general unions. Because of their diverse membership general unions tend to be divided internally into a number of 'trade groups' based on the main industrial concentrations of membership. The T&G, for instance, groups its membership into four main industrial sectors for the purpose of participation, administration, and servicing: food and agriculture, manufacturing, services, and transport. Because they organize many low-skilled workers with limited bargaining power, general unions may attach particular importance to political action in order to secure protective legislation.

genuine occupational qualification (GOQ) A legal sanction in the UK that allows an organization to discriminate on the ground of gender or race/ethnicity because of an essential requirement of the particular job. For example, when casting for a play or a film, the director can audition only women for a female role; similarly, the proprietor of an 'authentic Indian restaurant' can choose to employ only Indian waiters by claiming it adds to the credibility and commercial viability of the establishment. The key word is 'genuine'—it would not be sufficient to claim, for example, that you want to employ a male porter because 'a man has always done that job' or to employ a female secretary because 'it is women's work'. [See **discrimination; direct discrimination.**]

geocentric management is an approach found in international firms where managers are appointed to posts across the subsidiary businesses and in head office irrespective of their nationality. [See **ethnocentric management; polycentric management; regiocentric management.**]

Ghent system A system of relief from unemployment involving government subsidies to unemployment funds run by **trade unions**. The name is derived from the Ghent municipal authority, which supplemented local trade union unemployment insurance schemes with public funds in 1901. The Ghent system spread widely in the early decades of the twentieth century but today only four countries rely upon it as the primary means of allocating unemployment relief: Belgium, Denmark, Finland, and Sweden. In these countries unions are involved in administering unemployment insurance and also play a role in finding work for the unemployed. The effect is to boost union membership by providing incentives to join and retain membership, even when unemployed.

glass ceiling is a term used to describe how some organizations claim to have equal opportunities but block progression upwards for women. The metaphor of the glass ceiling conveys the idea that although women can see the opportunities and positions at the higher levels of the organizational hierarchy, there is a barrier denying them access to these positions. The reasons for this barrier can range from outright prejudice (**direct discrimination**) against women to unintentional discrimination where unnecessary conditions or qualifications are being used to decide on promotions.

The effect is the same: there is **vertical segregation** in the workplace. Commentators often extend the metaphor and describe policies or actions that allow greater progression for women as 'cracking', 'breaking', or 'shattering' the glass ceiling.

globalization is the process of creating links between organizations and individuals that transcend national boundaries and are not subject to political interference. There are four main forms of globalization: markets, production, finance, and communications. Information technology, and particularly the internet, is considered to be an important catalyst in the globalization process. Theorists often talk of the collapse of time and space, meaning that geographical boundaries and distances are no longer as relevant or important as inhibitors of trade and communication. More commonly, the phrases 'the world is getting smaller' or 'the global village' are used to describe the tendency towards globalization.

glocalization is a business strategy adopted by a multinational enterprise which allows each of its national subsidiaries to operate as free-standing businesses that conform to the business and employment practices that prevail in the host country.

goal displacement The idea that the formal goals of an organization can be supplanted by a new set of objectives that reflect the interests of organizational leaders. The concept is applied particularly to the analysis of trade unions and is associated with the belief that union leaders are often unresponsive to the interests of ordinary members. In the most influential version of this argument the source of goal displacement lies in union leaders' responsibility for maintaining the security and finances of their organizations. This responsibility, it is believed, leads to a cautious and moderate policy, even when the interests of union members are best served by militant action. [See **rank-and-filism**; **union bureaucracy**.]

goals see objectives

goal-setting theory is based on the idea that the behaviour of employees can be altered by influencing their goals and targets.

It comprises four general principles designed to elicit high performance and increase motivation: (1) goals should be challenging but attainable; (2) goals should be specific rather than vague; (3) employees should be involved in the process of setting their own goals; and (4) goals should be measurable in terms clearly understood by employees: quantity, quality, time, and cost. [See **management by objectives; SMART**.]

going rate The accepted rate of pay or pay increase within a particular occupational labour market or industrial sector. The 'going rate' might be used to refer to the accepted rate of pay for occupational groups working in a particular labour market or the rate of increase which is set within the process of annual wage negotiations in the motor industry or some other industrial sector. The term has connotations of fair and equivalent payment and is often used by union wage negotiators to ground claims for wage levels or wage increases which are comparable with those in other employing organizations. As such, the notion of a going rate may be resisted by employers who are keen to tie wage rates and wage increases either to company or to individual performance within a particular employing organization. There is evidence from the CBI's Pay Databank, which collects information on the factors influencing pay settlements, that employers have been successful in shifting **pay determination** away from the notion of a going rate since the early 1980s. The result has been that pay levels and the pattern of increase have become more variable between firms. [See **ability to pay; comparability; rate for the job**.]

golden formula The principle established by the UK Trade Disputes Act 1906 that a **trade union** organizing **industrial action** should have legal **immunity** if the action is 'in contemplation or furtherance of a trade dispute'. A **trade dispute** includes those over terms and conditions of employment, work allocation, dismissal, discipline, union membership, union recognition, and the introduction and operation of industrial relations procedures. The restriction of immunity to matters of trade is intended to limit lawful strikes to those that are non-political.

golden handcuff A reward system that is used to discourage valued employees from leaving the enterprise. An example would be a **share option** scheme for executives which can only be exercised after a minimum period of service.

golden handshake A signing-on fee or one-off payment made to employees who bring valued skills to the organization. A golden handshake is a recruitment tool used to attract scarce talent to the organization and may take a number of different forms, including the payment of a **bonus** or the offer of **share options**. The recipients of golden handshakes are normally executives. [See **Enterprise Management Incentive**.]

golden parachutes are severance agreements for senior managers in an organization which guarantee them substantial payments if they are dismissed following a **takeover** by another company.

good employer A concept that is sometimes applied to the analysis of employment relations in the public sector. It expresses the view that states and state agencies have subscribed to a norm of good practice in managing their own employees. This norm embraces **procedural rules**, such as **recognition** of trade unions, reliance on **collective bargaining**, and **joint consultation**, and the use of formal **procedures** and **arbitration** in resolving employment disputes. It has also embraced **substantive rules**, such as meritocratic selection and promotion, **security of employment**, relatively generous **benefits**, fair wages and **comparability**, and the adoption of a formal **equal opportunity policy**. Critics have argued that the good employer commitment was only ever partial and largely restricted to salaried employees and that elements of good practice have been forced on public sector managers through union pressure. There is a consensus, however, that the commitment has worn increasingly threadbare in recent years as a result of financial constraints and the restructuring of the public sector. [See **model employer**.]

go-slow A form of **industrial action** in which workers restrict output and possibly **work to rule** in order to pressurize management for concessions.

grade A grouping of jobs with equivalent demands which are offered the same rate or range of pay. Jobs are often allocated to grades through a formal process of **job evaluation**, which can be used to establish their relative demands. A pay structure will typically comprise a hierarchy of grades with less demanding jobs occupying the lower grades and more demanding jobs occupying the higher. Reflecting the movement towards flatter organizational structures (see **delayering**), there has been a simplification of grade structures in many companies in recent years through the process of **broad-banding**.

grade drift is the process whereby jobs may be regraded, and so migrate up a graded **pay structure**, without any significant change in their content. As a consequence, jobholders will receive a higher rate of pay without assuming any additional or more demanding job functions. Grade drift is an indicator of the **degeneration** of a graded pay structure and may arise for a number of different reasons, including weak management control systems, labour market pressures, and the possession of bargaining power by jobholders. It has been a particular feature of public service organizations, where managers have allowed grade drift as a means of maintaining rates of pay of employees in the face of **incomes policy**, which threatens to erode earnings. Symptoms of grade drift include the gradual emptying of jobs from the bottom grades of a pay structure and a clustering of jobs in the middle and highest grades over time.

grandfather appraisal is a technique designed to limit bias in the **appraisal** process (see **halo effect**) by having the appraisal undertaken by the employee's line manager's manager, rather than the line manager him- or herself. It also helps to ensure consistency, although the problem is that it burdens the more senior manager with a greater amount of work. The less sexist term 'grandparent' appraisal is preferred in some organizations.

graphic rating scales see **trait rating**

graphology is the analysis of handwriting and is sometimes used as a selection technique. In theory, a person's handwriting is supposed to reveal aspects of their personality and character, so a company might use a graphologist to produce profiles of the candidates based on handwriting samples. Graphology has extremely low **validity** but this does not stop some firms from using it among their selection techniques. Surveys reveal it to be widely used among organizations in France.

greedy institution A social institution that demands total commitment from its members and overrides the established separation of social life into different spheres, such as work, home, leisure, politics, and religion. The best examples of greedy institutions are religious sects, monastic orders, and revolutionary political parties. Companies that seek to develop high levels of **organizational commitment** and promote a **strong culture** may also approximate to this form, however, and place heavy demands on their committed employees. [See **work–life balance**.]

greenfield site A location outside a city that has been developed specifically for existing businesses to relocate, or for new businesses to start up. A greenfield site might be attractive to a business for a number of reasons: lower business rates, more space, opportunity for expansion, a customized building, the opportunity to acquire a new workforce, logistics (e.g. location near to a motorway), etc. Some commentators have noted that a particular feature of firms in greenfield sites in the UK is that they are less likely to recognize trade unions (see **recognition**). This has led some critics to suggest that the move to a greenfield site is therefore driven by management's desire to establish new terms and conditions of employment without trade union involvement. Others reject this and claim that whilst labour relations and union **derecognition** might be one of the factors in deciding to locate on a greenfield site, operational and financial considerations are far more influential.

grievance procedure An industrial relations procedure through which employees can raise problems or complaints about their employment, working conditions, and management behaviour. In most cases procedures consist of a number of stages, which begin with the individual employee raising a grievance with his or her immediate supervisor. If there is no resolution at this level, the grievance can proceed upwards, with more senior managers and possibly more senior trade union representatives becoming involved at each successive stage. The final stage of the procedure may involve **third-party intervention** and a resolution of the dispute by an independent arbitrator. Grievance procedures are very common in UK industry, though they are found with greater frequency in companies that recognize trade unions. Under the Employment Relations Act 1999, individuals have a right to be represented in company grievance procedures by a trade union officer if the grievance deals with a serious issue, such as an allegation of unlawful action by the employer.

grievances are sources of discontent amongst employees. Common grievances concern **management style** and treatment of workers, **deductions from wages**, work organization that leads to **job stress** or **health and safety** problems, and poor facilities for rest and refreshment at work. In many organizations grievances can be raised and addressed through a formal **grievance procedure** and 'grievance handling' is an important function of **trade unions**.

gross misconduct is conduct at work that represents a serious transgression of disciplinary rules and which is normally punished through **dismissal** without notice. Examples of gross misconduct might include fighting at work, abusive behaviour, drunkenness or being in possession of illegal drugs, theft, fraud, and the **harassment** of co-workers. According to ACAS, gross misconduct is 'generally seen as misconduct serious enough to destroy the employment contract between the employer and the employee and make any further working relationship and trust impossible'.

group The widely accepted definition of a group is by psychologist Edgar Schein. He described it as a collection of people who interact with each other, are psychologically aware of each other, and who perceive themselves to be in a group. A *workgroup* meets these criteria, but in addition the members have task-centred goals. Importantly, whilst the group members support each other, they each have their own area of responsibility for which they are individually accountable. In comparison, a work *team* is composed of members with complementary skills who are involved in a common set of goals for which they are collectively accountable. Some commentators suggest that teams are expected to exhibit **synergy**, whereas no such expectations are made of groups. It is worth noting that the definitions of *group, workgroup* and *team* vary from commentator to commentator. Indeed, some people use the words interchangeably. The distinctions made above are the ones we judge to be the most widely accepted by contemporary writers on HRM.

group development see **stages of group development**

group incentive see **team-based pay**

groupthink is the tendency for group members, when faced with a problem, to seek consensus and in so doing ignore or suppress alternative ideas and minority viewpoints. The result of groupthink can be poor-quality decisions because it discourages full assessment of the problem, thorough information search, and proper evaluation of a wide range of alternatives. The concept of groupthink was developed by organizational psychologist Irving Janis, who identified six symptoms: (1) an illusion amongst group members that the group 'knows best'; (2) a tendency to rationalize away information that contradicts the group's beliefs/opinions; (3) the presence of 'mind guards' who protect the group from contradictory information; (4) a confidence in the group's legitimacy/moral authority; (5) a tendency to produce negative **stereotypes** of other groups or individuals; (6) the emergence of coalitions that pressurize individuals/minorities into conformity.

guarantee payment A statutory payment to employees who are laid off because of a reduction in their employer's business. Employees with one month's continuous service are entitled to up to five days' guarantee pay in any single three-month period.

guild Guilds were the collective organizations of crafts or trades that existed in pre-industrial Britain. They wielded their powers under warrant from the crown, regulated entry to the trade through **apprenticeship**, enforced monopolies, and upheld customary standards of **reward**, status, and work. In medieval times guilds embraced both masters and journeymen, though over time they evolved into organizations of workers and were the precursors of craft trade unions. [See **craft union**.]

guru see **management guru**

H

halo effect A halo effect is when you have an overall positive view of someone because they have one or two characteristics you admire. For example, in a work situation, because people are sociable, you might assume they are good salespersons; or because they have degrees in engineering you assume they will be competent managers. In other words, it is a form of bias which overemphasizes one quality in a person and ignores other, equally important characteristics. The opposite of the halo effect (sometimes called the horns effect) can also occur: you judge a person negatively because of one characteristic. For example, if you think modesty is a good quality in a person, you are likely to take an instant dislike to strangers who start boasting about their achievements as soon as they meet you. It is particularly important for managers to be aware of the halo effect when judging people (for example, **selection**, **appraisal**, **grievance**, **reward**) because it is a form of prejudice that can have serious consequences in terms of fair treatment and **equal opportunities**.

handmaiden A role that can be adopted by a manager who is primarily responsible for personnel/human resources. Handmaidens react to the requirements and demands of line managers, often adopting a **firefighting** role when personnel problems surface. They are tactical, rather than strategic, and tend to have a subservient, attendant relationship to line managers (hence the label, handmaiden). The term 'handmaiden' was coined by management theorist John Storey to describe one of four potential styles of managing human resources (the others being **adviser**, **changemaker**, and **regulator**).

handwriting analysis see **graphology**

harassment is unwanted behaviour that an employee finds intimidating, upsetting, embarrassing, humiliating, or offensive. It can take many forms including physical contact, joking, the use of offensive language, obscene posters and graffiti, isolation and exclusion from social activities, intrusion through pestering or stalking, coercion for sexual favours, and pressure to participate in political or religious groups. Harassment is not defined in terms of the intentions of the harasser but rather in terms of whether it harms the victim and whether it includes behaviour that is regarded as unacceptable by normal standards. There is no general legal prohibition of harassment but **sexual harassment** and racial harassment are regarded as unfair discrimination and are covered respectively by sex and race discrimination law. Employers may be liable for failure to deal effectively with other forms of harassment under the obligation to provide a safe working environment and under the general **duty of care** owed to the employee. To combat harassment it is recommended that employers develop an anti-harassment policy, often known as a **dignity at work policy**. This should provide a statement that defines harassment, establish a procedure for dealing with complaints, offer support through advice and **counselling**, and allow for disciplinary action to be taken against harassers. It is also recommended that the policy be communicated to employees and that guidance be offered as to what might be regarded as unacceptable behaviour. [See **workplace bullying**.]

hard contract An agreement between two parties where each specifies the terms and conditions of their association with each other. In particular the contract will clearly specify what they expect from the other party and what they will deliver. The parties each have their own separate interests and will pursue these within the limits of the contract. [See **soft contract**; **spot contract**.]

hard HRM see **soft HRM**

harmonization The movement away from separate terms and conditions of employment for manual hourly paid and white-collar salaried employees, towards **single status**, i.e. common basic terms and conditions of employment. Harmonization most frequently affects holiday and leave entitlement, redundancy pay, and occupational pensions. It may also have a symbolic element involving the use of common restaurant and car-parking facilities or a standard company uniform.

Hawthorne effect This concept was derived from the **Hawthorne studies** in which the investigators noticed how the subjects of their experiments responded positively to being singled out as a special group worthy of study. Consequently, the term is used to describe how aspects of the investigation itself might be influencing the results, especially where such investigation is based on an experimental research design. Consequently, some researchers reject any social research based on experimental design on the grounds that it can never accurately reproduce the real social context. Others argue that experimental design is a legitimate form of social research providing that the possible influence of the experimental artefacts (the Hawthorne effect) is taken into account.

Hawthorne studies A pioneering set of research investigations in the 1920s exploring the effects of physical working conditions on employee productivity. However, the studies are widely known not because of their findings about worker productivity but because they revealed the importance of the social dimension of workplace relations. In particular the investigations highlighted the influence of group norms and informal rules on individual behaviour at work. [See **human relations theorists**.]

Hay Management Consultants is one of the premier management consultancy firms, and specializes in the fields of **performance management** and **reward**. Hay is best known for its proprietary **job evaluation** system, the Hay Guide Chart-Profile Method, which is one of the most widely used in business, particularly for managerial and professional jobs. The scheme is an analytical system of job evaluation based on three core factors, Know-how, Problem-Solving, and Accountability, and was originally developed by the company's founder, Edgar N. Hay, in the 1950s. One of the attractions for employers using the Hay scheme is that it is possible to use the results of job evaluation in tandem with those from **salary surveys** from a sample of other employers using the same system. As a consequence salaries can be set in line with those for jobs with an equivalent job evaluation score in the same business sector or labour market. Other consultancy firms that offer job evaluation services include KPMG Management Consulting, PA Consulting, PE Consulting, Saville and Holdsworth, and Towers Perrin. While proprietary job evaluation schemes are widely and increasingly used, they have been criticized for not being tailored sufficiently to the requirements of individual organizations, for being biased towards managerial jobs, and for being insufficiently receptive to the issue of equal pay for work of **equal value**.

hazardous substances include chemicals, dangerous metals, dust, fumes, and bacteria that are present in the workplace and pose a threat to health. In the UK there are strict regulations designed to minimize the risk of exposure to substances of these kinds and which require the provision of emergency procedures in the event of exposure. The key regulations are the Control of Substances Hazardous to Health Regulations 1994 (COSHH), the Control of Lead at Work Regulations 1998, and the Chemicals (Hazard Information and Packaging for Supply) Regulations 1994. [See **health and safety regulations**.]

headcount is the number of employees in an organization.

headhunters see **executive search consultants**

health and safety is that aspect of human resource management concerned with identifying hazards and risks to health within work processes and taking steps to minimize or remove those risks. Given its importance and given the fact that there may be financial and operational pressures on managers to neglect health and safety, it is an area of the **employment relationship** that is closely regulated by law. The European Union has adopted a series of directives on health and safety, while in the UK the Health and Safety at Work Act 1974, with its associated **health and safety regulations**, provides a legal framework to guide management action (see **risk assessment**). Significantly, health and safety law provides for the appointment of both **safety representatives** and **health and safety inspectors** to ensure that the law is adhered to and that companies develop good practice in health and safety management. Despite regulation, workplace death continues to be a feature of hazardous industries, such as fishing, agriculture, and construction, and workplace injury and disease are major problems that blight the lives of thousands of workers and impose a heavy cost on business. **Job stress**, **repetitive strain injury**, and **workplace violence** are among the issues that have come to the fore in health and safety management in recent years. In the UK, the **Health and Safety Commission** and its operational arm, the **Health and Safety Executive**, have overall responsibility for monitoring and improving health and safety at work.

Health and Safety Commission (HSC) A tripartite agency including representatives from business and labour that has overall responsibility for **health and safety** in the UK. The **Health and Safety Executive** is its operational arm. The functions of the HSC are to secure the health, safety, and welfare of people at work, to protect the general public from health risks that emanate from work activities, to review legislation and recommend reform, and to conduct research, promote training, and provide information and advice. The HSC is formally accountable to government ministers.

Health and Safety Executive (HSE) The UK government agency that is responsible for **health and safety** and accountable to the **Health and Safety Commission**. The HSE is responsible for reviewing and developing health and safety laws and producing **Approved Codes of Practice** and standards that ensure safe working across business. It also publishes advice and guidance and commissions research. The HSE is responsible for enforcing health and safety law and regulations and employs **health and safety inspectors** who visit employers' premises to ensure the law is being complied with. As part of this enforcement role the HSE can initiate legal proceedings against employers who contravene health and safety law, though it has been criticized by safety campaigners for resorting too infrequently to legal sanctions. [See **corporate killing**.]

health and safety inspector In the UK health and safety inspectors (previously factory inspectors) are employed by the **Health and Safety Executive** and are charged with enforcing health and safety law. Inspectors have the right to enter any workplace without giving notice and on a normal inspection will examine the workplace and work activities and the management's health and safety practice to ensure there is compliance with the law. They may also speak to workplace **safety representatives**. Inspectors offer guidance to employers and may offer informal advice to put right any minor breach of health and safety law. They also have powers to issue an improvement notice to force compliance with the law or a prohibition notice, where there is an immediate threat to safety or health. In serious cases inspectors can initiate prosecution of employers. If an improvement or prohibition notice is served, the 'dutyholder', the manager with formal responsibility for health and safety, has the right to appeal to an **Employment Tribunal**. While health and safety inspectors have considerable powers, the system of inspection has been criticized by safety campaigners on the grounds that the power of prosecution is used sparingly and that the inspection service is under-resourced. [See **environmental health officers**.]

health and safety regulations are issued under the Health and Safety at Work Act 1974 and specify particular obligations for employers. The majority of UK safety regulations now originate in the European Union and include regulations dealing with **manual handling**, **hazardous substances**, **vibration**, display screens, **noise at work**, electricity, and gas. There are also regulations for specific industries, such as railways. Regulations are supported by **Approved Codes of Practice** and are enforced by the **Health and Safety Executive** and local authority safety inspectors. [See **environmental health officers; risk assessment; VDU regulations**.]

health education Under a 'good employer' obligation many organizations provide health education to the workforce as part of **occupational health care**. Health education at work is often tailored to the particular organization and its working practices but, in addition, may cover general topics, such as diet, smoking, stress, exercise, alcohol and drugs, and AIDS.

health insurance Increasing numbers of employers in the UK offer private health insurance to their employees as a **benefit**. Health cover typically provides employees and their immediate family members with access to private health services and can be an important feature of **remuneration**, particularly for managers and professionals in the private sector. The provision of private health insurance in this way points to the emergence of a two-tier system of health care, in which public services occupy a residual position with the private sector catering to the better off.

helicopter vision means taking a broader perspective; seeing the big picture rather than concentrating on the detail.

heroes/heroines Heroes or heroines (in relation to **organizational culture**) are people who personify the organizational values and provide role models.

Herzberg's two-factor theory This theory suggests there are two sets of factors that impact upon an employee's feelings of satisfaction at work. The first set (hygiene factors) concerns the employee's need for fair treatment in compensation, supervision, and working conditions. If these are not met, employees feel dissatisfied. However, if managers devise ways of meeting these needs, it will still not lead to job satisfaction. In addition, a second set of needs (motivator factors) concerning personal growth and development in the job (promotion, achievement, responsibility, etc.) must be met for employees to experience job satisfaction. The distinction between these two sets of factors is important because it means that different factors are responsible for job satisfaction and job dissatisfaction. The theory was developed by psychologist Frederick Herzberg in the 1960s and had an influence on methods of **job redesign**. Critics argue that the theory is inadequate because it does not take into account situational variables, the measures of satisfaction are questionable, and it tends to assume that job satisfaction will lead to improvement in productivity.

hierarchy of needs see Maslow's hierarchy of needs

high commitment management (HCM) is an approach to the management of people that emphasizes the need to develop organizational commitment amongst the employees, on the assumption that this will lead to positive outcomes such as lower labour turnover, better motivation, and improved performance. The importance of increasing commitment has been recognized in various approaches to people management (for example, theory Y (see **theory X and theory Y**), **high trust, responsible autonomy**, and **employee involvement**) but was popularized in the 1980s by management theorist Richard Walton, whose **normative approach** advocates that organizations move from a strategy of 'control' to a strategy of 'commitment' in the management of employees. This reflects a concern amongst commentators at that time (particularly in the USA) that traditional methods (see **Fordism**) were no longer an appropriate means of organizing and managing people. This seemed particularly pertinent given that US organizations were faced with increasing competition from Japan and other countries in South-East Asia, all of which had a different approach to management (see **theory Z; Japanization**) that seemed to be delivering good results in terms of productivity, profitability, and market share. More recently, HCM is being used as a general term that embraces a diverse range of human resource practices and techniques (sometimes labelled high commitment practices—HCPs) designed to improve the overall performance of the organization through generating commitment amongst the workforce. An alternative term, high involvement management, is used by some commentators. [See **high performance work practices; empowerment; soft HRM**.]

high commitment practice (HCP) see high commitment management

high involvement management see high commitment management

high performance management see high performance work practices

high performance work practices (HPWP) are management techniques that supposedly increase the overall performance and/or effectiveness of the organization by making better use of the skills of employees and improving their commitment to the organization. Typically such techniques would include **teamworking, functional flexibility, empowerment, employee development, appraisal, counselling,** and **performance-related pay**. The term HPWP is particularly associated with research undertaken by **bundles theorists**. The problem is that different theorists do not agree upon the precise bundle of human resource practices that is supposed to account for better organizational performance. To some extent this is reflected by the range of terms that different researchers use to label their particular bundles of practices, for example, **high commitment management**, high involvement management, high performance work systems, high performance management, and human capital enhancing HR systems.

high performance work systems see high performance work practices

high road The 'high road' to competitiveness is based on the cultivation of employee commitment and an exchange of high wages for high productivity. German manufacturing companies, which develop a skilled and flexible workforce as a basis for the production of high value-added goods for global markets, are said to embody this approach to **competitive strategy**. [See **low road**.]

high trust is a description given to a pattern of employment relations based on the assumption that employees are committed to the organization and motivated to work on its behalf and therefore do not require close supervision or financial **incentives**. On the contrary, it is argued that high-trust relations flourish where employees are offered **security of employment**, are paid a **salary** tied only notionally to measures of worker performance, and are allowed wide scope for discretion at work. High-trust relations are found most readily in managerial and professional employment, although experiments with **employee involvement** and **high commitment management** are meant to reproduce the pattern for other categories of employee. [See also **low trust**.]

hiring hall The supply of skilled labour to employers by **craft unions**, such that the union acts as a **labour market intermediary**.

homeworking is an arrangement that allows 'employees' to undertake their work in their own home. For the employers this has the advantage of reducing overheads, because homeworkers are normally classed as **self-employed**. For employees it can have the advantage of providing greater flexibility to manage their working time in line with domestic responsibilities and social life. Homeworking ranges from low-paid manual work (such as finishing goods or packing) to high-paid professional work (such as graphic art and design). [See **teleworking**.]

horizontal loading is the technique of adding a greater range of tasks to an existing job. The extra tasks will require a similar level of skill. [See **job redesign**.]

horizontal segregation is a concept that describes a workplace where different types of jobs in the organization can be distinguished by the particular characteristics of the employees doing those jobs. Examples of horizontal segregation can be found in most organizations—for instance, in many university departments almost all the secretarial staff are women and most of the technicians are men; or in a hotel, the receptionist is more likely to be a woman and the porter is usually a man. In these examples, the horizontal segregation is on the basis of sex, but it can also apply to other characteristics such as race/ethnicity, age, and disability. Whilst the type of segregation can differ, its impact is similar because it ghettoizes certain people into particular jobs and thereby limits their opportunities. It is also frequently based on **stereotypes** of what is considered appropriate work for particular groups. When it is combined with **vertical segregation** it has a particularly adverse effect on **equal opportunities**.

horns effect see halo effect

host-country national (HCN) In an international firm, an HCN is a person whose nationality is the same as that of the country in which the company is operating: for example, a UK manager working for a UK-based subsidiary of a Japanese company. [See **parent-country national; third-country national.**]

hot-desking describes a situation where an employee has no fixed desk space in the office, but instead uses any available workstation. It is deemed appropriate for employees whose main activities are outside the office—for example, meeting clients—and in organizations that thrive on human interaction and creativity. Not only does it reduce costly office space, it also discourages territoriality amongst employees.

hourly rate is the basic rate of pay per hour. Hourly rates are used largely, though not exclusively, as the means of expressing the rate of pay for manual occupations. Hourly rates contrast with annual salaries, in which the rate of pay is based on the number of weeks worked per year and which are used for most non-manual occupations. A feature of the movement towards **single status** in industry has been the abandoning of hourly rates and the use of salaries for all categories of employee.

HRMism is a term coined by industrial relations theorist Tom Keenoy to signify all the various meanings and practices that have come to be subsumed within HRM.

human capital enhancing HR systems see **high performance work practices**

human capital theory is based on the assumption that individuals can affect their value in the labour market by choosing whether or not to take advantage of educational opportunities and training. If they do so, they increase their human capital and consequently will increase their value to employers. Human capital theory suggests employees should be treated as individuals with specific sets of skills and abilities, so it emphasizes **competence-based pay** as an effective remuneration system. Proponents argue this leads to a very **meritocratic** system and helps to achieve **equal opportunities** based on talent and ability, and regulated by a market economy. Critics argue that one of the major problems with the theory is that it assumes that everyone has the same chance to invest in their human capital, but, in reality, people have different life opportunities that are outside their control from birth, not least because of the relative wealth or poverty of their parents. In other words, human capital theory is not as meritocratic as it might first appear.

human relations theorists in the 1920s and 1930s challenged the conventional wisdom of the time that people were motivated simply by money and other forms of **extrinsic rewards**. Instead their research revealed that a range of social factors satisfied and motivated people; thus **intrinsic rewards** (such as receiving praise, feelings of achievement, a sense of pride in one's work) were often just as important for some individuals. The ideas raised by these theorists persist today and find expression in management concepts such as **empowerment** and **teamworking**.

human resource accounting is the technique of treating expenditure on the development of employees as capital investment. Accountants are frequently dismissive of this, arguing that it is impossible to put a monetary value on human assets that would be generally acceptable. Other commentators suggest that it is not just a technical problem, but also an ethical one: should free human beings be regarded as assets in the same way as legally owned property?

human resource development (HRD) is the process of encouraging employees to acquire new skills and knowledge through various training programmes, courses, and learning packages. For the organization, the aim is to build **competency** amongst its employees, which will contribute to achieving the overall business objectives. For the individual, development provides opportunities that might be beneficial in four ways. (1) It makes the employee more valuable to the organization and thereby improves job security. (2) It enhances career opportunities within the organization. (3) It increases an individual's **employability** outside the organization because of his or her broader skill/competency base. (4) If it broadens the scope and responsibility of work, it can raise the **intrinsic reward** employees derive from their jobs. If HRD is to be successful, it requires commitment from senior management in terms of allocating sufficient resources. In addition, line managers increasingly are expected to be involved in the delivery of training (see **devolution**) and so their commitment to HRD is vital. Critics argue that HRD frequently requires a long-term focus, whereas many organizations have short-term objectives (often set by tough financial performance targets) and, consequently, are reluctant to commit resources to HRD initiatives (see **short-termism**). Indeed, when there is a downturn in the market, the training/development budget is typically the first area where managers in an organization seek to make cutbacks. [See **personal development plan**.]

human resource flow is a term used to describe the process by which employees pass through the organization. It encapsulates a number of sub-processes: inflow (**recruitment** and **selection**), throughflow (**promotion** and **lateral career moves**), and outflow (**resignation, retirement, dismissal,** and **redundancy**). Monitoring human resource flow is vital to ensure accurate **human resource planning** since it allows data to be collected that can help to predict any shortfall or oversupply of labour.

human resource management (HRM) is a term that has many definitions. In the UK it has been the subject of considerable academic analysis, and there is no common agreement on what HRM means. In particular there have been debates about whether HRM is different from personnel management, and whether there are different types of HRM. As a result, we offer ten definitions that attempt to summarize the various approaches you might encounter in the textbooks.

1. *A label*. HRM is simply another name for **personnel management**. Organizations might adopt the title HRM because it is seen as contemporary term that gives a modern image of the personnel department. In the USA the term HRM has long been in use as a way to describe the various activities that are considered part of the personnel function in the UK. Therefore, there is nothing distinctive or special about HRM.

2. *A convenient shorthand term*. HRM is simply a way of grouping together the range of activities associated with managing people that are variously categorized under employee relations, industrial/labour relations, personnel management, and organizational behaviour. Many academic departments where research and teaching in all these areas take place have adopted the title department of human resource management.

3. *A map*. HRM is a map that can help guide students and practitioners through concepts and ideas associated with the management of people and in so doing reveal to them a choice of routes and destinations.

4. *A set of professional practices*. HRM is a co-ordinated approach to managing people that seeks to integrate the various personnel activities so that they are compatible with each other. Therefore, the key areas of employee resourcing, employee development, employee reward, and employee involvement are considered to be interrelated. Policy-making and procedures in one of these areas will have an impact on other areas, therefore human resource management is an approach that takes a holistic view and considers how these various areas can be integrated. This definition suggests that HRM is a systematic approach to personnel management, as advocated by organizations representing the personnel profession (such as the **Chartered Institute of Personnel and Development** in the UK).

5. *A method of ensuring internal fit*. HRM is a co-ordinated approach (as in definition 4) but one that also considers how the policies will fit with other aspects of the organization. In other words, there is a concern with **internal fit**, in line with strategic

decisions that have been made higher up the organization. In addition, there is emphasis placed upon the consequences of personnel policy for the organization and the individual. This approach is exemplified in the USA by the Harvard version of HRM (proposed by Michael Beer, Bert Spector, Paul Lawrence, D. Quinn Mills, and Robert Walton) and in the UK by David Guest's version of HRM. Both versions suggest a causal link between human resource policies and outcomes; in other words, making the correct choices in terms of policy intervention will lead to positive outcomes that benefit both the organization and the individual. In the Harvard version, these choices are constrained by a range of situational factors—business strategy amongst them. In addition, in both versions there is an emphasis on the need for greater involvement of all managers (from corporate executive down to line managers) in human resources issues and practices (again part of ensuring internal fit).

6. *A method of ensuring external fit.* HRM is a fully integrated approach that seeks to match the policies, procedures, and activities of people management with the demands of the external environment. In this sense there is an emphasis on **external fit** between the environment and the business strategy, of which human resource management is considered to be a vital component. Whilst this viewpoint is shared by various theorists, they disagree about which aspects of a firm's strategic position should influence the human resource policies and procedures. For example, the Michigan version of HRM (proposed by Charles Fombrun, Noel Tichy, and Mary Devanna) matches human resource strategy to the extent of diversification; Tom Kochan and Thomas Barocci match it to the organization's stage of business development (start-up, growth, maturity, and decline); Randall Schuler and Susan Jackson match it to the organization's competitive strategy (innovation, quality enhancement, or cost-reduction); and Raymond Miles and Charles Snow match it to the organization's strategic orientation (**analyser, defender, prospector, reactor**). [See also **strategic human resource management**.]

7. *A competitive advantage.* HRM is the means through which an organization can gain a competitive advantage. The employees are

one of the key resources in an organization, and through carefully developing and managing them, they will ultimately be the critical factors that distinguish successful organizations from unsuccessful ones. This definition is exemplified by the cliché 'people are our most valued asset'. Recently this perspective has been revived through growing interest in the **resource-based view**.

8. *A market-driven approach*. HRM is an approach to people management based on assumptions of **unitarism** and an emphasis on **individualism**, consistent with a **neo-liberal** political perspective. The needs of the business determine the way employees are treated—some being valued and developed as important resources, others being treated as expendable commodities. This means that whilst there is a need for loyalty and commitment from some employees, there is simply a requirement for performance from others. Consequently, HRM can embrace a wide variety of practices. [See **soft HRM**.]

9. *A manipulative device*. HRM is rhetoric to disguise the exploitative nature of capitalism and make new management techniques more palatable. Human resource management is the means through which managers, as agents of capital, conceal the exploitation inherent in the **labour process**, control employees, and encourage them to consent to techniques of work intensification.

10. *A hologram*. HRM is a projection that shifts its appearance, depending on where we are standing. This perspective has been developed by one of HRM's foremost critics, Tom Keenoy. He suggests that the HRM hologram explains how a precise definition of HRM cannot be established. It gives HRM a fluid identity and multiple forms. Furthermore, after perceiving HRM in their own particular way, employers, employees, managers, consultants, and academics 'project' it back to others, and further change its form and image, thereby adding to its fluid identity.

human resource planning (HRP) (sometimes called manpower planning) is the process of analysing an organization's need for employees and evaluating how this can be met from the internal and external labour markets. It should be an ongoing process of monitoring that helps identify the need to attract, allocate, develop, and retain human resources to meet the wider business objectives of the organization. It encourages managers in organizations to plan ahead. Good-quality human resource planning will involve analysing data on existing employees (**demographics, competencies, training**, etc.) in order to assess the overall balance of existing resources and to predict possible future issues such as skill shortages, **promotion** opportunities, and **retirement** patterns. [See **human resource flow**.]

human resources (HR) are employees, personnel, or the workforce of an organization. The term has become increasingly fashionable in recent years and expresses the view that employees are a resource that must be harnessed and managed effectively alongside the other resources used by business organizations, such as capital, property, raw materials, and energy. Partly for this reason some commentators are unhappy with this description of the workforce because it expresses the view of labour as a mere commodity or factor of production. Reflecting this unhappiness, some firms that aspire to practise **soft HRM** refer to the employees as **associates**, members, partners, or **stakeholders**.

human resource strategy is the set of objectives guiding human resource policies within an organization. In theory the human resource strategy can (some commentators argue *should*) be linked to the wider business strategy (see **strategic integration; strategic human resource management**).

hygiene factors are features of work that affect job dissatisfaction, according to **Herzberg's two-factor theory**. They include quality of supervision, pay, physical working conditions, job security, relations with others, and organization policies.

hysterisis is the long-lasting or permanent effect on the economic or the **industrial relations system** that results from a crisis or catastrophic event. Thus, the oil crisis of the early 1970s is sometimes viewed as a key turning point in recent economic history that generated a seemingly permanent increase in **unemployment** across the developed world. In the sphere of British industrial relations the recession of the early 1980s or the miners' strike of the mid-1980s are sometimes viewed in a similar light, as catastrophic events that halted one line of development and pushed the system along a different course.

immunity Under UK law **trade unions** do not have a positive right to strike and organize other forms of **industrial action** akin to that which exists in most other European countries. Instead, the law has granted the organizers of industrial action immunity from liability in tort. Essentially this means that, provided certain conditions are met, trade unions and their members and officers are protected from civil legal action by those adversely affected by industrial disputes. The reform of trade union law by the Conservative governments of the 1980s and 1990s had the effect of narrowing union immunity by introducing more exacting conditions before lawful industrial action could be taken. Thus, for action to retain immunity today it must be preceded by a properly conducted **strike ballot**, notice must be given to the employer, action must be taken in furtherance of a **trade dispute**, and it must not be **secondary action**, targeted at third parties. The law has also been changed to allow trade unions themselves to be targeted in civil action and not just their individual members and officers. In some cases this has led to unions suffering major claims for damages and to the sequestration of their assets. The terminology of 'immunity' is often criticized because it suggests that unions are above the law and uniquely privileged. In fact, the provision of statutory immunity is simply the way in which British law has provided unions and their members with the basic social and political right to withdraw labour. [See **golden formula**.]

implied term An implied term is part of the contract of employment that has not been expressly agreed by the employer and employee. Implied terms may be inferred from accepted practice; for example, there may be an implied mobility clause within a contract if a worker has accepted previously that he or she should work temporarily at another site. [See **express term**.]

impression management is the process of deliberately creating an image designed to impress others for the purpose of gaining credibility and influence. Successful impression management is the triumph of image over substance.

incentive A cash payment or some other **reward** that is offered to employees conditional on an improvement in performance. The purpose of an incentive is to induce **motivation**.

Incomes Data Services (IDS) A company which specializes in the production of pay data and industrial relations, management, and legal briefings for employers. IDS is a specialist publisher producing a series of regular bulletins and reports on aspects of the labour market, labour law, and human resource management. The main publications produced by IDS include *IDS Brief*, *IDS Report*, *IDS Study*, and *IDS European Review*.

incomes policy A state policy directed at restraining the growth in earnings, usually in order to combat inflation. Incomes policies can take a number of different forms. In extreme circumstances a pay freeze may be initiated, which blocks any increase in pay for its duration. In other situations, in contrast, there might be a target percentage figure below which pay increases must fall. With this arrangement there may also be provision for higher increases provided they are matched by increases in productivity. Incomes policies can be 'statutory', which means they are inscribed in law, or 'voluntary', in which case they are typically agreed with the central **confederations** of business and labour. Where there is agreement of this kind, the government may enter into a corporatist exchange and in return for pay restraint agree changes in employment law, welfare, tax, or investment policy to secure the agreement of the social partners (see **corporatism**). The Social Contract between the UK Labour government of the 1970s and the trade unions took this form, with pay restraint being exchanged for a series of changes in employment law and improvements in the state pension. In the UK incomes policies have been successful in depressing earnings growth and have also narrowed the **pay dispersion**. They have generated fresh problems, however, and have been associated with wage militancy and the outbreak of large public sector strikes as employees who believe they have lost out rebel against the policy's constraints.

income tax is a tax on earnings which is normally progressive. That is, no income tax is paid on small amounts of income and the amount due increases proportionately to the amount earned. Moreover, above a given point it is normal for the amount of tax on each unit of income to increase. In the UK income tax is collected from most employees through the **pay-as-you-earn** system. Under the Labour government elected in 1997 the income tax system has become more progressive, largely through reducing the tax burden on the lower paid via mechanisms like the Working Families Tax Credit. [See **National Insurance Contributions; social charge**.]

incorporation is the absorption of trade unions in the process of economic and conflict management, such that they lose their radical potential, cease effectively to represent their members, and become instruments of government and employers. [See **goal displacement**.]

incremental scale A pay or salary range which is divided into a series of fixed, even steps between the minimum and maximum salary points. Ideally, employees are appointed at the bottom of the scale and then progress towards the top depending on seniority, skill acquisition, or performance. Fixed incremental scales of this kind are a particular feature of public service employment, where annual increments are awarded for each year of service. The reform of the public services in recent years, however, has led to some displacement of seniority with performance-based progression. Where the latter is used, high-performing employees might be awarded two or more increments at any one time or a 'merit bar' might operate which restricts the upper reaches of the scale to those with a high performance rating. [See **grade; salary progression**.]

independent contractor see **self-employed**

indexation An arrangement where pay is up-rated on a regular basis in accordance with indexes of average earnings or inflation. Indexation is rarely used in the UK, although the police and firefighters have their pay determined in this way. Since the Edmund-Davies inquiry of 1977, police pay has been up-rated annually in line with the monthly index of average earnings. Indexation, in this context, provides a means of maintaining the relative earnings of a group of workers who are denied the right to strike. Indexation has been advocated as a means of maintaining the relative value of the **National Minimum Wage**.

indirect discrimination see **direct discrimination**

indirect participation is a system of worker participation in management decision-making that is conducted through worker representatives. Examples include **collective bargaining**, **joint consultation**, or **worker directors**. [See **direct participation**.]

indirect pay is an alternative term for employee **benefits**. 'Indirect pay' refers to those elements of remuneration, including **pensions**, **health insurance**, and benefits in kind, which are made in addition to the basic wage or salary and regular incentive payments.

individual conciliation see **conciliation**

individual contract see **personal contract**

individual employment law is the law governing the relationship between individual workers and their employers. In the UK, it is composed of two main elements: the common law of contract and statutory employment rights. The latter have expanded greatly in number since the mid-1960s, in part as a consequence of the UK's membership of the European Union. Both statutory rights and common law entitlements can be enforced by workers at **Employment Tribunals**. [See **collective employment law**; **contract of employment**; **employment law**; **legal regulation**; **voluntarism**.]

individualism is an approach to managing people that emphasizes the importance of the individual as the prime unit of analysis. In other words, policies and procedures are devised that focus on the rights and obligations of employees as individuals, rather than as groups—for instance, individually negotiated pay, rather than collective bargaining over pay levels. Collectivism is the opposite approach whereby managers recognize that employees can be dealt with as groups that have aspects of their work in common (collective interests). In these circumstances, the employees have to elect or nominate representatives to act on their behalf when dealing with management. In practice there are individualistic and collectivist elements in most workplaces, and managers might adopt different approaches according to different circumstances. However, management styles are sometimes described as individualist or collectivist when one or the other of these aspects tends to dominate; likewise, organizations are sometimes categorized as being individualist or collectivist.

individualism–collectivism is one of the measures of national culture used by Geert Hofstede in his study on international differences in work culture. It refers to the extent to which society is viewed as being composed of separate individuals or of social groups, with individual identity being attached to that of the family, clan, or organization. [See **power-distance**; **uncertainty avoidance**.]

individual labour law see individual employment law

individual performance-related pay (IPRP) see performance-related pay

induction is the formal process of acclimatizing a newcomer to an organization. Typically, it involves an introduction to the organization by a senior manager; a guided tour of the workplace; introductions to co-workers and managers; an explanation of health and safety procedures; the completion of employment documentation, for payroll, pensions, etc.; a discussion with a personnel specialist (or the line manager) about employment policies and procedures (appraisal, grievance, equal opportunities, etc.); and a discussion with the line manager about the expectations and requirements of the job and the immediate training needs. If a trade union is recognized, the newcomer will be introduced to their representative and provided with information about joining the trade union. Induction can last from several hours to a week, depending on the complexity of the work organization and job responsibilities. [See **probation; socialization**.]

industrial action is the use of sanctions by trade unions and employers in the course of an industrial **dispute**. On the union side industrial action can take a wide variety of forms including the **strike, overtime ban, go-slow**, and **work-to-rule**. On the employers' side it may involve a **lockout** or the dismissal and replacement of strikers. The regulation of industrial action is an important function of **collective employment law** and in all liberal democracies there is an extensive body of statute and case law dealing with this issue. In the UK an important distinction exists between trade union action which is lawful and which enjoys civil **immunity** and action that is unlawful and vulnerable to civil action for damages by the employer.

industrial conflict Most academic observers regard conflict as an intrinsic, unavoidable feature of the **employment relationship** and believe that, while manifestations of conflict rise and fall over time, they can never wholly disappear. The reason is that there is a conflict of interest within the employment relationship, which finds expression in the employer's search for higher output, stricter control, and reduced costs while the employee wants protection from overwork, autonomy, and higher wages. In analysing industrial conflict several important distinctions can be drawn. The first is between latent and manifest conflict and refers to the distinction between conflict of interests and actual resort to conflict behaviour by workers and their managers. The second is between forms of conflict. These may be individual and informal and embrace behaviour such as **absenteeism**, quitting, **restriction of output**, and **sabotage**. Alternatively, conflict may assume a collective, more organized form and embrace **strikes** and other forms of **industrial action**. It must also be recognized that employers engage in conflict, including the disciplining and **dismissal** of workers, the threat of closure, and the use of the **lockout** and victimization to counter trade unions. [See **unitarism**; **pluralism**.]

industrial democracy is a term that has both precise and looser meanings. It is sometimes used to refer specifically to the existence of **worker directors**, who are elected to sit on the **supervisory board** of companies in some European countries. Alternatively, it can embrace a variety of forms of worker **participation** in management, including **collective bargaining**, **joint consultation** and the existence of **works councils**. Underlying the term is a normative sentiment that employing enterprises and their managers should be accountable to the workforce and that hierarchical control in business should be tempered with worker participation. As such, the term is akin to the notion of industrial citizenship and the belief that the citizens of liberal democracies should have the right to participate in the governance of industry in the way that they participate in the governance of the wider society.

industrial dispute see dispute

industrial relations (IR) is a term with two primary meanings. In everyday parlance it refers to the actions of **trade unions** and their relations with employers and government. Industrial relations coverage in the media is thus largely restricted to the reporting of industrial **disputes**. However, industrial relations is also an academic field of study, the subject of which tends to be defined more broadly in terms of the institutions and processes of **job regulation**. In this second sense industrial relations is the study of the employment relationship and its management and regulation. As such it embraces the issues of management strategy, work organization and working practices, employee involvement and participation, and state regulation of employment relations, in addition to the study of trade unions and collective bargaining. Industrial relations is a multi-disciplinary field of study and its researchers draw upon a number of core disciplines, including history, sociology, psychology, law, and economics. It is also an applied field and much of the work undertaken by IR researchers is policy evaluation, concerned with examining and assessing the strategies of employers, trade unions, and governments. The field of industrial relations embraces a number of **frames of reference**, though the dominant perspective in the UK is that of **pluralism**. [See **comparative industrial relations; employee relations; employment relations; international industrial relations.**]

industrial relations system A conceptual model developed by John Dunlop in the 1950s to guide the analysis of **industrial relations** in national economies. Dunlop contended that the IR system was a subsystem of the wider society that existed to resolve economic conflict. It comprised four elements: actors, contexts, a body of employment rules that are the outcome of the interaction between the actors, and a binding ideology. The actors were identified as employers and their organizations, employees and any representative body of workers, such as trade unions, and the government and public agencies. The main contexts that shaped the conduct of industrial relations were technology, market and budgetary constraints, and the distribution of power within the wider society. Within these constraints the actors develop **substantive** and **procedural rules** by unilateral action, by **joint regulation**, or by tripartite action involving the state. Finally, the whole system is bound together by shared understandings and beliefs, including acceptance of the main elements of the IR system itself. The model has been widely used in the industrial relations literature and the structure of many industrial and **employee relations** courses at universities is derived from its elements. It has also been criticized, however, for exaggerating the stability and self-contained nature of the sphere of industrial relations and for the limited scope it affords for the analysis of social and industrial conflict.

Industrial Tribunal see **Employment Tribunal**

industrial union A **trade union** that recruits workers within a single industry or sector with the aim of uniting all occupational groups in one industry organization. In the UK, industry unions have included the National Union of Mineworkers, the Graphical, Paper, and Media Union, Unifi the finance union, and the National Union of Rail, Marine, and Transport Workers. The principle of industrial unionism has never been dominant in the UK, although it has been the main form of trade unionism in other countries, the most notable of which is Germany. Since the Second World War most German trade unionists have been grouped in a small number of industrial unions, though recent mergers and the blurring of industrial boundaries through technical change have begun to undermine the principle. In Germany today the main unions are effectively multi-industry, multi-occupational **general unions**.

industry bargaining Collective bargaining that results in the signing of an industry agreement between trade unions and an **employers' association** representing employers within a particular industrial sector. In many cases, industry agreements of this kind will be supplemented by enterprise or **workplace bargaining** in individual firms. Industry bargaining has declined in importance in the UK since the 1950s, and in many sectors, including engineering, banking, and independent television, it has collapsed altogether. It continues to be important, however, in public services, in a number of traditional manufacturing industries, and in the arts and entertainment industries. In continental Europe industry bargaining retains its importance and the tradition of **collective agreements** setting industry-wide terms and conditions continues. [See **decentralization of bargaining**.]

inflow see **human resource flow**

infringement proceedings By virtue of Article 227 of the EC Treaty, the European Commission can initiate infringement proceedings in the **European Court of Justice** against a member state for failing to transpose a **directive** into national law. The Commission instituted such proceedings against the UK in 1982 for failure to enact provisions giving the right to equal pay for work of **equal value**.

in-house agency The situation where the personnel department or some of its activities are designated a cost centre and services are cross-charged to other management departments.

injunction see **interlocutionary injunction**

innovation strategy A **competitive strategy** through which a company seeks **competitive advantage** by developing new products and services ahead of its competitors.

input-based pay see **payment system**

insourcing is the provision of a labour force on a long-term basis by an **employment agency**. The agency may also undertake aspects of workforce management, such as selection, discipline, and reward, on the client company's behalf, though the deployment of workers may be the responsibility of client company managers. For example, call centres operated by large companies in the UK can be staffed by **agency workers**, resourced and managed by one of the large labour-supply firms. Insourcing is reportedly becoming more common and is indicative of the growth of relational contracting between employment agencies and client companies. In effect, there is little to distinguish insourcing from outsourcing or **subcontracting** apart from the fact that labour is supplied by an employment agency.

Institute of Personnel and Development (IPD) see **Chartered Institute of Personnel and Development**

Institute of Personnel Management see **Chartered Institute of Personnel and Development**

instrumentalism is an orientation to work in which employees are focused on **extrinsic rewards** and work for money rather than because they find their work interesting, challenging, or satisfying.

integrated pay structure see **pay structure**

integrative bargaining is an approach to **collective bargaining** that is **positive-sum** and seeks to identify mutually beneficial outcomes. Integrative bargaining often takes the form of joint problem-solving, in which management and union come together and try and resolve a problem to the benefit of both sides. For instance, a 'problem' of worker discontent over pay might be addressed through the negotiation of changed working practices which yield higher productivity and therefore permit higher earnings. Integrative bargaining rests on mutual trust and acceptance of the bargaining partners and contrasts with distributive or **zero-sum** bargaining. [See **distributive bargaining**; **mutual gains**.]

interim manager A manager supplied by an **employment agency** to provide temporary cover for absence or to manage a project of fixed duration.

interlocutionary injunction A prohibitive order issued by the High Court in the UK ordering a particular course of action to cease while the issue is pending trial. Injunctions of this kind are occasionally sought by employers faced with **industrial action** by a **trade union** that they believe to be unlawful. The usual effect is that the union complies, the strike is called off, and the employer's legal action is abandoned. If the union fails to comply with the injunction it can be fined heavily for contempt of court and may even have its assets sequestrated; that is, the Court can appoint commissioners to seize the union's financial assets. [See **immunity**; **trade dispute**.]

internal consultancy is an arrangement where a specialist department (for example, personnel) sells its services to other departments in the organization. The managers purchasing the services are free to look for alternative services and make use of external consultants if they are not happy with the service provided.

internal consultant A person from another department or another area of the organization who offers expert advice. For example, some organizations are developing their human resource department into an **internal consultancy** whereby they offer expert advice on specific employment matters to line managers and 'sell' services such as **training**, **recruitment**, and **selection**. [See **management consultant**.]

internal customer This is a concept that encourages employees to treat their co-workers as though they were customers. In practical terms it means that whoever works in the next stage of the process should be considered *your* customer because they are receiving your output. Like real customers they will expect your work to be of a certain standard and they have the right to reject work that fails to reach the quality they require. Similarly, you too are the internal customer of the employee who precedes you in the work process, and so you can behave as a customer. The purpose is to raise quality consciousness within an organization, particularly when many employees do not deal directly with the real (external) customers. [See **Total Quality Management; just-in-time; total quality control**.]

internal fit is the process of ensuring that the various human resource policies are sufficiently integrated to produce a coherent human resource strategy. In other words, the key activities of resourcing, development, and reward should be composed of policies and processes that are directed towards achieving the same or complementary objectives. [See **external fit**.]

internal labour market (ILM) The supply of employees within the organization who could fill a job vacancy. [See **recruitment**.]

internal recruitment see **recruitment**

international industrial relations is the study of international institutions and processes of **job regulation**. The subject matter includes HRM in multinational enterprises, international trade unionism, and international labour regulation. The latter includes the issuing and enforcement of global labour standards by bodies like the **International Labour Organization** and the regulation of employment within regional trading blocs, like the European Union and the North American Free Trade Area. [See **industrial relations**.]

International Labour Organization (ILO) The United Nations specialized agency that promotes social justice and internationally recognized human and labour rights. It was founded in 1919 and formulates **international labour standards** in the form of

Conventions and Recommendations. It also provides advice, conducts research, collects statistics, and promotes the formation of independent employers' and workers' organizations and **social dialogue** between the two sides of industry. The ILO embodies the principle of **tripartism** and the representative organizations of business and labour participate as equal partners with governments in the work of its governing organs. The latter comprise the annual International Labour Conference, which meets each year in Geneva and which is attended by representatives of all the member states of the ILO, and the Governing Body, the ILO's executive council. The latter consists of 28 government members, 14 worker members and 14 employer members, with 10 of the government seats being reserved permanently for states of 'chief industrial importance'. In addition, there is a permanent secretariat, the International Labour Office, with headquarters in Geneva and forty field offices across the globe. The secretariat consists of officials and technical experts who implement the policy of the ILO. Interest in the ILO's work has increased in recent years in line with pressure for higher labour standards in the context of **globalization** and the campaign for a **social clause** to be attached to world trade agreements. Reflecting this pressure, the ILO itself has become more active and in 1999 agreed a global treaty banning the worst forms of **child labour**—defined as slavery, forced labour, child prostitution and pornography, drug trafficking, and work that harms children's health, safety, and morals. Its powers of enforcement remain limited, however, and its commitment to consensual, tripartite decision-making has led to criticism from those who want stronger and more urgent action to promote higher labour standards.

international labour standards are formulated by the **International Labour Organization** and establish core labour rights, principles of labour management, and minimum acceptable conditions that are applied across the globe. Standards are adopted by the ILO's tripartite International Labour Conference and are set out in Conventions and Recommendations. The former create binding obligations on states that ratify them to implement their provisions through national legislation, while the latter provide guidance on policy, legislation, and practice. Since 1919, Conventions and Recommendations have been adopted covering many aspects of employment. What are often regarded as the core labour standards deal with the following: abolition of forced labour; the **freedom of association** of workers and employers; the right to **collective bargaining**; **equal pay** between men and women; the elimination of discrimination on the grounds of race, colour, sex, religion, political opinion, and social origin; and the abolition of **child labour**. The ILO has established a supervisory procedure to ensure Conventions are given effect in law and practice, which is based on evaluation by independent experts. There is also provision for special investigations into infringements of freedom of association. The issue of international labour standards has risen to prominence in recent years as a result of the **globalization** of the economy and increasing pressure from labour organizations for a **social clause** in world trade agreements. [See **corporate code of conduct**; **Declaration of Philadelphia**.]

internet recruitment see e-recruitment

interorganizational means *between organizations*. So, interorganizational conflict is conflict between two or more separate organizations—for example, between competitors. Similarly, interorganizational communication is communication between two or more organizations—for example, a company and its suppliers. [See **intraorganizational**.]

interview Interviews are undertaken at various stages in an employee's career and are considered to be a useful method of gaining information and insight into the person. They serve different purposes according to requirements of the particular situation, so a selection interview will have different objectives from, for example, an **appraisal** interview, a **discipline** interview, or an **exit interview**. There is a large amount of research evaluating the effectiveness of various interview methods and techniques, all of which stress the importance of ensuring fairness and consistency. The overall thrust of the findings is that interviews should be planned in advance, well structured, and involve interviewers who have been trained in interviewing skills. The information gained from the interview should be considered alongside other sources of data in order to provide a more rounded picture of the interviewee. [See **selection**.]

intranet learning is the delivery of education and training material to employees through the organization's internal computer network.

intraorganizational means *within the organization*. So intraorganizational conflict means conflict within the organization—for example between different functions, or between managers and employees. Similarly, intraorganizational communication means communication within the organization—for example between different teams, or between levels in the hierarchy. [See **interorganizational**.]

intraorganizational bargaining is the bargaining that takes place within management or within a trade union before interorganizational bargaining occurs between the two sides. It occurs because there may be different interests and perspectives within each side and these have to be resolved through bargaining to produce an agreed set of objectives to take to the other side. [See **collective bargaining**.]

intrapreneur is a term coined by **management guru** Rosabeth Moss Kanter to describe employees who behave in an entrepreneurial manner within an organization. For example, they might use their initiative to develop new ideas for products or services, devise new ways of working, or suggest systems and processes to improve efficiency.

in-tray exercise (or in-basket exercise). A technique sometimes used in the **selection** process, particularly in **assessment centres**. It entails a candidate dealing with an accumulating and confusing amount of information which requires prioritization and action, and in this respect it is designed to simulate the work of a busy manager. The information is usually in the form of a series of memos and other documents, although it could also be e-mails and telephone calls. The candidate is given strict time constraints and during the exercise is frequently interrupted with new information and issues that require immediate action. If designed carefully, the in-tray exercise can be an effective simulation to test how candidates might organize and prioritize work, and how they might cope with pressure. In-tray exercises are also used in **management development** programmes, although their effectiveness as a learning tool is dependent on having good-quality feedback once the exercise has been completed.

intrinsic reward A reward that is integral to work and which is obtained by performing work tasks. Examples of intrinsic rewards include **job satisfaction**, challenge, autonomy, pride in work, and a sense of achievement. [See **extrinsic reward**; **reward**.]

Investors in People (IiP) is a national standard of action and excellence in the UK. It specifies good practice for improving an organization's performance through its people—thus making such organizations attractive for employees to work in. Organizations applying for the IiP award must (1) demonstrate commitment to invest in people to achieve business goals; (2) undertake planning about how skills, individuals, and teams are to be developed to achieve these goals; (3) take action to develop and use necessary skills in a well-defined and continuing programme directly tied to business objectives; and (4) constantly evaluate outcomes of training and development in terms of employee progress towards goals, the value achieved, and future needs. In theory, it is designed to raise the standard of training and development in UK organizations, but in practice research reveals a mixed picture of success. Some organizations are fully committed to training and developing their employees, and are convinced that it will lead to improvements in performance. Others do the minimum possible to achieve the IiP recognition because they believe it is good for the company image, but will have little impact on performance.

involuntary part-time work is **part-time** work that is undertaken because an individual cannot find a suitable full-time job. There is evidence that the proportion of part-time work that is involuntary is growing and that male part-timers in particular would prefer full-time work. There is also evidence, however, that many women employees would prefer to lengthen their working hours, while many male full-timers would like to shorten their working hours. [See **working time**.]

Involvement and Participation Association (IPA) A UK-based business organization that exists to promote **employee involvement** and worker **participation**. In recent years the IPA has been an advocate of **labour–management partnership**.

iron law of oligarchy A theory of trade unions and socialist political parties formulated by the sociologist Robert Michels in the early years of the twentieth century. It expresses a deeply pessimistic viewpoint that progressive social movements inevitably become undemocratic and dominated by a conservative elite. The theory has had most influence on the analysis of trade unions and is associated with the view that unions are controlled by an unaccountable bureaucracy. Critics of the theory believe that it exaggerates the extent of leader control of unions and argue that the trend towards oligarchy is reversible. [See **goal displacement; union bureaucracy**.]

itemized pay statement In the UK there is a statutory right of employees to receive an itemized pay statement providing details of their earnings and any deductions from their wages.

J

Japanization is the term used to describe changes in western industry that involve the adoption of techniques of managing and organizing production that were developed by Japanese-owned companies in Japan. In particular it centres on the use of production techniques such as **just-in-time** that require particular forms of external buyer–supplier relations and internal work organization, such as **teamworking** and **kaizen**. The term has been criticized for: (1) assuming that there is one 'Japanese way of managing' when in Japan there is a diverse range of strategies; (2) obscuring the viewpoint that the techniques are new methods of management control that have more to do with the conflict between management (capital) and employees (labour) than with that between nations; (3) overstating the extent of change and failing to acknowledge developments in the West, such as **Total Quality Management** or **functional flexibility**, that share similarities with the supposed Japanese model. Whilst accepting some of these criticisms, the main proponents of Japanization, organization theorists Nick Oliver and Barry Wilkinson, argue that the term remains an appropriate shorthand to describe the changes in UK industries that depend on ideas of organizing and managing transferred from Japan.

job advertisement see recruitment advertising

job analysis is the process of analysing the content of jobs in order to guide **recruitment** and **selection**, identify training needs, or for the purpose of **job evaluation**. Job analysis can be carried out in a number of ways, including interviewing jobholders and supervisors, observation of work activity, and the completion of a job-analysis questionnaire. The result should be an account of the tasks and competencies that comprise a particular job, which can then be used to inform a wide range of personnel management practice. [See **job description**.]

job board see e-recruitment

JobCentres are the offices of the UK Employment Service that exist to help those seeking work to find work. JobCentres play an important part in administering the government's **Welfare-to-Work** programme and are charged with identifying employers who will provide New Deal placements for the long-term unemployed. Equivalent labour market services are operated by governments in most other developed economies.

Job Characteristics Model (JCM) The Job Characteristics Model, developed by organizational psychologists J. Richard Hackman and Greg Oldham, is a **normative approach** to job enrichment (see **job redesign**). It specifies five core job dimensions that will lead to critical psychological states in the individual employee. The first three dimensions are: (1) skill variety (the range of tasks performed); (2) task identity (the ability to complete the whole job from start to finish); and (3) task significance (the impact of the job on others). These three dimensions contribute to the meaningfulness of the work—in other words, the higher the task variety, identity, and significance, the more meaningful the work is to the employee. The fourth job dimension is **autonomy** (the extent of discretion and freedom an employee has over his or her tasks) and the higher this is, the more the employee feels responsible for the outcome of his or her work. The fifth dimension is feedback (the extent to which the job provides the employee with information about the effectiveness of his or her performance) which allows the employee to appreciate the outcome of his or her efforts. As a consequence of providing positive psychological states, the JCM suggests that positive outcomes will occur for the individual and the organization: high **motivation**, high-quality performance, high **job satisfaction**, low **absenteeism**, and low **labour turnover**. The model is used to assess the motivational potential of particular jobs and thereby suggest which of these jobs could be redesigned. To do this, a motivational potential score (MPS) is calculated from a questionnaire consisting of the components of the JCM. The score is an index based on the following formula:

$$\text{MPS} = \frac{\text{skill variety} + \text{task variety} + \text{task significance}}{3} \times \text{autonomy} \times \text{feedback}$$

job description This is a document that outlines the purpose of the job, the task involved, the duties and responsibilities, the performance objectives, and the reporting relationships. It will give details of the terms and conditions, including the remuneration package and hours of work. It is used in the recruitment process and provides the basis for developing a **person specificiation**.

job description index (JDI) see job satisfaction

job enlargement see job redesign

job enrichment see job redesign

job evaluation (JE) is a procedure for assessing the relative demands of jobs with a view to allocating jobs to positions within a pay structure. Job evaluation involves **job analysis**, the production of **job descriptions**, and an assessment of the 'size' of jobs (i.e. how demanding they are) so that they can be placed in rank order and divided into **grades**. The latter will thus consist of jobs with equivalent demands, which will receive the same basic rate of pay or be allocated to the same salary scale or **pay range**. There are a number of different techniques of job evaluation including 'non-analytical' schemes which compare whole jobs (e.g. job ranking, grade classification, paired comparisons) and 'analytical' schemes which compare jobs on the basis of their component elements or '**factors**' (e.g. factor comparison, **points rating**). There has been considerable debate in recent years on the merits and demerits of job evaluation. Critics claim that the technique is costly, inhibits flexibility in work organization, and is often discriminatory. Defenders reply that costs can be minimized through computerization of job evaluation, that factors can be selected which reflect new and more flexible job roles, and that schemes can be redesigned so that the demands of typically 'female' jobs are recognized in the process of evaluation. The **Equal Opportunities Commission** has recommended that non-discriminatory job evaluation be used to promote equal pay for work of **equal value**.

job family A set of jobs based around common activities but conducted at different levels of the organization. For instance, a finance and accounting job family could embrace junior finance officers, senior accountants, and the finance director of the enterprise. A job family may form the basis of an integrated **pay structure**, such that all jobs within the family are managed using a common set of pay rules and procedures. The reason for basing pay on job families is that it allows rates of pay for each family identified to be set with regard to the external labour market. For example, the rates of pay for those within the finance job family can reflect the going rate for accountants and finance directors, with different rates of pay being established for those in other job families, such as operations or personnel management.

job for life is a concept that is increasingly rare for most employees. There was a time when people entered an occupation fairly certain that they would be able to pursue the same line of work until they retired. Nowadays, technological developments and economic demands mean that flexibility and constant change are required in all jobs. Theorists suggest that career and job changes are increasingly common, and some prophesy that in the future everyone will be expected to undertake a variety of jobs and experience periods of unemployment throughout their working life. [See **portfolio career**.]

job redesign is a range of techniques that attempt to increase the variety of tasks that employees perform in order to improve motivation and satisfaction at work. Job enlargement is the technique of increasing the scope of employees' jobs by increasing the amount of tasks they do that require a similar skill level. Sceptics argue that, in practice, this means instead of workers undertaking one boring task, they undertake several boring tasks. An alternative technique of job enrichment is considered preferable because it not only extends the range of tasks but also involves employees undertaking some tasks of a higher skill level. In many contemporary organizations jobs have been enriched by making employees responsible for quality improvements in their work. Finally, job rotation means that employees within a particular work area have the ability to perform a variety of tasks and will move from one to another at various times within the working day or working week. This technique means that employees are fully flexible and it might (although not always) require them to undertake tasks of various skill levels—in such instances rotation involves both enlargement and enrichment. [See **teamworking**; **quality circles**.]

job regulation Academic industrial relations was defined by Hugh Clegg, one of its founders in the UK, as the study of job regulation. The concept of job regulation refers to the rules that govern the content of the employment relationship and the behaviour and activities of employees, employers, and their representatives. The study of job regulation is therefore the study of the creation, application, and effects of job or employment rules. Employment rules can be classified in a number of different ways. An important distinction can be drawn between those rules that are formal, and written down in company handbooks, collective agreements, and employment statutes, and those which are informal and take the form of customary understandings or norms about appropriate workplace behaviour. A second distinction can be drawn between **substantive rules**, which govern the content of the employment relationship, and **procedural rules**, which govern the behaviour of workers, managers, trade unions, employers' associations, and others who become involved in industrial relations. A third distinction relates to the way in which rules are created. Some employment rules are simply inherited from the past and take the form of

custom and practice; that is, a taken-for-granted way of behaving or relating to co-workers or managers. Other rules are created through processes of **joint regulation**, in which employers and employees come together to regulate the employment relationship through **collective bargaining, joint consultation**, or some other joint mechanism. A third method is **unilateral regulation**, in which either managers or, more rarely, workers one-sidedly decide what the content of regulation will be. Finally, rules may be generated by the state through the process of **legal regulation** and the creation of laws which directly determine the content of the employment relationship (e.g. through a statutory **minimum wage**) or regulate the behaviour of employers and trade unions through **collective employment law**.

job rotation see **job redesign**

job satisfaction is a central concept within work psychology. It is defined by Edwin Locke as 'a pleasurable or positive emotional state resulting from the appraisal of one's job or job experience'. Psychologists have identified a number of dimensions or sources of job satisfaction, including attitudes to pay, working conditions, co-workers and superiors, career prospects, and the intrinsic features of the tasks performed. Job satisfaction is normally measured through surveys of employee attitudes and several instruments have been developed and used repeatedly by researchers. These include the Job Description Index (JDI), Job Satisfaction Scales (JSS), and the Occupational Stress Indicator (OSI).

job security see **security of employment**

jobseeker is the preferred official term in the UK for those who are unemployed and available for work. Most jobseekers are entitled to the Jobseekers' Allowance, a state insurance payment for those without work.

job-sharing is a work arrangement in which two people share one job. In effect, both employees work **part-time**, although their combined hours make up the equivalent of a full-time job.

The employees do not have to work exactly the same number of hours, but their proportion of working hours is specified in their contract. Some employers are reluctant to offer job-sharing arrangements because they consider it to be inconvenient for their business or administratively too complex. Their reluctance disadvantages women more than men because a greater proportion of women seek job-share arrangements. In fact, the predominant number of job-sharers are women, which is not surprising, given that the greatest proportion of employees working part-time are women.

jobshift refers to the claim that **post-industrial societies** are moving to a 'jobless' state, in which the open-ended, long-term career with a single employer will largely disappear. In its place, it is argued, workers will develop mobile or **portfolio careers**, based on self-employment and short assignments with a large number of clients/employers. Despite predictions of the 'end of work' and the 'death of the job', empirical studies of **job stability** in both the UK and the USA indicate that there is little evidence of a collapse of long-term employment across the economy.

job stability is a measure of **security of employment** used by labour economists. It is based on estimates of average **job tenure** for the entire workforce or groups within it. Despite concern over rising insecurity, there is evidence of only a modest decline in job stability since the 1970s.

job stress is a condition where an aspect of work is causing physical or mental problems for an employee. Two sets of stressors can be identified. (1) Work-related stressors include **role ambiguity**, **role conflict**, **work intensification**, interpersonal conflicts, and **harassment**. (2) Individual stressors include financial worries, family and marital difficulties, and dual-role pressures between work and home life (see **work–life balance**). The symptoms of stress reveal themselves in the behaviour of the employee (for example, aggression, **absenteeism**, decreased performance, and increased accidents), in the mental condition of the employee (for example, anxiety, tension, irritability, and depression), and in the physical condition of the employee (for example, digestive problems, high blood pressure, insomnia, and alcohol/drug dependency). Commentators on stress suggest that the toleration of stress differs from person to person. Some people thrive on stressful environments whilst others flounder. Therefore, it is important to get a match between an individual's tolerance of stress and the stressors in the job. From this perspective, job stress only occurs when there is a mismatch. However, other commentators suggest that whilst this analysis of stress may be adequate, it fails to take into account a general tendency amongst contemporary work towards a greater range of stressors in all jobs. In other words, there is an increasing expectation that both employees and managers will be able to cope with an increased amount of stress at work. As a result, the incidence of job stress is on the increase. [See **stress management**.]

job tenure is the length of time that an employee holds a particular job.

job territory is that segment of the economy or labour force in which a **trade union** seeks to recruit and represent workers. It is a concept, therefore, that refers to the scope of recruitment of an individual trade union. The job territory of a trade union can be broad, embracing a range of industries and occupations, or it can be narrow and confined to workers in a particular enterprise, occupation, or industry. [See **closed union; open union**.]

joint consultation is the process through which employers and **trade unions** share information and exchange views within a joint consultative committee (JCC). Joint consultation differs from **collective bargaining** in that it addresses issues of shared, not opposed, interest and does not result in a joint decision. Under joint consultation the union (and possibly non-union) representatives have the opportunity to influence management decision-making, but actual decisions remain in management hands. Partly for this reason it has been viewed as of limited value by some trade unionists and has often been restricted to less important issues: tea-towels, toilets, and trivia. [See **consultation; Joint Industrial Council**.]

joint consultative committee (JCC) see **joint consultation**

Joint Industrial Council (JIC) JICs or Whitley Councils were a product of the Whitley Report of 1918. They were industry-level joint boards of employers and trade union representatives, which were to form the basis of a co-operative system of industrial government. As such, their intended functions included **collective bargaining** but also **joint consultation** over the modernization of their respective industries. Seventy-four JICs were established between 1918 and 1920 but most were short-lived and those which survived and continue to exist today primarily act as forums for the negotiation of basic terms and conditions within public services and mature industries. [See **Whitleyism**.]

jointism is the principle that employment issues and problems should be handled jointly by employers and employee representatives. [See **integrative bargaining**; **mutual gains**; **mutuality**; **labour–management partnership**.]

joint regulation is the process of joint rule-making by employers, trade unions, and other workplace representatives through **collective bargaining** and **codetermination**. Employment rules developed in this way may be either substantive or procedural. Substantive rules set the terms of the employment relationship (e.g. rates of pay, hours of work, working practices) while procedural rules govern the behaviour of the parties to the relationship (managers, workers, trade union representatives) by specifying how particular issues (e.g. discipline, disputes, grievances, harassment, redundancies, regrading) should be handled. Joint rule-making of this kind can be contrasted with **unilateral regulation**, where employers or trade unions alone make employment rules, and with **legal regulation**, where employment rules are framed in statute and case law.

joint shop stewards' committee (JSSC) The joint shop stewards' committee is a common form of workplace trade union organization in traditional manufacturing. It consists of workplace trade union representatives who are elected to the committee from different trade unions operating within the same establishment. The JSSC, therefore, is a means through which the divisive effects of **multi-unionism** are controlled at the level of the workplace. [See **combine committee; shop steward.**]

joint working party (JWP) A technique advocated by ACAS as a means of preventing industrial **disputes.** JWPs are chaired by ACAS staff and consist of a group of employer and employee representatives who work together to devise mutually acceptable solutions to specific workplace problems. JWPs are often established following an approach to ACAS from a company that is experiencing industrial relations problems. They can operate with seeming effect in both unionized and non-union companies.

juridification is the process of increasing legal intervention in the employment relationship that can be seen in an expanding volume of **legal regulation** of employment and increasing recourse to legal process to resolve employment disputes. In the UK, for instance, there has been a steady increase since the 1960s in the number of statutes that regulate aspects of the **employment relationship**. There has also been a marked increase in the number of individual employment disputes that are referred to **Employment Tribunals** for adjudication. Critics of juridification hold that the process imposes a burden on the economy through the increase in demand for legal representation and that employment disputes are best handled without recourse to law through negotiations between employer and employee representatives.

just-in-time (JIT) is a production system developed in Japanese manufacturing industries. It is based on the principle that the most efficient way to run production is to eliminate all types of waste (time, materials, labour, rework, etc.), since this adds cost rather than value. By concentrating upon ways of organizing production so that components, sub-assemblies, and goods arrive just in time at the next stage of the process, the system is designed to be more efficient than Fordist mass-production techniques which frequently had costly buffers built in, such as contingency time, high stock levels, and surplus labour. The overarching principles of the JIT system are the minimization of stock and a reliance on demand 'pulling' products through the system rather than production schedules 'pushing' them; the reduction of set-up times to improve flow and responsiveness to the market; employees' flexibility to work where required at any given time; and a drive for continuous improvement (see **kaizen**). Underpinning all this is an emphasis on **total quality control**. JIT puts both workers and managers under greater pressure because, by eliminating any slack from the system, any hold-ups or poor-quality operations will mean a greater likelihood of failing to deliver to the customer on time.

K

kaizen or continuous improvement is a concept that encourages employees and managers to look constantly for ways of making changes to any system or process that will improve performance. This idea stems from Japanese production systems, in particular those of the motor giants such as Toyota. Once an improvement has been suggested, it is evaluated and, if found to be of benefit, standardized across the operations. Critics sometimes argue that such a system is exploitative, since it captures the ideas of shopfloor employees, adopts them across the organization, and leads to performance improvements, but does not reward those who came up with the idea in the first place. Defenders of the system argue that employees experience the **intrinsic reward** of seeing their ideas put into practice and getting recognition from management—which in some cases might lead to more favourable appraisals or one-off bonuses.

key performance indicator (KPI) A measure of achievement that can be attributed to an individual, team, or department. KPIs should be constructed using the **SMART** principles of objective-setting, and are normally developed as part of a **performance management** system.

key-time working is a form of **numerical flexibility** where employees are brought into the organization to cover busy periods—such as 12–2 p.m. in retailing. Effectively, these employees are part-timers, although their hours are not specified in advance and will fluctuate according to the employer's requirements.

knowledge-based companies are organizations whose success derives from their ability to create new knowledge, and use this as the basis for new products and services. Within the organization, the emphasis is on 'knowledge management' whereby the processes and operations of the organization are directed towards the creation of knowledge and its dissemination throughout the organization. Essential to these processes are employees at all levels whose ideas and insights form the basis of knowledge creation, and provide the potential competitive advantage for the organization. The idea of the knowledge-creating company has been developed by management theorists Ikojiro Nonaka and Hirotaka Takenchi, who draw upon Japanese companies such as Matsushita, NEC, and Kao to substantiate their arguments.

knowledge management see knowledge-based companies

Kolb's learning cycle A theory developed by psychologist David Kolb that describes how four stages influence the way that people learn. (1) Concrete experience: being involved in the world. (2) Observation and reflection: thinking about these experiences. (3) Abstract conceptualization: drawing conclusions from these experiences and making generalizations—thereby constructing new theories, or building on existing theories. (4) Active experimentation: testing these theories, especially by using them to solve problems and guide future action. A person can start at any stage of the cycle but successful learning is accomplished only when the full cycle is completed. The theory also recognizes that people have strengths or learning preferences that mean they are comfortable at some of the stages, but not at others. This therefore can inhibit progress through the full cycle.

L

labour code A statutory code that sets out the national framework of **employment law**. Examples include the Code de Travail in France, the Workers' Charter in Spain, and the Workers' Statute in Italy.

labour correspondent A journalist who specializes in the coverage of collective **industrial relations**. Labour correspondents were once ubiquitous within the UK media but the decline of trade unions and strike activity has reduced their number. Increasingly, the broadsheet newspapers cover a fuller range of employment topics, with business and economics pages carrying stories regularly on various aspects of HRM.

labour court Many countries have a specialist system of labour or employment courts that deal with disputes arising from the **employment relationship**. These courts are often less formal than the primary system of justice and may involve lay adjudicators, nominated by employers' organizations and trade unions. The intention is to provide accessible and flexible resolution of disputes that draws upon specialist knowledge. In the UK labour courts are known as **Employment Tribunals**.

Labour Force Survey (LFS) The LFS is a quarterly survey of around 60,000 private households throughout the United Kingdom that provides a broad range of information on the working population. Since 1989 LFS has collected information on trade union membership and the survey produces the most accurate estimates of **union density** and **bargaining coverage** for the UK.

labour law see employment law

labour–management partnership A collective agreement between a **trade union** and an employer that gives effect to the concept of **social partnership** at enterprise level. Agreements of this kind have been negotiated by a growing number of UK companies and trade unions in recent years and there are also several well-known examples in North America. Partnership agreements typically consist of a joint declaration of commitment to the principles of mutual respect and co-operation and a number of substantive and **procedural rules**. The main substantive elements usually embrace employer commitment to employment security, training, equal opportunities, and **employee involvement** in return for union acceptance of flexible working practices and long-term pay agreements. The main procedural clauses usually involve reduced reliance on **collective bargaining** and the introduction of new consultative machinery. In many cases partnerships have also involved the use of joint working parties, made up of management and union representatives, to find mutually acceptable solutions to shared problems or address areas of common interest. Labour–management partnerships are advocated by the TUC and have been endorsed by the UK government. They have been criticized by some in the trade union movement, however, on the grounds that they promote the **incorporation** of unions into management and produce few concrete benefits for workers, while providing employers with higher productivity and lower labour costs.

labour market see **external labour market**; **internal labour market**

labour market intermediary An organization that exists to connect workers seeking work with employers who are offering employment. Public agencies, such as the Employment Service, can fulfil this role, though it is increasingly undertaken by a range of specialist firms that include **employment agencies**, **recruitment consultants**, and **executive search consultants**. Trade unions may also act as labour market intermediaries when they operate a **hiring hall**. [See **JobCentres**.]

labour power is a term coined by Karl Marx in *Capital* and refers to the capacity of workers to work. Marx held that when employers hired workers in the labour market they were effectively buying this capacity to work rather than work itself. For this reason the **employment relationship** is indeterminate and the actual amount of work produced for each unit of wages is variable and dependent on the success of the employer in managing workers within the labour process. [See **porosity**; **Marxism**.]

labour process theory is concerned with analysing how a workforce's **labour power** (its ability to work) is directed towards the production of commodities (goods and services) that can be sold at a profit. The control of this labour process by managers is essential because profit is accumulated in two stages: first, through the extraction of the surplus value of labour (the price of a commodity greater than the costs incurred in its production); and second, through the realization of that value when commodities are actually sold. These two stages are frequently referred to as valorization. In other words, managers seek to control the way work is organized, the pace of work, and the duration of work because these are crucial to profitability. Labour process theorists are therefore particularly concerned with the social relations of production, and issues of workplace conflict, control, and regulation.

labour productivity see productivity

labour relations see industrial relations

labour standards see international labour standards

labour turnover is an index of the number of employees who leave the organization during a particular period, expressed as a percentage of the average number of employees during that period.

last-in-first-out (LIFO) is a principle used in selecting workers for **redundancy**. It means that those with least **seniority** are the first to lose their jobs in the event of redundancies being imposed. LIFO has often been seen as a fair method of selection and is a principle to which many trade union negotiators are attached.

Managers may prefer, however, to select people on the criteria of competence, performance, or the ease with which their skills can be replaced. LIFO has also been criticized on the grounds that it can discriminate indirectly against women and young workers who may have less seniority, respectively, than men and older workers.

lateral career moves occur when an employee changes job, department, or location in an organization, but remains at a similar level in the hierarchy. The increase in delayering means there are fewer promotion opportunities and so employees are encouraged to see lateral career moves as a positive opportunity to broaden their portfolio of skills and experience. For example, an employee might face new challenges and responsibilities by being seconded to a different department or working on a series of projects, rather than being promoted. Of course the problem is that promotion is normally associated with higher salary and enhanced status, whereas lateral career moves do not necessarily entail either of these. Therefore, it is obviously difficult to persuade employees that a lateral career move is a satisfactory alternative to promotion up the hierarchy.

lay-off is the temporary or permanent ending of the employment relationship because of a decline in business activity. [See **guarantee payment; redundancy**.]

lay representative A trade union officer or representative who acts in a voluntary capacity and whose status differs from that of a **full-time officer** who is a union employee. Most union officers in the UK are lay representatives and are elected to their positions by union members. Lay representatives include **shop stewards**, **convenors**, and **branch** officers at local level and the elected members of union executives, councils, conferences, and committees at regional and national levels.

leader A leader is defined in psychology as an individual who is given responsibility for directing and monitoring a group's activities or who assumes primary responsibility for the group's tasks. There is a body of psychological research that has attempted to identify the personality and other characteristics of individuals who attain leadership positions.

leadership embraces the personal qualities, behaviours, styles, and decisions of a **leader**. A common distinction drawn in studies of leadership is that between 'transactional' and 'transformational' styles. Transactional leaders clarify the task requirements of their subordinates and ensure they are rewarded for appropriate behaviour. In the Multifactor Leadership Questionnaire (MLQ) developed by Bass in the 1980s, transactional leadership is measured by the extent to which leaders provide rewards that are contingent on effective performance and manage by exception, so that work methods are not changed provided performance goals are met. Transformational leaders, in contrast, articulate a vision or mission and challenge their followers by providing a personal example. In the MLQ **transformational leadership** has three components: **charisma**, individual consideration for followers, and intellectual stimulation by encouraging subordinates to question, reason, and innovate.

lean production is a system of organizing that combines the use of **Total Quality Management**, Japanese management techniques (such as **just-in-time**, **statistical process control**, and **kaizen**), and job design techniques such as **teamworking**. It is based on a number of key elements: minimizing waste (material, time, rework, people, etc.), low inventories, zero defects, continuous improvement, emphasis on the **value chain**, and **benchmarking**. The main proponents of lean production are management consultants James Womack and Dan Jones. They emphasize the need for lean production to be underpinned by 'lean thinking' amongst managers, which involves five key principles: (1) specifying value as defined by the end customer; (2) identifying the value stream; (3) making the value-creating steps flow; (4) allowing customers to pull value from the organization; and (5) seeking perfection. Critics argue that lean production has become associated with employing fewer people and relies on **downsizing** and **work intensification**. Defenders suggest that whilst some organizations have taken this approach, it is not solely the result of lean thinking but occurs as a result of changes in the competitive environment. Moreover, they argue that job loss is not inevitable within the lean thinking approach: redeployment being an alternative.

leapfrogging is a situation in which a pay deal secured by one group of workers is matched and exceeded by a second group, followed by a third, and so on, generating an upward spiral of earnings. Pay leapfrogging is likely to be a feature of a fragmented structure of **collective bargaining**, in which pay negotiations are frequent and cover relatively small groups of employees. Central to the process is the principle of **comparability**, that earnings and pay increases should be based on those achieved elsewhere, outside the enterprise. [See **whipsawing**.]

learning is the process through which individuals acquire knowledge, **skills**, and attitudes. It may be achieved through experience, reflection, study, or instruction. [See **action learning**; **employee development**; **open learning**.]

Learning and Skills Council (LSC) The national body in England and Wales that assumed responsibility for the planning and funding of all post-16 education and training in 2001. The council oversees a network of fifty local LSCs. The LSC has combined the functions delivered previously by two separate sets of institutions, the Training and Enterprise Councils (TECs), an employer-led system of vocational training, and the Further Education Funding Council, which oversaw vocational education. An important feature of the new local LSCs is that, although employer representatives form the largest group, they no longer constitute a majority as they did on the TECs. Increased representation has been given to government agencies, voluntary organizations, and **trade unions**, which represents a step back towards **tripartism** in government training policy. [See **vocational education and training**.]

learning climate The concept of creating an environment where it is possible to experiment with new ideas and ways of working, and to learn through this direct experience. The aim is to encourage innovation and improvement, and thereby contribute to **organizational learning**. Obviously an encouragement of trial and error means that a **no blame culture** is essential. Constant feedback from others is also necessary to ensure that good ideas are developed and shared, whilst poor ideas are dropped.

learning curve The time it takes for a person to learn a new task and perform it competently. Therefore, a 'steep' learning curve means that the person is expected to become competent in a relatively short space of time; a 'flat' learning curve means the opposite.

learning cycle see **Kolb's learning cycle**

learning organization (LO) An organization that has developed the ability to adapt continuously. Instead of remaining fixed to standard ways of operating, the learning organization is constantly looking for new ideas and approaches. Underpinning the concept is the notion of a shared organizational vision (see **unitarism**) with collaboration and co-operation amongst all organizational members. This means that a learning organization also emphasizes 'openness' and stresses the importance of communication across all levels and boundaries. However, this also means tolerating criticism and nurturing a culture that allows employees of all levels to speak their minds without fear of criticism or punishment (see **no blame culture**). Critics of the learning organization argue that the concept can never work in practice because it fails to recognize the important role of organizational politics and power imbalances.

leased car A **company car** that is leased by the employer from an external supplier on the employee's behalf. Increasingly company cars are provided through this mechanism, representing the trend towards the **subcontracting** of non-essential functions.

legal regulation is the creation of **procedural** and **substantive rules** through legal processes. The latter include **statutory regulation**, the introduction of **employment law** through an Act of Parliament. Another form of legal regulation is through judicial action or case law, where the decisions of courts amend or extend the framework of law that governs the employment relationship.

legends (in relation to **organizational culture**) are popular stories based partly on fact, about people or groups in the organization's history, which help to reinforce organizational values and beliefs.

liberal collectivism is a school of thought within academic **industrial relations** in the UK. Central to the school is a commitment to **voluntarism** and limited state intervention in the employment relationship, combined with support for collective organization of workers in **trade unions** and reliance on **collective bargaining** as the primary means for determining conditions of employment. [See **collective laissez-faire; frame of reference**.]

lifeboat democracy is a rather cynical approach to **employee involvement** whereby employers communicate openly with their employees during a crisis to help secure the co-operation and support of employees—particularly if the organization is fighting for survival in severe market conditions. Once the crisis is over, the employer reverts to limited or non-involvement of employees, and asserts the **management prerogative**. [See **cycles of control**.]

lifecycle see **business lifecycle**

lifelong learning is the concept that employees need continually to update their knowledge and skills in order to ensure they are employable in the future. It stems from the view that the pace of change has increased and will continue to do so, particularly through technological developments, economic changes, and **globalization**, therefore skills must be constantly updated. The concept applies to people both in and out of work: they are encouraged to update existing skills, where appropriate, or to retrain and acquire new skills and knowledge. It particularly stresses the importance of education and learning continuing beyond normal years of schooling, and lasting throughout a person's working life. It also emphasizes that it is the responsibility of the individual to ensure his or her skills are up to date, and to seek opportunities for self-development from a variety of sources provided by the public and private sectors.

line manager This is a role with two common meanings. (1) A person directly responsible for achieving the objectives of the organization. The line manager is supported in this role by **staff managers** who provide support functions, such as pay administration, training, or maintenance. In many respects, line manager is an ambiguous term because it depends on the specific context: it will be used to describe varied roles in different organizations. (2) A person to whom one is accountable as an employee. Irrespective of the functional role or level of the manager, he or she will have a number of employees (**direct reports**) working under them and is responsible for allocating work and monitoring their performance.

lockout The exclusion of the workforce from the workplace by the employer as a tactic in an industrial **dispute**. A lockout effectively denies the opportunity to earn and puts pressure on trade unions to settle disputes as their members become dependent on **strike pay** or have to use their savings. Lockouts are rare events in the UK and in some countries they are unlawful. In Germany, however, they are an established feature of industrial relations and are used by employers in response to selective or **pin-point strikes**. In this context they serve to escalate **industrial action** and pressure the unions towards settlement.

London allowance A **premium payment** made by some organizations to their employees who work in London. It is designed to offset the higher cost of living in the area. Some commentators argue that this principle of regional variations in pay should be extended across the UK, resulting in differential wage rates for similar jobs thereby reflecting local variations in the cost of living.

long-hours culture An accepted and approved pattern of working characterized by long hours, overwork, and **presenteeism**. It is believed to be a particularly problematic feature of many British workplaces and comparative statistics on **working time** indicate that the UK has a much larger proportion of its workforce who regularly work excessive hours than any other European state. [See **workaholic**.]

long-term incentive (LTI) see executive pay

lower earnings limit (LEL) The annually adjusted rate of pay below which neither British employees nor employers have to make National Insurance Contributions (NICs). Critics of the LEL point to the fact that it provides an incentive to employers to offer short-hours part-time jobs with very low earnings. Employees may be attracted to these jobs to avoid paying NICs, but then are excluded from a series of statutory benefits, such as **Statutory Sick Pay** and **Statutory Maternity Pay**.

low pay There is no standard definition of low pay. Commonly it is considered as **hourly rates** falling within the lowest 10 per cent of earnings (the lowest decile), but this figure can vary quite widely depending on the data source used. Another way of calculating low pay is in terms of a percentage of median earnings, though again this can lead to widely varying estimates because median earnings can be calculated in different ways. The **Low Pay Commission** (LPC), in its first report recommending the level of the **National Minimum Wage** (NMW), adopted a working definition of low pay as gross earnings at or below £3.50 per hour at 1997 pay rates. There has been mounting concern at low pay in recent years, which has resulted in the establishment of the NMW. This concern has arisen because of a widening of the distribution of earnings in the UK since the 1970s and evidence of substantial and growing in-work poverty. Many low-paid workers supplement their earnings through state benefits, such as Family Credit, and there is concern at the health, social, and economic costs which are associated with a substantial pool of low-paid workers. The incidence of low pay is variable across the economy and is concentrated in certain industries and amongst certain categories of employee. The analysis of low pay by the LPC indicated that the following groups are more likely to be low paid than others: women, young people, ethnic minorities, people with disabilities, part-time workers, lone parents, temporary and seasonal workers, and homeworkers. It found that low pay occurs disproportionately in certain regions, such as the north east, Wales, and Northern Ireland, and that it is concentrated in particular industries, with clothing and footwear, retail, hospitality, contract cleaning, agriculture, hairdressing, social care, and security having particularly poor records. Low pay is also more common in small firms and companies which do not recognize trade unions.

Low Pay Commission (LPC) The LPC was appointed in July 1997 by the newly elected Labour government to recommend the level at which the **National Minimum Wage** (NMW) should be introduced and how it should be applied to young workers. The remit of the LPC also required it to take into account the likely social and economic consequences of the NMW and to consider the impact on levels of employment, inflation, the competitiveness of UK industry, and costs to business and the Exchequer. The first report of the LPC, *The National Minimum Wage: First Report of the Low Pay Commission*, was published in June 1998 and recommended an initial NMW of £3.60 per hour, rising to £3.70 in June 2000, with a lower rate of £3.20 per hour for young workers and trainees. It also provided detailed advice on how the NMW should be calculated and enforced, and reviewed and commissioned evidence on the likely social and economic consequences. The majority of its recommendations were incorporated in the National Minimum Wage Act 1998, though the government opted for a lower initial youth rate of £3.00 per hour. Subsequently, the LPC has been retained in order to review the introduction, operation, and impact of the NMW.

Low Pay Unit (LPU) An advocacy group that campaigns on behalf of the lower paid. The LPU played an important part in raising the question of a statutory minimum wage for the UK and helped turn trade union and Labour Party opinion in favour of a statutory **pay floor**. Since the introduction of the **National Minimum Wage** it has been highly critical and argued that the rate is too low to have a major impact on working poverty. The LPU's principal objective is a minimum wage set at the Council of Europe's 'decency threshold' of 68 per cent of national average earnings. This is more than £7.00 per hour and, if introduced, would cover more than 10 million UK workers.

low road refers to the search for competitiveness on the basis of low labour standards and **cost minimization**. It is an approach to management that critics claim is characteristic of many UK firms and which is encouraged by state **policies** of labour market **deregulation**. [See **competitive strategy; high road**.]

low trust is a description of employment relations that derives from the assumption that the natural tendency of workers is to shirk. As workers cannot be 'trusted' to work effectively on the organization's behalf, managements institute a variety of controls to secure employee compliance. These can include the design of jobs so as to minimize scope for worker discretion (and disruption), close supervision, and the use of **incentives** to motivate worker performance. Controls of this kind, however, may institute a low-trust dynamic as employees reciprocate with the kind of **instrumentalism** and hostility to management that were assumed to exist in the first place. [See **high trust**.]

Luddite The original Luddites were early nineteenth-century **outworkers** who engaged in machine breaking and riot in protest at unemployment and the displacement of workers by new and more productive machinery. Since then the term has been applied to any individual or group that resists technical change or to an attitude of mind that is resistant to innovation.

lump labour or 'the lump' is the traditional term for **false self-employment** in the UK construction industry.

luncheon voucher (LV) A benefit in kind that can be exchanged for food at many restaurants, shops, cafés, and sandwich bars and which is given to many city centre office and service workers. Luncheon vouchers, like many other **benefits**, are defined in law as comprising part of the wage.

M

McGregor's theory X and Y see **theory X and theory Y**

machiavellianism is the belief in doing whatever is expedient in order to succeed. Machiavellian people are manipulative, ruthless, single-minded, and arrogant; they waste no time on issues of ethics or social responsibility. This means that fair play, loyalty, friendship, and decency are easily sacrificed if they get in the way. The term derives from the sixteenth-century Italian philosopher Niccolò Machiavelli, whose novel *The Prince* set out a strategy for seizing political power.

macho management is an aggressive management style characterized by very little **consultation** with employees, a distrust of and hostility towards trade unions, an emphasis on **unitarism**, and the assertion of the **management prerogative**.

McJob A pejorative term for a low-paid, low-skill job in the service sector, typified by those in large fast food outlets. [See **minimum wage job**.]

McKinsey 7-S framework A framework for analysing and implementing organizational change based on the interrelationship between seven key factors that contribute to organizational effectiveness: structure, strategy, systems, style, staff, skills, and superordinate goals. The framework was devised by the McKinsey consultancy firm in 1980 to encourage managers to extend their thinking beyond the commonly accepted key variables of strategy and structure.

mainstreaming is consideration of issues of gender and equality in all aspects of government or company policy and practice.

For example, in developing a training or reward policy a company with a commitment to mainstreaming would consider the likely impact on the relative treatment of men and women and members of majority and minority ethnic groups. [See **equal opportunity policy**.]

management board The operational board of a company, which is formally accountable to a **supervisory board**, under the system of **corporate governance** that exists in Germany and other continental European countries. In some circumstances in Germany workers have the right to agree the appointment of the 'labour director' or director of personnel who sits on the management board.

management by objectives (MbO) is a technique for managing performance that emerged in the 1950s but receives little attention these days. However, many of the ideas it is based upon are still relevant to contemporary **performance management** methods. MbO is a goal-directed process that relies upon setting clear targets for each employee and reviewing his or her performance against these targets. The targets (objectives) are established through a joint discussion between the employee and his or her line manager. The participation in objective setting is designed to increase the employee's commitment to achieving the targets. The objectives should be clearly defined, measurable, and set at a level that is challenging yet attainable. This is a difficult balance to get right: if set too high, the employee will consider them unattainable and become demotivated; if set too low, they fail to stretch the employee and so performance falls short of her or his full potential. An assessment of whether the objectives have been met by the employee occurs at a specified time and this feeds through into remuneration and development (like most **appraisal** systems). The problem with MbO (as with most goal-directed processes) is that objectives might not be achieved because of reasons beyond the employee's control, and that targets can become out of date or inappropriate. This means that a short-term focus is essential, but this itself can cause problems because the long-term needs of the employee, department, and the organization can easily get overlooked. [See **goal-setting theory**; **SMART**.]

management by stress is a characterization of modern work systems, based on **just-in-time** and **lean production**, which is favoured by writers with a radical **frame of reference**. The central claim is that new forms of work intensify labour and pressurize workers, leading to **job stress**. This view is a corrective to optimistic interpretations of workplace change that emphasize **empowerment**. [See **disciplined worker thesis**.]

management by walking about (MBWA) became a buzzword in the 1980s. It is based on the concept of managers leaving their desks and becoming more involved in the work processes they are managing. This forces them to communicate with their staff and makes them more available and approachable. It is a hands-on, proactive approach to managing.

Management Charter Initiative (MCI) An employer-led initiative launched in 1988 to improve the quality of management education in the UK and raise the status of management as a profession. The MCI was founded on a belief that deficiencies in management competence were one of the reasons for the relative underperformance of the UK economy. Since its launch the MCI has become the government's designated 'lead body' for the development of standards of competence for the occupation of management (see **National Vocational Qualifications**). Its early ambition to create a professional chartered institute for management, however, has been dropped.

management consultant A person who offers advice on a commercial basis to an organization. Normally a consultant will be brought in to solve a particular problem or set of problems identified by managers within the organization, or to advise on a change programme. The consultant is supposed to offer independent expertise and bring a fresh view, uncontaminated by previous experiences within the organization and by organizational politics. In reality, of course, the consultant will have his or her own prejudices and preferred solutions, and will become embroiled in organizational politics through the consultancy process. Sceptics argue that external consultants rarely tell organizations anything they do not already know and are nothing more than pawns that help the most influential managers get the solution they wanted. Some of the fiercest cynics are managers, who argue that consultants do not have to live with the consequences of their ideas—they walk away from the organization and are not accountable for any problems or difficulties that occur. However, management consultancy is a thriving and lucrative business, particularly due to the perceived need for constant change amongst organizations operating in dynamic environments. [See **internal consultant**.]

management development is the process of ensuring the organization has the appropriate management competencies to meet its business needs. This means assessing existing skills and abilities and identifying actual or potential shortfalls and problem areas. Management development is typically a mixture of reactive and proactive intervention: reactive in the sense of responding to recognizable needs to enhance management skills brought to light by problems; proactive in attempting to predict future needs in line with the strategic objectives of the business. In practice management development is a set of policies that operate in two areas: (1) developing existing managers by assessing their current competences, agreeing their performance objectives, and identifying any development/training required to ensure the objectives are met; and (2) developing future managers by identifying achievements and potential at lower managerial levels and rewarding them through career enhancement opportunities based on **personal development plans**. Management development can be seen as part of a broader policy of **human resource development**.

management guru A person whose ideas and opinions have had an influence on business managers and who has become a well-known figure as a result. The original meaning of the term guru is a spiritual teacher or revered mentor, and it is applicable because many management ideas are pursued with almost religious fervour whilst their proponents (the gurus) become highly respected in management circles. Management gurus such as Tom Peters, Rosabeth Moss Kanter, or Peter Drucker can command high fees for attendance at seminars where they convey their ideas to senior managers. Gurus are concerned with 'big ideas' illustrated with anecdotal evidence and presented through a charismatic performance on stage (see **charisma**). These ideas can then be taken away by the managers in the audience and adapted to their own organizations. [See also **management consultant**.]

management jargon consists of words and phrases that prevent wider understanding of particular ideas or actions. Jargon can be used to bemuse and confuse people, and management jargon in particular is seen as a way of hiding sinister intentions behind benign words. For example, management debunker and cartoonist Scott Adams (see **Dilbert**) points out that, over the years, increasingly happier sounding management jargon is being used for making people redundant: from 'you're fired' to 'you're laid off' to 'you're downsized' and, nowadays, 'you're rightsized'. He suggests the following possible changes in the future: 'you're happysized', 'you're splendidsized', and 'you're orgasmsized'.

management prerogative is the concept of the right of managers to control and direct the work process, unhindered by interference from employees, trade unions, or the law. In reality, there are always constraints on managers—these include (1) externally imposed legal requirements such as health and safety or equal opportunities; (2) organizationally agreed arrangements, such as union recognition or employee consultation; (3) individually determined moral and social obligations to employees, such as treating people with respect or giving praise. Whilst few people would argue that managers should have no constraints on their action whatsoever, there is considerable disagreement as to where the limits of the management prerogative should be drawn and the extent to which the state should have a role in regulating the employment relationship. [See **voluntarism**; **corporatism**.]

management style is the preferred way of managing people that has been adopted either by an individual or by the whole organization or a department within the organization. For instance, at the individual level the **managerial grid** is a tool for assessing individual management styles based on the balance between a manager's concern for people and for operations. At the organizational level, management and industrial relations theorists such as John Purcell and Keith Sisson have sought to identify styles of managing employee relations based on the extent to which **individualism** or collectivism is emphasized.

management succession planning is the process of ensuring that managerial posts are filled with effective managers through either identifying and developing talent with the organization (through **career management**), or recruiting suitable people from outside the organization. The process is supposed to be proactive, in the sense that it should include planning for both certainty—such as retirement—and eventuality, such as resignation and vacancies as a result of internal promotions or transfers.

managerial grid A diagnostic tool developed by organizational consultants Robert Blake and Jane Mouton which allows managers to assess their leadership style. In a self-completion questionnaire, managers indicate their behaviour preferences and the overall score is plotted on two dimensions: concern for people and concern for task. From this, different styles of management can be identified and managers can assess whether they need to change their style. Implicit in the managerial grid approach is the assumption that the most desirable style is a high concern for people and task. However, critics argue that this **normative approach** is problematic because it fails to take into account the needs of particular circumstances, and that the appropriateness of particular styles will vary from situation to situation.

managerialism is an approach to work that emphasizes the objectives of the business above all other concerns. It is often used in connection with public sector and voluntary organizations, since they are not primarily profit driven, and might legitimately be focused on a variety of social and ethical objectives. For example, a doctor in a hospital might make a decision whether to administer a drug based on the needs of the patient and in line with the ethics of the medical profession. If, however, the doctor was to base the decision on the cost of the drug and how this would affect the hospital's budget, he or she might be accused of being managerialist (and even unprofessional). Private sector professionals (such as accountants, research scientists, and corporate lawyers) can also face similar dilemmas of balancing business objectives with professional concerns. For some people, managerialism will therefore be considered an insult; other people will see it as a compliment because it suggests focused dedication to business needs.

managers of discontent is a phrase coined by the American sociologist C. Wright Mills to describe **trade unions**. It expresses the view that unions channel **industrial conflict** through industrial relations procedures and thereby moderate its disruptive impact on the economy. The phrase also captures the notion that unions harness discontent and use it to exert bargaining pressure on employers, resulting in higher pay and better conditions of employment for their members.

managing diversity (MD) is the concept of recognizing the wide variety of qualities possessed by people within an organization. It emphasizes the individuality of people, and the importance of valuing each person for his or her unique combination of skills, competences, attributes, knowledge, personality traits, etc. Advocates of managing diversity often present it as an alternative to **equal opportunity**. The latter is condemned for being obsessed with treating people the same, when people ought to be treated differently, in order to reflect their diversity. It is considered a new approach to fair treatment which values the individual: respect for the individual is stressed, and policies emphasizing **individualism** are preferred. Critics argue that the concept of managing diversity underestimates the extent to which people share common interests, values, and belief, and have similar needs. By focusing on the individual it ignores the importance of a shared, collective identity and the reality of social groupings. Moreover, rather than addressing fair treatment, it abandons the idea entirely and appeals to the selfish and self-serving aspects of human nature. In between the advocates and the critics are commentators who argue that management of diversity has an important practical application because it allows organizations with an increasingly diverse workforce to address the varying needs of both individuals and groups. Importantly, it can provide a means of putting fairness and respect for differences on the agenda in organizations with managers who previously have been resistant (or even hostile) to equal opportunities.

manpower planning see **human resource planning**

manual handling is transporting or supporting loads by hand or by bodily force and is a major source of workplace injury to the back, arms, hands, and feet. More than a third of all injuries that cause more than three days' absence from work are the result of manual handling. In 1992 the UK government issued the Manual Handling Operations Regulations to guide work practice and reduce the hazard involved in this kind of work.

market failure arises when the optimum social or economic effect is not generated by the interaction of supply and demand. For example, it is often argued that training in **transferable skills** is subject to market failure. Although such training is beneficial to the economy, it can prove costly to the individual employer who runs the risk of losing trained workers to competitors before the fruits of investment have been recouped. A condition of market failure is often used to justify state intervention in the employment relationship; for example, that skills be developed through publicly funded programmes or that training be financed by a levy on employers.

marketization is the progressive exposure of the public sector to market forces. This might be effected in a number of ways including the creation of internal markets, **compulsory competitive**

tendering, and **privatization**. It is motivated by the conviction, elaborated by public choice theorists, that the public sector is prone to inefficiency, its workforce to shirking, and its managers to empire-building. Marketization is designed to provide a salutary shock, in order to keep these tendencies in check.

marriage bar A ban on the employment of married women, so women employees who get married have to give up their employment. Operation of a marriage bar was common in many industries in the UK until the 1960s but the practice is now unlawful under sex **discrimination** legislation.

Marxism is the body of social theory that derives from the work of the nineteenth-century German philosopher Karl Marx. The influence of Marxism within the social sciences has declined in recent years, though the study of **employment relations** in the UK continues to be shaped by Marxist theory. The work of critical management theorists, labour process theorists, and other radical **industrial relations** researchers and sociologists, is informed by aspects of Marxism. For many writers within these traditions it is axiomatic that capitalist relations of production are based on the exploitation of wage labour and that this provides the basis for an ongoing class struggle between capital and labour. [See **Trotskyism**; **labour process theory**.]

Maslow's hierarchy of needs is a motivation theory that suggests human beings will function most effectively when their needs are met. The well-known hierarchy devised by psychologist Abraham Maslow is composed of the following five needs: (1) physiological, (2) safety, (3) social, (4) esteem, (5) self-actualization. The lower-order 'deficiency needs' (1 to 3) have to be met before the higher-order 'growth' needs (4 and 5) can be satisfied. As each of the needs is satisfied, so the need at the next level becomes more important to the individual. In the workplace, it means managers must seek to satisfy all the needs of their employees if they want optimum performance. Whilst many workplaces address the deficiency needs, it is far more challenging to find ways of satisfying the growth needs, although attempts to do so can be seen in **job redesign** initiatives, **empowerment**, and **teamworking**. [See also **self-actualization**.]

mass consumption is the purchase of standardized products or services by large numbers of customers. Traditionally it has been associated with **mass production** and the techniques of **Fordism**. However, some recent commentators (see **post-Fordism**; **flexible specialization**) argue there has been a demise of mass consumption and mass production, and a growth in forms of work organization that allow for greater variation in the production of goods and services to meet the demands of increasingly discerning customers, constituting increasingly differentiated niche markets (**mass customization**).

mass customization is the high-volume creation of products or services which can be varied according to customer preferences. In this sense, the products or services are customized rather than standardized and are therefore designed to satisfy a large range of niche markets, rather than a single mass market. The concept is used to contrast high-volume, variable production with the standardized **mass production** associated with **Fordism**.

mass picketing see **picketing**

mass production is the high-volume creation of products or services that are standardized to one particular design or set of specifications. It is a concept closely associated with **Fordism** and based on the principle of **economies of scale**. Allegedly, Henry Ford characterized the production methods used to produce the Model T Ford cars as 'Any colour you want as long as it's black'. This phrase sums up the mass-production approach which is focused on the producer's needs rather than the customer's requirements. More recently, the term **mass customization** has been coined to contrast the traditional mass-production approach with methods that provide greater variation in products and services.

maternity leave is the period of time away from work that a woman is entitled to take during and immediately following the birth of her child. Most countries provide a legal entitlement to maternity leave, although the length of time varies from country to country, and some organizations provide enhanced leave beyond the statutory legal minimum. There is a legal entitlement to leave of this kind under the EU Pregnant Workers Directive 1992 and the UK Employment Relations Act 1999. The latter has strengthened the rights of UK women in this field and defines three types of maternity leave. All women are entitled to 'ordinary maternity leave' of eighteen weeks' duration (raised from fourteen weeks). During this leave the woman is entitled to the benefit of all the terms of her **contract of employment** apart from pay and is entitled to return to the job in which she was employed before her absence. 'Compulsory maternity leave' covers a period of two weeks immediately after the birth of her child during which a woman must not work for the good of her own health and that of her infant. 'Additional maternity leave' can be taken by women who satisfy a one-year **qualifying period** (down from two years) and will end twenty-nine weeks after the birth of the child. The contract of employment continues during additional maternity leave, with the exception of pay, but at its end a woman does not have the right to return to the same job. Rather, she is entitled to a job 'of a prescribed kind'; i.e. broadly similar employment. If all three types of leave are taken in full, a woman is entitled to a total amount of forty weeks' maternity leave. [See **Statutory Maternity Pay**.]

maternity pay is payment to a woman employee immediately prior to and following childbirth. The purpose of maternity pay is to provide income security to mothers during a period of **maternity leave**, when their normal work pattern, and hence their capacity to earn, is disrupted. The payment is also intended to reduce the risk of health problems which might arise from women continuing to work up to childbirth or returning to work too early after giving birth. In Britain, many women qualify for **Statutory Maternity Pay**, though companies often supplement the statutory entitlement through occupational maternity pay.

measured daywork (MDW) is a **payment system** in which a flat day-rate is made to employees provided they achieve output targets derived from **work-study** estimates. Measured daywork has traditionally been used as a payment for manual workers and was advocated widely in the 1960s and 1970s. Its introduction formed part of a widespread reform of workplace industrial relations, designed to introduce greater stability of earnings and reduce the volume of workplace bargaining associated with **piecework**.

mediation is a means of resolving **disputes** between employers and trade unions which represents a 'halfway house' between **conciliation** and **arbitration**. A conciliator helps the parties to a dispute find a mutually acceptable solution, while an arbitrator makes an award that both parties agree in advance to accept. A mediator, in contrast, makes recommendations for the solution of a dispute but the parties do not undertake to accept them in advance. Mediation is a service provided by ACAS though, as with arbitration, ACAS officers themselves do not serve as mediators. Rather, ACAS appoints a mediator or mediation board from its panel of arbitrators.

medical suspension is the suspension with pay of an employee on medical grounds under health and safety regulations. It relates specifically to those in hazardous occupations involving exposure to ionizing radiation, lead, and certain other chemical substances.

mentor A formal role that can be taken by anyone with experience in an organization. It is a person who takes a long-term, direct interest in the development of a more junior employee, and who is there to guide, listen, and advise. The mentor is not normally the employee's **line manager**, so there is no direct reporting relationship between the two individuals.

mentoring is the process whereby a senior employee takes an active role in developing a junior colleague. Typically this occurs at managerial level or amongst professions. The mentor provides advice on how the mentee can develop his or her skills, competencies, knowledge, and experience in order to progress along a successful career path. As well as giving advice, the mentor might also prove useful in providing contacts that help the mentee to engage in the process of **networking**.

merger occurs when two companies join together in order to combine resources and produce a new, more successful organization. Elements of both companies mix together although the merger rarely results in an equal combination and some employees and managers frequently bemoan and resent the loss of the old **organizational culture**. In such circumstances, the merger is sometimes referred to as a **takeover**.

meritocratic organization The guiding principle of a meritocratic organization is that everyone is promoted and rewarded according to their ability. Of course this laudable aim is rarely achieved in practice. Whilst many organizations have procedures in place that are supposed to produce fairness, they do not always result in the most deserving person benefiting the most. Organizational politics, bias, favouritism, prejudice, and ignorance can intervene to distort the decision-making processes and undermine the meritocratic principle. Whilst most people would support a merit-based system publicly, many people in positions of power and influence have benefited from past privileges (family connections, wealth, social status, etc.) that are decidedly not meritocratic. [See **equal opportunity**.]

merit pay is an individualized system of payment in which earnings are related to an assessment of employee performance in the job. Merit pay is also known as appraisal-related and individual performance-related pay and is usually based on a system of annual performance **appraisal**, which is used to allocate employees to one of a small number of performance bands. The level of performance rating then determines either the award of cash bonuses or **salary progression** through a scale or range. Merit pay is a long-established system of payment for white-collar and managerial workers in the private sector but has spread to other categories over the past two decades. It has been used more widely for manual and public service employees and its application to the latter has often been justified in terms of the promotion of a 'performance culture' within risk-averse bureaucratic organizations. There has also been a trend towards greater use of 'merit only' salary awards in which all of the annual increase received by employees is linked to the results of performance review. Under this more radical arrangement cost of living increases are done away with and employees rated as poor performers will be denied any upward adjustment in salary. Merit pay remains a hotly disputed form of payment, with critics claiming that it can demotivate workers, erode **teamworking**, and generate **perverse effects**, as workers focus on performance targets at the expense of other dimensions of their work. Supporters, in contrast, claim that the principle of individual reward is intrinsically fair and accepted by many employees and that merit pay can contribute to the targeting of worker behaviour and raising performance. [See **appraisal-related pay**; **competence-based pay**.]

meta-competencies are 'overarching' competencies that are relevant to a wide range of work settings and which facilitate adaptation and flexibility on the part of the organization. Meta-competencies are usually said to include learning, adapting, anticipating, and creating change. [See **competency**.]

M-form is the term used to describe a company with a multi-divisional structure. It is composed of units or divisions that are relatively autonomous, with their own resources, operating procedures, and management structure. One way of visualizing such a company is to see it as composed of several smaller companies (divisions) each of which is operating independently, but which are ultimately accountable to the main board of directors at corporate level. Some M-form organizations (particularly **multinational corporations**) are very complex, being composed of many divisions within which are many operating units producing a vast range of products and services.

militancy is the propensity of a **trade union** or group of workers to engage in strike action and other forms of **industrial action**. A militant orientation on the part of a union is often counter-posed to union moderation or 'partnership'. Militancy is one of the key indicators used in definitions of 'union character'. Militancy can also refer to the act of striking.

militant A militant is a trade unionist who advocates resort to **strike** and other forms of **industrial action** on a frequent basis, while a militant **trade union** is one that frequently takes industrial action.

milkround is a term used in the UK to refer to the annual process of recruiting graduates by large organizations. Typically, representatives from organizations attend recruitment fairs in universities around the country at which prospective recruits can find out about the opportunities offered by the company.

mind-set is a term used to describe a person's way of thinking that remains relatively fixed. Their mind-set will guide the way they behave and approach issues or problems. **Culture change programmes** in particular talk about changing the mind-set of managers and employees where they deem certain ways of thinking and behaving to be detrimental to achieving the organization's objectives.

minimal compliance is an orientation to work in which employees comply with management instructions but restrict their level of **motivation** or engagement in work tasks to a minimal level.

minimum wage A basic, minimum rate of pay below which earnings cannot fall. Minimum wages can be established either through **multi-employer bargaining** or through statutory mechanisms. The British **National Minimum Wage**, established in 1999, is an example of the latter. However established, minimum wages introduce a **pay floor** to the labour market and are a means of combating working poverty and income inequality. Virtually all developed economies now have provisions for establishing a minimum wage and international bodies, like the **International Labour Organization** and the European Union, advocate the adoption of minimum or fair wage standards. [See **monopsony wage**.]

minimum wage job A job that is paid at the statutory minimum rate and for this reason is unattractive to jobholders and likely to be low skilled and associated with low productivity. In the USA and other developed countries there has been concern at minimum wage jobs replacing better-paid manual work in manufacturing, leading to an overall degradation in the quality of employed work that is available.

mission statement A published declaration of the organization's goals. Its purpose is to communicate the goals to the organizational **stakeholders** and to rally support for these goals.

model employer The belief that the public sector should be a repository of good employment practice and provide a model or standard to which private sector companies should aspire. The notion that the state should act as a model or **good employer** was influential through much of the twentieth century, however imperfectly it was realized in practice. Increasingly, though, it is assumed that best practice is found in the private sector and that the public sector should follow, not lead. A concrete manifestation of this change in policy in the UK has been the appointment of private sector managers to senior positions in public services and state enterprises.

Modern Apprenticeship is a UK government training initiative launched by the Conservatives in 1993. It seeks to revive and improve **apprenticeship** training in sectors where it is established and extend it to new areas of the economy. Modern Apprenticeships share some of the features of traditional apprenticeship in that they are based on a contract of apprenticeship, combine work-based and off-the-job training, and share the costs of training through lower wage rates for apprentices. However, they also differ in that they are based on industry standards, monitored externally, result in the acquisition of a competence-based **National Vocational Qualification** Level 3, and attract government subsidy for off-the-job training. Since its inception 250,000 young people have been involved in the programme.

modular organization An organization where there has been extensive **subcontracting** of non-core functions to a range of other, independent organizations that offer specialist services. A modular organization might subcontract locally or globally, depending on their business needs.

moments of truth A phrase used within **business process re-engineering** to denote key instances in a process where value can be clearly identified as being added to a product or service.

money purchase pension scheme With a money purchase or defined contributions pension scheme the employer and employee make contributions to an investment fund to create a 'pot of money'. The latter will fund the employee's pension on retirement and is usually used to purchase a pension from a financial services company. Money purchase schemes differ from defined benefit pensions in that the financial risk associated with the investment of pension contributions is transferred to the employee. Money purchase pension schemes are becoming more common because they carry a series of advantages for employers. It is possible to have a mixed benefit scheme, which effectively combines final salary and money purchase principles. [See **final salary pension scheme**; **occupational pension**.]

monopoly wage is a term used by economists to refer to the higher average wages enjoyed by unionized workers compared to their non-union equivalents. It expresses the idea that unions act as coercive monopolies within the labour market that control the supply of labour and therefore raise wages above the level that they would otherwise reach. [See **monopsony wage**; **sword of justice**; **wage-gap**.]

monopsony wage The theory of monopsony wages has been developed in economics to account for the results of research on statutory minimum wages. Economists have found that, contrary to expectations, the establishment or increase in a statutory **minimum wage** can lead to higher levels of employment. This finding has been explained by claiming that employer monopsony in the labour market effectively depressed wages below their 'true' market rate before the minimum wage was introduced. The minimum wage raises pay to the market rate and improves labour market functioning, with a consequent rise in employment. Employer monopsony in the labour market may arise where there is one dominant employer or where employers can identify a source of labour which is immobile or constrained in its choice of employment. An example might be women workers who are seeking twilight employment (evening work) to complement domestic responsibilities. [See **National Minimum Wage**.]

moonlighting means secretly doing extra work for another employer and (usually) being paid **cash in hand**. It is frowned upon because it quite often involves tax fraud, and means that the second employer is benefiting without investing in the training of the employee. Moonlighting is not the same as having several legitimate jobs, as might occur in the case of a **work portfolio**.

motivation is the propensity of the individual to expend effort in work. Psychologists sometimes distinguish three aspects of motivation: the direction in which people are motivated to act, the effort they are willing to expend, and the persistence with which they will work. Given its relevance to the question of business performance, motivation has been a major concern of social psychologists, who have developed a variety of theoretical models to explain how and under what conditions individuals become motivated to work. These theories can be loosely classified in two ways. First, there are content theories of motivation that are concerned with what motivates people at work and, second, there are process theories of motivation that concentrate on how the content of motivation influences behaviour. Content theory is also known as **needs theory**. Needs theories are based on the idea that there are psychological needs, probably of a biological nature, which underpin human behaviour. These needs might include the need for subsistence, esteem, **self-actualization**, achievement, or power. Examples of needs theories include **Maslow's hierarchy of needs** and **Herzberg's two-factor theory**. Process theories are concerned with the processes through which individuals become motivated and are generally based on cognitive psychology; that is, they assume that individuals engage in a rational calculating process in choosing to pursue particular objectives. Examples of process theories include **expectancy theory**, **goal-setting theory**, and **equity theory**. [See **demotivation**.]

motivation-hygiene theory see **Herzberg's two-factor theory**

motivator factors are features of work that affect job satisfaction according to **Herzberg's two-factor theory**. They include promotion opportunities, opportunities for personal growth, recognition, responsibility, and achievement. [See also **self-actualization**.]

multi-divisional structure see **M-form**

multi-employer bargaining Collective bargaining that results in a multi-employer agreement covering a multiplicity of individual firms. On the employers' side multi-employer bargaining is conducted through an **employers' association**. The bargaining may affect all firms in a particular industry, all firms in the national economy, or all firms in a particular region. [See **industry bargaining**.]

multinational corporation (MNC) A large organization with subsidiary businesses in more than one country.

multi-skilling involves an increase in the range of skills possessed by an individual worker or an occupation. It is often used to describe a situation where craft workers, such as electricians, learn and make use of the skills of an adjacent occupation, such as engineers. Multi-skilling may be a feature of **teamworking** and a pattern of labour use based on **functional flexibility**.

multi-source feedback see **360-degree feedback**

multi-unionism is the presence of two or more **trade unions** within a single workplace, enterprise, or industry. Multi-unionism is a relatively common feature of traditional industries in the UK and reflects the occupational basis of trade union organization. It has been criticized on the union side as leading to rivalry and division and on the employer side for reinforcing skill demarcations and generating inter-union disputes. These problems can be exaggerated, however, and in many organizations there are joint union committees and bargaining forums, which reduce some of the harmful effects of division. In recent years the trend has been towards the rationalization of union representation through processes of union merger, **derecognition** of smaller unions by employers, and the creation of **single-table bargaining** arrangements.

multi-unit manager A manager responsible for managing a number of different service outlets usually within a single service brand, such as a particular brand of pub or fast food outlet.

mushroom management is a joke term to describe a style of management where employees (like mushrooms) are kept in the dark and periodically given a load of manure.

mutual gains The notion that enterprises should be managed in the interests of both shareholders and employees. The mutual gains enterprise is one that is responsive to all its stakeholders and ideally should be characterized by a flexible, **high performance work system**, coupled with job security, high wages, **profit-sharing**, and **employee involvement**. A mutual gains strategy is an approach to workforce management that seeks to promote shared interests and co-operation, while mutual gains bargaining involves attempts by management and union to identify common interests. [See **integrative bargaining; labour-management; partnership**.]

mutuality is the concept of shared interests in the workplace. In other words, managers and employees have mutual goals, influence, and responsibilities, and receive mutual respect and rewards. In practical terms, the principle of mutuality means that changes in work organization should be negotiated with employee representatives (usually trade unions), essentially giving the employees the power of veto over workplace change. Critics argue that, although a laudable aim, such mutuality is rarely found because, ultimately, there is an imbalance of power, which means managers always have the upper hand. [See **unitarism; pluralism**.]

Myers-Briggs type indicator A self-assessment questionnaire for measuring personality traits, and using these to identify a person's overall personality type.

mystery shopper A person hired by an organization to evaluate secretly the performance of its staff or aspects of its operations by pretending to be a customer. For example, a supermarket might use a mystery shopper to assess product availability or how well their staff deliver good customer service. Similarly, some airlines use mystery shoppers (known as 'ghost riders') to assess the overall in-flight experience and the demeanour of the flight attendants. [See **consumer reports**.]

myths (in relation to **organization culture**) are explanations of past events that are designed to explain or legitimize the present situation. They do not have to be true, but they always convey powerful messages about organizational values and beliefs.

N

National Action Plan (NAP) Under the terms of the 'employment chapter' of the Amsterdam Treaty 1997, member states of the European Union are required to submit a National Action Plan (NAP) on employment each year in a standard format. The plan must be based on four common 'pillars': improving **employability**; developing entrepreneurship; encouraging adaptability (flexibility) in business and amongst employees; and strengthening the policies for equal opportunities. It must also conform to the principle of **social partnership** and allow for consultation with business, labour, and other interests. The plans are submitted for review to the European Commission, which assesses them and provides feedback to member states. The creation of this system of planning stems from the adoption by the European Union of a formal objective to promote 'a high level of employment'.

National Insurance Contributions (NICs) are payable by employers and employees in the UK on earnings from employment above a **lower earnings limit** and below an upper earnings limit of £575.00 per week in 2001 (i.e. NICs are only paid on the first £575.00 of weekly income). The contributions are used to finance a range of social insurance payments, including old age pensions, **Statutory Sick Pay**, and **Statutory Maternity Pay**. [See **social charge**.]

National Minimum Wage (NMW) Following the report of the **Low Pay Commission**, the NMW was established in the UK by the NMW Act of 1998 and came into force in April 1999. The Act gives an entitlement to a minimum hourly rate of pay to all workers (with the exception of the genuinely self-employed, children, apprentices, members of the armed forces, voluntary workers, prisoners, and share fishermen), though there is a lower rate for young workers (aged 18–21) and for those on the first six months of an accredited training contract. The NMW is calculated by dividing the total hours worked in the 'pay reference period' (a period up to a maximum of one calendar month) into total pre-tax earnings received for that period. The latter include incentive payments and tips paid through the payroll but exclude cash tips direct from customers, shift and overtime premiums, unsocial-hours payments, and employment benefits (with the exception of accommodation). The current rate for the NMW is £3.70 per hour for adults and £3.20 per hour for young workers and trainees. Employees can enforce their entitlement to the NMW at an **Employment Tribunal** and there is also a statutory obligation on employers to ensure they pay the NMW and maintain adequate records, which is backed up by inspection and the risk of criminal prosecution. Britain has never previously had a statutory minimum wage, though until 1993 the **wages councils** were empowered to set minimum rates in a number of low-wage industries. The introduction of the NMW has brought the situation in Britain in line with most other developed economies, which have had statutory minimum wages or equivalents for several decades.

National Vocational Qualifications (NVQs) and Scottish National Vocational Qualifications (SNVQs) are certificates of competence for particular occupations and professions. There are five levels within an NVQ and the standards for each of these levels are established through industry lead bodies, which bring together employers, professionals, trade unions, and other experts. Skills are acquired through on-the-job **training** and accredited by the NVQ. This means achievements beyond just educational qualifications can be recognized through nationally agreed standards for each occupation and each industry. Theoretically, NVQs provide employees with wider opportunities in the labour market than firm-specific training schemes or educational qualifications alone.

natural wastage is the process of reducing the number of employees through a combination of three techniques: **recruitment freeze**,

voluntary redundancy, and **early retirement**. The advantage of natural wastage is that there are no **compulsory redundancies** and so it provides a more acceptable method of reducing headcount—particularly for trade unions. However, the disadvantage is that management has very little control over who exits and typically it will be those people who have a better chance of getting employment elsewhere that are likely to leave the organization. Therefore, natural wastage can result in the organization retaining its least effective staff and losing its best performers.

needs theory This theory (developed by David McClelland) identifies three different needs that can act to motivate people in the workplace. (1) The need for achievement (nAch) is the drive to excel and succeed and to improve upon set standards and past performance. (2) The need for power (nPow) is the desire to influence and control others. (3) The need for affiliation (nAff) is the desire to be accepted and liked by others. Each person has within them a different balance of needs, and it is important to get the correct fit between the needs of the individual and the job in order to ensure optimum performance. To apply the theory, the needs for a particular candidate are assessed through various psychological tests, resulting in comparable overall scores of nAch, nPow, and nAff. [See **Maslow's hierarchy of needs; ERG theory; Herzberg's two-factor theory; motivation.**]

negative reinforcement see **reinforcement theory**

negotiation of order is the idea that the pattern of HRM practice is not solely the product of management policy and action but is negotiated with employees and partly reflects their interests. Such negotiation may be formal and be conducted through **trade union** or other workforce representatives. In other cases, however, it may simply involve 'give and take' between workers and their supervisors, in which employees co-operate with management and accept direction in return for managers tolerating a variety of informal workplace practices. [See **fiddles; frontier of control.**]

negotiation track The negotiation track of the European Union was established by the **Social Protocol** attached to the Maastricht

Treaty of 1993 and was designed to extend the **social dialogue** between business and labour. Under the procedure the **social partners** can negotiate **framework agreements** on aspects of employment, which can subsequently be adopted as legally binding **directives** by the Council of Ministers. To date, the social procedure has resulted in directives on **parental leave**, **part-time** work, and **fixed-term contracts**. If the social partners decline to negotiate or fail to reach agreement, the European Commission remains free to propose legislation directly to the Council of Ministers under the 'legislative track'.

neo-corporatism see corporatism

neo-Fordism is the term used to describe an approach to work organization that is essentially Fordist, but has been adapted to incorporate a greater degree of flexibility. This adaptation has occurred because even though there is still a market for mass-produced goods and services, customers expect a greater degree of variation and choice than ever before. Within manufacturing, commentators argue that techniques such as **just-in-time**, **lean production**, **kaizen**, and **business process re-engineering** are merely refinements to the traditional techniques associated with Fordism. Commentators also argue that many of the new, service sector industries that supposedly demonstrate a post-Fordist approach to work organization also rely on Fordist techniques. For example, there has been a massive growth in call centres but neo-Fordist commentators consider these to be the factories of the future where rows of alienated white-collar workers sit processing information, under a system of electronic surveillance that constantly monitors their output. So neo-Fordism stresses the continuity of current systems of work organization with traditional systems of the past, but recognizes that **globalization** and information technology will change the location and form of the work. This contrasts with **post-Fordism** which emphasizes the extent of dramatic change and discontinuity.

neo-liberalism is an intellectual and political perspective that is suspicious of state intervention in economy and society and advocates maximum scope for the free play of market forces. For neo-liberals, liberty is best preserved by a minimal state and economic utility best secured through free markets. Prominent neo-liberals have included the political philosopher Frederick von Hayek and the monetarist economist Milton Friedman. The ideas of these and associated thinkers have shaped the policies of governments, most notably those of Margaret Thatcher in the UK and Ronald Reagan in the United States. In the field of HRM neo-liberalism is associated with the call for freer and more 'flexible' labour markets and a policy of **deregulation**.

nepotism is the action of appointing and promoting family and relatives. In an organization, it means that family members are favoured over others, even though they may not be as qualified or skilled. Family businesses, by definition, rely on nepotism. In other contemporary organizations the meaning of nepotism is often extended to include any sort of favouritism towards family and friends of existing employees. Critics of nepotism consider it bad practice because it favours connections over talent, and therefore does not lead to a truly **meritocractic organization**. Defenders of nepotism argue that it has the virtue of producing a loyal and trusted workforce. [See **equal opportunity**.]

networking is the process of establishing useful links and contacts with various individuals in key roles in different organizations in order to enhance one's career opportunities. For example, trade shows and conferences are less about getting information on new products, services, ideas, techniques, etc. than making contacts across the industry and getting known to others. Networking is always beneficial to the individual, and often useful to the organization.

New Deal see **Welfare-to-Work**

New Earnings Survey (NES) An annual UK government survey of earnings based on a representative sample of those within the **pay-as-you-earn** (PAYE) tax system. It is thus derived from companies' **payroll** information and is the main data source on earnings (including incentive payments and overtime) and hours of work in the UK. However, because the data are based on PAYE they exclude a large number of low-paid employees and for this reason the NES is not considered a satisfactory instrument for measuring the incidence of **low pay** within the UK economy.

new pay is a term coined by the American management writer Edward E. Lawler III and has been used increasingly in the USA and more latterly in the UK to refer to current developments in **reward management**. It encapsulates the belief that changes in business structure and environment require new approaches to the management of reward which break decisively with the 'old pay' of job-evaluated pay structures, seniority-based progression, time-rates, and extensive fringe benefits. The 'new pay' refers essentially to a model of good practice in the field of reward, and its advocates urge that reward be managed in accordance with a set of broad principles which are derived from the wider, normative literature on **high commitment management**. These principles include the following. First, that pay should be 'strategic' and pay management integrated with the wider management of the business. In practice this has led to an interest in rewards which can promote quality and innovation, such as quality incentives or share options. Second, that rewards should promote flexibility in work organization, and several new pay writers urge the use of **team-based pay** and flat, broad-banded pay structures, which maximize the scope for flexible working. Third, that there should be a focus on **paying the person** rather than 'paying the job' and that reward management should be individualized, with pay linked to the competence, market value, and performance of the individual employee. Lawler himself is a keen advocate of **skill-based pay**. Fourth, that there should be an extensive use of incentives and **variable pay** to guide employee behaviour and ensure it conforms to the needs of the business. New pay writers tend to favour non-traditional incentives such as award and recognition schemes or pay systems which tie earnings to novel indicators or performance, such as customer satisfaction. Fifth, that **line managers** should assume greater responsibility for the management of rewards and, in particular, retain extensive discretion over the distribution of payments amongst employees. Sixth, that employee commitment to systems of reward be secured, involving employees where possible in their selection, design, and operation. Lawler advocates **employee involvement** in project groups tasked with developing employee involvement in pay awards through peer review. While the 'new pay' has influenced current thinking on reward it has been subject to criticism. It has been suggested that its constitutive principles may be contradictory rather than reinforcing, that a number of techniques advocated by adherents may have serious disadvantages, and that the central prescription of expanding variable pay is unethical because it involves a transfer of economic risk from shareholders to employees.

New Realism was the policy adopted by the **Trades Union Congress** in the 1980s that involved acceptance of the Conservative government's programme of **collective employment law**. The term is also used to refer to the eschewal of **militancy** by trade unions and the search for a more co-operative relationship with employers. In the 1980s this found expression in the signing of **single-union agreements**. The current vogue for **labour–management partnership** represents a continuation of this policy.

new-style agreement see **single-union agreement**

no blame culture is the phrase used to describe the tolerance of mistakes within an organization providing that people learn from these mistakes. It is usually associated with **empowerment** and the **learning organization**, where employees are responsible for making their own decisions. An empowered employee must be free to make mistakes and then learn from these by evaluating the outcomes and discussing the issues with work colleagues. For many managers, the no blame culture presents particular problems because they must resist the temptation to tell employees what to do and instead persuade and encourage them to reach their own decisions. This is often more time-consuming.

noise at work is a major workplace hazard that can result in hearing loss and premature deafness. In the UK, the Noise at Work

Regulations 1989 apply and require the monitoring of noise levels and the provision of ear protection in work situations where there is a noise hazard. [See **health and safety**.]

nominal group technique is a method of group problem-solving that involves individual group members writing down their ideas in private, then presenting one of their ideas to the group and recording this on a flipchart. The process continues until all the ideas are listed. The group then discusses the ideas for a set period of time. Each member then privately ranks the ideas and the final decision involves adopting the idea that has achieved the highest aggregate ranking. [See **brainstorming; Delphi technique**.]

non-accelerating inflation rate of unemployment (NAIRU) The level of **unemployment** in a national economy that is seemingly compatible with an absence of inflationary pressure. In the 1980s it was widely assumed by economists that the NAIRU had risen, such that higher levels of unemployment were required to maintain monetary stability. Since then, however, the recent period of non-inflationary growth in countries such as the UK and the USA has suggested that the NAIRU has fallen, perhaps because of the supply-side reforms to the labour market of recent decades.

non-standard contract is any contract of employment that is not issued on a full-time, permanent (open-ended) basis. It normally refers to **part-time, temporary, fixed-term**, and **zero-hours** contracts, as well as **subcontracting** arrangements. Commentators suggest that the increasing emphasis by employers on achieving numerical flexibility has led to a rise in the number of non-standard contracts being offered, and a decline in standard, permanent contracts.

non-standard work is work that does not conform to the male norm of permanent, full-time employment. Forms of non-standard work include **part-time** work, **homeworking, temporary contracts, self-employment**, and **agency labour**. There is evidence of an increase in a number of forms of non-standard work in the developed economies over the past two decades. [See **atypical work; contingent work.**]

non-union workplace An organization where management does not recognize a trade union for individual representation, **joint consultation**, or **collective bargaining**. Until recently in the UK whether or not to accept a union was purely a matter for management decision. Under the Employment Relations Act 1999, however, employers can be obliged to concede **recognition** if there is majority support for the union. The Act has also established a statutory **right to representation**. It is sometimes assumed that employment relations in non-union companies typically follow a co-operative pattern, characterized by **employee involvement** and **soft HRM**. In reality, many non-union companies have a poor record for involving their staff and on many dimensions employment conditions tend to be inferior to those found in the unionized portion of the economy. [See **black hole; bleak house; derecognition; representation gap.**]

non-verbal communication see **body language**

Nordic system This refers to the common and distinguishing features of industrial relations in Denmark, Finland, Norway, and Sweden. At the heart of the model is a 'basic agreement' between the central **confederations** of business and labour, which provides far-reaching **joint regulation** of the labour market and reduces the need for an extensive statutory labour code. Further components include high levels of collective organization amongst employers and employees, centralized trade unions and employers' associations, and a three-tier system of wage bargaining at national, industry, and workplace levels. The Nordic system was associated for many years with low inequality, low inflation, low unemployment, strong welfare provision, and industrial peace. Greater exposure to world markets has placed the system under strain, however, and particularly in Sweden its future is in doubt. [See **solidaristic wages policy.**]

normative approach A set of guidelines that state how things ought to be done. Therefore a normative theory or model typically tells us how various concepts or ideas should be linked together in order to produce certain desirable outcomes. A normative theory or model is not based on **empirical evidence**, but is a set of ideas that have been theoretically derived through a process of logical thinking.

normative commitment occurs when an employee remains with a particular organization because he or she feels obliged to do so due to pressure from others. [See **organizational commitment**.]

norming is the third stage of the five-stage model of group development. [See **stages of group development**.]

norms are standards of expected behaviour. They indicate to people how they ought to act in a particular situation. Learning the norms is an important part of the **socialization** process when joining an organization, or being accepted into a group. Typically, when a person violates the norms of any group he or she is quickly brought into line by the other group members.

no-smoking policies Increasingly organizations are committed to providing smoke-free environments for their employees and therefore adopt no-smoking policies. These restrict smoking to certain areas in a building or ban it totally. In any city it is often easy to identify offices with smoking bans because at coffee breaks there are frequently small huddles of employees outside the front door or in the car park puffing away on their cigarettes.

no-strike clause A clause in a collective agreement that stipulates that a trade union will not take strike action in the event of a **dispute** but will rely instead on **third-party intervention** to resolve conflict. No-strike clauses were a controversial feature of the **single-union agreements** signed by a number of British trade unions in the 1980s.

notice period The period of advance notice that an employer or an employee must give to the other side before terminating an employment contract. In the UK, the Contracts of Employment Act 1963 established the principle that employees were entitled to a minimum period of notice before **dismissal**. The current provisions are set out in the Employment Rights Act 1996 and stipulate one week's notice for employees with less than two years' service and, for employees with longer service, one week for each year up to a maximum of twelve weeks. The contract of employment may provide for a longer period of notice but a contract cannot override the statutory minimum. If an employee is dismissed without proper notice, he or she can take a claim for **wrongful dismissal** to an **Employment Tribunal**. [See **dismissal with notice**.]

numerical flexibility is the policy of ensuring that the appropriate amount of labour is employed for the needs of the organization. This involves putting people on a variety of contracts to ensure that fluctuations in the demand for employees across the working day, week, or year are matched with the appropriate supply of labour. The most common forms of numerical flexibility are: (1) **part-time working**, (2) **temporary/fixed-term contracts**, (3) **subcontracting**.

O

objective justification is a legal principle within European law that allows unequal treatment of employees when there is a prima facie case for equal treatment. For example, the **Fixed-Term Contracts Directive** states that a fixed-term worker's terms and conditions must be no less favourable than those of a comparable permanent employee unless the difference can be justified objectively. There is a four-stage test for objective justification: (1) there must be a clearly defined business need that shows measurable benefits arising from unequal treatment; (2) the requirement or condition that leads to unequal treatment must be an appropriate way of achieving that business need; (3) the requirement or condition must not be tainted by **discrimination** in any way; (4) the benefit to the business must far outweigh any discriminatory impact on the individual. This test is also applicable in cases of **equal pay** and the equal treatment of **part-time** workers.

objectives (or goals) specify what is to be achieved and when. They do not specify *how* the required results are to be obtained.

occupational community Where there is an interlinking of work and non-work social activities, an occupational community can develop. Typically it means that workers socialize more with people of their own occupation in non-work hours than they do with members of other occupations. In many instances this is emphasized by geographical location; for example where a community has a dominant employer such as a steel works, factory, call centre, or retail outlet. Importantly, however, the term implies there are shared values and beliefs that are perpetuated outside the workplace.

occupational culture The shared values, beliefs, and norms associated with a particular occupation or type of work. An occupational culture is independent of the particular organization where the employee works. Such cultures can be associated with both blue- and white-collar workers—for example, fishermen, accountants, police officers. The developments in flexibility and the decline of traditional careers have led some commentators to argue that the notion of occupational culture is ceasing to be relevant. Others, however, point to new occupational groups, such as computer technicians or financial traders, as evidence of emergent occupational cultures.

occupational health care is the provision of health and medical services by the employer at the place of work. In large companies it is common to have an occupational health centre with full-time medical staff and smaller companies sometimes band together to provide group occupational health services. The original purposes of occupational health were to identify and control work-related injuries and diseases and reduce time lost through **absenteeism**. Additionally, however, it may be used to promote the general health and well-being of the workforce and many organizations, in agreement with trade unions, have established 'well man' and 'well woman' clinics that provide health checks and advice on healthy living. [See **health education; stress management**.]

occupational language consists of two types of words. (1) Technical words and phrases that are peculiar to a particular occupation. These develop because everyday language does not contain appropriate words to describe the activities and processes. (2) Occupational argot (slang) that develops among the occupational group. This has the important social function of creating social cohesion amongst those within the occupational group, and distancing them from those outside the occupation (who obviously would not understand the argot). Both forms of occupational language are often labelled as 'jargon' by outsiders. Jargon is frequently condemned as being inaccessible, incomprehensible, and even elitist— but that is the point of it. All forms of work have their own jargon.

This dictionary is concerned with explaining much of the **management jargon**.

occupational pension A pension scheme operated by an employer or group of employers. Occupational pensions can be contrasted with the state pension schemes or personal pensions, which are taken out by individuals. Schemes can assume a number of different forms though common to all is the principle of employer contributions to the pension fund. In many cases, though not always, employees will also make regular contributions through deductions from their weekly wage packet or monthly salary. Occupational pension schemes cover a large proportion of the working population in the UK and are a valued 'security benefit'. Schemes are closely regulated through legislation and a variety of tax incentives are in place to encourage companies to establish schemes and employees to join them. The Occupational Pensions Regulatory Authority has responsibility for the overview of occupational pensions in the UK. [See **benefits**; **deferred pay**; **indirect pay**; **pension**.]

occupational stress see **job stress**

occupational stress indicator (OSI) see **job satisfaction**

occupational union A union whose **job territory** is restricted to members of a particular occupational group. **Craft unions** of skilled manual workers take this form as do unions of professionals, such as doctors, midwives, teachers, lecturers, and nurses. [See **closed union**.]

Office of Manpower Economics (OME) The UK Office of Manpower Economics is a civil service secretariat which provides support to the **Pay Review Bodies**, charged with recommending pay levels for more than a million public servants. It was created in 1971 and its main role today involves the collection of evidence from employer and employee organizations and the carrying out of original research into public service pay levels, pay systems, and other aspects of remuneration. The OME is the latest in a series of specialist agencies that have provided research which can inform the setting of fair salaries for public servants, and much of its work is concerned with the question of the **comparability** of public sector pay with pay in the private sector. The assumptions underlying its creation and operation have been, first, that the absence of a functioning labour market for certain groups of public servants requires the use of an administrative mechanism to determine pay and, secondly, that a consensus about appropriate levels of pay for doctors, dentists, military personnel, judges, nurses, and teachers can best be created on the basis of objective research into comparative pay levels and related issues. The OME, therefore, reflects the distinctiveness of pay determination within the public services but also the need to maintain 'fair' levels of pay which will secure an adequate supply of motivated employees and minimize the risk of **industrial action** in politically sensitive public services.

off-the-job training see **training**

old boys' network is a colloquial term for the informal contacts that exist between people which can lead to favouritism and unfair advantages at work. In particular it applies to the way men gain advantages in managerial circles through their social connections with other men. [See **networking**; **halo effect**; **equal opportunity**; **nepotism**.]

omission see **reinforcement theory**

on-line learning is the delivery of interactive training and educational material via an organization's internal computer network (intranet) or the world wide web (internet). [See **computer-assisted instruction**.]

on-line recruitment see **e-recruitment**

on-the-job training see **training**

open door policy Literally, it means the manager's door is always open for any employee to air grievances or concerns, or to offer suggestions. Such policies are designed to encourage individual employees to bring any problems directly to the attention of any of their managers, rather than going through an employee representative.

Typically, open door policies are found in workplaces where there is no recognized trade union. They are considered by some commentators as evidence of a move away from collectivism towards **individualism** in the employment relationship. Sceptics argue that open door policies are ineffective because employees are naturally reluctant to bring grievances or problems to the attention of their immediate managers, since it might adversely affect their promotion chances, their appraisals, and their pay. Many open door policies address this problem by allowing employees to raise issues with managers more senior than their immediate line manager.

open learning has two elements. First, it comprises a philosophy of **learning** that involves reducing the barriers to access and giving learners control over the process through which they acquire knowledge and skills. Second, it consists of a set of methods based on self-study and non-traditional media, including audio cassettes, television, and computers.

open union A **trade union** with a broad **job territory**; that is, it recruits and represents workers across a range of industries, enterprises, and occupations. In the UK, the Transport and General Workers' Union is an example of an open union because its membership covers a broad range of, largely manual, occupations in industries as diverse as air transport, docks, road transport, engineering, chemicals, oil refining, retail, local government, and the voluntary sector. There has been a trend for trade unions in the UK to become more open over time. Many craft unions, for instance, which used to restrict their membership to an elite of skilled workers, now recruit amongst semi- and unskilled manual workers and clerical and technical workers. The process of merger between trade unions has contributed significantly to the genesis of more open unions. [See **closed union**; **general union**.]

operating time is the time that an organization is open for business or the delivery of services. [See **working time**.]

opportunistic managers are those who take advantage of the particular circumstances they find themselves in. They are not concerned with strategy and planning, but instead look for quick fixes to current problems. They are content to accept the latest ideas and fads, and are followers of management fashion.

Opportunity 2000 is a business-led initiative in the UK with the aim of improving the 'quality and quantity of women's participation in the workforce'. Organizations from the public and private sectors sign up to Opportunity 2000 to make a public commitment to the aims of the initiative. The voluntarist approach means that each member organization sets its own objectives and monitors progress towards these. Awards are given each year for outstanding achievements and progress. Opportunity 2000 was renamed Opportunity Now in 2001.

oral warning The first sanction within many company **disciplinary procedures** is the issuing of an oral warning to an employee that his or her conduct must improve if he or she is to avoid further sanctions. The warning will typically be given by a **line manager** and will be recorded on the employee's personal record for a set period of time, after which it will be excised. [See **written warning**.]

organizational commitment refers to an individual's psychological attachment to an organization. It is often measured by three attitudinal factors: identification with the goals and values of the organization; a desire to belong to the organization; and willingness to display effort on behalf of the organization. For some commentators, an individual can only be considered truly committed to the organization when all three factors are in evidence. For others, one of these factors would constitute adequate evidence of commitment. [See **dual commitment**.]

organizational culture There are two main approaches to organizational culture which give the term different meanings. (1) Organizational culture is the set of shared understandings and assumptions the members of an organization have about what the organization is (**beliefs**), how it ought to be (**values**), and how organizational members should behave (**norms**). The culture is perpetuated through symbols and language (for example, **stories**, **myths**, **legends**, **heroes/heroines**, **rituals**, and **ceremonies**). The culture is shared by all members of the organization, and reflects a management style based on **unitarism**. Newcomers are introduced to the culture through **socialization** and must learn to accept it, rather than question it. Those who do not accept the culture are encouraged to leave. Some commentators use the term 'corporate culture' and tend to stress the importance of the founders, leaders, and senior management as the creators of a particular culture. This line of thinking suggests that culture is managed from the top, and can be devised strategically to help support the business objectives. In summary, in this first approach organizational culture is a variable; it is something an organization has; and it is something that can be managed. (2) Organizational culture is created through the social interaction of the members of the organization. It emerges as a result of the interpretations and meanings constructed by employees (including managers) as they work together, talk with each other, make sense of their surroundings, and deal with conflict. Symbols and language are the manifestations of the culture—they are physical and verbal expressions of the deep-rooted meanings and understandings of the organization's members. As these meanings and understandings are constantly changing, so too organizational culture is in a state of flux. In summary, in this second approach, organizational culture is the outcome of social interaction; something an organization is; and something that cannot be manipulated or managed. [See **strong culture**; **weak culture**; **culture management**.]

organizational development (OD) is a term used to cover a set of tools and techniques designed to improve the effectiveness of an organization. In particular it has been used to assist in the process of managing change. Typically, external change agents (consultants) are brought in to diagnose the organization and propose a set of techniques (usually based on social psychology) to improve human interaction in the internal processes of the organization. Such interventions might include tools and techniques designed to improve communication, or develop team spirit, or assess the appropriateness of one's leadership style. The focus of OD is on people: improving social interaction. It is therefore often disparaged as the 'soft side', or 'touchy-feely' side of management. It focuses on attitudes and values, so managers are often sceptical of the techniques and methods that OD practitioners use. OD was popular in the 1970s and the term is currently out of fashion, although many of the ideas are alive and kicking in a new guise—for example, techniques for analysing group roles and stages of group development have received new impetus with the current emphasis on teamworking in organizations; similarly, techniques for improving communication and creative thinking have re-emerged with the interest in **Total Quality Management**. In other words, although the term OD is rarely used in organizations and not often found in management textbooks, the basic techniques and ideas have been repackaged and are still being used by consultants and practitioners to address contemporary organizational problems and initiate change—particularly the management of culture.

organizational learning is the process through which knowledge gained by individuals within an organization is shared collectively. This means that instead of knowledge being the property of individuals it is 'possessed' by the organization. In this way the organization can be said to learn lessons and this is seen as a necessary first step towards becoming a **learning organization**.

organizer A union officer or representative who concentrates on the tasks of recruiting new members and developing union organization. In North America there is a long tradition of trade unions establishing separate organizing departments to extend trade unionism to unorganized companies. In recent years in the UK there has been a similar trend and a movement towards unions employing organizers in a bid to try and reverse the long decline in union membership since the 1970s. Indicative of this trend is the establishment in 1998 by the TUC of an Organizing Academy to provide a yearlong traineeship in organizing methods. [See **full-time officer**.]

organizing model This refers to an approach to **trade union** recruitment and organizing developed by American trade unions in the

1980s which has since influenced union practice in a number of countries, including Australia, Canada, New Zealand, and the UK. At the heart of the model is the notion that unions should rest upon the 'self-activity' or activism of their members. Recruitment of workers into trade unions, therefore, should not be done on the basis of providing member services but through mobilizing workers in campaigns that result in the creation of an effective and self-reliant workplace organization. Organizing in this way is often contrasted with the **servicing model** and is informed by the concept of **social movement unionism**.

outdoor management development (OMD) see **outward bound courses**

outdoor training/learning see **outward bound courses**

outflow refers to the means by which individuals leave jobs and organizations, in particular **dismissal**, **redundancy**, **resignation**, and **retirement**. [See **human resource flow**.]

outplacement is the process of helping employees who are made redundant to find jobs elsewhere. Rather than simply handing out redundancy notices, some more progressive employers arrange for their employees to receive career advice and assistance in seeking alternative work. This usually involves bringing in outplacement consultants to offer specialist expertise. The increase in **downsizing** amongst contemporary organizations has led to a growth in demand for outplacement services. The services offered may include financial planning and advice, career counselling, skills assessment, and the development of job search skills such as CV writing, completing application forms, and interviewing and networking skills. [See **redundancy**.]

output-based pay see **payment system**

outsourcing see **subcontracting**

outward bound courses (outdoor training/learning) are sets of physical activities in which participants work as teams to complete various tasks, such as building a bridge to cross a river or orienteering through a forest. They have become increasingly popular as a tool for management development—in particular developing leadership skills, team-building, and group problem-solving. The advantage of outward bound courses is that the activities are normally fairly simple and not related to the participants' day-to-day jobs, so the problems and deficiencies of the team can be analysed with the help of a facilitator, thereby leading to collective and individual learning. The disadvantage is that the artificial situations can make it a poor simulation of how the team might behave in a work environment, faced with complex, job-related problems. Moreover, there is sometimes a credibility gap which leads some participants to fail to see any link between the outward bound course and their job requirements—thus a person might protest, 'How does building a raft to cross a river in mid-Wales help me to manage my sales team?' Only by clearly specifying the learning objectives and undertaking thorough debriefing sessions can such scepticism be reduced.

outworker A worker who works away from the employer's premises. Outworking was a pronounced feature of early systems of manufacturing when employers distributed raw materials to home-based craftworkers and later collected finished goods. This method of production was also known as the putting-out system. Contemporary manifestations of outwork include **homeworking** and **teleworking**.

over-reward inequity A condition that occurs when employees believe their remuneration and recognition are greater than their contribution merits, compared with other employees. The resultant feelings of guilt can lead to the employees increasing their effort in an attempt to redress the balance. [See **distributive equity**; **equity theory**.]

overtime is the term used to describe work undertaken on top of an employee's normal contracted hours. Normally employees are paid for overtime at an enhanced rate (usually equivalent to time and a half or, in some cases, double time). Usually overtime is voluntary and is welcomed by employees as a means of supplementing their basic wage. However, in some circumstances overtime is compulsory. For many employees, particularly in white-collar jobs and especially amongst professionals and managerial grades, there is no additional overtime payment, even though working beyond the contracted hours is expected. Indeed, in some organizations there is a culture of **presenteeism**, whereby employees are expected to get into the office early and work late, even though they are not paid for this overtime.

overtime ban A form of **industrial action** in which the sanction taken against the employer is the refusal to work **overtime**. Given the dependence of many UK companies on overtime working, an overtime ban can be highly effective.

P

paid holiday see **annual leave**

panel interview An interview situation where two or more interviewers take it in turns to ask questions.

panopticon control refers to a system of work organization in which employees can be monitored by managers at any time, but are unaware of when they are being monitored. This has the same effect as if they were being continuously monitored by managers. The term 'panopticon' derives from the design for a prison of the nineteenth-century social philosopher Jeremy Bentham. He envisaged a circular array of individual prison cells facing a central tower, in which would be located the prison guards. The prisoners would be clearly visible to the guards, but an elaborate system of screens would prevent the prisoners from seeing the guards—so they would not know when they were being monitored. This is akin to the concept of Big Brother in George Orwell's novel *1984*. More recently the term has been popularized by the postmodern theorist Michel Foucault, who applied the notion of panopticon control to the way employees are increasingly monitored through means of electronic **surveillance**.

parental leave is leave that is taken by fathers, mothers, and adoptive parents to cope with their parenting responsibilities. The Parental Leave Directive of 1996 gives parents across the European Union a legal entitlement to leave of this kind and incorporates a European **framework agreement** negotiated by the **social partners**. The directive has been implemented in the UK through the Employment Relations Act 1999. This confers a right to a maximum of thirteen weeks' unpaid leave per child on parents of children under 5 born after 18 December 1999 (there are separate provisions for adoptive parents). There is a **qualifying period** of one year's continuous service. During parental leave the **contract of employment** remains in force (with the exception of pay), such that **seniority** and **pension** rights are preserved. At the end of leave the parent has the right to return to the same job or, if this is no longer available, to a similar or better job. Flexibility in the application of parental leave provisions can be obtained through a **collective agreement** or, where there is no union, through a **workforce agreement**. The UK's parental leave regulations have been heavily criticized by **trade unions** and campaigners for **family-friendly policies** because leave is unpaid, there is a qualifying period, and parents of children born before December 1999 are denied the entitlement.

parent-country national (PCN) or expatriate. In an international firm, a PCN is a person whose nationality is the same as that of the firm, but different from the country in which they are working: for example, a Japanese manager working for a UK-based subsidiary of a Japanese company. [See **host-country national**; **third-country national**.]

participation is the inclusion of employees or their representatives in the process of management decision-making. It can occur through a wide variety of mechanisms and several dimensions or aspects of participation have been identified. First, it is possible to differentiate systems of participation in terms of who participates. **Direct participation** allows individual employees to shape business decisions, while **indirect participation** is based on employee representatives, who may or may not be trade unionists. Second, participation can occur at different levels of an organization. Thus, task-based participation allows workers to influence their immediate job and work environment, while participation at higher levels allows influence over business policy and management strategy. Third, participation can be directed at different categories of decision and a central distinction can be drawn between **financial**

participation, where employees participate in the ownership of the company, and participation in various aspects of business practice. Within the latter, employers tend more readily to concede participation in decisions that relate to employee welfare, are rather less ready to concede participation on pay and working conditions, and least likely to concede on issues of business operations and strategy. Fourth, participation can be weak or strong in the sense that employees can have more or less influence over the final decision. An **escalator of participation** has been identified, with weak forms, like information sharing, at the bottom, and strong forms, such as **codetermination**, at the top. Fifth, systems of participation can be distinguished in terms of their originator. Typically, managers favour relatively weak forms of participation located at the level of the work task, unions prefer participation through the medium of **collective bargaining**, and governments promote participation which confers rights to information and consultation on citizens (e.g. **works councils**). Sixth, the rationale for participation can vary. It is often justified through a **business case** argument on the grounds that participation can promote co-operative employment relations, facilitate change, and allow managers to draw upon the **tacit skills** of employees in resolving business problems. Participation may also be defended, however, on the grounds of industrial citizenship; that it extends the principles of democratic decision-making and accountability to the enterprise.

partnership see labour–management partnership; social partnership

part-time work denotes jobs where the number of hours is less than the standard working week. The problem is that there is no general agreement on what constitutes a standard working week, although there are sometimes industry or establishment norms. This means that the term part-time can be applied equally to someone working three hours a week and someone working thirty hours. Therefore, when you are using the label 'part-time' it is important to define clearly the range of hours covered by the term.

Part-Time Workers Directive Adopted by the European Union in 1997, this directive implements a **framework agreement** on **part-time** work negotiated by the European **social partners**. It has two objectives: the removal of discrimination against part-time workers and the development of part-time work on a voluntary basis. In the UK, the directive has been implemented through the Part-Time Workers (Prevention of Less Favourable Treatment) Regulations 2000. The latter give part-time **workers** the right in principle not to be treated less favourably than full-time workers of the same employer who work under the same type of employment contract. These rights are enforceable through application to an **Employment Tribunal**. In addition, the government has issued best-practice guidance to employers to remove obstacles to part-time work. [See **negotiation track**.]

paternalism is a style of management that involves looking after employees in a 'fatherly' manner. It is an approach that assumes managers know best and that they have the welfare of their employees at heart. Therefore, decisions are made on behalf of employees, rather than involving employees in the decision-making process through trade unions. It also signifies a clear division between managers and employees—a power and status difference. Paternalism is often associated with small firms where there are close personal interdependencies.

paternity leave is paid or unpaid leave taken by a father following the birth of his child. There is a legal entitlement to paternity leave in the European Union under the **parental leave** directive and in Scandinavian countries governments have provided financial incentives for fathers to take leave of this kind.

path dependent Change within an organization or national employment system is path dependent when it builds upon and is constrained by pre-existing practice. The inheritance from the past, therefore, limits and shapes what can be attempted in the present and future. Path dependency is often counter-posed to **contingency theory**, with its belief that organizations have to adapt continually to the demands of an external environment. [See **divergence**.]

pattern bargaining is a form of **collective bargaining** in which agreements negotiated in lead firms provide a model or 'pattern' for agreements in other companies within the same industry. Pattern bargaining was for long characteristic of the industrial relations of mature manufacturing industry in the United States, where unions focused bargaining pressure on target companies with the aim of spreading concessions to other firms. It provided a means of co-ordinating bargaining within a decentralized system and hence reduced pay inequality. The weakening of trade unions since the 1980s has eroded pattern bargaining, though in the USA and other countries it remains that collective agreements within sectors tend to converge. [See **co-ordinated bargaining; leapfrogging; shunto; whipsawing**.]

patterned behavioural description interview A method of **selection** interviewing that asks for specific examples of past behaviour. The approach begins with a **critical incident job analysis** and questions are framed that ask candidates to describe how they have responded to situations with similar characteristics in their previous employment.

pay see **remuneration**

pay-as-you-earn (PAYE) is the system for collecting **income tax** from employees in the UK that relies on deduction of tax from gross earnings by the employer. The amount deducted depends on the level of gross earnings in the pay period (month or week) and the individual's tax code, which determines their level of liability for tax in the light of their annual earnings and a range of other factors. PAYE is used for employees who are taxed under the rules of Schedule E. The **self-employed** are taxed under Schedule D and are responsible for making their own income tax payment. [See **National Insurance Contributions**.]

pay club A grouping of employers who exchange information and perhaps co-ordinate their policies on wage determination. Pay clubs may consist of employers in a particular sector or locality and may be more or less formalized arrangements. In some cases, the pay club may co-ordinate a **salary survey** amongst its members whereas in other cases there may be a less structured exchange of information. The purpose of pay clubs is to allow employers to maintain rates of pay which are equivalent to those in other companies, and so avoid recruitment and retention problems. They may also be used as a means of co-ordinating employer responses to bargaining pressure so as to prevent a general rise in wage costs across a given labour market. The functions of pay clubs may also be discharged by a formally constituted **employers' association**.

pay determination is the process of setting rates of pay, including increases in pay. Pay determination can be classified in a number of different ways, in terms of those involved in the process and the factors taken into account in deciding what pay should be. An important distinction can be drawn between three systems of pay determination: those which rely on unilateral decisions by managers; those which involve employees through **collective bargaining**; and those which rest on statutory mechanisms and involve government ministers and officials. The system of **Pay Review Bodies** and the **National Minimum Wage** are examples of statutory forms of pay determination, in which boards and commissions recommend pay increases that are adopted by the government. In setting rates of pay managers and others can take into account a wide range of influences and pressures. Some of these may be internal to the organization, such as the level of profit, productivity, and the need to secure employee co-operation with change. Others may be external, including the state of the labour market for particular occupations, the rate of inflation, and movements in earnings both in comparable organizations and across the economy. In recent years the system of pay determination in the UK has altered. There has been a decline of joint systems of pay determination based on collective bargaining and an increase in unilateral decision-making by employers, supplemented by increased statutory regulation. According to some there has also been a shift to reliance on internal principles of pay determination, with **ability to pay** taking precedence over fair comparisons and the need to maintain the real value of earnings by matching pay rates to the rate of inflation.

pay dispersion is a measure of the range of pay which is used by economists as an indicator of inequality within the labour market. Pay or wage dispersion is most commonly expressed in terms of the ratio of the 90th to the 10th percentile of the wage distribution in a given national economy. Comparative research indicates that pay dispersion is influenced by two key features of national labour markets: it is lower where there is a high trade **union density** and where the national system of **pay determination** is centrally co-ordinated through effective minimum wage provisions and a system of multi-employer collective bargaining. Pay dispersion has widened considerably in a number of developed economies in recent years, including New Zealand, the UK, and the USA, in large part because of the decline of trade unions and the deregulation of the labour market. In the UK's case, the introduction of the **National Minimum Wage** should alleviate this trend.

pay equity is the term used in North America to refer to **equal pay** between men and women.

pay flexibility is the use of payment and reward systems which allow total labour costs to rise and fall in line with business performance. Pay flexibility can therefore be achieved through the introduction of systems of **variable pay**, based on profit and performance. The concept forms part of the wider model of the 'flexible firm' and, within the model, pay flexibility serves the same end as **numerical flexibility**, to adjust labour costs to the vagaries of the business cycle.

pay floor A minimum rate of pay below which earnings cannot fall. The most obvious pay floor is the **National Minimum Wage**, established through statute in 1998, which provides for a minimum hourly rate of pay for adult workers of £3.70 across the entire UK economy. A pay floor might also be established within a particular industry through the mechanism of **multi-employer bargaining**. Industry-wide collective agreements have traditionally fulfilled this role of setting a pay floor, which might then be supplemented by further increases negotiated at company level. The benefit of establishing a pay floor, either through a statutory mechanism or through collective bargaining, is that it affords protection for the most vulnerable, least-skilled employees. It might also encourage companies to seek profit through improvements in the use of labour rather than by seeking reductions in wage rates and labour costs. [See **minimum wage**.]

pay-for-knowledge is a **payment system** in which pay increases are linked to the successful completion of training. Pay-for-knowledge can form part of a set of **high performance work practices** because it promotes skill formation and employee development. It can also support a system of **teamworking** in which employees are required to work flexibly, moving across traditional task and occupational boundaries within the team. [See **skill-based pay**.]

paying the person is a principle increasingly advocated by writers on reward, who argue that earnings should be based on the attributes of employees rather than the nature of the job role they occupy. Person- as opposed to job-based pay involves reliance on **payment systems** that link earnings to the skill level or performance of the individual employee. It may also involve the abandoning of traditional **job evaluation** and the notion of paying the **rate for the job** and is indicative of a growing individualism within employment relations. [See **new pay**.]

pay level The rate of pay for a given occupation or grade of job. Pay levels can be expressed as **hourly rates**, weekly wages, or annual salaries and are established through the process of **pay determination**. [See **grade; rate for the job; salary**.]

payment by results (PBR) is a system of payment in which earnings are tied to estimates of worker output or performance. There are many forms of PBR, including **piecework**, work-measured incentives, and **appraisal-related pay**. The term therefore denotes a 'family' of **payment systems**, rather than any particular single type, and, as such, is analogous to 'performance pay'.

payment system A procedure for calculating employees' pay, in the vast majority of cases by relating earnings to some measure of work performed. There are many different forms of payment system but virtually all can be placed in either of two broad categories. Input-based payment systems link earnings to the time, experience, skills, or competencies which employees bring to their work. Output-based payment systems base earnings on the product of work, measured either in operational terms (e.g. units of output, achievement of goals, customer satisfaction) or financially (e.g. sales, profitability, value-added). Examples of input-based payment systems include **hourly rates** of pay, annual salaries, overtime premiums, call-out payments, service-related increments, career grades which link pay increases to qualifications, and **skill-based pay**. Examples of output-based payment systems include **piecework**, work-measured incentive schemes, **appraisal-related pay**, **gainsharing**, and **employee share ownership**. Output-based payment systems can be further classified in terms of whose output or performance is measured: it might be that of an individual, as in traditional piecework, a workgroup (as in **team-based pay**), or an organization (as in **profit-sharing**). Potentially, an individual employee may be subject to several payment systems at once which link earnings to a range of input and output measures. For example, an employee may receive: an annual **salary** (based on the number of weeks and hours worked); an unsocial-hours payment for late-working; progression through a salary range based on **seniority**; an annual performance bonus based on success at achieving agreed work objectives; and the award of share options triggered by company profits reaching a set minimum figure. Recent trends in the use of payment systems in the UK have included greater use of profit-sharing and individual performance-related pay and some experiment with skill-based pay, team-based pay, and quality incentives.

pay range A range or band of pay which is offered to workers in the same job or **grade**. A pay range consists of a minimum and maximum salary and a mid-point. The latter is usually considered to be the market rate for a fully effective performer in a given job. Workers who are paid below this rate will therefore be newly appointed, undergoing training, in plentiful supply, or classified as less than effective performers. Workers who are paid above the mid-point, conversely, will be experienced, highly skilled, in short supply, and rated as high performers. Salary ranges can be distinguished from **incremental scales** by the fact that they do not consist of a series of fixed steps: actual salaries can be set at any point between the minimum and maximum points and therefore managers have greater discretion in deciding what an individual's salary will be. Writers on reward report that there is a trend towards the broadening of pay ranges, in order to give greater scope for managers to respond to labour market signals and reward skill acquisition and performance. Adjacent pay ranges typically overlap so that workers at the top of one range will be paid as much or more than workers at the bottom of another. This arrangement allows recognition of the fact that a high performer in a less demanding job may be worth more to an organization than a new starter or indifferent performer in a more demanding position.

Pay Review Body (PRB) An advisory body created by the UK government to make recommendations on pay increases and pay systems for approximately 1.3 million public servants. There are five Pay Review Bodies (PRBs) at present: the Doctors and Dentists Review Body; the Armed Forces Review Body; the Senior Salaries Review Body (covering the justiciary and senior civil servants); the Nurses Pay Review Body (which covers nurses, midwives, health visitors, and professions allied to medicine, such as physiotherapists, radiographers, orthoptists, and occupational therapists); and the School Teachers Pay Review Body. The first three PRBs were established in 1971 as a means of determining fair levels of pay for groups not covered by **collective bargaining**. The nurses' and teachers' review bodies supplanted collective bargaining in 1983 and 1991, respectively, after major episodes of industrial action in the National Health Service and the schools. PRBs consist of a chair and committee of members appointed by the Prime Minister and are supported by an independent civil service secretariat, the **Office of Manpower Economics** (OME). All take evidence from interested parties, including employers and trade unions, and commission their own research. They make recommendations on pay increases and other aspects of remuneration to the appropriate government minister and, while these are not binding on the government, it is extremely rare for them to be ignored in their entirety. During periods of public sector pay restraint, however, it has been common for governments to defer or stage the implementation of PRB recommendations. In recent years the remit of PRBs has tended to broaden and, in addition to making recommendations on pay levels, they have been asked to comment on the use of pay and other reward systems to influence recruitment and retention, motivation and morale. PRBs comprise a collective system of **pay determination** which allows scope for independent representation of employees through trade unions but which is not based on collective bargaining between employer and employee. Discussion of the system has tended to concentrate on two issues: the independence of PRBs from government and the efficacy of the system in maintaining fair salaries for public servants. With regard to the first issue, there has been recurrent tension in the relationship between PRBs committed to maintaining fair levels of salary for public servants, and governments concerned to control the public sector pay bill. With regard to the second, there is evidence that groups covered by PRBs have secured higher settlements than other public servants, which has led to claims that PRBs have been 'captured' by occupational interests and to calls for the extension of the system to other groups, such as university teachers.

payroll A list of employees kept for the purpose of calculating wages. In most large organizations today the payroll is computerized and there are specialist software packages for payroll management. In addition to listing employees, the payroll must contain all data necessary to calculate gross and net earnings, including basic rate of pay, hours worked, incentive earnings, pension contributions, deductions from earnings, and tax code. Problems with payroll management are a frequent source of wage disputes and can result in cases being taken to **Employment Tribunals** for **deductions from wages**.

pay scale A salary band or **pay range** consisting of fixed-incremental steps, between the minimum and maximum points. Pay scales are a common feature of salary administration in public services and allow for **salary progression** based on a number of criteria. Individuals can advance through a scale on the basis of **seniority**, performance, or skill acquisition.

pay spine An extended series of pay or salary points which can be divided up into a series of grades to create a graded salary structure. Pay spines are a feature of salary administration in a number of public services, such as health and local government. They are sometimes created as part of a movement towards **single status**, the extensive range of points covering rates of pay typical of both manual and non-manual occupations. [See **grade**; **pay structure**.]

pay structure The wage or pay structure is the hierarchy of rates of pay which exists within an employing organization. Economists also sometimes use the term to refer to the structure of pay within an industrial sector or national economy. Within companies pay structure has two main components. Pay groups are broad groupings of employees who have their pay managed in accordance with a common set of rules. A large manufacturing company, for instance, might have several pay groups including a senior management group, middle management, supervisory and technical, skilled workers, semi-skilled and un-skilled operatives, and clerical and secretarial. Pay **grades**, in contrast, are divisions in pay within a pay group, such that managers with higher levels of responsibility are graded above and paid more than managers with lower levels of responsibility. Pay structures can be configured along two dimensions. First, they can be integrated, so that effectively there is a single pay group and a single hierarchy of pay grades, or they can be fragmented, with a number of pay groups, each with its own set of grades. In recent years there has been a trend to rationalize pay structures and move to greater integration, particularly by merging manual and non-manual pay groups through **single-status** agreements. A counter-trend seen in some organizations, however, has been to divide the pay structure between different **job families**, so that there is a distinct set of pay grades for the accountancy and finance function, for operations management, for information technology, and so on. Second, pay structures can be taller or flatter. Where the former obtains there will be a large number of pay grades within a particular pay group, while a flat structure will consist of a small number of grades. The dominant trend at present appears to be towards the flattening of pay structures as companies delayer and introduce more flexible forms of organization. The main technique which managers rely upon in generating a graded pay structure is **job evaluation**, which can be used to assess the relative demands of different jobs and thus sort them into grades. [See **broad-banding**; **differential**.]

peer appraisal is the technique of evaluating the performance of your work colleagues. Traditionally, the **appraisal** process relies on the views of managers, but some organizations are recognizing the value of getting a wider range of opinions about an employee's performance, and so work colleagues are an important source of information. Of course no organization is likely to rely entirely on peer appraisal, but it is used in conjunction with the line manager's evaluation of performance and the employee's own assessment of his or her performance (**self-appraisal**). [See **360-degree feedback**.]

peer review see **peer appraisal**

pendulum arbitration is a form of collective **arbitration** in which the arbitrator must choose between the position of the employer or trade union and so has no right to recommend a third solution drawn from the demands of each side. The claimed benefit of removing the arbitrator's right to 'split the difference' is that it leads to the adoption of more realistic bargaining positions by the two sides and so reduces the chance of an industrial **dispute** developing.

It is felt that the two sides are more likely genuinely to seek agreement if they risk losing everything through the arbitrator's decision. However, critics claim that pendulum arbitration is likely to sour relationships by leaving one party aggrieved and that it is poorly suited to the resolution of complex, multi-issue employment disputes. Pendulum arbitrationced was widely advocated in the 1980s and features in a number of the single-union recognition agreements signed at that time.

pension A regular payment to those who have retired from work due to age or ill health paid by the state or an employer. In the UK the basic state pension is based on **National Insurance Contributions**, though there is also provision for a State Earnings Related Pension (SERPS) (see **stakeholder pension**). An **occupational pension**, in contrast, is derived from regular payments into a pension fund made by the employer and (in many cases) the employee over the course of a working life. A third arrangement is for the individuals to take out a personal pension with a financial services company. Occupational pensions are a vital employment benefit for many employees and provide for security in old age at a level above the minimum provisions of the state pension. They can take a number of different forms, including final salary, money purchase pension, and hybrid schemes. Schemes also typically provide for payments to the spouses and dependants of members who die, with a lump-sum payment for death in service. Recent trends in pension provision include the equalization of male and female treatment and entitlements, inclusion of part-time workers in pension schemes, and a movement towards greater portability of pensions.

performance appraisal see **appraisal**

performance management is the process of linking the overall business objectives of the organization with departmental objectives, team objectives, and individual objectives. It involves setting targets, constantly reviewing progress towards those targets, and taking remedial action where there are training/development shortfalls. Typically, to keep people focused on their objectives, the process is underpinned by frequent employee feedback and performance-related pay. So how does performance management differ from **appraisal**? Basically, appraisal systems focus on each employee separately in order to review his or her performance over the previous year and set new objectives for the next twelve months. In contrast, performance management systems have an organization-wide approach that tries to integrate various objectives across the business and established procedures to ensure progress towards these objectives is constantly monitored. In practice many organizations combine appraisal with performance management, and the particular systems will vary greatly from organization to organization. Performance management has become more popular during the last decade, not least because it provides (in theory) a method of achieving better **strategic integration**. [See also **management by objectives.**]

performance management cycle A continuous process of performance planning, performance development, and performance measurement to ensure that the actions of individuals, teams, and departments contribute towards the overall business objectives.

performance-related pay (PRP) The term performance-related pay is used in two senses. First, it can describe the broad class of **payment systems** which relate pay to some measure of work performance. As such, it can embrace **profit-sharing**, **merit pay**, **gainsharing**, **piecework**, **sales incentives**, and other output-based based pay systems. Second, it can refer to individualized systems in which salary increases are related to the results of performance **appraisal**. This latter usage corresponds to **appraisal-related pay** or merit pay. To avoid confusion some writers refer to individual performance-related pay (IPRP).

performing is the fourth stage of the five-stage model of group development. [See **stages of group development.**]

periphery workers are those who undertake activities considered by management to be important to the functioning of the organization, but not vital to its success. These workers typically are

(1) employees with contracts of employment that emphasize **numerical flexibility** or (2) subcontracted workers. The term is normally used in connection with the **flexible firm model**.

personal contract A contract of employment that is negotiated by the individual employee and employer and which is not determined by and does not include clauses that are the result of **collective bargaining**. In many cases 'personal contract' is something of a misnomer because these contracts take the form of 'standardized packages individually wrapped'. In other words, the terms of personal contracts within a single organization are likely to be standard and set by the employer, rather than being tailored to the individual case through meaningful negotiations.

personal development plan An action plan devised for a particular employee that sets out a programme of training and learning (both on and off the job) that will allow the employee to increase his or her competencies in line with the organization's requirements. For the individual, this may have the benefit of improving his or her career opportunities within the organization. The plan should be devised in partnership with the employees so that it can incorporate their interests and reflect their willingness to develop particular aspects of their work roles. [See **human resource development**.]

personality tests see psychological tests

personnel management is a term that can be used in at least three ways. First, it can refer to the management of people within organizations, including **recruitment** and **selection**, **training** and **employee development**, **appraisal** and **reward**, **discipline** and **dismissal**, and **employee involvement** and **participation**. As such, personnel management can form part of virtually all management jobs. Second, it can refer to the specialist group of **personnel managers** who concentrate on the development of personnel management policy and practice. In this sense it describes a management occupation. Third, it can refer to a particular approach to the management of people that is contrasted, usually unfavourably, with **human resource management**. In this case, personnel management, unlike HRM, is operational rather than strategic, bureaucratic rather than flexible, and collectivist rather than individualist. Comparative analysis of prescriptive models of personnel management and HRM, however, indicates that there is very little significant difference between them.

personnel manager A manager who specializes in the field of **personnel management**. Personnel managers are one of the primary management groups within UK business and have their own professional organization, the **Chartered Institute of Personnel and Development** (CIPD). The jobs of personnel managers are highly variable and researchers who have examined the profession have identified a number of different types, including the **architect model**, the **clerk of works model**, and the **contracts manager model**. A large percentage of personnel managers are female and the occupation continues to provide the main channel into managerial work for women. However, as in other female-dominated occupations, men are disproportionately likely to occupy senior personnel posts and those that involve direct negotiations with trade unions. Studies have indicated that personnel management is often regarded as a rather marginal function by other managers and the profession of personnel management suffers from something of an inferiority complex, concerned about the extent to which it influences strategic management within organizations. An indicator of the status and influence of personnel managers that has been used by researchers is whether or not there is a personnel director on the main board of the company. [See **big hat, no cattle**; **handmaiden**; **strategic integration**; **trash can activity**.]

personnel officer is a common job description for a lower-grade **personnel manager** involved in largely routine administration of **personnel management** systems and procedures. [See **clerk of works model**.]

personnel record system The set of documents accumulated for each employee covering all aspects of their employment.

It contains information from when the person first applied for the job, details of current position and salary, training records, appraisal forms, attendance records, any disciplinary notices, in fact anything related to the employee's terms and conditions of employment. In short, it forms a complete employment profile of the employee, and it is vital not only for developmental reasons, but also to provide documentary evidence in instances where there is a legal dispute between the employee and the organization. Increasingly organizations are using computer-based personnel record systems, although it is usual for such organizations to maintain a separate paper-based system for original documents, such as references. All personnel record systems are subject to legal regulations, such as the UK's Data Protection Act 1998, which can give employees the right to see the information stored and restricts publication of that information to a third party without prior permission of the employee. [See **data protection**.]

person specification This is a document that describes the skills, knowledge, and qualities needed to perform a particular job. It is used in the recruitment process in order to translate the job requirements (specified in the job description) into tangible features that applicants need to demonstrate they possess in order to be deemed suitable for the vacancy. Typically a person specification will outline the criteria that are (1) essential, and (2) desirable, in terms of qualifications, experience, work-based **competencies**, and behaviour-based competencies. Using the person specification it is possible for the managers involved in the selection process to decide upon the appropriate selection techniques to use in order to assess and compare the candidates.

perverse effect An unforeseen negative consequence of an action or policy which produces exactly the opposite to the intended effect. Free-market economists often claim that labour market regulation has perverse effects; for example, that the introduction of a **minimum wage** hurts the very people well-meaning reformers are trying to help by raising wages and thereby depressing the demand for low-skilled labour. Free marketeers are not the only ones to use this kind of argument, however, and free-market reforms have themselves been said to generate perverse effects. For example, attempts to stimulate the economy through **deregulation** simply encourage companies to adopt strategies of **cost minimization**, which in the long term depress the rate of economic growth. The opposite of a perverse effect is a benign effect, an unanticipated positive consequence of change. It is claimed that minimum wages can generate benign effects; for instance by raising wages they can reduce labour turnover which, in turn, provides more incentive for employers to invest in **training** to raise labour productivity.

PEST analysis is an audit of an organization's environmental influences with the purpose of using this information to guide strategic decision-making. The PEST technique involves assessing four sets of factors: Political/legal, Economic, Socio-cultural, and Technological. The assumption is that if the organization is able to audit its current environment and assess potential changes, it will be better placed than its competitors to respond to changes.

picketing is a tactic used by workers taking **strike** action which involves placing a picket line at the entrance to the workplace to discourage or dissuade co-workers and suppliers from entering. During some of the large strikes in the UK in the 1970s there was use of mass picketing, to blockade workplaces, and secondary picketing, which targeted companies along the supply chain that were not party to the original dispute. For example, strikes in the car and mining industries involved picketing at docks. To counter action of this kind, the Employment Act 1980 specified that lawful picketing was limited to the worker's own place of work. In the same year the government issued a Code of Practice on Picketing that stated (amongst other things) that the number of pickets should not exceed six at any entrance to a workplace.

piece-rate The payment per unit of output offered under a **piece-work** payment system. Piece-rates traditionally are determined by a rate-fixer or by **work study** and may be the subject of intense bargaining between shopfloor managers and workgroups in mature manufacturing industry. Partly for this reason there has been a movement away from reliance on piece-rates in recent years, though they remain an important feature of industries such as textiles and clothing.

piecework is an output-based **payment system** in which workers are paid a flat rate (piece-rate) for each item/operation completed. It is common for the piece-rate to be set through **work study** and for workers to be guaranteed a fall-back rate of pay if machine breakdown or the non-availability of materials makes it impossible for them to earn piecework. Under differential piecework systems the piece-rate can vary for each unit of output, typically with a lower rate for every additional unit above a predetermined level, the aim being to stabilize production at an optimum rate. Piecework is a feature of traditional manufacturing industry such as clothing, footwear, and engineering and operates most effectively in industries where output can be easily measured and the rate of production is controlled directly by employees, either individually or in small workgroups. Although piecework can be highly effective in motivating employees, a number of problems have been identified by researchers. These include poor quality of output, the neglect of work tasks for which workers are not paid, contravention of safety standards, and the manipulation of performance targets in order to maximize or stabilize earnings. Piecework can also generate industrial relations problems as workers and management dispute what are reasonable and attainable piece-rates. [See **degeneration**.]

pin money is a pejorative term for women's earnings which suggests that most women work to obtain a modest supplement to the earnings of their male partners. It is based on the assumption that men are the primary **breadwinners** within the labour market and that the involvement of women in paid work is temporary and of secondary importance. It may also be used to justify lower earnings for women, on the grounds that women's pay is not the means through which the primary needs of subsistence are met. [See **family wage**.]

pin-point strike A form of **strike** action used particularly by trade unions in Germany. A pin-point strike involves the withdrawal of labour in key supplier firms with the objective of disrupting economic activity across an entire sector. It can be a cost-effective form of action for trade unions because **strike pay** is paid only to a minority of workers while others who are laid off may be entitled to social security payments. For this reason the German government amended the Work Promotion Act in 1986 to end the entitlement to unemployment and short-time working benefit for employees indirectly affected by strike action.

pluralism is a **frame of reference** that emphasizes the different interests of the members of an organization. It assumes there are diverse goals and objectives that reflect the many (plural) interests present in all organizations. These differences occur not only between employees and managers but also within these groups. In other words, different managers at different levels in the hierarchy and responsible for different functions will have competing goals; similarly, different groups of employees will frequently have diverse needs and requirements. Therefore, the pluralist viewpoint assumes that conflict is a normal part of organizational life and can never be eliminated. Consequently a pluralist will seek ways to manage conflict and thereby limit the negative effects whilst developing some of the positive, creative aspects that emerge from differences of opinion and ideas. Pluralism is the opposite of **unitarism**—both terms were coined by industrial relations theorist Alan Fox.

plussage is any addition to **base pay** made because of particular working conditions or employee capability.

poaching is the management tactic of attracting fully trained and highly experienced specialist employees and managers from other organizations. The purpose of a manager using this tactic is that it avoids the cost of training and developing people in the manager's own organization, only to find that these employees/managers are poached by competitors. The poachers usually attract people by offering high salaries or enhanced working conditions. In fast-moving areas of business where cutting-edge skills and experience are in short supply (such as e-commerce), poaching is seen as the most feasible method of keeping up with competitors, although not necessarily the best way of gaining competitive advantage.

poet's day is an office workers' term for Friday: Pissing Off Early Tomorrow's Saturday.

points rating is an analytical, factor-based method of job evaluation. Under a points-rating scheme, jobs are scored under a number of different job characteristics or **factors**. The latter might include, skill, effort, know-how, level of responsibility, working conditions, and decision-making. The total score for the job across all factors determines where it will be placed in a graded **pay structure**. Points rating is the most common form of analytical job evaluation used in the UK.

policies are rules and guidelines that define and limit action, and indicate the relevant procedures to follow.

political fund A special fund established by trade unions in the UK to finance their involvement in the political process. Political funds are used by some unions to affiliate to the Labour Party but many others use their funds to finance lobbying activity, while remaining neutral in a party-political sense. Under the Trade Union Act 1984 it is a requirement that unions establish a separate fund for political purposes and that they ballot their members every ten years to gain authorization for such a fund. It is also a requirement that union members who do not wish to contribute to the political fund can 'opt out'.

political strike Strike action that is taken with the explicit aim of challenging the government or influencing its policy. Political strikes are an important feature of the industrial relations of a number of countries, and in France, for example, there is a tradition of unions using large-scale protest strikes to influence the legislative process. In the UK political strikes are rare and are unlawful as they do not involve action in 'furtherance of a **trade dispute**'. [See **golden formula; immunity**.]

polycentric management is an approach found in international firms where **host-country nationals** manage the subsidiaries. Decision-making is devolved to the subsidiaries, although head office in the parent country controls the overall business strategy. From this perspective, host-country nationals are considered important because they can bring local knowledge and understanding to the day-to-day operations of the subsidiary businesses. [See **ethnocentric management; geocentric management; regiocentric management**.]

polyvalent is a description given to workers who are multi-skilled and capable of completing a broad range of work tasks. For example, polyvalent craftworkers might be qualified to undertake both electrical and engineering maintenance tasks. Polyvalent workers are a feature of systems of work organization, like **teamworking**, that require flexibility. [See **functional flexibility**.]

porosity normally refers to the spaces or gaps (the 'pores') in the working day when employees are not working. Managers seek to reduce the porosity (close up the gaps) by increasing the workload. This sometimes leads to accusations of **work intensification**, although managers argue that it is simply the result of increasing organizational efficiency by reducing the non-productive work time.

portfolio career An increasingly popular concept that describes how a person develops his or her career through acquiring a diverse set of skills and experiences. Instead of a person's career being evaluated simply in terms of upward progression through the organizational hierarchy (see **career ladder**), it is seen as a collection (portfolio) of varied work experiences that demonstrate practical expertise, knowledge, and ability acquired through **lateral career moves** within an organization or across organizations. The concept of portfolio career is one of several that have been advanced by management writers, such as Charles Handy, who suggest we are witnessing a fundamental shift in the structure of the labour market and the decline of long-term employment. [See **jobshift**.]

portfolio planning is an approach to business strategy that was influential in the 1980s and 1990s. At its core is the belief that strategy is concerned with deciding the mix of activities and range of product markets in which the company invests. Portfolio planning is based on the assumption that the enterprise consists of a series of separate companies that are controlled from the centre through measures of financial performance. The head office, therefore, acts like an investment banker rather than a strategic planner of company operations. Within a portfolio of companies it is suggested that there should be a mix of types, including 'cash cows', mature businesses that generate revenue, together with start-up and innovative enterprises that may become the cash cows of the future.

positive action is any policy initiative designed to promote equality of opportunity through the provision of facilities, procedures, or actions that redress the disadvantage suffered by a particular group. Examples of positive action are recruitment campaigns targeted at a specific group currently under-represented in the workplace, career break schemes, company crèches, and race awareness training. Positive action should not be confused with **positive discrimination**, which is unlawful in the UK. [See **equal opportunity targets**.]

positive discrimination (sometimes called reverse discrimination) is the preferential treatment of a disadvantaged group. For example, if an organization appointed a female candidate to a senior management position because of her gender, rather than her managerial skills, this would be positive discrimination. In the UK, not only would this be an unlikely scenario, it would also be unlawful. Similarly the European Court of Justice has ruled against the use of quotas operated by some public organizations in Germany because it contravened the EU Equal Treatment Directive. However, in some states in the USA, positive discrimination can be used as part of an affirmative action programme that sets **quotas** for particular disadvantaged groups. Such quotas are usually designed to ensure that the organization has a workforce that is broadly representative of the wider community in which it is located. The quota system is designed to redress the imbalance over time. It should not lead to employees being judged solely because of, for example, their ethnic group, but does allow ethnicity to be used as one of the criteria on which to judge a person. [See **discrimination; positive action**.]

positive reinforcement see **reinforcement theory**

positive-sum An exchange is positive-sum when both parties benefit. For example, **productivity bargaining** can be a positive-sum activity because workers gain above-average pay increases while the employer obtains changes in working practices that increase labour productivity. [See **integrative bargaining; zero-sum**.]

postal balloting Under the employment legislation introduced by the Conservative governments of the 1980s and 1990s UK trade unions are required to use secret, postal ballots to elect members of their executive committee and to authorize strike action and the establishment or renewal of a **political fund**. Such ballots have to be overseen by an independent scrutineer and they are usually conducted on behalf of trade unions by specialist balloting agencies. The primary motive of the Conservatives in requiring unions to rely on postal ballots was to influence their behaviour. It was assumed that the views of a moderate union majority, which was less likely to strike, want a political fund, or vote for a militant executive, would be reflected in the results of such ballots. Critics have argued that the legislation privatizes the process of democratic decision-making in unions and involves an unwarranted intrusion into the affairs of private voluntary organizations. [See **strike ballot**.]

posted worker A worker who is sent by his or her employer to work in a foreign country either under an existing contract of employment or under one amended to take new responsibilities into account. In the European Union the Posted Workers' Directive entitles workers in this category to the minimum pay and conditions for their class of work established by law, regulation, or collective agreement in the host country. [See **expatriation**.]

post-Fordism is the term used to describe an approach to work organization that relies upon flexibility, adaptation, and innovation. Whereas Fordism was oriented towards mass production and mass consumption of standardized goods, post-Fordist methods of organizing are seeking to satisfy a greater diversity of customers in niche markets, demanding varied and customized products and services. Post-Fordism therefore incorporates a wide range of methods of work organization—for example, **empowerment** of teams, **subcontracting**, **flexible specialization**, **homeworking**, **hotdesking**. Furthermore, there is increasing emphasis on service sector industries, relying on information technology, and operating at a global level through new media—in particular the internet. Critics argue that whilst there are new ways of organizing work, there has not been a fundamental change but rather an adaptation of Fordist techniques—consequently, they prefer the term **neo-Fordism**.

post-industrial society or post-industrialism is a concept within sociology that refers to the changes in work, organization, and employment relations that are attendant on the evolution from an economy based on manufacturing to one based on services. Theories of post-industrialism fall into broad categories. On the one hand are optimistic theories, which predict the upskilling of the workforce, the emergence of flexible knowledge-based organizations, and a decline in **industrial conflict** (see **flexible specialization**; **post-Fordism**). On the other hand are pessimistic theories that claim the service economy is characterized by low skill, insecurity, and wider inequality and identify new sources of exploitation and social conflict (see **emotional labour**). A third position, adhered to by theorists influenced by **Marxism**, claims that the movement from manufacturing to services is a change in the surface form of economic activity but that the essential characteristics of the capitalist mode of production remain unchanged. [See **neo-Fordism**; **regulation theory**.]

postmodernism is a perspective on organizations that can be divided into two approaches. (1) Postmoderism as an epoch (i.e. a period of time). This approach suggests that there has been a fundamental change in the way organizations operate because of significant changes in the nature of capitalist society, in particular the increasing importance of **globalization** and information technology. Theorists of postmodernism argue that the rational, bureaucratic, Tayloristic (see **scientific management**) and **Fordist** modes of organizing are being replaced by new methods based on flexibility, constant change, and uncertainty. Consequently, the employment relationship is changing and new techniques are being used to manage employees. Postmodernism is therefore considered to be a new period in which the dominant management techniques and theories of the past have to make way for different methods and ideas. In the field of HRM, this can be characterized by features such as changes in the **psychological contract, flexibility, empowerment**, quality (see **Total Quality Management**), and the **virtual organization**. (2) Postmodernism as an epistemology (i.e. a way of understanding). This approach suggests that the change is not simply structural and economic, but that it goes much deeper into the way we understand the world and the nature of reality. It suggests that increasingly the previous assumptions about the basis of knowledge must be challenged through examining how symbols and language are important in creating the meanings which inform our understanding of the social world. Within HRM, this approach is, in part, reflected in the analysis of **organizational culture** and the wider impact of HRM on sociocultural life outside organizations. Organization theorist Karen Legge explores the implications for HRM of both postmodern approaches in her key text *Human Resource Management*.

power-distance is one of the attributes of national cultures identified by Geert Hofstede. It refers to the degree to which members of a group or organization accept an uneven distribution of power amongst their members. In some cultures with large power-distance it is regarded as acceptable that power is concentrated in the hands of senior managers, while in other cultures there is an expectation that power will be diffused. [See **individualism–collectivism; uncertainty avoidance**.]

pragmatic managers are those who do whatever is practical and expedient. They do not concern themselves with theories or big ideas. They want to get the job done and are happy with a satisfactory outcome rather than striving for the optimal outcome.

precarious employment is employment that is uncertain or non-permanent, either because employees work to a fixed-term or temporary contract or because their employer is involved in subcontracting and may have to make them redundant if a contract is not renewed. According to some commentators, an increasing proportion of employment falls into this category. [See **contingent work**.]

predictive validity see **validity**

prejudice means holding negative attitudes towards a particular group, and viewing all members of that group in a negative light, irrespective of their individual qualities and attributes. Typically we think of prejudice being against a particular group based on gender, race/ethnicity, religion, disability, age, and sexual orientation. However, prejudice extends much further and is frequently directed at other groups based on features such as accent, height, weight, hair colour, beards, body piercings, tattoos, and clothes. It is extremely rare to find a person who is not prejudiced against any group—although most of us are reluctant to admit to our prejudice. [See **discrimination; stereotyping**.]

premium payment An enhanced rate of pay which is offered when employees work **overtime**, on a shift system, at weekends, or in accordance with some other arrangement of working time which requires attendance at unsocial hours. Premium payments traditionally have been expressed as a multiple of the hourly rate for a given job, so, for example, a worker working overtime may earn 'time and a half' or 'double time' (i.e. one and a half or twice the hourly rate). Underlying payments of this kind is the assumption that the time workers commit to their employer is of variable value and time spent at work after the course of a normal shift or at night time and weekends is more valuable and therefore deserving of a higher rate of **compensation**. In some industries there has been a movement towards the removal of premium payments through annual-hours schemes and seven-day working. Employers seeking greater **flexibility** in the organization of working time have tried to eliminate premium pay, particularly for weekend working, arguing that in service industries Saturday and Sunday should be counted as normal working days. [See **hourly rate; time-rate**.]

prerogative The right to act in a particular way, without any restrictions from others. [See **management prerogative**.]

presentee A person who works long hours in order to be seen at work, thereby giving the impression he or she is a committed and loyal employee. [See **presenteeism**.]

presenteeism is the opposite of absenteeism. It means being ever present at work. In some organizations there is a culture of presenteeism whereby employees are expected to put in many hours, often at the weekends, without overtime pay. 'Being seen' is important in order to give the impression of dedication to the organization (see **organizational commitment**). However, being present and being productive are not necessarily the same thing, therefore more progressive organizations encourage their employees to work *smarter* rather than work *longer*. Presenteeism is sometimes associated with occupational health problems, particularly stress, although causality may be hard to establish: is someone stressed about their workload because they are always in the office, or are they always in the office because are stressed about their workload?

principal–agent Principal–agent theory has been developed by economists to analyze employment contracts and particularly the employment contracts of senior executives. Since business owners cannot undertake the running of the organization entirely themselves, they must employ agents to act on their behalf (i.e. managers).

However, the problem is that the interests of the agent are likely to differ from those of the principal (the business owner). The standard assumption is that employers want high levels of effort relative to pay, while all employees (including managers) want the reverse, though other assumptions may also figure. For example, that principals desire obedience, whereas agents value autonomy and independence. The principal–agent problem, therefore, is to minimize these differences of interest and secure an arrangement within the employment contract which maximizes the shared interests of the two parties. The typical recommendation which flows from this kind of analysis is that principals should adopt incentive schemes in order to control agents and ensure their interests are complementary to their own. For example, the theory is sometimes used to justify the payment of bonuses and the award of **share options** to senior executives, out of a belief that this will lead to shared interests and encourage executives to maximize shareholder value. [See **executive pay**.]

private recruitment industry The private recruitment industry consists of private sector **labour market intermediaries** that engage in four kinds of activity. First, there are companies that provide 'permanent' recruitment services and assist clients in filling job vacancies. In many cases this work embraces **outplacement** and headhunting (see **executive search consultants**; **recruitment consultants**). Second, there are **employment agencies** that provide temporary staff and contract workers. Third, there are specialist agencies in the entertainment sector that act as personal managers and representatives and who are allowed to charge workers for this service. Finally, there are job vacancy information providers, which include newspapers and magazines and internet websites (see **e-recruitment**). The private recruitment industry has grown markedly in the UK and other advanced economies in recent years. According to UK government estimates the industry tripled in size between 1992 and 1999.

privatization is the sale of public assets to the private sector, such that erstwhile state enterprises become privately owned and managed. In the UK an extensive programme of privatization since the 1970s has returned nearly all the major utilities to private hands with major consequences for HRM. [See **marketization**.]

proactive managers are those who constantly think ahead and plan. They attempt to predict future problems, based on past experiences. Their minds are focused on the future and they make decisions guided by a strategic vision of what they want to achieve. [See **reactive managers**.]

probation is the initial period of employment, often lasting several months, during which an employee is assessed in terms of his or her capability and suitability for permanent employment.

problem-solving group An alternative name for a **quality circle**. [See **employee involvement**.]

procedural equity is the perception of fairness felt by an employee about the procedures and processes within the organization (such as appraisal, performance-related pay, and promotion). [See **equity theory**.]

procedural justice is the ethical principle of fair treatment within either judicial or company procedures. A commitment to procedural justice within a company **disciplinary procedure** would lead to the following: common treatment of all like cases; reliance on evidence and the calling of witnesses; entitlements to a defence, representation, and an appeal; the separation of the 'prosecuting' and adjudicating managerial roles; and the award of a punishment that fits the offence. [See **business ethics; distributive justice**.]

procedural rule An employment rule that governs the behaviour of workers, managers, trade unions, employers' associations, state officials, and others who become involved in the process of **job regulation**. Examples of procedural rules can be found in industrial relations procedures governing **discipline** and **dismissal**, the handling of employee grievances, the **recognition** of trade unions, and cases of sex or race **discrimination**. In each of these cases the rules state the rights and obligations of employers, employees, and others and describe how particular cases of discipline, dismissal, or discrimination will be dealt with. A **disciplinary procedure**, for example, will specify the circumstances under which the employer is entitled to initiate disciplinary action and a set of rules (to do with the collection and hearing of evidence, the involvement of representatives, the right of appeal, etc.) that determine how a particular disciplinary case will be handled. Procedural rules can be created in a number of different ways. They can be developed unilaterally by managers, negotiated jointly with trade unions, or set down in legal regulations or statutes. For example, a disciplinary procedure may be negotiated by a trade union and govern the treatment of disciplinary cases within a single enterprise. If an employee is dismissed under this procedure, however, and takes a claim for **unfair dismissal** to an **Employment Tribunal**, then a second set of procedural rules will come into play, which govern the treatment of such cases in the legal system.

procedure A **procedural rule** devised to process issues and disputes that arise within the employment relationship. The most common employment or industrial relations procedures govern the recognition of trade unions, **discipline**, grievances, job grading, and disputes. [See **disciplinary procedure**; **disputes procedure**; **grievance procedure**; **recognition**.]

procedures are step-by-step sequences of actions that should be taken to attain particular **objectives**.

process owner Within **business process re-engineering**, a process owner is a person responsible for the re-engineering of a specific process.

process theories of motivation see motivation

producerism is the operation of a public service to the primary benefit of its workforce while neglecting the needs of clients or 'customers'. The accusation of producerism is often laid against public service professionals, such as doctors and lecturers, and is used as a justification for the reform of public services. The latter may take the form of **marketization** (i.e. reforms that are meant to create an element of consumer choice) and **managerialism** (i.e. reforms that limit professional autonomy by making professionals accountable to a management hierarchy).

productivity The amount of output per unit of input achieved by a business organization, industrial sector, or national economy. In the field of human resource management the primary interest is in labour productivity; that is, the amount of output per unit of labour input. Labour productivity can be expressed in a variety of different ways, including the volume or value of output per worker, per day, per shift, or per person-hour. Labour productivity can be increased by lengthening working hours, intensifying effort, or improving skills. It can also be raised by investment in labour-saving machinery or by improvements in the system of work and co-ordination of work activities. Attempts by employers to raise productivity may be resisted by workers, particularly when these involve extending working time or intensifying effort levels. [See **effort bargain**; **lean production**; **work intensification**.]

productivity bargaining is a form of **collective bargaining** in which increases of pay are secured in return for changes in working practices which allow labour productivity to be raised. Productivity bargaining has a long history in UK industrial relations and the term was coined in the 1960s when the first productivity agreements were negotiated at the ESSO oil refinery at Fawley in Kent. The practice of linking pay settlements to changes in work organization and patterns of labour use continues to this day, however, and is an important feature of many **collective agreements**, even when the term 'productivity bargaining' is not used. Recent examples can be seen in partnership agreements between trade unions and employers which link guarantees on pay and **security of employment** to acceptance of **teamworking**, **flexibility**, and annualized hours. [See **annual-hours contract**.]

productivity coalition A form of enterprise industrial relations founded on management–union co-operation to raise productivity and ensure security of employment. A stimulus to the emergence of a productivity coalition might be the intensification of competition through globalization. In this case an external threat encourages co-operation between the two sides to ensure mutual survival.

professional association A collective organization of professional workers, such as doctors, dentists, nurses, midwives, lawyers, and accountants. Professional associations provide a number of services to their members, including the provision of training, indemnity insurance, advice, and representation, and in some cases they may also become involved in collective representation and **collective bargaining**. In addition to servicing their members in a manner equivalent to trade unions, however, professional associations may be licensed by the state to regulate entry to the occupation through a system of examination and vocational training and to determine and uphold standards of professional expertise and practice. Because of this latter role professional associations typically aspire to speak on behalf of clients as well as their members and may be active in campaigning for improvements in professional services, particularly within the public sector.

professional union A **trade union** that represents professional workers. Examples in the UK include the specialist associations of doctors, teachers, nurses, midwives, probation officers, lecturers, and physiotherapists. Professional unions are often distinctive in aspiring to speak on behalf of client interests as well as representing their members and they often campaign actively on behalf of the public services where their members tend to work. In some cases they eschew the use of industrial action because this is seen as incompatible with professional commitment and responsibility to clients. [See **job territory**.]

profit-related pay (PRP) is a **payment system** in which a proportion of earnings is related directly to the profitability of the enterprise. Profit-related pay became more common in the UK from the late 1980s as a result of tax incentives which reduced the requirement to pay income tax on that portion of earnings related directly to profitability. The motive was to encourage greater **pay flexibility** and therefore a higher level of employment across the economy. The Conservative government at the time believed that flexible, profit-related pay systems would provide an alternative means of reducing labour costs to redundancy during an economic downturn and would therefore reduce unemployment. There is no firm evidence that the profit-related pay schemes encouraged by the government did have this effect.

profit-sharing is an arrangement under which a proportion of profits above a given level is distributed to employees in accordance with a set formula. Profit-sharing assumes two main forms: cash-based profit-sharing under which profits are allocated in the form of a cash payment, usually an annual **bonus**; and share-based profit-sharing where profits are used to purchase shares in the company which can then be distributed amongst employees. Profit-sharing can be viewed as a form of **incentive** payment system, though clearly the element of direct incentive is weak because profits are not solely determined by the efforts of employees and the link between individual or workgroup performance and profit is likely to be tenuous. Profit-sharing can also be viewed as an **employee involvement** technique and is often introduced out of a belief that it fosters the identification of employees with the company and its senior management. In the UK and other countries profit-sharing is regulated by taxation law which provides incentives for employers and employees to participate in schemes. The incidence of profit-sharing in the UK has risen markedly since the early 1980s as a result of a series of changes in taxation law which have stimulated the introduction of new share-based schemes and greater reliance on **profit-related pay**. The European Union, largely at the UK's behest, has also adopted a policy of encouraging member states to promote profit-sharing.

proletariat is a term used within Marxist theory to refer to waged labourers or the working class.

promotion is the act of moving an employee up the organizational hierarchy, usually leading to an increase in responsibility and status and a better **remuneration** package. It is linked with upward career progression and usually arises as a result of excellent performance. Fair and transparent promotion procedures are vital to ensure equal opportunities, and research reveals that a **glass ceiling** often inhibits the promotion of women, in spite of their abilities and performance. Ironically, promotion takes the person away from the job that he or she can do well into one that is more challenging and sometimes unfamiliar. This has led to the cynical notion of the Peter Principle: people are promoted to their level of incompetence. [See **career ladder**; **career track/path**.]

proportionate representation is the requirement in systems of **union government** for the proportion of elected officers to reflect the proportion of women members. Proportionate representation has become increasingly common in recent years and is a feature of the systems of government of several well-known British unions, such as GPMU, UNISON, and TGWU. The adoption of the principle reflects a growing **feminization** of unions and an attempt to ensure union image and union policy reflect fully the concerns of women workers. Unions are increasingly dependent on attracting women into membership and proportionate representation is a means of ensuring the interests of actual and potential women members are reflected in union conferences, executives, and policy committees.

prospector A type of firm identified by Raymond Miles and Charles Snow in their typology of 'strategic types'. It is a firm that seeks to exploit new opportunities, develop new products, and create new markets. Its core skills will lie in marketing and research and development and it will tend to have a broad range of technologies and product types. Its HR policy, ideally, will be directed at supporting innovation and expansion into new markets. [See **analyser**; **defender**; **reactor**.]

protective practice An alternative term for **restrictive practice** that is used by sociologists and industrial relations researchers who are sympathetic to labour. Whereas 'restrictive practice' implies criticism and adopts a managerial viewpoint, 'protective practice' is a more sympathetic description of job controls developed from the worker's perspective. It is associated with the view that restrictions on management's control of labour imposed by workers arise from a real conflict of interest and can have the legitimate purposes of preserving employment and autonomy and preventing overwork.

pseudo-participation is an approach to management in which managers cultivate an impression of openness but are careful to retain decision-making in their own hands. It is associated with the use of **direct communication** and other weak forms of employee **participation**.

psychological contract The beliefs of each of the parties involved in the employment relationship about what the individual offers and what the organization offers. For example, an individual employee might be willing to offer loyalty to the organization and in return expects to get security of employment. Unlike the employment contract, the psychological contract is not written down and changes over time as new expectations emerge about what employees should offer and what they can expect to get back in return. Some commentators suggest that the psychological contract is undergoing a fundamental transformation because of the increasing need for flexibility and adaptability in conditions of intense competition. In particular, it is suggested that the employee should be willing to offer commitment and high performance to the organization and expect to receive individual development in return.

psychological tests are techniques used in the selection process and can be divided into two types. (1) Cognitive tests measure a person's mental abilities, such as IQ, spatial awareness, reasoning, logic, numeracy. Although reliable, such tests are often questionable in terms of their validity. (2) Personality tests measure a person's attitudes, values, and beliefs. There are a variety of personality tests in use but typically they involve a lengthy questionnaire containing a series of value statements to which candidates must indicate their preferences. Taken together the answers produce a personality profile of the candidate which can then be compared with the profile the assessors deem appropriate for the job. For example, a candidate whose personality profile reveals 'extroversion' is more likely to fit the salesperson profile than a candidate who scores high on the 'introversion' scale. Personality tests have gained in popularity as a selection technique, not least as a result of managers wanting employees whose existing values are in line with the corporate culture.

psychometric test The generic term used to describe a wide range of tests that measure mental abilities, behavioural preferences, and attitudes/values. The tests produce a quantifiable result—a test score—that can be used to compare a person with others, or against a particular standard. Such tests can be used as part of the **selection** process, although they ought to be administered and interpreted by qualified professionals with psychology training. [See also **psychological tests**.]

public interest disclosure see **whistle-blowing**

punishment see **reinforcement theory**

pupillage is the period of on-the-job training undertaken by prospective barristers before they enter their profession.

Q

qualified majority voting (QMV) is a system of voting used by the European Council of Ministers which was first introduced by the Single European Act 1986. Under the procedure a total of 87 votes are distributed across the 15 member states, in proportion to population size, and 62 of these have to be cast in favour for a **directive** to be adopted. The purpose of QMV is to speed up the pace of European decision-making and integration and prevent any single country, even a large one, vetoing legislation. QMV was originally restricted to measures to do with the creation and operation of the Single European Market but its scope was extended to include employment matters by the **Social Protocol** of the Maastricht Treaty. The latter allowed for QMV in the areas of health and safety, working conditions, the information and consultation of workers, sex equality, and the integration of persons excluded from the labour market. In other fields of employment policy (e.g. **codetermination**) unanimity is still required and a third set of issues (e.g. freedom of association, strikes, and lockouts) are explicitly ruled out of the sphere of European legislative competence.

qualifying period The length of time a **worker** or **employee** has to spend with a single employer before acquiring statutory employment rights under UK law. For example, the right to a redundancy payment and protection from **unfair dismissal** are only acquired after twelve months' service, while the entitlements to paid **annual leave** and to join a **stakeholder pension** are acquired after three months. There is no qualifying period for certain employment rights, such as the right not to suffer discrimination on the grounds of sex, race, marital status, and trade union membership.

quality see Total Quality Management

quality circles (QC) Originally a concept devised in the 1950s, the idea underwent a revival in the 1980s with the emergence of TQM. Organizations began to encourage groups of workers to devise ways of improving the product, process, or service. The original idea of quality circles involved small groups of volunteers meeting on a regular basis, but in its contemporary form, quality groups are often compulsory and organized around specific work teams. Some organizations have even gone as far as setting targets for the number of suggestions quality groups are expected to come up with. [See **kaizen**.]

quality enhancement is a **competitive strategy** based on producing better-quality goods or more responsive services than those of competitor firms in the same industry. [See **customer care**; **Total Quality Management**.]

quality incentive The spread of **Total Quality Management** has led to experiment with **payment systems** designed to secure worker commitment to quality objectives. Quality incentives are output-based payment systems which usually link a **bonus** payment to the achievement of a quality objective or target. The latter might be operational (e.g. number of defects, delivery to time) or be based on customer reports (e.g. number of complaints, survey estimates of customer satisfaction). While there are reports of increased use of quality incentives by employers, some commentators question their value and argue that employee commitment to quality goals is best secured through intrinsic motivation and supported by **training**, **direct communication**, and **empowerment**.

Quality of Working Life (QWL) is a generic term for a range of techniques and processes that are designed to give employees greater discretion and control over their work, such as those described under **job redesign**. The principle behind all QWL initiatives is that greater participation and involvement in decision-making by employees will lead to increases in satisfaction, motivation, and commitment, which, in turn, might lead to improvements in performance. The label QWL emerged in the 1960s and was associated with many of the ideas of **human relations theorists**. It is less frequently used today although techniques such as **empowerment** and **teamworking** are contemporary expressions of QWL.

quotas are the proportions of employees from different groups (ethnic minorities, disabled, ages, etc.) that an organization is required to have in order to make it representative of the local community, or its customer/client base. In addition to overall representativeness of the workforce, quotas also require the various levels in the organizational hierarchy to reflect the wider community. In other words, if a 20 per cent quota is set for particular ethnic minority, this would apply to each level of management, as well as to the employees as a whole. Consequently, for quotas to be achieved, appointments and promotions must be made on the basis of **positive discrimination**. [See **equal opportunity targets**.]

R

race is the concept of classifying people according to physical characteristics such as skin pigmentation and facial features. It is a social construct because there is no biological basis to the classification. In biological science the notion of race has long since been rejected because there are no distinct genepools that allow humans to be categorized into subspecies or races. Everyone is of mixed race. The social race classification produces some very broad categories which group people together who share no common ancestry or culture. For example, 'black' may refer to people of African descent, native Australians, and Caribbean people. Similarly, the 'white' category would subsume, for example, anyone who is Irish, Polish, or Jewish. In spite of this, race-based classifications are used in the UK, thus the **Commission for Racial Equality** recommends the following nine categories for collecting data for the purpose of equal opportunities monitoring: white, black-African, black-Caribbean, black-other, Indian, Pakistani, Bangladeshi, Chinese, other.

Race for Opportunity is a business organization that exists to promote equal treatment of ethnic minorities in employment in the UK. It is modelled on **Opportunity 2000** but has been less successful in attracting companies into membership.

race to the bottom is the competitive **deregulation** of labour markets by nation states to make their economies attractive to multinational companies seeking the maximum return on inward investment.

racial discrimination see **discrimination**

racial groups see **race**

racism is the ideology and practice of discriminating against someone on the basis of their race or their ethnic group. Typically it is based on categorizing people according to physical attributes such as skin colour, and ascribing negative characteristics to some categories. These characteristics are then used to justify the unequal treatment of people who fall into particular racial categories. Racism is normally perpetrated by a dominant racial/ethnic group over a racial/ethnic minority group. Some commentators suggest that racism can also occur between minority groups; others reject this by asserting that racism is a phenomenon emerging out of white imperialism and is characterized by the ideology of white supremacy. [See **race**; **ethnicity**; **equal opportunity**.]

radicalism see **frame of reference**

rank and file The rank and file consists of ordinary workers who are members of trade unions. Use of the term is often associated with the belief that the interests of the rank and file are neglected by the official trade union movement, the **union bureaucracy**, and can only be met by the mobilization and direct participation of workers in trade union activity.

rank-and-filism is an approach to the study of trade unions based upon the belief that there is a sharp divergence of interests between ordinary trade union members and union officialdom. Effective trade unionism, on this view, is based on the mobilization of ordinary members and their direct participation in union activity, in order to hold union officers and other representatives to account. It is also assumed that effective unions must be **militant** and that **militancy** has its origins amongst the rank and file, who are exposed directly to exploitative working conditions. Union officers, who are remote from the point of production, it is believed, are less inclined to be militant and prefer to rely on the formal procedures of industrial relations rather than direct action by union members. The renewal of trade unions, on this view, must originate in a 'challenge from below', both to employers and to the **union bureaucracy**. [See **goal displacement**; **union renewal**.]

rate-buster An employee who is highly productive and exceeds the formally agreed rate of output for the particular task. Whilst this is advantageous for management, rate-busters are usually disliked by their colleagues because their action provides managers with the excuse to raise the rate of output for all the other employees. Typically, there is informal social regulation of work in most workgroups where rate-busting is deemed antisocial behaviour and potential rate-busters are brought into line by their work colleagues through a mixture of persuasion and coercion.

rate for the job The concept of a basic rate of pay for a particular form of work, paid regardless of the circumstances of the individual employee or employer. The rate for the job may be expressed as an hourly or weekly rate of pay or an annual **salary** paid to a particular occupation or grade of employee. It has a strong connotation of fair payment and is often used by trade unions or workers to combat systems of variable or individualized pay which result in differential earnings for employees doing the same class of work. [See **base pay**; **hourly rate**.]

reactive managers are those who respond to problems as they arise. They are frequently firefighting and are unable (or unwilling) to plan ahead beyond the short term. Whilst they lack strategic vision, they are often highly pragmatic. [See **proactive managers**.]

reactor A type of firm identified by Raymond Miles and Charles Snow in their typology of company types. Reactors are firms with little control over their environment and lack the ability to adapt to external competition. These are companies that are ill matched to their market context and lacking in effective internal control mechanisms. [See **analyser**; **defender**; **prospector**.]

realistic job preview Information provided to candidates during the recruitment process which gives an accurate picture of what the organization expects from its employees, and the conditions of work. The tendency of organizations to sell themselves to prospective employees by giving attractive, but unrealistic, impressions increases the likelihood of **entry shock** and can result in the newcomer leaving after only a short time in the job (hence the recruitment process has to be undertaken again). The downside of realistic job previews is that they can deter applicants—including the best-qualified applicants who, research shows, tend to place more weight on negative information than less-qualified applicants.

real working time is the actual time spent working by employees and is a proportion of **attended time**, in that it excludes breaks, mealtimes, cleaning up, and other 'dead' or non-productive time spent at the workplace. [See **porosity**; **working time**.]

reasonableness In defending a case for **unfair dismissal** the employer must be able to prove that the dismissal was reasonable in the circumstances. The latter include the size and administrative resources of the employing organization, the substantial merits of the case, and equity. In determining reasonableness a key issue for the **Employment Tribunal** is the extent to which the dismissal was procedurally fair. For example, was the employee given the opportunity to change behaviour, mount a defence, and seek representation, were equivalent cases dealt with in the same manner, and was the punishment of dismissal proportionate to the offence? In deciding whether a dismissal was reasonable, a tribunal can have regard to the ACAS Code on Disciplinary Practice and Procedures. The result of this has been the formalization of **disciplinary procedure** within employing organizations and the modelling of those procedures on the ACAS code. In other words, employers have used the code to ensure they do not fall foul of the test of reasonableness if a dismissal is taken to an Employment Tribunal.

recession fatigue A situation when employees become tired of the constant fear of losing their jobs, and begin no longer to care what might happen. It is most likely when there has been a sustained period of recession and where this has led to **work intensification**. [See **security of employment**.]

recognition Employer acceptance of a **trade union** as the authorized representative of the workforce. Recognition is usually inscribed in a formal recognition agreement that states the rights and obligations of the recognized trade union. Within such an agreement, the terms of recognition might include the right of the union to recruit and organize workers, the entitlements of its representatives to time off work (see **facilities agreement**), the right of the union to represent its members in company procedures, and the right to negotiate collectively on the workforce's behalf. The agreement might also specify the limits to union recognition, i.e. that it is confined to workers within a particular **bargaining unit** or that it excludes particular issues or categories of decision which remain subject to the **management prerogative**. The extent of recognition rights can vary substantially; in some companies recognition will be restricted to the right of the union to recruit and represent members, while in others it will embrace **collective bargaining** and **joint consultation**. In the early 1970s approximately three-quarters of UK workers were covered by trade union recognition agreements but this percentage has dropped substantially in the intervening period. Today only a third of employees work in organizations where unions are recognized for the purpose of pay bargaining. The passage of the Employment Relations Act 1999, however, seems to be halting the downward trend in union recognition and in recent years there have been a number of prominent recognition deals signed by trade unions. The Act introduced a statutory recognition procedure which unions can use to secure recognition in the face of employer opposition. Under the procedure an employer is required to recognize a union for the purpose of collective bargaining on pay, hours, and holiday entitlement if either of two conditions apply. The first is that the union can demonstrate that it has more than 50 per cent of the proposed bargaining unit in membership, while the second is that the union has won a majority in a recognition ballot in which at least 40 per cent of the workforce took part. The operation of this statutory recognition procedure is overseen by the **Central Arbitration Committee** (CAC). Although there is now a legal route to recognition, many recognition agreements are voluntary and unions prefer to use the legislation as a means of pressing employers to concede a voluntary recognition agreement. [See **certification**; **derecognition**.]

recruitment is the process of generating a pool of candidates from which to select the appropriate person to fill a job vacancy. Typically the recruitment process involves identifying a job vacancy, specifying the requirements of the job (**job description**) and the skills needed to perform the job competently (**person specification**), deciding on the appropriate method of application, choosing the appropriate method of advertising the vacancy, and devising the procedures for dealing with applications. Whilst the terms recruitment and selection are frequently used together, they constitute different stages in the overall process of employee resourcing (see **selection**). External recruitment is the process of attracting applicants for a vacancy from the available pool of labour outside the organization (the external labour market). Internal recruitment is the process of filling a job vacancy through promotion or transferring an existing employee within the organization (the internal labour market). In practice, when a job vacancy arises, many organizations allow both internal and external applications (see also **extended internal labour market**). Internal recruitment is particularly important in ensuring there are career opportunities within an organization. In this way an organization can seek to retain its valued and high-performing employees by providing a career structure. However, recent trends towards **flat structures** and **delayering** have reduced promotion opportunities and forced employees to think more about **lateral career moves** within the organization.

recruitment advertising is the advertising of jobs through the local, national, and specialist press and other media, including the internet. Its purpose is to attract sufficient numbers of qualified candidates to fill job vacancies. Advertisements themselves should be clear, informative, tailored to the kind of job being advertised, and should avoid discriminatory content, including the inclusion of age-related criteria or age barriers. They should also seek to appeal to as broad a cross-section of the population as possible and avoid language or images that are gender or culture specific.

recruitment consultants are specialists that provide a service for organizations that want to outsource their recruitment and selection processes.

recruitment freeze is a policy of non-replacement of existing staff (when they choose to leave or retire) and non-recruitment of trainees. A recruitment freeze can be an effective short-term measure when an organization needs to reduce headcount as a result of structural change or changing economic conditions and has reliable human resource planning data. For example, a large corporation that typically takes graduate trainees on an annual basis may have a recruitment freeze for a year in order to ensure there is not an oversupply within the **internal labour market**.

red-circling A job is red-circled when the results of a **job evaluation** exercise reveal that it has been 'over-graded', resulting in a higher rate of pay for those doing the job than would otherwise be justified. Red-circling typically results in existing employees in these jobs having their earnings 'protected'; but new entrants to the job will start on a lower rate of pay, matched more exactly to the demands of the job.

redeployment is the act of moving employees to other jobs in the organization, rather than making them redundant. Normally redeployment involves a period of retraining and readjustment. It may also require employees to move to a different location, and a **relocation allowance** is usually offered.

red tape is a widely used colloquial term for **bureaucracy**. Typically people complain of 'too much red tape', which means they consider there are too many rules and restrictions.

redundancy is a form of **dismissal** that takes place because of a cessation or reduction in the employer's business or because the class of work carried out by employees is no longer required. Redundancy is closely regulated by employment law and in the event of redundancy employees have a number of rights that can be enforced at an **Employment Tribunal**. If there is a **collective redundancy** there must be **redundancy consultation** and for many employees there is entitlement to **redundancy pay** and time off to look for new work or for training. The rules used to select workers for redundancy must also be fair if a claim for **unfair dismissal** is to be avoided (see **compulsory redundancy**; **voluntary redundancy**). Employer use of redundancy in the UK and other countries has increased in recent years and there is growing concern over the impact of what can be a very traumatic event on employees, business, and the wider community. [See **corporate anorexia**; **downsizing**; **outplacement**; **survivor syndrome**.]

redundancy agreement A **collective agreement** that determines the procedure to be followed in the event of a redundancy in a unionized employing organization. Redundancy agreements typically provide for reliance on **voluntary redundancy**, enhanced **redundancy pay**, and more extensive support in seeking work for those made redundant.

redundancy consultation Under EU law there is a requirement on employers to consult with representatives of their workforce in the event of a **collective redundancy**. Consultation is also widely recommended as good practice. Under UK law there is a statutory duty to consult representatives of any recognized **trade union**, or, if no union is recognized, other elected representatives of the affected employees. Employee representatives may be elected solely for the purpose of consultation about redundancies or they could be part of an existing consultative body. The consultation must cover ways of avoiding redundancies, reducing the numbers to be made redundant, and mitigating the effects. It must also be undertaken with a view to reaching an agreement with the workforce representatives and must begin in good time: at least 30 days before the first dismissal takes effect if 20 to 99 employees are to be made redundant and at least 90 days before the first dismissal if 100 or more are to be made redundant. A failure to consult can result in a case going to an **Employment Tribunal**, which can make a 'protective award' as compensation to the employees.

redundancy pay is payment to an employee to compensate for loss of a job due to redundancy. In the UK, there is an entitlement to statutory redundancy pay for employees with one or more years' service. This payment is calculated on the basis of average earnings per week, years of service, and the employee's age. In many organizations this statutory payment serves as a minimum and is supplemented by an occupational redundancy scheme providing more generous payments. Redundancy payments are often negotiated by trade unions and a union presence is associated with a level of payment in excess of the statutory minimum. Occupational schemes can play an important part in inducing employees to take **voluntary redundancy**. Like the statutory scheme, they typically calculate the payment on the basis of average earnings and length of service.

redundancy procedure A redundancy procedure sets out the steps to be followed in the event of redundancy. Typically, such a procedure will include: (1) a statement of intent to maintain employment security where practicable; (2) details of consultation arrangements with trade union or other workplace representatives; (3) measures for minimizing or avoiding **compulsory redundancies**; (4) the selection criteria to be used where redundancy is unavoidable; (5) details of redundancy payments; (6) details of relocation expenses, hardship funds, and appeals procedures; and (7) the policy on helping redundant employees obtain training or search for alternative work.

re-engagement In a case of **unfair dismissal** an **Employment Tribunal** can order an employer to take back the employee and find him or her 'employment comparable to that from which he was dismissed or other suitable employment'. However, in only a minority of unfair dismissal cases is re-engagement ordered and the majority of employees receive financial compensation for the loss of their job. If an employer refuses to accept re-employment, then an 'additional award' can be made to the employee.

re-engineering tsar A key role in **business process re-engineering** (BPR), the tsar is a manager responsible for developing the re-engineering tools and techniques to be used, overseeing the whole process, and creating **synergy** from the different BPR components. The term was coined by BPR consultant Mike Hammer.

reference checks normally occur at the end of a **selection** process after a candidate has been offered a job. They are straightforward checks of factual information from referees nominated by the candidate, one of which is usually the candidate's current employer. [See **reference letters**.]

reference letters are statements of support for job applicants from people nominated by the applicant—usually previous employers, educational establishments, or clients. Not only do reference letters provide some factual information, they often include opinions about the abilities and qualities of the candidate. There are mixed views about the value of references and appointments are rarely made based on references alone. However, references can be useful when treated as another piece of information in the overall profile of the candidate being built up from various parts of the **selection** process.

refreezing (in relation to Lewin's change theory), see **unfreezing, moving, and refreezing**

regime competition refers to the pressure on nation states to provide a framework of employment law and industrial relations that is attractive to inward-investing multinational enterprises. Such pressure has intensified in Europe as a result of the creation of the Single European Market and has encouraged governments to adopt policies of labour market **deregulation**. [See **race to the bottom**.]

regime shopping is the selection of a country for inward investment by a multinational enterprise on the basis of the framework of employment law and industrial relations.

regiocentric management is an approach found in international firms where **host-country nationals** manage the subsidiaries and co-ordinate operations on a regional basis. In this sense, there is local autonomy for day-to-day decision-making and regional control over strategic aspects of the subsidiary businesses. However, the top jobs at head office are dominated by **parent-country nationals**. [See **ethnocentric management**; **geocentric management**; **polycentric management**.]

regulation theory suggests that capitalism is characterized by a regime of accumulation guided by an associated mode of regulation. The regime of accumulation is the ability to extract surplus value, whilst the mode of regulation is the mechanism through which control is exerted (particularly class relations, institutional arrangements between firms, and management–employee/capital–labour relations at work). Regulation theorists argue that historically capitalism has survived through adjusting to exploit new circumstances. They argue that the nineteenth-century accumulation regime was based on small firms/artisans with 'extensive' growth productivity and unregulated competition between firms/traders. The early/mid-twentieth-century accumulation regime was **Fordism**, with 'intensive' growth through fixed capital (for example, technical advances) under the regulation of monopoly capital. The late twentieth-/early twenty-first-century accumulation regime is **neo-Fordism**, with growth through new management techniques (such as **flexibility**, quality (see **Total Quality Management**), **teamworking**, and **just-in-time**) under the regulation of multinational capital and **globalization**. Regulation theory was pioneered by French economists, in particular Michel Aglietta, Alain Lipetz, and Robert Boyer.

regulator A role that can be adopted by a manager who is primarily responsible for personnel/human resources. Regulators devise and monitor rules and procedures for managing people. They have a hands-on approach to people management, thereby intervening rather than leaving issues to line managers. Their interventions are largely tactical; they are not involved in strategic issues. The term 'regulator' was coined by management theorist John Storey to describe one of four potential styles of managing human resources (the others being **adviser**, **changemaker**, and **handmaiden**).

rehabilitation is the provision of therapy to people who have left work because of illness or injury in order to allow them to return to employment.

reinforcement theory is based on the idea that human behaviour can be shaped through a system of reward focused on reinforcing desirable behaviour. Psychologists suggest that in a work setting managers must identify and explain to employees the desired behaviour and then devise methods of reinforcement. Reinforcement is the attempt to elicit a desirable behaviour through either the introduction of a pleasant aspect of work (positive reinforcement) or the removal of an unpleasant aspect of work (negative reinforcement). For example, in order to reward the representative with the best sales record at the end of each month, he or she could be given a bonus payment (positive reinforcement) or relieved from the tedious post-sales paperwork for the next month (negative reinforcement). For reinforcement to have full effect, psychologists have found that the reward must be valued by the person concerned, and it must follow quickly the behaviour it is designed to reinforce. So, for example, if a person does a good job, he or she should be given a reward (praise, bonus, etc.) immediately, rather than several weeks later. Reinforcement not only provides feedback about the desired behaviour, it also helps to sustain motivation. It is important not to confuse negative reinforcement with punishment—they do not mean the same thing. Punishment is the attempt to eliminate an undesirable behaviour through either the introduction of an unpleasant aspect of work or the removal of a pleasant aspect of work (sometimes called 'omission'). Whereas reinforcement is focused on the desired behaviour, punishment is focused on undesired behaviour. Therefore, punishment is considered an inferior approach because it tells employees what not to do but does not inform them about the desirable behaviour. It also fails to have any motivational effect. In reality, most workplaces have systems of both reinforcement and punishment to guide behaviour. [See also **reward**.]

reinstatement An **Employment Tribunal** can recommend reinstatement of an employee who has been unfairly dismissed; that is, the employee will return to the job that she or he held prior to the **dismissal**. If an employer refuses to accept reinstatement, the tribunal can award additional financial compensation to the employee. When the law on **unfair dismissal** was first introduced it was assumed that most employees would be either reinstated or re-engaged. In fact, this is a rare occurrence and in most cases employees accept compensation rather than return to a workplace where the working relationship has broken down. [See **re-engagement**.]

relational contract An economic exchange that assumes the characteristics of a social relationship. In many cases the **employment relationship** takes the form of a relational contract in that it is long term, open ended, and characterized by a degree of mutual trust and commitment. [See **spot contract**.]

relativity see **differential**

relayering is the process of putting back levels (layers) in the hierarchy of the organization that had previously been removed through a process of **delayering**. It occurs when the supposed benefits of delayering have not materialized and problems have emerged—particularly a loss of senior managerial control (too much lower-level autonomy), overburdening of lower-level managers (too much responsibility), or a lack of organization-wide co-ordination (too much fragmentation).

reliability When a particular selection technique is used to decide between job applicants, it ought to be reliable. This means that the particular technique will produce consistent results. For example, if a person takes two separate IQ tests on different days, in similar circumstances, they ought to yield similar results. If they fail to do so, the IQ test can be said to be unreliable. However, it is not sufficient for a selection technique simply to be reliable, it must also be valid. [See **validity**.]

relocation allowance A one-off payment made to an employee who is obliged to move to another geographical location because of the requirements of his or her job. In some circumstances, such as when managers decide to move the whole organization to a **greenfield site**, relocation might be paid to the whole of the workforce. In managerial and professional occupations, relocation allowances are sometimes offered to new members of staff to assist their move—particularly where this requires selling their home and relocating a family.

remote conferencing see video-conferencing

remuneration is payment for work, which can assume a number of different forms, including a basic wage or **salary**, supplementary cash payments, such as **shift pay** and overtime pay, and **benefits** in kind. A series of legal judgments at the European Court of Justice have effectively expanded the legal definition of remuneration, which is now very broad. Ex gratia payments and **occupational pensions**, for instance, are now legally defined as aspects of remuneration within European equality law.

remuneration committee A subcommittee of the board of directors within an enterprise that is charged with setting the pay package for individual executive directors. It is generally recommended that remuneration committees be composed solely of non-executive directors to minimize the risk of executives determining their own income. The use of remuneration committees has increased in the UK in recent years as a result of public concern over levels of executive remuneration and the recommendations of the Cadbury and Greenbury committees on corporate governance. [See **executive pay**.]

repatriation is the process of returning managers from abroad to their own country after they have been working for a subsidiary of a multinational organization. On return, the process should include a programme of readjustment to the parent organization, debriefing, and career planning.

repetitive strain injury (RSI) is a generic term used for a group of industrial injuries that are caused by fast, repetitive work (for example, tenosynovitis, carpal tunnel syndrome). Usually they affect the hands and arms, but can also be associated with neck and back strain. [See **vibration**.]

Reporting of Injuries, Diseases, and Dangerous Occurrences Regulations (RIDDOR) These regulations came into force in 1995. They give effect to European legislation in the UK and require employers to report injuries, illnesses, and dangerous occurrences either to the environmental health department of a local authority (for office, retail, hospitality, and similar businesses) or to the **Health and Safety Executive** for other kinds of business. [See **health and safety regulations**.]

representation gap The representation gap refers to the fact that a significant proportion of workers in non-union enterprises would like to be represented either by a **trade union** or by some other form of representative body. It is a product of the decline of trade unionism and **collective bargaining** and the continued aspiration of many employees to participate in the government of industry through representative institutions. The existence of the representation gap suggests that for many workers management communication and attempts at **employee involvement** are not an adequate substitute for independent representation at work.

reserved seat A stipulation that a place or places on trade union executive committees are reserved for women or members of minority groups. Reserved seats are used by trade unions to increase the presence of women and minorities in important policy-making forums and correct their under-representation in the past. They form part of a wider reform of **union government** designed to provide greater voice for women and other groups whose interests previously have been marginal to union concerns.

reservism see zero-hours contracts

resignation is the voluntary termination of a **contract of employment** by an employee, usually to take up a job at another employing organization. Having handed in a letter of resignation an employee in most cases is contractually obliged to work a **notice period** before leaving his or her employment. [See **garden leave**.]

resource-based view A perspective that theorizes how firms can achieve sustained **competitive advantage**. It has become of interest to those studying human resource management because it suggests that human capital resources (training, experience, judgment, knowledge, relationships, etc.) can be one of the key resources that a firm might use to develop a value-creating strategy. For a resource to provide sustained competitive advantage it must have the following four characteriztics. (1) Value—the resource must have the capacity to exploit opportunities or neutralize threats in the firm's environment. (2) Rarity—the resource must be very rare or unique so that current or potential competitors cannot exploit the resource in the same way. (3) Imperfect imitability—it must not be possible to copy the resource. This lack of imitability is likely to come from the firm's unique historical conditions, its social complexity, and the causal ambiguity between the resources possessed by the firm and its sustained competitive advantage. (4) Non-substitutability—it must not be possible to replace the resource with a similar resource, or a different resource that has an equivalent effect. Only when a resource exhibits all four of these characteristics can it be said to be a source of sustained competitive advantage. One of the key commentators on the resource-based view is management theorist Jay Barney.

responsible autonomy and direct control are terms coined by sociologist Andrew Friedman. Responsible autonomy is the management technique of allowing employees more discretion and greater variety in their work (using methods suggested by **job redesign**). In contrast, direct control is the technique of closely supervising the work of employees, who are allowed to undertake only a narrow range of tasks (using methods suggested by **scientific management**). Responsible autonomy is more likely to enlist commitment from employees, but does not guarantee compliance with management wishes. Direct control is more likely to ensure compliance, but does not create or encourage commitment from employees. Within an organization, both techniques might be used for different groups of employees; for example, responsible autonomy for highly skilled **core employees** in scare supply, but direct control over low-skilled **peripheral workers** who are easily replaced. [See **high trust; low trust**.]

restriction of output is the deliberate limiting of output by individual employees and work groups. Restriction of output has been widely observed and is a feature of work behaviour in many different occupations. Understanding and eliminating the problem has also been a major concern of the social and management sciences. Taylor's system of **scientific management** was developed to overcome what he called systematic **soldiering** by employees, and in the 1930s the **human relations** school explained restriction of output in terms of the psychological pressure on individuals to conform to workgroup **norms**. More recently, restriction of output has been viewed as economically rational behaviour by employees intended to reduce effort levels and counter management attempts to intensify work. Despite the vogue for 'high performance' and 'high commitment' work systems, restriction of output continues to be a feature of many work situations.

restrictive practice A method of working that is enforced by a **trade union** or workgroup that limits management's freedom to organize work and deploy labour. Examples of restrictive practices might include the specification of minimum staffing levels, a requirement that work tasks are undertaken by members of a particular union or trade, or customary norms over the amount of work to be completed in the course of the working day. The elimination of restrictive practices has been a major concern of successive attempts to reform British industrial relations. Evidence for the intensification and restructuring of work since the recession of the early 1980s suggests that many such practices have been abandoned or have been broken in a period of management ascendancy. [See **protective practice**.]

résumé see **curriculum vitae**

retention is the ability to hold on to employees. Where an organization finds that it is losing valuable staff (such as those with scarce skills or specialist knowledge) it may be said to have a 'retention problem'. However, irrespective of whether an organization has retention problems, it is seen as good practice to develop a retention plan based on collecting and analysing data from (1) an ongoing **attitude survey** (typically once a year) to test the climate of opinions within the organization; (2) a regular **salary survey**; (3) a **training needs analysis**; and (4) **exit interviews**. The retention plan should form part of the broader **human resource plan** because retention is a critical component in managing **human resource flow**.

retirement occurs when someone leaves employment, not for another job, but because their normal working life has come to an end. It occurs usually because an individual has reached the contractual age for retirement (commonly 60 or 65), though individuals may take **early retirement** before this point either for medical reasons or as an alternative to **redundancy**. When people retire they rely on an occupational, state, or personal **pension** for their income. In the UK the state pension used to be available to women at 60 and men at 65 but under European equality legislation the age is being harmonized at 65. This state retirement age influences the age of retirement in many **contracts of employment**. It should be noted that many retired people continue to work on a voluntary basis or in part-time employment. Indeed, some companies deliberately target retired people in their **recruitment** because they are thought to be particularly reliable employees.

retraining is the process of teaching employees new skills so that they can be redeployed in the organization. It is particularly relevant where changes in technology have meant that employee skills have become obsolete. Retraining is an alternative to redundancy, although managers might not deem it appropriate to offer retraining to employees, preferring instead to recruit skilled staff from the **external labour market**. Similarly, some employees might be unwilling or unable to retrain, and might prefer to accept a **redundancy payment** and seek similar work elsewhere.

reverse discrimination see **positive discrimination**

reward In its broadest sense 'reward' is used to refer to the benefits which employees receive in return for working on behalf of an employing organization. Rewards can therefore assume a number of different forms, though there are two main forms: **extrinsic rewards**, which take the form of cash payments and employment **benefits**, like staff discounts, **occupational pensions, health insurance**, and **company cars**; and **intrinsic rewards** such as **job satisfaction**, recognition, **personal development**, and the social status which may be attached to particular job roles. There is increasing attention to the use of non-traditional or intrinsic rewards by management, and recognition or award schemes are now commonplace in many companies and are used to celebrate and reinforce high performance. Despite this shift, 'reward' is also commonly used in a narrower sense to refer to pay and benefits. In this respect, it is simply a fashionable term for an established aspect of HRM which has a more positive connotation than equivalent labels, such as **compensation** or **remuneration**.

reward management is that aspect of HRM that deals with the management of **remuneration** and, potentially, with the management of **intrinsic rewards**, such as recognition of employee achievement. The term 'reward management' has partly replaced earlier labels that were applied to this field, such as 'compensation and benefits' and 'salary administration'. While the change is partly a matter of fashion, the inclusion of the word 'management' is meant to signify a more proactive, deliberate approach, in which **payment systems** are used as tools to secure strategic business objectives. [See **new pay**; **strategic pay**.]

rightsizing means getting rid of employees. Some organizations use this term instead of **downsizing**, which is considered too negative a word because it suggests a decline in the organization's fortunes. Rightsizing supposedly conveys the more positive image of the organization achieving the correct number of staff to meet its business needs. But whether you have been rightsized or downsized, it means the same thing: you no longer have a job.

right to representation Under the Employment Relations Act 1999 workers in the UK have the right to be represented by a trade union officer in company disciplinary and grievance **procedures**. The right is restricted to serious cases, where there is a prospect of dismissal or an accusation of unlawful action by the employer. Despite these limitations the provision of the right to representation has been widely regarded as presenting an organizing opportunity to trade unions because it confers a legal entitlement to enter non-union companies. [See **recognition**.]

right-to-work laws are laws that outlaw the 'union shop' or **closed shop** in many of the states of the USA. Where the 'right to work' is framed in state legislation there is no compulsory unionism and union membership tends to be lower.

ripple effect When an employee is promoted or transferred, it automatically creates a job vacancy. If this vacancy is filled through internal recruitment, a second vacancy arises, which in turn may be filled through internal recruitment leading to a further vacancy. In other words, the promotion can create a ripple effect throughout the organization, which only comes to a halt when a vacancy is filled through external recruitment.

risk assessment Under **health and safety regulations** employers are required to undertake a risk assessment to identify possible threats to **health and safety** within the workplace. There is an obligation to identify and record hazards, review the risk assessment periodically in the light of workplace change and the record of accidents, and apply methods to prevent or reduce risks. The obligation on employers to identify and remove risks at work is qualified to the extent that employers must only do what is 'reasonably practicable'. This does not mean, however, that employers can avoid their obligations by saying they cannot afford them.

rituals (in relation to **organizational culture**) are routines undertaken on a regular basis which help to reinforce the organizational beliefs and values.

role ambiguity occurs when employees are unclear about the responsibilities and the remit of their job. This may arise because of the absence of an up-to-date job description. However, role ambiguity can also occur when employees are encouraged by management to increase their **functional flexibility**, without specifying the boundaries to this flexibility. [See **job stress**.]

role conflict occurs when employees are faced with incompatible demands from different parts of their job, or from different people and groups at work. It can also be experienced when people attempt to juggle their work and home commitments to satisfy the expectations of their managers and their families. [See **job stress**.]

Roman-German system A model of industrial relations in which the state plays a dominant role. **Freedom of association** and the right to withdraw labour are guaranteed in a written constitution and there is an extensive statutory labour code, which regulates all major aspects of the employment relationship. Countries that approximate to the Roman-German system include Belgium, France, Germany, Italy, and the Netherlands. Because of the dominance of this model within Europe it has necessarily influenced the social policy of the European Union, and member states with a tradition of **voluntarism**, such as the UK, Ireland, and Denmark, have moved towards the Roman-German pattern in recent years.

rookie A person who is new to a job or an organization. [See **induction**; **socialization**.]

S

sabotage is the deliberate breaking of machinery or disruption of business processes by aggrieved employees. Sabotage can take a wide variety of forms including tampering with equipment, adulterating food, wilfully damaging products, insulting customers, or manipulating software. In most cases it is initiated by individuals or small groups of employees and is usually classed as a type of informal **industrial conflict** or protest. It can arise for a number of reasons but two interpretations are dominant in the academic literature. The first sees sabotage as a response on the part of workers to alienating work that is tedious and lacking in meaning for those who perform it. The second views sabotage as economically rational behaviour that is used by employees to reduce the intensity of work or as a means of pressurizing management to make concessions. [See **Luddite**.]

sacking and 'getting the sack' are colloquial terms for **dismissal**.

safety and health is the term used for **health and safety** in North America.

safety committee Every employer requested in writing to do so by two or more **safety representatives** must establish a safety committee. The size and functions of the committee must also be agreed with safety representatives. The typical work of safety committees includes analyzing trends in accidents and workplace diseases, developing safety rules, arranging for safety training, and advising on safety education and advice.

safety culture The set of attitudes and work practices within an organization that either inhibits or promotes risk-taking and other forms of behaviour that threaten workplace **health and safety**.

safety representatives Under the Safety Representatives and Safety Committee Regulations (SRSCR) 1997 workers have rights in UK law to appoint safety representatives. Where there is trade union **recognition**, these representatives must be appointed by the union from among its members within the enterprise. Where there is no recognized union, employers must consult directly with employees or with non-union representatives elected specifically for this purpose. Safety representatives have a number of rights in law and are also protected from victimization. Their role is to carry out inspections of the workplace, receive information from management, investigate accidents, and represent workers' concerns about **health and safety** to the employer. Under the SRSCR safety representatives have the right to paid time off work to carry out their safety functions and to undergo training.

salariat is a pop-sociological term to refer to salary earners; in other words, wage earners in higher-status, better-remunerated employment. The term is derived from, but also used as a counter to, the Marxist notion of the **proletariat**, with its associated belief in the formation of a relatively undifferentiated and exploited working class.

salary The annual rate of remuneration for a job, which is based, at least notionally, on the number of weeks or hours worked per year. The payment of an annual salary has been associated particularly with managerial, professional, and other white-collar employment but has spread in recent years to manual work as part of the movement to **single-status** employment. Receipt of a salary has often formed part of a relatively diffuse employment relationship in which payment takes the form of a 'consideration' for loyal and dedicated service in a managerial or professional role. The spread of **performance management** and **performance-related pay** schemes in recent years, however, has led to a tighter definition of the employment contract for many salary earners and it is now common for **salary progression** to be dependent on the formal assessment of performance.

salary matrix A chart that can be used to determine the annual salary award and rate of **salary progression** of an individual employee. A salary matrix allows two variables to be taken into account in deciding the level of an award: the individual's performance rating and the position already attained within the salary range. An individual with a 'fully acceptable' performance rating, for example, could receive a 5 per cent increase when at the bottom of the range, a 3 per cent increase at the mid-point, and 1 per cent above the mid-point. The same level of performance rating, therefore, results in different levels of salary award depending on existing salary.

salary progression Increases in salary that result from movement up an **incremental scale**, **pay range**, or band. Such movement may be determined by several factors, including **seniority**, performance rating, assessments of skill or competence, or success in obtaining formal qualifications. Seniority-based progression, in which increases in salary are awarded with each year of service, is based on the assumption that competence or performance increases as employees become more experienced. There has been a trend in recent years, however, to try to measure competence and performance directly, and it is now common for payment to be determined through a formal system of **performance management**. As a consequence, employees with the same level of seniority may progress through scales and ranges at different speeds and to different levels. Other recent changes include greater discretion for line managers in determining progression and greater scope for progression (i.e. to increase salary while staying in the same grade) within broad-banded salary structures.

salary review The regular review of an individual's salary conducted most frequently by the employee's immediate **line manager**. Salary reviews may involve a degree of negotiation between manager and subordinate and in many cases are based on an assessment of performance. Where the latter is the case, there may be a right of appeal to the line manager's line manager or 'grandparent'. Salary reviews are an important feature of an individualized system of human resource management in which there is at least the semblance of managing individual employees in accordance with their individual requirements and capabilities.

salary survey Salary or pay surveys seek to establish rates of pay for particular occupations within given industrial sectors. Their purpose is to allow employers to set rates of pay that are broadly in line with those offered by companies using the same types of labour. As such, salary surveys are a means of managing labour supply and avoiding **recruitment** and **retention** problems. In many cases the results of the survey are provided only to those employers who take part in the survey, thereby encouraging participation. Salary surveys may be regular, annual events or intermittent, designed to inform a one-off pay determination exercise. They are usually commissioned, rather than undertaken by companies themselves, and **management consultants** and **employers' associations** frequently provide this service. Companies typically use the results of surveys to decide their 'salary posture'; where they will 'sit' in the external labour market. A blue chip firm, anxious to attract high-calibre recruits, may position its salaries above the upper quartile of the range revealed by the survey. A less prominent company, in contrast, may choose to set rates of pay at or below the median.

sales commission A form of **sales incentive** which provides employees with a bonus proportionate to the financial value of sales.

sales incentive An output-based **payment system** which is widely used in retail and other sectors and which links the remuneration of sales staff, either individually or collectively, to the value of sales. Sales incentives take a number of different forms, including 'commission-only' schemes, in which all earnings are dependent on sales, and schemes which offer bonuses and commission on top of a basic salary. It is also common for the reward to assume a non-cash form with successful sales staff being rewarded through holidays, consumer goods, recognition awards, and enhanced benefits. Underlying all of these schemes is the assumption that sales staff can be motivated to sell more goods if earnings are related to the value of sales or dependent on the attainment of a sales target, and in many situations they can prove highly effective. There are cases, however, of sales incentives generating severe **perverse effects**, most notably in the financial services industry where they have been associated with the mis-selling of private pensions, endowment mortgages, and insurance. Some companies in this sector now explicitly state in their advertising that their sales force does not work to an incentive in order to reassure customers about the accuracy of the information and advice given.

satisficing The management of an organization to attain acceptable rather than optimal levels of performance.

Save-As-You-Earn (SAYE) share option scheme The SAYE **share option** scheme was introduced in the UK in 1980 as part of the Thatcher government's policy to create a 'shareholding democracy'. Under the scheme employees open a saving plan and make regular contributions from their earnings for a period of three, five, or seven years. The accumulated sum can then be used to exercise a share option and buy shares in the company at a pre-arranged price. If the shares are subsequently sold, employees do not pay tax unless the income gained is high enough to qualify for capital gains tax. SAYE schemes are all-employee, Inland Revenue-approved schemes and to qualify for tax incentives all employees and directors must be able to participate on similar terms. An alternative name for SAYE schemes is Sharesave. [See **employee share ownership**; **financial participation**.]

scab is the traditional, abusive term used by trade unionists to describe those who refuse to join or take other action to break a strike, including accepting employment as a replacement for a striking worker.

scientific management (or Taylorism) is a management theory based on a belief that there is one best way of organizing work.

It advocates the use of 'scientific techniques', such as time and motion studies, to measure work activities to find the optimum method of performing them. Once analysed, the activities can be centrally planned by managers and specialized, simple tasks clearly prescribed for each employee. In organizing the work, managers must be guided by four principles: (1) the division of manual and mental labour; (2) careful selection and training of employees to fit the job; (3) control of employees through close supervision; (4) rewards linked directly to productivity through **piece-rate** payments. The result is highly fragmented and prescribed work, no opportunity for employees to use their discretion, and constant supervision to monitor performance. The ideas of scientific management were proposed by Frederick W. Taylor (hence Taylorism) at the beginning of the twentieth century, yet they still remain relevant at the beginning of the twenty-first century because some of the world's leading companies (such as McDonald's) organize aspects of their work according to Tayloristic principles.

Scottish National Vocational Qualifications (SNVQs) are the Scottish equivalent of the **National Vocational Qualifications**.

seasonal-hours contracts are contracts of employment that allow for variation in the length of the working week at different time of the year to match peaks and troughs in demand. This means that instead of hiring and firing employees, they are given permanent contracts with variations in contracted weekly hours across the year.

secondary action is industrial action by a trade union that is directed against employers other than the one with which it is in dispute. The aim is to disrupt the primary employer's business and exert pressure by spreading the action to other companies located in the same industry or along the primary employer's supply chain. Secondary action can take various forms, such as the refusal to handle material or components bought from or being supplied to the primary employer. It might also involve sympathy action by workers in other unions remote from the dispute, as when coal miners strike in support of nurses. In the UK, the Employment Act 1990 rendered all forms of secondary action unlawful, including sympathy action and action directed at the primary employer's customers and suppliers. This represents a significant weakening of the right to strike and effectively confines lawful strike activity to the individual enterprise or a group of associated enterprises.

secondary boycott see **secondary action**

secondary picketing see **picketing**

second job An additional job that may be held in either of two circumstances: first, where an employee has a primary full-time job but takes on an additional job (e.g. evening bar work) to supplement his or her income and, secondly, where an employee has a number of separate **part-time** jobs to secure a 'full-time' income. [See **component wage job; moonlighting**.]

second-order strategy is a term coined by management theorists John Purcell and Bruce Ahlstrand in relation to **M-form** companies to refer to decisions concerning the internal operating procedures and relationships between parts of the firm—in particular the looseness or tightness between the corporate office, divisions, and operating subsidiaries. [See **first-order strategy; third-order strategy**.]

security of employment is the policy of guaranteeing continuity of employment for employees as long as they meet performance expectations and show loyalty to the organization. However, security of employment is increasingly rare because of the contemporary emphasis on **numerical flexibility**. [See **psychological contract**.]

segregation see **horizontal segregation; vertical segregation**

selection is the process of assessing job applicants using one or a variety of methods with the purpose of finding the most suitable person for the organization. It is the stage that follows the recruitment process, whereby a pool of possible candidates has been generated. A wide range of selection techniques can be used and ideally these are chosen according to the type of job vacancy to be filled.

The techniques are designed to reveal attributes, skills, and qualities of the individual that indicate their suitability for the job. This means that only appropriate selection techniques ought to be used. The use of techniques that have **reliability** and **validity** is more likely to lead to an appropriate selection decision and the appointment of a suitable candidate. Selection techniques include: **assessment centres**, **biodata**, **graphology**, **interviews**, **psychometric tests**, **reference checks**, and **work sampling**.

selective strike A **strike** that involves only a proportion of the union members involved in an industrial **dispute** and therefore reduces the cost of **industrial action** to the union. Selective strikes typically rely on groups of workers in particular workplaces or occupations who are well organized and who can have a significant disruptive effect on the employer's business. Less well organized and less militant groups of union members are thereby sheltered from the demands of taking industrial action. [See **pin-point strike**.]

self-actualization is the process of achieving one's full potential as an independent, fulfilled, free-thinking, human being. Normally it is used in connection with **motivation** theory—most notably **Maslow's hierarchy of needs**, where self-actualization is considered the pinnacle of human needs that can be satisfied after lower-order needs are met. Self-actualized employees are working at their full creative potential and are clearly valuable to an organization. However, relatively few people achieve self-actualization through work, others self-actualize outside work, and the remainder fail to satisfy their self-actualization needs at all.

self-appraisal is the technique of evaluating your own performance and then discussing this with your **line manager**. Some organizations use this technique as part of their **appraisal** process because it provides employees with an opportunity to reflect on their own performance and explain the reasons behind their own evaluation. This is thought to lead to a more positive and less judgmental appraisal interview. [See **peer appraisal**.]

self-directed team see **self-managed team**

self-efficacy is an individual's belief that he or she will be able to complete tasks, acquire knowledge, or achieve goals. Self-efficacy is a psychological theory of **motivation**, in that individuals are more likely to be motivated to attempt tasks or pursue goals when their sense of self-efficacy is high. The practical significance of the theory is that employing organizations should rely upon training, development, and positive reinforcement to build the sense of self-efficacy of employees.

self-employed In the UK the self-employed make up about 13 per cent of the total workforce. They are made up of individuals who work for a living but who do not have a **contract of employment**. Instead they sell their services to employers and in law are said to have a contract *for* service, rather than a contract *of* service. Amongst the self-employed it is important to distinguish between the self-employed with employees of their own and the self-employed who rely solely on their own labour. The **employment status** of self-employed workers can be a matter of dispute and in some cases employers may attempt to rely on **false self-employment** to disguise the fact that an employment relationship exists. [See **freelance**.]

self-managed team (SMT) A group of functionally flexible employees that have the responsibility for directing and controlling their own work. They do not have a supervisor, but will nominate a team leader, who will co-ordinate the activities of team members and act as a central point of communication. The team leader role will rotate amongst members of the team. Truly self-managed teams also have the responsibility for hiring and firing, setting pay levels, handling grievance, and managing disputes—although few organizations have gone this far. Self-managed teams are a logical extension of the concept of **teamworking**, but, in practice, the meaning of the term 'self-managed team' varies extensively between organizations. [See also **empowerment**.]

self-organization is a principle increasingly adopted by **trade unions** in which women and minority groups are encouraged to develop their own forms of organization. The most prominent example is UNISON, whose founding constitution allows for the creation and resourcing of a number of self-organized groups (SOGs), for women, black workers, the disabled, and gays and lesbians. The SOGs are meant to provide a space in which these groups can independently develop their own policy agenda, without their interests and identity being lost within the 'mainstream' union. SOGs also provide a mechanism through which women and minorities can inform and influence wider union policy. The adoption of the principle of self-organization is indicative of an increased trend within unions to accommodate and represent diversity, which according to some reflects the fragmentation and multiplication of social identities within a postmodern society.

seniority is the principle that employment rewards should be contingent on length of service within the employing organization. Examples of seniority include the payment of an annual salary increment for each year of service and allocating promotions or selecting employees for redundancy on the basis of length of service. Reliance on the principle of seniority derives from two sources: from a belief that competence is related to experience and from a conviction that seniority is fair, especially because it removes the scope for managers to exercise discretion and favouritism when making decisions on reward, deployment, promotion, and redundancy. There might also be an assumption that long-serving employees have demonstrated loyalty to the employing organization and so are entitled to reciprocal treatment. Despite these arguments, the principle of seniority has been subject to considerable attack in recent years. It has been argued that managers should take decisions on reward and labour use and that seniority rules lead to the sub-optimum use of human resources. **Salary progression**, **promotion**, deployment, and selection for **redundancy**, it is felt by many, should be based on performance. From a different perspective, it is argued that seniority is indirectly discriminatory and can work to the systematic disadvantage of women workers, who are more likely to experience breaks in their employment. There have been legal judgments which have found seniority-based pay and redundancy systems to be discriminatory and there have also been legal challenges to the use of the seniority principle in employment protection legislation, much of which requires twelve months' service before employment rights are obtained. [See **last-in-first-out**.]

sequential interview Several interviewers undertake separate, individual selection interviews with each of the candidates.

servicing model A form of trade unionism in which activism and self-representation by union members are discouraged in favour of the provision of services by paid **full-time officers**. These services may include **collective bargaining** or the provision of advice, representation, and consumer benefits to individual union members. The servicing model is often counter-posed to the **organizing model**.

7-S framework see McKinsey 7-S framework

severance pay see redundancy pay

sex discrimination see discrimination

sexism is the ideology and practice of discriminating against someone on the basis of their sex. It is based on the belief that there are innate natural abilities of men and women which justify their unequal treatment. Almost invariably this leads to a woman being treated less favourably than a man, thus sexism has become associated with women's disadvantage. In theory, sexism could work to men's disadvantage, but the important point to recognize is that whilst men dominate positions of power and influence such a scenario is implausible. However, there are instances where discrimination on the basis of sex has unfairly disadvantaged men, and some successful legal claims have been made against employers. It is important not to confuse sexism with simply recognizing that men and women differ. Sexism is where one group uses this difference to justify worse treatment of the other. [See **equal opportunity**.]

sex-typing of jobs is the process through which some jobs come to be labelled as 'women's work', appropriate to a female workforce, and others are regarded as 'men's work'. The gendering of jobs in this manner is an important source of **horizontal segregation** in the labour market. Sex-typing often reflects the division of labour in the home, and many women's jobs involve caring work and extend the province of female domestic labour into the sphere of paid work. It is important to recognize, however, that the assumed sex of particular jobs and occupations can shift over time; clerical work for instance was once male dominated but was progressively feminized during the twentieth century. [See **feminization**.]

sexual contract The sexual contract refers to the normal domestic division of labour, in which the majority of unpaid housework is performed by women, thus releasing men for full-time involvement in the labour market. The different types of employment contract for men and women, therefore, and the fact that women are much more likely to work **part-time**, reflect this prior sexual contract.

sexual harassment is defined by the EU as 'unwanted conduct of a sexual nature, or other conduct based on sex affecting the dignity of men and women at work'. The perpetrators of this conduct may be colleagues, superiors, clients, or customers. Research indicates that sexual harassment is a common and disturbing experience for many women at work and has also been experienced by a significant minority of men. Research also indicates that harassers are often superiors who use their position of power and authority to bully, victimize, or exploit members of the opposite sex. Importantly, sexual harassment, like other forms of **harassment**, is defined in terms of the experience and perceptions of the person who is harassed and not in terms of the perceptions of the harasser. The EU issued a Code of Practice on sexual harassment in 1992 together with a Commission Recommendation (1991) that member states adopt the code. Pressure is building currently for further legislative action and the Commission issued a proposed amendment to the Equal Treatment Directive in 2000 that will outlaw sexual harassment. Under UK law there is some protection from sexual harassment under the Sex Discrimination Act 1975, which outlaws detrimental treatment on the grounds of sex. [See **workplace bullying**.]

sexual orientation refers to the sexuality of individuals and the nature of their sexual preferences, including those of gays and lesbians. It is an issue of relevance to human resource management because it is argued widely that employers should take action to prevent discrimination against individuals because of their sexuality. There is also mounting legal pressure to outlaw such discrimination. The European Court of Human Rights has ruled that the UK government's ban on the employment of gays and lesbians in the armed forces is unlawful and this has prompted a review of employment practice across the public sector. In 2000 the Department for Education and Employment issued a voluntary code to minimize discrimination against workers on the grounds of their sexual orientation. The European Commission has also proposed amending the Equal Treatment Directive to outlaw this kind of discrimination. [See **gender reassignment**.]

sex work is paid employment in the sex industry, comprising prostitution and pornography. The term is used to emphasize the commonality between work in this industry and other, more conventional occupations. Thus, campaigners for the decriminalization of prostitution use the term to stress that sex workers should have the same status and legal protection as others engaged in paid employment. [See **body work; emotional labour**.]

shadowing is a training technique whereby trainees spend time with experienced employees closely observing how they undertake their work, and then undertaking the tasks themselves (with guidance from the experts). Typically it has been used to familiarize trainee managers with the work of various departments to give them an understanding of the overall process. [See **training**.]

shared-screen conferencing is a process that involves connecting the computers of participants so that information can be shared or interaction (via the keyboard) can take place in real time. Unlike **video-conferencing** there is no audio or visual image of the conference participants.

shared services are HR services that are concentrated in a call centre or service centre within an organization and accessed by managers from different business divisions and **strategic business units** via telephone or company intranet. In large multinational companies shared services may be provided from a single centre to managers across the globe, with service centre staff fielding enquiries and offering advice to managers on a broad range of company policy.

share option The opportunity to buy shares at a future date at the price when the option is made available. Share options are an important feature of the remuneration of executives, though other groups may also have access to this benefit. Their rationale is to allow employees to share in the success of the company and provide an incentive to contribute to that success, as an increase in the share price will enable the recipient to gain when the option is exercised. Most employees, including executives, sell their shares to reap an immediate dividend on exercising the option. Share options for executives have been widely criticized because they have allowed lacklustre managers to reap enormous windfall gains that reflect general movements in the stock market rather than their own level of input. [See **Company Share Option Plan; employee share ownership; Enterprise Management Incentive; executive pay; Save-As-You-Earn (SAYE) share option scheme**.]

sharesave see Save-As-You-Earn (SAYE) share option scheme

shift pay is a **premium payment** made to shiftworkers to acknowledge the demands and inconvenience of early or late shifts and night work. Shift pay, like other premium payments, is typically expressed as a multiple of an **hourly rate**. Thus, a shiftworker on an early or late shift might receive time and a fifth or time and a third of the basic hourly rate for the job or grade, while a worker on permanent nights might receive time and a half or even double time.

shiftworking allows establishments to work continuously by deploying a large workforce across (typically) three segments in the working day: early shifts, late shifts, and night shifts. In many instances employees will rotate across these shifts from week to week, although in some organizations employees are on fixed shifts for longer periods of time, or are even permanently on a particular shift. Of course shift patterns and arrangements differ from establishment to establishment, and may be combined with other forms of **temporal flexibility**. Shiftworking may be required by the organization because of the work processes involved—for example, the postal service and supermarkets with twenty-four-hour trading—or it may be due to the desire by management to make full use of equipment and plant—for example, the oil industry.

shop steward A lay trade union officer who represents co-workers at workplace level. Shop steward representation originated in traditional manufacturing industries in the UK but has since spread widely throughout the economy and the central role of the shop steward in workplace industrial relations has long been a distinctive feature of the UK system. Essentially, shop stewards are the face of trade unionism within the workplace. Potentially they can perform a wide range of functions including recruitment of new union members, representation of individuals involved in disciplinary and grievance cases, advising members on union services, employment law, and welfare matters, and negotiating with managers on terms and conditions of employment. In large workplaces shop steward organization may be relatively sophisticated, with a hierarchy of steward roles, headed by a senior shop steward or **convenor**, and with formal policy developed by a **joint shop stewards' committee** (JSSC), comprised of steward representatives of different unions. In large companies, steward organization may extend beyond the workplace, with a **combine committee** acting as a co-ordinating body. In the 1950s and 1960s shop steward numbers increased greatly and the rise of the shop steward was seen to constitute a 'challenge from below' both to the established leadership of trade unions and to the formal system of multi-employer collective bargaining. Since that period the formalization of workplace and company-level bargaining has led to greater acceptance by unions and employers of the shop steward role and, indeed, it is common practice for managers to support steward organization through **facilities agreements** which provide for paid time off work for union representatives. According to some critics, management sponsorship of stewards in this way has led to the '**incorporation**' of workplace leadership and a decline in the radical potential of workplace trade unionism. While employer support for steward organization continues in unionized companies, there have been cases of support being withdrawn or scaled down. The growth of **employee involvement** and **teamworking** is also regarded by some as a means of bypassing the shop steward and developing new lines of direct communication between management and workforce.

short-termism is the tendency to judge a policy or course of action by assessing its effects using a relatively short time horizon: for example, assessing the payback of investing in a piece of new technology by evaluating efficiency improvements within six months. Whilst short-termism is clearly of value in encouraging managers to make decisions that can be judged relatively quickly—such as the next quarter, or within the financial year—it dissuades them from longer-term investment. For some aspects of personnel, this can have particularly disadvantageous effects, especially where there has been a **devolution** of decision-making to **line managers**. For example, line managers might be reluctant to invest in employee **training** if the advantages of such an investment are likely to be realized in the medium or long term, rather than the short term. Such a scenario is particularly likely when line managers themselves are judged against short-term performance objectives. Therefore, short-termism is often seen to be counter to some of the human resource management rhetoric that advocates valuing and developing employees.

shunto The Spring Labour Offensive in Japan, when the Japanese trade union movement submits wage demands to the employer.

The shunto provides a means of co-ordinating wage bargaining within Japan, which has a seemingly highly fragmented system of industrial relations based on **enterprise unions**. The degree of co-ordination results in relatively narrow **pay dispersion** (wage inequality) across the Japanese economy. [See **co-ordinated bargaining**.]

sick building syndrome (SBS) occurs when work-related health problems are prevalent among the occupants of a particular building. SBS is recognized by the World Health Organization, which lists a range of symptoms, such as eye, nose, and throat irritation, skin rash, mental fatigue, headaches. Cynics argue that there is no such thing as SBS because it is difficult to establish any causal links between the building and the health problems. Defenders of SBS reply that such a view is naive and point out that the same dismissive attitude has proven to be both wrong and damaging in the past regarding other occupational health problems—for example, pneumoconiosis from working in coal mines or asbestosis from working in buildings with asbestos insulation. The causes of SBS are thought to be related to features of the building, such as ventilation, lighting, and airborne pollutants, and aspects of the working conditions, such as workload and breaks.

sick pay is payment to employees during a period of illness. In most occupational sick pay schemes there is provision for full pay during an initial period illness with payment at a reduced rate for more extended illness. In the UK, there is also a **Statutory Sick Pay** scheme based on National Insurance Contributions.

single-employer bargaining is **collective bargaining** between trade unions and a single employer, which potentially can be conducted at different levels within the company. Single-employer bargaining can take the form of **enterprise bargaining** or may be conducted at a lower level and result in agreements that cover a particular workplace, business division, or business unit. All these forms can be contrasted with **multi-employer bargaining**, where agreements cover a large number of different firms and are conducted at industry level. In the UK the historical trend has been for single-employer bargaining to assume greater importance. [See **decentralization of bargaining**.]

single status refers to the provision of common terms and conditions of employment to all employees of a single enterprise. It means, essentially, that all workers of whatever grade will share the same set of employment **benefits** (pension, sick pay, annual leave, parental and maternity provisions) and be paid through the same mechanism (e.g. annual **salary**). Single status contrasts with the traditional 'status divide' between hourly paid manual workers and salaried staff and may arise either from trade union negotiating pressure or from a desire on the part of the employer to foster teamwork and commitment. The achievement of single status can be costly and for this reason there may be only incomplete **harmonization** of employment conditions across the workforce hierarchy.

single-table bargaining The arrangement whereby multiple unions within an enterprise act as a single representative entity for the purpose of **collective bargaining** with the employer. Single-table bargaining is a means of reducing the divisive effects of **multi-unionism** and has increased in frequency as a result of an employer policy to rationalize collective bargaining arrangements.

single-union agreement A form of trade union **recognition** pioneered in the UK by the electricians' union EETPU (now part of the AEEU) during the 1980s. Single-union agreements are also known as 'new style' and 'strike-free' agreements and involve the granting of recognition to a single **trade union** in return for guarantees on the avoidance of conflict and the promotion of co-operation between management and employees within the workplace. These agreements typically comprise a package of measures including, on the one hand, employer support for the union and the granting of facilities to its representatives and commitments to training, involvement, and **single status** for employees. On the other, it can embrace union acceptance of flexible working, binding

arbitration to resolve **industrial disputes**, and representation through a **company council**, which might include non-union representatives and have only an advisory or consultative role. Single-union agreements were seen by some as a basis for reconstructing British industrial relations on a more co-operative basis, and recently concluded **labour–management partnerships** embrace many of their elements. They led to controversy in the trade union movement, however, largely because unions bid for agreements from employers through competitive '**beauty contests**' and because, in a number of cases, agreements resulted in the **derecognition** of rival unions. This controversy led to the expulsion of the electricians' union from the TUC in the late 1980s. Single-union agreements have not spread widely and are primarily a feature of **greenfield** manufacturing sites developed by inward investors. Notable examples exist at Nissan, Toshiba, Sony, Panasonic, and Pirelli General in south Wales. There is evidence in some of these companies of low union membership, which suggests a problem of perceived union ineffectiveness where this form of recognition is adopted. [See **no-strike clause; pendulum arbitration**.]

sit-down strike A **strike** in which workers occupy the workplace. Sit-down strikes, sit-ins, or factory occupations are rare events but when they do take place can be very dramatic. They were an important feature of the unionization drive of the American unions in the 1930s and there were several notable sit-down strikes in the 1970s in the UK, including those at the Upper Clyde shipyards in Glasgow.

sitting-with-Nellie is a term used to describe poor-quality on-the-job training where a trainee is not instructed by a qualified trainer but instead is expected to learn how to do the job by observing someone who has been doing the job for years (i.e. Nellie). Such training is not planned or systematic, but instead is haphazard and variable. Although the trainee might glean much of Nellie's expertise, he or she will also pick up her bad habits. And although Nellie might well be personable, she does not necessarily have the skills to train others. [See **training**.]

situational interview A technique used in selection interviews where candidates are presented with scenarios based on realistic situations that might be encountered in the job and asked to explain what they would do. The 'situations' are derived in advance of the interview and the possible responses are rated on a scale denoting the appropriateness of the response. Thus, when the interviewee responds, his or her answer is matched to the list of possible responses and allocated a score. The interviewee will be given a number of different situations and an overall score will be calculated. All interviewees are given the same situations, and are rated on the same scales. Situational interviews are considered to have high **reliability** and **validity**.

16PF personality test A self-assessment questionnaire for measuring personality traits.

skill A task that a person can perform to a satisfactory level (or higher). Or, if referring to a specific individual, it means the person's current level of performance. [See **competency**.]

skill-based pay is an input-based **payment system** in which employees receive increases in pay for undergoing training and adding to their range or depth of skills. Schemes are often based on a modular training programme (which may itself be linked to a **National Vocational Qualification**) which enables employees to acquire a series of work-relevant skills. The reward typically takes the form of progression through an **incremental scale** with the successful completion of each unit of training leading to an enhanced **salary** or **hourly rate**. Skill-based pay is most commonly applied to manual or technical workers and is associated with forms of work organization, like **teamworking**, which require **functional flexibility**. In the United States skill-based pay is often referred to as **pay-for-knowledge**. [See **paying the person**.]

skill shortage A skill shortage occurs when the demand for a particular skill outstrips supply. Imbalance of this kind is recurrent in the UK economy, largely due to failings in the **vocational education and training** system. The results of a skill shortage typically are to generate an upward spiral in earnings as employers compete to attract scarce labour while simultaneously acting as a brake on economic growth.

small to medium-sized enterprises (SMEs) are organizations employing less than 500 people. Sometimes this categorization is subdivided: medium-sized enterprises have 100–499 employees; small enterprises have 10–99 employees; micro-enterprises have less than 10 employees.

SMART An acronym standing for Specific, Measurable, Agreed, Realistic, and Timed, though the precise words derived from the initials vary from organization to organization and from theorist to theorist. For example, some replace 'Specific' with 'Stretching' and others replace 'Agreed' with 'Appropriate' or 'Achievable'. SMART refers to either business or employee objectives adopted within a formal system of **performance management**. The theoretical rationale for the adoption of SMART objectives is derived from **goal-setting theory**.

smoke-free offices see no-smoking policies

social charge A payment made by employers and/or employees to a social insurance fund to provide for state **pensions**, **sick pay**, and other security **benefits**. They are normally linked to employee earnings. In the UK social charges take the form of **National Insurance Contributions**, which are payable by employers and employees if the latter earn more than the **lower earnings limit**. The issue of social charges is a controversial one in Europe because in many EU states they comprise a large proportion of total labour costs and there is pressure for their reduction. Advocates of **deregulation** claim that high social charges discourage employment, while their defenders dispute this and claim they form an equitable means of providing social security.

Social Charter The European Social Charter of 1989 was a 'solemn declaration' that listed twelve fundamental social rights. These included freedom of movement, fair wages, social security, **freedom**

of association and **collective bargaining, health and safety**, and equal treatment of men and women (see **equal opportunity**). The Charter itself had no legal force but was rather an expression of the normative standards to which the member states of the European Community were committed. It did give rise to an Action Plan, however, and a number of **directives** were subsequently adopted in the fields of health and safety and **working time**. The UK Conservative government refused to endorse the Charter, but it was finally accepted ten years after the Charter's inception, following the election of a Labour government in 1997.

social clause This refers to a proposal to attach a clause to a multilateral trade agreement obliging the signatory governments to respect the fundamental rights of workers, as articulated in the core conventions of the **International Labour Organization**. The question of a social clause has risen to prominence in recent years as a result of the campaigning of trade unions, some national governments, and development and human rights organizations for the adoption of a social clause by the World Trade Organization (WTO). At the 1999 meeting of the WTO in Seattle President Clinton called for labour standards to be included in trade agreements, with reinforcing sanctions; a proposal that was rejected by the majority of the 135 countries attending. The argument for a social clause is premissed on the belief that increased trade liberalization is leading to the erosion of national labour standards. In many developing economies, however, arguments of this kind are regarded as a form of protectionism designed to shelter the industrialized economies from competition. [See **Battle of Seattle; race to the bottom; regime competition**.]

social dialogue refers to meetings and discussions between the central organizations of business and labour at European level that have been encouraged by the European Commission since the mid-1980s. The Commission is anxious to develop the co-operative involvement of the **social partners** in policy-making and has sponsored meetings and encouraged joint policy-making and negotiations between the **European Trade Union Confederation** on the one side and the European employers' organizations on the other (i.e. CEEP, UNICE). The concrete expression of this dialogue to date has been the negotiation of a series of **framework agreements** (e.g. on **parental leave** and part-time work) that have been adopted as directives by the Council of Ministers. As well as a general dialogue between the social partners at European level, the Commission has also promoted a 'sectoral social dialogue' within particular business sectors.

social dimension A term coined by Jacques Delors when he was President of the European Commission to suggest that the integration of European economies through the creation of the Single European Market should be accompanied by the development of European social and employment policy.

social dumping This term has two similar meanings. (1) Within the context of Europe, social dumping is the use of low labour standards by a member state of the European Union to attract jobs and investment from other member states. Essentially it refers to the export of unemployment from countries with low labour standards to those with higher standards. The European Commission and member states, such as France, Germany, and the Netherlands, have argued that there must be relatively high minimum labour standards across the European Union in order to discourage social dumping. (2) Social dumping is the process whereby a transnational organization shifts production from a country with relatively high employment costs to a country with lower costs (see **regime shopping**). Critics argue that this is one of the negative consequences of **globalization** because it means that companies can switch production from developed economies with regulated employment conditions and protection for employees to developing countries with cheap labour and unregulated working conditions.

Social Europe refers to the social and employment policy of the European Union and is often used as a slogan; that is, to emphasize the need for European social policy to complement economic and political integration.

socialization is the process through which newcomers become familiar with an organization or workgroup, learn its norms and begin to share its values. There is usually a formal process of **induction**, whereby new employees are introduced to co-workers and managers, given a tour of the workplace, and told about rules and procedures. However, socialization is an informal, gradual process whereby the newcomer learns about the organization and the values and beliefs of its members through social interaction, and, in turn, existing members of the organization form an understanding of the newcomer.

social loafing is when individuals exert less effort whilst working in a group than they would if they were working on their own.

social movement theory is a branch of sociology that is concerned with the analysis of social movements and popular protest. Social movement theory has attracted considerable interest within academic **industrial relations** in recent years as a means of analyzing the process of collective action by workers within **trade unions**. Theorists in this tradition have sought to identify the conditions under which collective action will arise. These include a sense of grievance or injustice, attribution of that grievance to action by the employer, the existence of collective organization (a mobilizing structure), a belief that collective action is likely to be effective (instrumentality), and the presence of a mobilizing leadership. The role of leaders is assumed to be particularly important within this theory, as leaders 'frame' issues and provide an interpretative scheme through which workers can justify and legitimize collective action.

social movement unionism is a form of trade unionism advocated originally by critics of **business unionism** in the United States and Canada. Social movement unionism is a form of trade unionism that is mobilizing and campaigning and has three distinguishing features. First, it adopts broad goals oriented towards the achievement of social justice and is not confined to the narrow economic agenda of traditional **collective bargaining**. Second, it seeks to extend the terrain of union action outwards beyond the enterprise to the community and advocates the creation of broad labour–community alliances. Third, it seeks to recreate unions themselves as social movements which mobilize their members against workplace and wider social injustice. Although of North American provenance, the idea of social movement unionism has influenced academics and activists in the UK and Europe. It is associated with attempts to extend union organization to low-paid, marginal employees through aggressive organizing campaigns.

social pact is the term used in the countries of the European Union to describe an agreement between government and either or both of the **social partners** to regulate the economy. Social pacts have been an important component of the **industrial relations system** in several European countries, including Belgium, Ireland, and the Netherlands. They are associated with a system of **corporatism** and typically involve agreements limiting the growth of incomes in return for government policies that promote economic growth or which protect welfare expenditure. [See **incomes policy**; **social dialogue**; **social partnership**.]

social partner is the term used within the European Union to refer to economic interests, such as business and labour. The representatives of the social partners are deemed to be the central **confederations** of trade unions and employers, and it is assumed that both partners are equally legitimate, should be consulted by national governments and the European Union, and can, in principle, co-operate to promote economic and social well-being. [See **social dialogue**; **social partnership**.]

social partnership is the principle of co-operation between the **social partners**; that is, the organized interests of business and labour. It is a complex term that can be used in a number of ways, though two meanings are paramount. In mainland Europe social partnership refers primarily to a co-operative relationship between the central **confederations** of business and labour and to their joint involvement with government in the task of economic and social management. Its meaning in this first sense is close to the notion of **corporatism**. In the UK, however, social partnership is also used to describe co-operative relations between business and labour at the level of the enterprise. A concrete expression of social partnership at this level is the conclusion of a **labour–management partnership** between a trade union and the management of an individual company.

Social Protocol The Social Protocol with its Agreement on Social Policy was annexed to the Treaty on European Union (Maastricht Treaty), which was ratified by eleven of twelve member states in 1993 (the UK secured an opt-out). The protocol had two main elements. It extended **qualified majority voting** and introduced a mandatory consultation process to draw the **social partners** more fully into European policy-making. Central to the latter is provision of a **negotiation track** through which the social partners can negotiate the content of European **directives**. In 1997 the newly elected Labour government accepted the Social Protocol and its elements have since been confirmed by all member states and incorporated in the social chapter (Articles 117–19) of the Treaty of Amsterdam 1997.

soft contract An arrangement between two parties that recognizes their mutual benefit from collaborating. The contract is 'soft' in the sense that it does not specify exactly what is to be delivered by each party, but does clarify the relationship between the two parties and their respective roles in securing mutually beneficial deliverables. [See also **hard contract**; **relational contract**.]

soft HRM is a term used to describe the developmental aspects of managing people. It is an approach that emphasizes the need to treat employees as assets which must be looked after, trained, and developed in order to get the best out of them. This approach stresses the importance of getting **organizational commitment** from employees (see **high commitment management**). In contrast, hard HRM views people as factors of production which, like other assets, can be treated dispassionately in line with business requirements. Thus, under hard HRM the important concepts are **flexibility** and performance (see **high performance work practices**). There is no particular need to develop and train employees or to elicit their commitment, unless the business requirements demand this. Indeed, hard HRM is seen by some commentators to be the pernicious side of managing people since it means that all actions are justifiable providing they are in line with business needs—employees are merely a variable cost. Some critics have argued that the soft/hard dichotomy is a misleading concept because it fails to account for the fact that many organizations may be engaging in both hard and soft HRM simultaneously for different groups of employees.

soldiering is a traditional American term for **restriction of output** by employees which entered the social science lexicon following its use by F. W. Taylor in his writing on **scientific management**. Taylor attributed 'soldiering' to the 'natural indolence' of employees and his system of scientific management was designed to eradicate the problem by transferring control over work organization to professional managers and instituting incentive schemes to encourage high and sustained levels of effort.

solidaristic wages policy The traditional bargaining strategy of the Swedish **trade union** movement, which sought to establish uniform rates of pay for each occupation and the narrowing of wage **differentials**. The strategy was dependent on a highly centralized system of wage bargaining and for most of the post-war period was successful in reducing wage inequality. Its pursuit has become increasingly difficult, however, as employers and skilled workers have rebelled against its constraints. In Sweden in recent years bargaining has been decentralized, allowing workers in the most profitable firms to increase their level of earnings.

solidarity is often regarded as one of the core principles of trade unionism and embodies the belief that workers should join together and support one another in conflict with employers. Concrete expressions of the principle of solidarity include the conviction that it is wrong to cross a picket line of striking workers or that workers involved in a dispute should be backed through expressions of support, sympathy strikes, or donations of cash, food, and clothing. [See **women's support group**.]

solid citizen is a term sometimes used to describe an employee who is performing well, but who has reached a **career plateau**.

sophisticated consultative is a **management style** that embraces investment in employee development and involvement alongside an attempt to develop a co-operative or non-adversarial relationship with trade unions. [See **labour–management partnership**.]

sophisticated human relations is a **management style** that attempts to develop **organizational commitment** through an emphasis on **individualism**, thereby leaving no role for trade unions.

sophisticated modern is a term coined by industrial relations theorist Alan Fox to describe a **management style** that acknowledges the role of trade unions but seeks to contain and restrict their influence through formalized procedures.

sophisticated paternalist is a **management style** found in large non-union companies like Marks and Spencer. It is characterized by an attempt to develop employee commitment and loyalty through the offer of permanent employment and extensive employee **benefits**. Companies of this kind may also make use of internal communications and pay above-average wages in order to pre-empt unionization. [See **welfare capitalism**.]

specialization is the degree to which an organization's activities are divided between separate roles, such that management tasks, for instance, are performed by operational, finance, marketing, and personnel specialists.

special leave is paid or unpaid leave from work that is normally taken to deal with domestic emergencies. The provision of special leave arrangements is regarded as a **family-friendly policy** and may reduce the amount of absenteeism that arises from employees trying to reconcile their work and caring responsibilities. [See **domestic-incident leave**.]

Special Negotiating Body (SNB) A body that can be established under the European Works Council Directive 1994 for the purpose of negotiating an information and consultation procedure within large European companies; that is, to establish a **European works council**. The directive states that an SNB must be created by the employer where this is requested by 100 or more employees or, alternatively, that the SNB can be established on the initiative of central management. The SNB is required to have between three and seventeen employee representatives, with all relevant states having at least one member. Under the UK's regulations implementing the directive, British representatives on the SNB must either be elected by a ballot of the workforce or be nominated from the members of an existing consultative committee that was itself elected by ballot. Once established the SNB has three years to negotiate the composition, functions, administration, and financing of a European works council or an equivalent procedure for informing and consulting employees on transnational issues. These agreements are known as **Article 6 agreements** and more than 100 had been negotiated by the year 2000. If management refuses to negotiate or agreement cannot be reached, the subsidiary or mandatory provisions for an EWC set out in the directive come into force. The purpose of the special negotiating procedure is to allow companies covered by the directive to negotiate an EWC that fits the structure and traditions of the enterprise, thereby allowing a degree of flexibility within the regulations.

spot contract An economic transaction consisting of a single, transient exchange of money for goods or wages for labour. The closest approximation to a spot contract within the sphere of HRM is the hire of casual workers by the day or hour. In this situation there is no assumption of an ongoing social relationship between employer and worker and employment is stripped down to its bare economic essentials. [See **contingent work; relational contract**.]

spot-rate A single rate of pay for a job or **grade** expressed as an **hourly rate**, a weekly wage, or an annual **salary**. The defining feature of a spot-rate is that there is no scope for salary or wage progression through a **pay scale** or **pay range**. However, employees may have the opportunity to increase their earnings above the spot-rate through premium and other supplementary payments or by earning non-consolidated cash bonuses.

staff association A representative organization of employees which is confined to a particular enterprise and which is established with employer approval or support. Staff associations are a common feature in financial services and a number of other industries and have usually been seen as a moderate alternative to representation through an 'external' **trade union**. Critics have claimed that many staff associations are not truly independent of employers and that they are used by the latter as a means of forestalling the unionization of the workforce. In contrast, proponents of staff associations claim that they are more attuned to the enterprise-specific needs of employees and that they reflect the preference for co-operative industrial relations of white-collar and managerial employees. Although staff associations have a reputation for moderation, some have become increasingly militant and 'unionate' in recent years. This is particularly true of staff associations in banking and finance, where the restructuring of the industry has led to widespread job losses and the retreat by employers from a relatively paternalist management style. Reflecting this change, a number of staff associations in the UK have affiliated to the TUC (e.g. Independent Union of Halifax Staff) while others have merged with trade unions. Unifi, the banking union, was formed in 1999 from a merger of the industry union BIFU with the staff associations in Barclays and National Westminster banks. [See **company union**; **enterprise union**.]

staff forum An alternative and relatively common name for a non-union consultative committee.

staff manager Someone who assists and advises **line managers** in attaining their objectives.

staff turnover see **labour turnover**

stages of group development Organizational psychologists have identified five stages through which a group is likely to progress. (1) Forming: individuals get to know each other and establish ground rules about their objectives and acceptable behaviour. (2) Storming: members conflict with each other about the control and leadership of the group. When they arrive at a settlement, they move on to the next stage, otherwise the group disbands. (3) Norming: members begin to bond together as a group, relationships develop, and feelings of shared responsibility emerge. (4) Performing: the group begins to get on with the tasks it has been set. (5) Adjourning: the group breaks up because it has completed its task, or disintegrates because members leave or because the norms cease to be effective. The amount of time for each stage varies from group to group, and the boundaries between each stage are not as clear-cut as implied by the five-stage model.

stakeholder A person who has a legitimate or vested interest in the activities of an organization. The primary stakeholders are managers, employees, shareholders, and investors; secondary stakeholders are suppliers, distributors, and customers; tertiary stakeholders include the local community, consumer groups, the government (national and local), political groups, minority groups (such as ethnic minorities or the disabled), and pressure groups (such as environmental or health campaigners).

stakeholder pension A money purchase pension scheme that is required in law from October 2001 in UK companies with five or more employees that do not have an **occupational pension** scheme. Employees are not required to join the stakeholder pension, which operates in a manner equivalent to a personal pension, and at present employers are not required to contribute financially to the scheme. However, the employer has to deduct the employee's contributions from wages and is also responsible for designating a provider, in most cases a financial services company. Employees have the right to be consulted over the choice of provider and trade unions may offer pension schemes or recommend particular providers to employers. Employees are eligible to take out a stakeholder pension if they are over 18, have three months' service and earn more than the **lower earnings limit** (currently £67.00 per week). The purpose of the scheme is to improve pension provision for low earners who are less likely to be covered by an occupational pension.

Stakhanovite was the term for a 'hero of labour' in the old Soviet Union who achieved prodigious levels of productivity as an example to fellow workers. It is sometimes used today as a satirical description of a person who overworks. [See **rate-buster; workaholic**.]

standardization is the degree to which an organization applies standard rules and procedures to its operations.

standard modern is a term coined by industrial relations theorist Alan Fox to describe a **management style** that is essentially **pragmatic** and **opportunistic**, rather than principled.

state of emergency Under the UK's Emergency Powers Act the government has the right to declare a state of emergency in the event of severe disruption of the economy by **industrial action**. States of emergency were declared on nine occasions between 1945 and 2000 in response to strikes by power workers, dockers, seafarers, miners, and public service workers. The Act empowers the government to involve the military in industrial disputes, generally to carry out tasks normally undertaken by striking workers.

statistical process control (SPC) is a set of measurement techniques designed to monitor a production process in order to assess variability of machine performance and allow for predictions of when corrective action needs to be taken to prevent a problem occurring.

status divide The traditional division within business between salaried white-collar workers and hourly paid manual workers. In some companies this division has been challenged through

harmonization and the adoption of **single status**, or common employment conditions, across all groups of employees. According to some commentators, however, a new status divide has arisen between full-time and part-time employees.

Statutory Code of Practice see code of practice

statutory incomes policy see incomes policy

Statutory Maternity Allowance (SMA) see Statutory Maternity Pay

Statutory Maternity Pay (SMP) Provided certain qualifying conditions are met, a woman in the UK has a legal entitlement to Statutory Maternity Pay during a period of maternity leave. The entitlement is to six weeks at 90 per cent of average earnings before the period of leave and to twelve weeks at a rate equal to that paid under **Statutory Sick Pay**. To qualify a woman must have twenty-six weeks' service prior to the fifteenth week before the baby is due and have earned an average wage at least equal to the **lower earnings limit** over an eight-week period. Women who do not meet these conditions but who have been employed or self-employed for twenty-six weeks out of the sixty-six preceding the fourteenth week before confinement are entitled to receive Statutory Maternity Allowance. Again, earnings across these twenty-six weeks must be at or above the weekly lower earnings limit. In many organizations SMP is supplemented by an occupational maternity pay scheme. [See **maternity pay**.]

statutory regulation is the creation of **substantive** and **procedural rules** through legal statute. Statutory regulation forms an important element of the system of **employment law**. [See **legal regulation**.]

Statutory Sick Pay (SSP) A statutory payment during sickness absence to which employees in the UK are entitled provided they earn above the **lower earnings limit** and make National Insurance Contributions. Employees who do not fulfil these conditions are covered by state sickness benefit. SSP is payable to employees for up to twenty-eight weeks of sickness absence beginning on the fourth day. Employers have a legal obligation to pay SSP to qualifying employees, though they can recover payments from their National Insurance Contributions. In many cases an occupational sick pay scheme provides more generous payments than those required through SSP. [See **sick pay**.]

stereotyping is the act of judging people according to our assumptions about the group to which they belong. It is based on the belief that people from a specific group share similar traits and behave in a similar manner. Rather than looking at a person's individual qualities, stereotyping leads us to jump to conclusions about what someone is like. This might act against the person concerned (negative stereotype) or in their favour (positive stereotype). For example, the negative stereotype of an accountant is someone who is dull, uninteresting, and shy—which, of course, is a slur on all the exciting, adventurous accountants in the world. A positive stereotype is that accountants are intelligent, conscientious, and trustworthy—which is equally an inaccurate description of some of the accountants you are likely to encounter. The problem with stereotypes is that they are generalizations (so there are always exceptions) and can be based on ignorance and prejudice (so are often inaccurate). It is vital for managers to resist resorting to stereotyping when managing people, otherwise they run the risk of treating employees unfairly and making poor-quality decisions that are detrimental to the organization. [See **discrimination**.]

stick to the knitting is a phrase coined by Tom Peters and Robert Waterman in their best-selling management book of the 1980s *In Search of Excellence*. It means that a business should do what it is good at and not become distracted by diversifying into totally different activities or enterprises. Any acquisition or internal diversification is more likely to be successful the closer it is to the existing activities and expertise of the business.

stoppage A stoppage of work is an alternative term for a **strike**, although in some cases a stoppage might arise as a result of a **lock-out** by the employer.

stories (in relation to **organizational culture**) help to transmit the values and beliefs of the organization in an entertaining and understandable way. They are designed to be repeated so that the message is reinforced.

storming is the second stage of the five-stage model of group development. [See **stages of group development**.]

strategic business unit (SBU) A profit or cost centre within a larger organization that has a degree of independence in operational management and is controlled, not by bureaucratic rules, but through its 'bottom-line' performance.

strategic human resource management (SHRM) Some commentators draw a distinction between HRM and SHRM. The latter, they argue, is distinctive because it is concerned with attempting to integrate the use of human resources with the wider business strategy of the organization. In this sense, they are advocating **strategic integration** based on the concept of **external fit**. In other words, SHRM is most closely associated with HRM definition (6) listed under the entry for human resource management. Some commentators do not specifically use the term SHRM, but instead argue that HRM is, by definition, concerned with strategy. So, for example, management theorist David Guest identifies strategic integration as one of the four positive outcomes in his normative model of HRM, the others being flexibility, commitment, and quality.

strategic integration is a concept particularly relevant to recent developments in HRM. It usually refers to the importance of ensuring there is an appropriate match between the human resources policies and the wider business policies within an organization. Whilst this perhaps seems obvious, commentators have pointed out the way that human resource policies are often developed in isolation, with little concern for the wider business objectives, or else have emerged through developments in the organization's history. Consequently there is often a mismatch between current human resource policies and business objectives. To overcome this, some commentators argue that a human resource strategy should be integrated with the organization's business strategy—although there is considerable disagreement over which aspects of business strategy should guide the human resource policy (see **external fit**). Critics suggest that achieving this type of integration is either unnecessary (see **bundles theorists**) or unfeasible.

strategic pay is a term coined by management writer Edward E. Lawler III to express the belief that the selection of reward systems should be driven explicitly by the need to reinforce business strategy. Strategic pay can therefore be contrasted with reward management based on custom, universal models of best practice, legal regulation, or the demands of employees as expressed through trade unions. It is based on the conviction that business performance is the only appropriate standard against which reward practice should be judged. 'Strategic pay' is a prescriptive concept and leads to the search for incentive and other tools that can reinforce patterns of worker behaviour (innovation, customer responsiveness, high output) that allow business strategy to be implemented successfully within the enterprise. [See **new pay**.]

stress see **job stress**

stress management is concerned to help employees identify, cope with, reduce and avoid **job stress**. It can involve provision of health information and education, keep fit and relaxation classes, access to stress counselling through an **employee assistance programme**, and training in stress awareness and ways of coping with stress.

strike The withdrawal of labour by workers, usually as part of an industrial **dispute** with their employer. Most strikes involve the members of trade unions and the strike weapon is the best-known form of **industrial action** used by unions to pressurize employers for concessions. Strikes can occur over a wide number of reasons though most originate in disputes over pay and conditions of employment. They can also assume a wide variety of forms, including brief stoppages involving few workers, protest strikes directed at government policy, and major **trials of strength** over significant points of principle that involve large numbers of workers and last for weeks on end. Workers differ in the degree to which they are **strike prone** and national strike statistics indicate considerable variation across industries, while international statistics indicate variation across countries. Explaining these patterns has been a major concern of industrial relations scholarship and the sources of strike activity have been variously traced to the nature of occupational communities, forms of technology, systems of payment, the structure of collective bargaining, and the effects of government incomes policy. Since the 1970s the number of strikes has reduced in many industrialized countries and there has been speculation that the strike may be 'withering away'. Strike activity, however, has followed a cyclical or wave-like pattern through history and it is perhaps unwise to extrapolate from the current state of 'labour quiescence'. The regulation of strike action is an important function of collective labour law. In the UK this takes the form of granting strikers and their unions civil **immunity** provided certain conditions are met.

strike ballot A ballot of union members to determine whether strike action should be taken against an employer or employers. Under UK employment law it is essential for a union to hold a properly conducted strike ballot if its action is to retain legal **immunity** (i.e. protection from civil legal action by the employer). The law on strike ballots is complex and supported by a statutory code of practice issued by ACAS. It is a requirement that ballots are postal, that the voting paper details the action to be taken and warns union members that striking may be in breach of their contract of employment, and that seven days' notice be given to the employer before striking begins. The introduction of a legal requirement to ballot for strikes was introduced by the Trade Union Act 1984 and formed part of the Conservative government's reform of industrial relations. It was assumed that strike activity would decrease if (presumed moderate) union members were balloted, although opinion is divided on whether the law has had this effect. Since its inception unions have become adept at using the law as a bargaining tactic and may hold strike ballots as a means of pressurizing employers to improve pay offers during negotiations.

strike-breaker A worker who refuses to join a **strike** or accepts work as a replacement for a striking worker and thereby undermines strike action by a **trade union**. Within the trade union movement, strike-breakers are pejoratively labelled **scabs**.

strike in detail A term coined by the social reformers Beatrice and Sidney Webb. It refers to the refusal of individual members of early craft trade unions to accept work below the union-recommended rate of pay, as opposed to a collective withdrawal of labour. If individuals refusing work in this manner were unable to find alternative employment, the union would provide them with unemployment benefit. The strike in detail, therefore, was a technique designed to enforce union regulation of craft labour markets by denying a supply of labour to low-paying employers.

strike pay or dispute benefit is paid by trade unions to their members during a **strike** or **lockout**. Some unions establish special funds for strike pay and may guarantee members in dispute a substantial proportion of their normal earnings. The aim is to strengthen support in the event of a strike and provide a credible threat of a prolonged stoppage to the employer. In other cases, however, the union may lack the resources to make all but a token payment. Despite this fact, under UK law it is assumed that strikers receive strike pay and an amount is deducted from social security benefits made to strikers' dependants.

strike prone An industry or a group of workers are strike prone when they display a high propensity to engage in **industrial action**. Strike proneness can be measured in a number of different ways including the number of strikes, the number of working days lost through strike action, and the number of workers involved and number of working days lost per thousand workers employed. UK industries that have traditionally been strike prone include car manufacture, docks, mining, shipbuilding, and steel. Today, the most strike-prone groups of workers are found in the public services and include schoolteachers, civil servants, and local authority administrators.

striker days A measure of strike activity calculated by multiplying the length of a strike in days by the number of workers involved. An aggregate figure for striker days can be calculated on an annual basis for the whole economy and this statistic is often used in **comparative industrial relations** in studies of **industrial conflict**. [See **working days lost**.]

strike wave A periodic surge of strike activity that involves large numbers of workers and affects a broad section of industry. In the recent past there were strike waves at the end of the 1960s and the end of the 1970s, which registered peak levels of **industrial action** across much of the industrialized world. The reasons for this wave-like pattern in strike activity are a matter of debate but it is widely recognized that strike waves can be very significant events. They may threaten public order and lead to the collapse of governments and they are often associated with significant reform in the institutions of industrial relations as governments, employers, and trade unions seek to re-establish industrial order.

strong culture refers to an organization that has a clearly identifiable set of values and beliefs that are widely shared by employees. The supposed advantage of a strong culture is that it unifies people around a common goal. However, it also has the disadvantage of getting everyone to think the same way, and behave in the same manner, thereby inhibiting innovation, originality, and even flexibility. It can also be problematic if the organization finds itself in a dynamic environment necessitating rapid and frequent change. [See **weak culture; organizational culture**.]

structured/unstructured interview A structured interview is planned in advance by the interviewers, the questions are put in a logical order, and the same format is applied to all the interviewees in order to ensure consistency. An unstructured interview is unplanned, haphazard, and inconsistent. The structured interview is therefore considered a superior method of gaining useful information and allowing comparisons to be made between interviewees.

subcontracting is the process of having certain tasks and operations in the organization performed by other businesses in accordance with a set of agreed terms and conditions. In other words, organizations are outsourcing aspects of their operations. Typically organizations will subcontract support services that are essential for the smooth running of the organization, but not part of its core operations—for example, catering, cleaning, portering. Increasingly organizations are using subcontracting as a means of reducing their overheads and concentrating on their primary activities. In some organizations, aspects of the personnel/HR department's work are being contracted out to specialist businesses, for example training and higher-level recruitment (executive search).

subsidiarity is the constitutional principle that the European Union should involve itself only in those areas of policy that cannot be dealt with or satisfactorily regulated at national level. The concept stresses the undesirability of highly prescriptive, detailed regulation at European level and has led to attempts to impart flexibility into European legislation. For example, there is scope to implement European **directives** at national level in a variety of ways, through legislation, regulations, administrative orders, or **collective agreement** by the **social partners**. The inclusion of **derogations** in community directives also allows flexibility, so that policy can be implemented to suit local circumstances.

substantive rule An employment rule that determines the content or 'substance' of the **employment relationship**. An example would be a rule stating that an employee in a particular job grade whose performance has been rated as 'exceptional' will receive a consolidated salary increase of 10 per cent. Substantive rules of this kind cover all aspects of the employment relationship including the design and organization of work and the recruitment, development, reward, appraisal, and exit of employees. Rules may be informal and take the form of implicit understandings about what is appropriate behaviour at work; for example, it may be accepted that people leave work slightly early on Friday evenings because it is the start of the weekend. Alternatively, substantive rules may be written down in contracts of employment, collective agreements, or statutes. The **National Minimum Wage** is an example of a formal, substantive rule as it states that all employees aged over 21 will receive a minimum payment currently set at £3.70 per hour. Substantive employment rules can be contrasted with **procedural rules** that govern the behaviour and interaction of workers, employers, and their representatives.

succession planning is an element within **human resource planning** in which the organization tries to identify likely candidates to take over management positions when incumbents leave or retire. In its most elaborate form succession planning will be based on a **management development** programme that prepares more junior managers to assume senior responsibilities. It can also draw upon a system of performance **appraisal** that rates more junior managers in terms of their suitability for **promotion**.

suggestion scheme A system of **employee involvement** in which employees can provide suggestions for improving company products, procedures, and work processes and receive cash payments or prizes to acknowledge any savings or increases in revenue that result.

summary dismissal see **dismissal without notice**

Sunday work is, quite simply, any paid work undertaken on a Sunday and is subject to restrictions in most European countries. In the UK the Employment Rights Act 1996 gives shop workers (except those employed only to work on Sundays) the right to choose not to work on a Sunday.

supervision is the act of co-ordinating, directing, monitoring, and correcting work behaviour and performance that is undertaken by a first-line manager or **supervisor**. Because it involves the exertion of control, supervision is a source of tension and conflict within work organizations.

supervisor A front-line manager who is responsible for the supervision of employees. Supervisors are often described as 'people in the middle' because they implement but do not shape management policy, and because they work alongside non-management employees but are distant from them by virtue of their responsibility for labour control. [See **chargehand**; **first-line manager**; **foreman**; **team leader**.]

supervisory board In countries such as Germany and the Netherlands, supervisory boards are an important part of the system of **corporate governance**. They are typically composed of different **stakeholders** in the enterprise, including representatives of shareholders, managers, and employers (see **worker directors**). Supervisory boards are responsible for the general direction of the company while the **management board** is responsible for ongoing operations.

Supported Employment Programme A UK government programme that subsidizes the employment of disabled people who have limited productivity but who work alongside the non-disabled.

surplus value is the price of a commodity greater than the costs incurred in its production. [See **labour process theory**.]

surveillance is the intrusive monitoring of employee behaviour at work, which may involve the use of electronic, video, and telecommunications equipment or management reliance on **consumer reports**. Companies may engage in surveillance in order to detect criminal activity, pilferage, and poor performance or simply to maintain a disciplined work environment. Some forms of surveillance, such as monitoring private phone calls and e-mails, may be unlawful under **data protection** and privacy law. The analysis of surveillance at work has been a key feature of the **labour process** school and some regard it is a defining feature of the contemporary workplace. [See **panopticon control**.]

survivor envy is the resentment sometimes felt by employees in organizations that have gone through the process of **downsizing**

and reorganization. Some of the employees who have survived experience envy against others who are perceived to have gained more from the reorganization process—for example, a better job, an enhanced remuneration package, higher status. [See **survivor syndrome**.]

survivor syndrome is the term used to describe a range of feelings experienced by employees who remain in an organization after it has gone through the process of **downsizing** and reorganization. Whilst there may be initial relief at keeping one's job, research reveals that this turns to feelings of betrayal (by management), anger (against management), guilt (at keeping one's job), resentment of others (**survivor envy**), and uncertainty (both about the survivors' current roles and about their job security). The consequent drop in morale can lead to a decrease in performance and an increase in stress. For some employees the survivor syndrome manifests itself in greater **absenteeism**, whilst for others it takes the form of **presenteeism**. The survivor syndrome is less likely to occur when the survivors perceive that the process has been handled fairly in terms of (1) selection of who should go, and (2) the reorganization of the jobs of those who remain.

suspension can be used by managers as part of the discipline procedure and involves temporarily relieving an employee of his or her duties and requiring him or her to leave the premises. The employee is normally suspended with pay where there has been a dispute that needs a full investigation of the circumstances. In some instances, the employee can be suspended without pay, providing the contract of employment specifies the conditions under which this applies. If investigation reveals the employee is in breach of contract, further action is taken, such as a **written warning** or even **dismissal**. If the investigation shows the employee is not in the wrong, he or she returns to work as normal, although possibly feeling he or she has been stigmatized by the suspension.

sustained competitive advantage see **competitive advantage**

sweating is a traditional term for **work intensification**.

sweetheart deal A colloquial term in the UK for a **single-union agreement** where an employer has agreed to recognize a trade union on the condition that they sign a **no-strike clause**, thereby prohibiting **industrial action**. Such deals were condemned by some trade unions as against the spirit of trade unionism; others saw them as an opportunity to gain a foothold in organizations that otherwise would be non-union. [See **beauty contest**.]

sword of justice refers to the effect of **trade unions** in promoting the redistribution of income and fair treatment of employees within the labour market. Indicators of unions' sword of justice effect include the narrower **pay dispersion** within unionized workplaces and the positive impact of union bargaining on the relative wages of women, ethnic minorities, and disabled people.

SWOT analysis is a technique for assessing whether the organization's strategy can cope with potential changes in the business environment. The procedure involves managers (1) identifying their current strategy; (2) drawing up a list of key changes in the environment; (3) identifying the current capabilities (Strengths) and limitations (Weaknesses) of the organization; (4) assessing each of these in turn against each of the environmental changes to identify whether (given the current strategy) they present Opportunities to overcome and benefit from the change, or Threats that will cause problems for the organization. Whilst systematic in its approach, the quality of the SWOT depends upon the knowledge of those undertaking it in relation to their organization's environment and its resource capabilities.

syndicalism is a revolutionary ideology that urges the overthrow of capitalism by trade unions through mass strikes, civil disorder, and the seizure of the means of production. Syndicalism was developed initially in France by Georges Sorel and was influential within the British trade union movement before the First World War. Several of its themes, such as reliance on rank-and-file mobilization, suspicion of **union bureaucracy**, and the educative effects of strike action, continue to influence the trade union left.

synergy is the positive benefit that occurs when two or more activities are combined. This means that the resultant combination is in some way superior to the separate entities—it is sometimes expressed as 2 + 2 = 5. It is a concept widely used in business strategy when assessing whether a particular takeover or merger might make sense.

T

table stakes are the resources that a company requires in order to enter a product market but which do not themselves confer **competitive advantage**. Table stakes might include investment, technology, product design, and a distribution network, aspects of business that are common to all companies within a given product market or easily imitated. To outperform competitor firms the business must possess additional resources that provide competitive edge. It is often claimed that a company's workforce and its distinctive approach to HRM comprise one of these differentiating resources. [See **resource-based view**.]

tacit skills or tacit knowledge are acquired through experience in an organization and arise from detailed familiarity with equipment, procedures, co-workers, and customers. One of the justifications for employee **participation** is that it allows managers to draw upon these tacit skills and feed them into the decision-making process.

take-home pay The earnings of an employee in any single pay period after tax, National Insurance, and other deductions from wages (e.g. pension contributions or trade union subscriptions) have been made.

takeover is when a strong company merges with a weaker company and the latter ceases to exist. [See **merger**.]

tall structure see flat/tall structure

tax efficiency A tax-efficient benefit is one which leads to the recipient incurring less **income tax** than would be payable on a cash payment of equivalent value. [See **benefits**.]

Taylorism see **scientific management**

team A group of people with complementary skills who are involved in a common set of goals for which they are collectively accountable. [See also **group**.]

team-based pay is a form of **performance-related pay** in which earnings or bonuses are related to the performance of a small group of employees who constitute an identifiable work team. While group-based incentives have long existed in traditional manufacturing industries, team-based pay tends to refer to recently developed systems, often applied to white-collar workers in the service sector, which are aimed deliberately at reinforcing new, team-based methods of working. In some cases team-based pay may be used to motivate the work of a temporary project team which is working to a deadline or series of targets. In other cases it may be used to motivate a permanent team involved in sales, production, or other ongoing activities. Central to all forms of team-based pay, however, is the notion of promoting teamwork through the offer of a shared reward and it is advocated as a corrective or alternative to the fragmenting effects of individual merit or **appraisal-based pay**. Despite its advocacy in recent years by writers on reward, the incidence of team-based pay appears to be limited and the main emphasis in white-collar work organizations continues to be on rewarding individual competence and performance.

team briefing (sometimes known as briefing groups). A communication technique that provides face-to-face meetings between managers and their subordinates on issues that have been identified by senior managers in the organization. The issues are cascaded down the organization from level to level, and at each stage the manager briefs his or her subordinates in a structured session that encourages open discussion and feedback. This is then passed back up the organization by the manager (see **cascade communication**).

team leader is the person in a group who is responsible for encouraging and co-ordinating the **teamworking** of the group's members. The role of the team leader is often said to be less directive and more facilitative than that of the traditional **foreman** or **supervisor**, although in reality there may be little difference.

team roles see Belbin's team roles

teamworking has become an increasingly popular means of organizing work in contemporary organizations. The idea of teams of workers is inextricably linked to the increasing importance of **flexibility**. Contemporary management thinking suggests that groups of workers who have been trained to perform a range of tasks are of greater use to the organization than the traditional view of workers undertaking specialized, segmented, repetitive tasks (see **scientific management**). Not only are flexible teams of workers able to undertake a greater variety of work (because there is no **demarcation** of tasks), there are also thought to be motivational advantages: from the collective spirit built up within teams, and the competitive spirit between teams in the same workplace. However, teamworking means different things in different organizations. One useful distinction is between groups of employees working *in* teams, as opposed to those working *as* teams. In the case of the former, employees might simply be working alongside others, and sharing a common work experience, but not truly engaging in teamworking. In this sense many organizations have teams, and many people would describe themselves as being part of a team. But it is the latter definition of working *as* teams that is sought by management since this brings the flexibility and motivational benefits. Whilst the idea of teamworking has received considerable management attention, it is not a new concept. Indeed, **human relations theorists** at the Tavistock Institute (UK) in the 1960s identified the supposed motivational effects of establishing autonomous workgroups. Teamworking might be seen as a contemporary expression of this in those organizations where the teams have been empowered with the authority to organize their work as they see fit in order to meet targets set by management (see **empowerment**). There are, in practice, relatively few instances where this extent of team autonomy actually occurs, although most teams would be expected to be responsible for monitoring their own quality standards. Research has also revealed negative aspects to teamworking: bullying and victimization of team members who do not fit in, who underperform, or who are in some way different.

technophile A person who is supportive of (or fanatical about) all technological developments. Such people often see technology as having a universal positive effect and argue that any negative effects are more than offset by the positive advantages offered by the technology.

technophobe A person who is fearful of all technological development, usually justifying his or her fear by focusing on the negative consequences of previous technological developments.

technosceptic A person who will highlight all the potential negative effects of a technological development. Unlike the **technophobe**, the technosceptic is not against technology *per se*, but wants to see evidence of how it will bring about advantages.

telecommuting see **teleworking**

teleconferencing is a training technique where a lecture or demonstration is broadcast live to trainees in various locations. There is some confusion about the term teleconferencing, and people sometimes use it when they really mean **video-conferencing**.

telecottaging is a form of **teleworking** where a person works in non-domestic premises that are rented from a third party. Typically such premises (the telecottage) will incorporate a range of facilities that are shared by self-employed teleworkers, thereby reducing overheads such as lighting and heating and pooling otherwise expensive equipment—such as photocopiers. Telecottaging also helps to produce social contact for teleworkers—often deemed to be one of the drawbacks of working remotely, especially on a self-employed basis.

teleworking is an arrangement that allows employees to work remotely from the office (normally from home) through the use of information and communications technology. Such teleworking, or telecommuting, is frequently associated with professional workers, but there are an increasing number of clerical jobs being undertaken through teleworking.

temp is a common colloquial term for an **agency worker** who provides short-term cover for absenteeism.

temporal flexibility is the variation in the numbers of hours worked and the timing of the work. Typical forms are **flexitime**, **overtime**, **shiftworking**, **zero-hours contracts**, **compressed working week**, **seasonal-hours contracts**, and **annual-hours contracts**.

temporary contracts specify the type of work for which a person will be employed, but not the exact duration of the work. In other words, the contract lasts until the particular task has been completed. For example, the tradespeople and labourers on a new residential development will be on temporary contracts—once their part of the building work has finished their contracts will end.

temporary-help agency is the term commonly used in North America to refer to an **employment agency**.

temp-to-perm payment A charge levied by an **employment agency** on its clients if they accept one of its temporary supply workers into permanent employment. Trade unions have lobbied unsuccessfully for the abolition of these payments because they reduce the chance of contingent workers finding a permanent job.

theory X and theory Y Management theorist Douglas McGregor coined these terms to describe two fundamentally different approaches to managing people. Theory X is based on the assumption that the average person has an inherent dislike of work (physical and mental effort), does not want responsibility, and lacks ambition. Therefore, managers must direct employees, control them through close supervision, and coerce them into putting in effort with threats of punishment. In contrast, theory Y assumes that the average person enjoys work, wants responsibility, and is ambitious. The manager must harness the employees' effort and creativity through gaining their commitment to the organization's goals, which entails allowing self-direction and discretion, reinforced through a system of feedback and rewards. By conceptualizing theories X and Y, McGregor drew attention to the assumptions about human nature that lie behind different approaches to managing people. In fact, he was describing two opposite extremes, and was suggesting that managers have a tendency more towards one than the other and that this influences their management style. McGregor advocated the superiority of theory Y in unleashing human potential, but theory X still thrives in many successful contemporary organizations.

theory Z An approach to managing employees in American organizations that advocates the adoption of aspects of Japanese management practice and techniques, such as long-term employment, consensual decision-making, and a holistic concern. The concept was devised by organization theorist William Ouchi as a way of suggesting how US organizations might adapt to changing competitive circumstances that seemed to require a fresh approach to managing, based more on developing **organizational commitment** through building a strong **organizational culture**. The label of theory Z was used by Ouchi to emphasize that this would constitute a new approach to management which lay between traditional US methods (especially **Fordism**) and management practices in Japan. In the UK, the term theory Z is not used, and instead commentators refer to **Japanization**.

therapeutic activity is work that is carried out by people with learning difficulties or other disabilities which is of primary benefit to the worker. Its purpose is to provide stimulus and facilitate social integration for those who otherwise would not work, rather than to contribute to the economic performance of an enterprise. Although therapeutic activity may be rewarded there is no requirement in the UK to pay the **National Minimum Wage**. People with **disability** who are engaged in productive work or involved in the **Supported Employment Programme**, however, are entitled to the minimum wage.

thinking outside the box A phrase used to describe the process of approaching a problem from a different angle and in so doing arriving at a creative or unusual solution.

third-country national (TCN) In an international firm, a TCN is a person whose nationality is different from that of the firm, and of the country in which the firm is operating: for example, a UK manager working for an Australian-based subsidiary of a Japanese company. [See **host-country national**; **parent-country national**.]

third-order strategy is a term coined by management theorists John Purcell and Bruce Ahlstrand in relation to **M-form** companies to refer to decisions concerning the approach to **employee relations**, and the structures and policies to support this approach. [See **first-order strategy**; **second-order strategy**.]

third-party intervention occurs when an outside person or body becomes involved in helping employers and employees find a solution to an industrial **dispute**. In the UK, third-party intervention is normally provided by ACAS. ACAS maintains a panel of arbitrators who can arbitrate or mediate in the event of a collective dispute between employers and trade unions. Members of this panel include retired civil servants, lawyers, academics, and others who have experience of industrial relations but who can be regarded as neutral between the parties. Another form of third-party intervention is **conciliation**, and this is a service that is provided directly by ACAS officers in both collective and individual employment disputes. The provision of third-party intervention is an important aspect of **dispute resolution** in all major liberal democracies. The involvement of a third party to arbitrate, conciliate, or mediate typically forms the final stage of a **disputes procedure**. [See **arbitration**; **mediation**.]

360-degree feedback is an **appraisal** technique designed to produce a rounded picture of the individual. It is based on the principle that the individual must receive feedback from all angles, not just his or her line manager. So, in addition, feedback comes from subordinates, peers, work colleagues from other departments, customers/clients—in fact anyone the individual comes into contact with as part of his or her normal work activities. These various **appraisers** describe the person's competences and behaviours, typically using an anonymous, questionnaire-based feedback form.

throughflow see **human resource flow**

tiger economies A label sometimes used to denote the newly industrialized countries of east Asia—in particular, South Korea, Taiwan, and Singapore.

time-and-motion study see **work study; scientific management**

time off Under UK employment law there is a right for employees to take time off work under certain circumstances. In some situations the law also stipulates that employees must be paid for this time. Thus, there is a right for trade union representatives, **safety representatives**, and employee trustees of pension funds to take paid time off to carry out their duties and attend training. There is also an entitlement to time off for those who undertake public duties, such as membership of a local council or health authority, though there is no stipulation in this case that employees should be paid. Apart from these circumstances women can take paid time off to attend antenatal care, those who are being made redundant can take paid time off to look for work, while carers are entitled to take unpaid **special leave** to care for dependants. A recent addition to this list of circumstances is contained in the Right to Time Off for Study or Training Regulations (RTOST) 1999. These give a right to **young workers** between the age of 16 and 18 to take paid time off to undergo training or attend a vocational educational course, provided certain conditions are met.

time-rate A rate of pay based on the amount of time that the employee spends at work. Examples of time-rates include **hourly rates** of pay, weekly payments, and an annual **salary**, which is based at least notionally on the number of weeks worked per year. Linking pay to the time spent at work, in this way, is the most commonly used method for determining wages in modern industry, though in many situations employees will receive additional payments based on qualification, skill, and performance.

tokenism is the practice of placing or promoting individuals from disadvantaged groups (for example, women, ethnic minorities, disabled people) into high-profile roles in the organization in order to give the impression that the organization practises **equal opportunities**. It represents a cynical move by managers to disguise or ignore the structures and procedures that disadvantage women, ethnic minorities, and disabled people. In this way, whilst the token individuals may benefit personally, their role does nothing to help further the cause of the disadvantaged group to which they belong. In fact it might have a negative impact because the token individuals become examples for organizational decision-makers to illustrate the **meritocratic** nature of the organization and to neutralize arguments for change.

total productive maintenance (TPM) is the technique of making improvements for the efficient use of machinery by benchmarking the existing overall equipment effectiveness and then identifying different ways of cumulatively and continually improving its performance. In particular it relies on the employees who use the equipment on a day-to-day basis taking ownership of the technology through cleaning tasks and basic maintenance. This familiarization encourages them to make suggestions for improvements in machine use and to be alert to potential problems before they happen.

total quality control (TQC) is a concept associated mainly with Japanese manufacturing organizations, although the idea of quality has spread to a range of organizations (see **Total Quality Management**). TQC stresses the importance of getting all employees to take responsibility for quality (i.e. delegating) yet ensuring that satisfactory standards are met by retaining systems of management control and monitoring. Quality, in this context, means finding ways of satisfying customer expectations; ensuring that processes, components, services, and products are 'fit for purpose'.

The emphasis lies on 'building quality in' rather than 'inspecting it out', thus employees are expected to 'get it right first time' because rework adds cost not value to the process. [See **just-in-time**; **quality circles**.]

Total Quality Management (TQM) is a collection of techniques that are designed to improve the responsiveness of the organization to the demands of customers. During the 1980s in particular, quality was considered to be the concept that could provide a competitive advantage for an organization. Thus, various management gurus and consultants devised packages of techniques that could make employees more quality conscious and more aware of the needs of both external and **internal customers**. In particular TQM became associated with a range of control techniques popular within manufacturing organizations (for example, **statistical process control** (SPC), **total quality control** (TQC), and **just-in-time** (JIT) production). Employees were encouraged (and in some cases obliged) to think of ways of making improvements to the product, process, or service in order to enhance quality and achieve greater customer satisfaction. TQM also emphasized that quality had to be adopted as one of the core values in the organization culture. This meant that rather than TQM simply being a set of techniques it also became a way of thinking—a philosophy of management. Managers were expected to 'think quality' when making any decisions. By the mid-1990s, the emphasis changed: rather than quality being seen as a competitive advantage it was considered to be an absolute necessity for an organization to survive in any intensely competitive environment. To this extent it ceased to be a fashionable management practice, although many of the ideas have passed into the mainstream of management thinking. [See **quality circles; kaizen**.]

total remuneration consists of three elements. The first is **base pay**, expressed as an **hourly rate** or annual **salary**. The second is **variable pay**, which consists of additional supplements, bonuses, and other payments that typically are linked to performance. The third component is **benefits** or **indirect pay**, including cash payments like occupational **sick pay** and **maternity pay** and non-cash awards like paid holidays and **health insurance**. Increasingly it is recommended that companies calculate and manage total remuneration for each employee as a means of securing tighter control of labour costs. It is also recommended, by advocates of the **new pay**, that the contribution of the three elements should be altered, such that variable pay makes up a larger proportion of the total. The purpose of this is to incentivize workers and ensure a tight link between reward practice and business strategy.

tough love is a term used to describe management actions that are of benefit to the organization but to the detriment of a minority of or, in some cases, all employees. For example, redundancies are often justified in terms of 'letting some people go' in order to ensure the survival of the organization. Similarly, management may justify the failure to give an above-inflation pay rise to employees on the grounds of the need to cut costs and remain competitive. Implicit in the term is the notion that 'management knows best' and hence it has undertones of **paternalism**.

trade association An association of employers that is largely concerned with matters of trade, such as export, competition, business promotion, and government regulation. Trade associations can be contrasted with **employers' associations** that are concerned primarily with employment matters, though the two kinds of activity can be combined in a single organization.

trade dispute Under UK law a trade union and its members and officers have legal **immunity** when organizing **industrial action** 'in contemplation or furtherance of a trade dispute'. A trade dispute is a dispute 'between workers and their employers which relates wholly or mainly' to the following: (1) terms and conditions of employment; (2) recruitment, suspension, and dismissal of employees; (3) work allocation and responsibilities; (4) discipline at work; (5) membership of trade unions and the rights of trade union officers; (6) procedural matters relating to trade union recognition, negotiation, and consultation. This definition excludes disputes that are not between workers and their employers, for example demarcation disputes between competing groups of workers. It also excludes disputes that are not about matters of trade, such as **political strikes**.

Trades Union Congress (TUC) The central organization of organized labour in the UK. The TUC is a **confederation** whose membership is comprised of individual affiliated **trade unions**. Currently the TUC has seventy-eight affiliates who represent 6.8 million trade unionists, about 87 per cent of the total in the UK. It is one of the oldest labour organizations in the world and was founded in 1868 to lobby Parliament for the passage of favourable trade union law. It continues to act as the political voice of the trade union movement and seeks to influence the development of employment law and social and economic policy at domestic and European levels. The TUC's role as a **social partner** has never been as extensive as that of its northern European counterparts but under the Labour government it has re-acquired some influence over public policy and continues to nominate representatives to a number of important tripartite bodies, including ACAS, HSC, and the **Low Pay Commission**. Other aspects of the TUC's work include mediating in jurisdictional disputes between affiliates, the provision of information and services, such as trade union education, and public campaigning on trade union and employment issues. The TUC employs a small professional staff in London and the regions which is headed by the General Secretary, John Monks. The latter initiated a formal relaunch of the TUC in 1994, which comprised a thorough reform of its decision-making machinery and the adoption of a more campaigning style. In recent years the TUC has become the most avowedly pro-European institution in British public life and has advocated the reform of British industrial relations on the lines of Dutch and German **social partnership**. It has also sought to promote organizing activity amongst its affiliates to try and reverse membership decline, and established an Organizing Academy in 1998 to train a new generation of paid trade union **organizers**. [See **tripartism**.]

trade union A representative or member organization of workers that exists to protect and advance the interests of working people.

Currently there are about 230 trade unions in the UK with a combined membership of 7.8 million. Unions are formally democratic organizations and their policy is developed through a system of **union government**, based on elected representatives, committees, councils, and conferences. In addition, however, large unions employ a staff of **full-time officers**, headed by a **general secretary**, which typically exerts a powerful influence over the direction of policy and the pattern of union activity. Trade unions act on behalf of their members in a number of different ways. They provide services directly to members, including insurance benefits, consumer discounts, and access to training, education, labour market services, welfare, and legal advice. They also play an important role representing individual members in company **procedures** and in the legal system, where unions may sponsor cases and provide advocates for workers taking cases to a **labour court** or tribunal. Perhaps the activity with which trade unions are most strongly associated, however, is **collective bargaining**, the negotiation of collective agreements with employers that determine employment conditions and regulate the employment relationship for unionized workers. Beyond collective bargaining unions may be involved in **joint consultation** or **labour–management partnership** with employers, where they contribute to the wider process of business decision-making. Finally, trade unions everywhere become involved in the political process, either by campaigning or lobbying governments for favourable legislation or by affiliating directly to a political party. Some of the largest trade unions in the UK, for instance, are affiliated to the Labour Party and seek to influence its policy from within. Trade unions come in a variety of forms and researchers have developed a number of classifications of unions. The most commonly used classify unions in terms of their membership base, the types of worker they recruit and represent. Thus, there are **closed unions**, which restrict membership to a particular occupation, enterprise, or industry, and there are general **open unions**, which recruit broadly across the occupational and industrial structure. Unions can also be differentiated in terms of their 'character'; that is some unions are **militant** and prepared to use a range of sanctions against employers, while others are moderate or embrace **social partnership** and may even have constitutional rules that outlaw **strike** action. In all countries with an established trade union movement there are central **confederations** of labour to which individual trade unions can affiliate. In the UK most large unions are affiliated to the **Trades Union Congress**, which acts as the voice of labour within the public sphere and the political process. In most industrial countries trade unions have declined in membership, influence, and power over the past two decades, due to changes in industrial structure, the election of hostile governments, and the emergence of a harsher, more competitive economic environment. Unions continue to play a significant role within the sphere of employment relations, however, and academic research on trade union effects indicates that union members tend to be better remunerated and enjoy more secure and closely regulated employment than workers in non-union firms.

traditionalist is a **management style** identified by **industrial relations** researchers that is said to characterize many small firms. Traditionalist companies are attached firmly to the principle of **management prerogative** and are resolutely hostile to trade unions.

training is the process of changing the skills, attitudes, and knowledge of employees with the purpose of improving their level of competence. It is a planned process, usually involving a series of stages where incremental improvements can be identified. It takes two main forms. (1) On-the-job training whereby an employee receives instruction within the place of work, usually through observing the tasks, being guided through them by experts, and then practising them. (2) Off-the-job training whereby an employee is instructed away from the place of work, either in a training room on the premises or at a separate location (such as a college). This training is more often theory based and might even take the form of self-learning packages.

training levy The compulsory collection of finance from all companies in a given sector by a state agency or **employers' association**

to fund training and correct **market failure** in training provision. Training levies were established in the UK in the early 1960s and operated by industry training boards. However, they were abolished by the Conservatives in the 1980s as part of their switch to 'employer-led' **vocational education and training**, with the exception of those in construction and engineering. The Labour government's White Paper of 1999, *Learning to Succeed*, raised the prospect of the reintroduction of a training levy across UK industry to correct a perceived shortfall in the amount of training being provided by British business.

training needs analysis (TNA) is the technique of assessing the training required to fill the gap between what skills and knowledge are currently possessed by employees, and what ought to be possessed. A training needs analysis can therefore not only address present deficiencies, it can also act as a developmental tool to allow managers to project future needs in line with the strategic aims of the organization. Typically the analysis will take place at three levels: first, the corporate level in order to establish organizational needs in line with the overall business objectives (see **human resource planning**); second, the departmental level, addressing the training required by different functional groups, project groups, and teams; third, the individual level, establishing specific employee requirements (see **appraisal**).

trait rating or graphic rating scales. A technique for evaluating the performance of an employee which can be used as part of the **appraisal** process. The technique involves listing the desirable traits that the jobholder should possess (such as reliability, integrity, drive, leadership ability) and rating (on a five-point scale, for example) each employee for each of these traits. These trait scores can then be aggregated into overall performance scores. This rating method is relatively simple to develop and administer, but suffers from two main drawbacks. (1) It is judgmental, rather than developmental, especially since the appraisee has no input into the grading decisions. (2) It is questionable whether some traits can be accurately and fairly rated. For example, whilst it might be possible to judge something like productivity, is it really possible to rate integrity or drive on a five-point scale? In order to address this problem, some organizations rate the employee's performance on job duties (for example, keyboarding skills, dealing with customers, running meetings) rather than traits. Other organizations reject the method entirely and instead adopt one of the alternative techniques such as **behaviourally anchored rating scales** (BARS) or **behavioural observation scales** (BOS).

transactional leadership see **leadership**

transaction costs are the indirect costs of economic exchange that are incidental to purchase and sale. For example, the transaction costs of hiring labour arise from the costs of **recruitment**, **selection**, **induction**, **training**, and **supervision** and not from the payment of wages.

transferable skills are skills that are developed in one context but which can be used in other contexts. Traditional **apprenticeship**, for instance, allowed craft workers to develop skills that could be used by a broad range of employers. The opposite of transferable skills are company-specific skills that are appropriate to a particular technology or business process but which attract no premium on the **external labour market**.

transfer of undertaking The transfer of all or part of an undertaking or business from one employer to another by sale or some other legal means. Under the terms of the Acquired Rights Directive of 1977 (amended 1998), employees have a number of protective rights in the event of such a transfer. In the UK these are set out in the 1981 **Transfer of Undertakings (Protection of Employment) Regulations**—known as TUPE. In a series of important judgments the **European Court of Justice** (ECJ) has clarified the circumstances in which these legal protections apply. It has determined that a transfer occurs when ancillary services, such as cleaning, are outsourced (see **subcontracting**), when public agencies are transferred from one authority to another, and when the control of non-profit-making organizations is transferred. It has also established through **infringement proceedings** against the UK government in

1994 that they apply where public services are transferred into private ownership as a result of **compulsory competitive tendering**. The UK's TUPE regulations stated explicitly that they did not apply to this situation but in the wake of the ECJ judgment they were amended in 1997 to cover most forms of transfer within and between public and private sectors. It should be noted that TUPE does not apply in the event of a transfer by share purchase, the main method by which businesses are transferred in the UK, because in formal terms the employer remains unchanged.

Transfer of Undertakings (Protection of Employment) Regulations (TUPE) The TUPE regulations give effect to the Acquired Rights Directive within the UK. They contain two main provisions. The first is a requirement to provide information to and consult on the transfer of an undertaking with the representatives of a recognized trade union or, in the absence of a union, workplace representatives. These requirements are akin to those that apply in the event of a **collective redundancy**. The second is an entitlement of employees to retain their existing contracts of employment and to protection from cuts in pay and conditions and from **unfair dismissal** arising from the transfer. The purpose of this second provision is to protect workers from the adverse effects of business restructuring set in train by the creation of the Single European Market. Its primary significance has been in the area of **compulsory competitive tendering** and the transfer of public services to private ownership. The regulations provide an element of protection for employees from the effects of cost reduction, have discouraged some private companies from bidding to take over public services, and have furnished trade unions with a degree of bargaining leverage. However, although the regulations establish that existing contracts and collective agreements are 'transferred' along with ownership, employers are free subsequently to negotiate new contracts or to offer altered contracts to new employees, provided these changes do not arise directly from the transfer itself.

transfiguration is the final stage that is supposedly achieved in the transition towards the **learning organization**. It is characterized by an organizational concern for society's welfare and betterment, acceptance of employees as members of an enterprise community, and a preoccupation with the personal development of all organizational members. Not surprisingly this communitarian vision has at best limited resonance with senior managers whose real preoccupation is with bottom-line performance. Furthermore, it has elicited scepticism from those who distrust **organizational development**.

transformational leadership is a concept that describes how some individuals can have such an impact that they fundamentally change an organization, particularly through affecting organizational culture. Transformational leaders are deemed to have the qualities of **charisma**, inspirational vision, intellectual stimulation, and a willingness to offer individualized support and encouragement of their followers.

transparency is the principle that management decisions should be based on demonstrable evidence. The term derives from legal judgments of the **European Court of Justice** and is applied particularly to the field of reward management. A transparent **payment system**, for instance, is one in which differences in earnings between employees arise from demonstrable differences in levels of qualifiation, effort, or performance, i.e. that one employee has a higher level of skill, has worked longer hours, or produced more output than another. The need for transparency in the management of reward is important because of **equal pay** legislation. If an employer cannot prove that differences in earnings are due to objective circumstances and a member of one sex is earning less than the other, then a court is likely to rule discrimination has occurred and award compensation.

trash can activity is a pejorative description of **personnel management** coined by the **management guru** Peter Drucker. It expresses the view that personnel management embraces a range of unrelated, low-level management functions that are avoided by higher-status management specialisms.

trial of strength A **strike** of long duration, involving large numbers of workers, over a fundamental issue that is central to the interests of both union and employer. Trials of strength can be bitter and occasionally violent events because a great deal may be at stake. An example is the long strike in the British mining industry in 1984–5 over management's right to close loss-making collieries. Trials of strength can be key turning points in the evolution of industrial relations and after the miners' strike, for instance, there was an extensive restructuring of the mining industry that resulted ultimately in **privatization**, extensive closure, and the effective **derecognition** of the National Union of Mineworkers.

tripartism is the principle that representatives of three primary interests will contribute to the public policy-making process: government, business, and labour. A tripartite public institution, therefore, is one with a governing council that comprises representatives of these three interests.

tripartite regulation is a process of **job regulation** that involves the three main actors in the **industrial relations system**, employers, trade unions, and government. [See **corporatism**; **joint regulation**; **unilateral regulation**.]

Trotskyism is a form of revolutionary **Marxism** derived from the work of the Russian thinker Leon Trotsky. Trotskyism is influential on the far left of the trade union movement and also influences academic writing on trade unions and industrial relations. Trotskyism is particularly associated with a critique of **union bureaucracy** and the advocacy of **militant** action by the trade union **rank and file**.

trust see **high trust**; **low trust**

twenty-four-hour society refers to the trend towards permanent opening of businesses to maximize consumer access to services and products. This trend has three major implications for HRM. First, it requires changes in the management of **working time** to ensure that the workforce is available to deliver services through extended **operating time**. Second, it has implications for **reward management** and is associated with the withdrawal of **unsocial-hours payments**, as all parts of the working day and week become classed as 'normal' working time. Finally, it raises the issue of **work–life balance**, as the cost of extended hours and greater choice for consumers may be the disruption of family and social life for workers.

2 + 2 = 5 see **synergy**

two-tier wages The payment of two separate rates of pay for the same class of work within a single, employing organization. Typically, the higher rate of pay is made to workers with **seniority**, while the lower rate is paid to new starters. The introduction of two-tier wages has been a feature of **concession bargaining** in American and British industry in recent years and has been sought by employers as a means of reducing labour costs.

U

U-form is the term used to describe a company with a 'unitary' structure. It is characterized by grouping the organization's activities into functional departments (marketing, sales, finance, personnel, etc.), each of which contributes a specialist expertise to the overall operation. The U-form is considered an appropriate way of structuring an organization that has a relatively narrow range of products or services. The greater the diversity of the product range, the greater the need for **divisionalization** around specific products or around geographical areas. [See **M-form**.]

unapproved share ownership scheme An **employee share ownership** scheme that is not registered with the Inland Revenue and which, as a consequence, is not eligible for the various forms of tax relief available to approved schemes.

uncertainty avoidance is the extent to which a national culture avoids uncertainty in life through career stability, formal rules, intolerance of deviance, belief in absolute truth, and attainment of expertise. It is one of the dimensions of national cultures identified by Geert Hofstede. [See **individualism–collectivism; power-distance**.]

unconstitutional strike An unconstitutional **strike** is one that is initiated before all the stages in an agreed **disputes procedure** have been exhausted. It is action, therefore, that contravenes the agreed rules established for regulating conflict within a sector or enterprise and to which the union has voluntarily agreed.

under-reward inequity A condition that occurs when an employee believes his or her remuneration and recognition are less than his or her contribution merits, compared with other employees. The resultant feelings of resentment can lead to employees reducing their efforts in an attempt to redress the balance. [See **distributive equity; equity theory**.]

unemployed Those who are without work. In the UK the official count of the unemployed is based on those who are without work but who are registered as seeking work and claiming benefit. Critics argue that this method leads to undercounting because it excludes discouraged workers who would like work but who are not claimants.

unemployment is the inability to find paid work when one is willing and able to perform work. Unemployment can be measured through official registration through a state agency, usually to claim unemployment benefit, or through self-assessment through a questionnaire survey. The latter generally produces a higher count. The unemployment rate is the unemployed as a percentage of the total workforce, defined as the employed plus the unemployed. The period since the late 1970s has been one of continuous high unemployment in most developed economies and this has had an important impact on the conduct of **industrial relations** and human resource management. It is generally believed that high levels of unemployment have shifted the balance of power in the **employment relationship** and endowed managers with greater freedom to redesign the system of work and employment to meet their own requirements. [See **non-accelerating inflation rate of unemployment**.]

unfair dismissal Since 1971 British employees have had a statutory right not to be unfairly dismissed that can be enforced at an **Employment Tribunal**. A **dismissal** may be judged unfair by a tribunal on two grounds. The first is the reason for dismissal, and the law declares certain reasons (e.g. dismissal for pregnancy or trade union membership) to be **automatically unfair**. The second is whether the dismissal satisfies the test of **reasonableness**, i.e. did the employer act reasonably and fairly given the circumstances of the case? If an employee wins a case for unfair dismissal, there are three possible remedies: **reinstatement** in the pre-dismissal job, **re-engagement** in comparable employment, and compensation.

Most successful cases result in the award of (usually modest) financial compensation. The latter has two elements: a basic award, calculated like **redundancy pay** on the basis of years of service and regular earnings, and a compensatory award. The maximum for the latter was set at £50,000 in 2000 and is up-rated in line with the retail price index. If the tribunal decides that the employee contributed to the dismissal the amount of financial compensation can be reduced. To qualify for unfair dismissal an employee must have twelve months' continuous employment apart from in cases where dismissal is for an automatically unfair reason. The number of unfair dismissal cases entering the Employment Tribunal system has risen in recent years and there are now more than 40,000 such cases per year.

unfreezing, moving, and refreezing is the three-stage model of change proposed by organization theorist Kurt Lewin. Although a simple idea, it captures the key stages in changing the dominant **beliefs**, **values**, and **norms** that are necessary to any programme of organizational change. The unfreezing stage is concerned with using techniques to show the need for change and freeing up the fixed views held by people within the organization (see **mind-set**). Moving is the stage where people are encouraged to accept new ideas and new ways of working. Refreezing is the process of fixing these new ideas into the minds of the employees and managers so that they form the new set of beliefs, values, and norms of the organization. The model uses the unfreezing and refreezing metaphor to emphasize that people can only be encouraged to change once the established ways of thinking and doing things have 'melted' and become fluid. The change agent's role (for example, the external consultant, or the internal **champion of change**) is to act initially like a source of heat, turning the solid state of thinking into a fluid (thereby gaining acceptance for the change programme), and then like a source of refrigeration transforming the fluid thinking back into a newly formed solid state (refreezing).

unilateral arbitration is **arbitration** of an industrial **dispute** that can be activated by either of the parties involved. At certain periods of time unilateral arbitration has been an important feature of UK industrial relations, particularly within the public sector. In the 1980s access to unilateral arbitration was withdrawn for some groups of public sector workers by the Conservative government. It was believed that the principle strengthened unions and compromised management's right to manage.

unilateral regulation is the one-sided creation and enforcement of employment rules by either employers or **trade unions**. Unilateral regulation of the employment relationship by trade unions is now a rarity but was once an important feature of craft labour markets, where unions controlled labour supply and set wages and working practices (see **strike in detail**). Unilateral regulation of work and employment by the employer, in contrast, is ubiquitous and has increased in importance since the 1970s as a result of the decline of trade unions and **collective bargaining**. The pay and conditions of most UK workers are today set unilaterally by their employers. [See **job regulation; joint regulation**.]

union see **trade union**

unionateness is a concept developed within sociology to measure the extent to which actual trade unions approximate to the characteristics of an 'ideal' **trade union**. The latter include reliance on **collective bargaining** and the **strike** weapon and participation in the broader labour movement through affiliation to a central **confederation** and a socialist political party.

union bureaucracy is a pejorative term for the **full-time officers** of trade unions that expresses the belief that official trade unionism is often ineffective or neglectful in advancing the interests of ordinary union members. The term is also used to refer to a particular kind of relationship between union members and their representatives, in which the latter take decisions and devise policy on behalf of members and therefore encourage passivity and dependence. [See **goal displacement; iron law of oligarchy; rank-and-filism**.]

union busting An attempt by an employer to break and remove a trade union in order to secure a non-union workforce. Union busting has been a particular feature of North American industrial relations and may take the form of a concerted campaign to secure the legal decertification of a trade union. Such a campaign might include unethical and illegal tactics including the harassment of union members and attempts to bribe employees to surrender their membership (see **captive audience meeting**). Union busting can also refer to attempts to pre-empt unionization and frustrate attempts at union organizing. In North America it is frequently conducted by specialist consultants, known colloquially as 'union busters'. [See **derecognition**.]

union democracy refers to the participation of trade union members in the government of their **trade unions**. Trade unions are membership organizations that are formally democratic and allow for member participation and control of policy-making through a variety of mechanisms. At local level, trade union members directly elect **shop stewards** and the officers of the local union **branch**. The branch, in turn, will typically nominate delegates to attend committees, councils, and conferences at regional and national levels of **union government**. In addition, under UK law voting members of the union's national executive must be elected by a secret **postal ballot** of all members. Postal ballots must also be used to endorse particular decisions, such as the setting up of a **political fund** and taking **strike** action, and, although not obligatory, they are used increasingly to decide the acceptance of wage offers from employers. Identifying the conditions under which union democracy flourishes, and the **iron law of oligarchy** is kept in check, have been major concerns of **industrial relations** researchers. According to one view, genuine union democracy is dependent upon the existence of competing factions or parties within a union which allow members to choose between alternative programmes and provide a source of opposition to the incumbent leadership. An alternative view stresses the value of 'direct' as opposed to 'representative' democracy and the scope for the union **rank and file** to participate in union activities at workplace level. Union democracy in the UK is subject to close legal regulation as a result of the Conservative reforms of trade union government of the 1980s and 1990s, which introduced the requirements to rely on secret postal balloting.

union density is the percentage of potential union members who are actual members, often expressed as the percentage of workers or employees in union membership. Union density can be calculated in a number of ways and there are several measures of actual and potential membership that can be used to make the calculation. In the UK the most frequently cited estimate is calculated from the government's annual **Labour Force Survey** (LFS). This is an estimate based on all those in employment, excluding members of the armed forces, and in 1998 provided an economy-wide union density figure of 29.6 per cent. Ten years earlier the same series produced an estimate of 39 per cent and there has been a sustained drop in union density in the UK since the 1970s. Union density varies considerably from country to country and is often used as an indicator of the strength of national trade union movements. According to the **International Labour Organization** (ILO) union density in the main European economies in 1995 was as follows: France (9.1), Germany (28.1), Italy (44), Spain (18.6), Sweden (91.1), and UK (32.9). Density can also vary substantially within national economies by industry, occupation, type of employment, age, and sex. In 1998, according to LFS, density was only 7 per cent in hotels and restaurants but 60 per cent in public administration, 52 per cent among associate professionals but only 11 per cent among sales staff, 33 per cent among full-timers but 20 per cent among part-timers, and 38 per cent among those aged 40–9 but only 6 per cent among those under 20. The gap in density between men and women, however, has nearly closed and according to LFS 31 per cent of male employees are union members and 28 per cent of female.

union exclusion A systematic attempt by governments and employers to reduce the influence of **trade unions** and deny them access to decision-making processes, either within the political system or within the employing enterprise. The term was first coined to describe the stance towards unions adopted by the UK Conservative governments of the 1980s, which systematically excluded unions from influence over government policy-making and disbanded a number of tripartite bodies (e.g. the National Economic Development Council) on which unions had representation. More latterly, the term has been used to describe the policies of employers and embraces attempts by the latter to derecognize unions or minimize their role within the firm.

union government is the system of rules and procedures that govern the election and appointment of representatives, the allocation of resources, and the determination of policy within **trade unions**. Within most UK trade unions the key institutions of internal government include a sovereign delegate conference that formally determines national policy, an elected executive that oversees the implementation of policy, and a staff of **full-time officers**, headed by a **general secretary**, that provides expertise and support to the executive. In addition, most unions have a system of local **branches** and intermediate levels of government consisting of regional committees and conferences and bodies that determine policy for a particular 'trade group'; that is, members within a particular industrial sector. In large unions the system of internal government can be extremely complex and can vary on a number of dimensions. It can be more or less centralized with decision-making concentrated in the hands of national leaders and institutions or devolved to local branches. It can also be bifurcated; that is, divided between procedures for determining policy for **collective bargaining** and for non-bargaining policy, such as the union's stance on political issues. Recent changes in union government in the UK have included the closer regulation of **union democracy** by statutes that require reliance on **postal ballots** and voluntary reform to allow for the expression of diverse interests amongst union members. For example, most unions in the UK now have separate women's committees and conferences and many have arrangements through which black workers, young workers, the disabled, and gays and lesbians can be consulted over and influence union policy. In the most ambitious of these attempts to represent diversity unions have committed themselves to **proportionate**

representation for women members and have introduced **self-organization** for women and members of minorities.

union merger The merger of two or more trade unions either through a 'transfer of engagements', in which a smaller union is absorbed in a larger union, or through the creation of a new trade union. UNISON, the largest trade union in the UK, was formed in 1993 from the merger of three previously separate public service unions. Researchers have identified three types of union merger. Defensive mergers are a response to membership decline, consolidatory mergers occur when two unions operating in the same industry decide to pool their strength, and aggressive mergers occur when growing unions take over smaller organizations in order to enter a new **job territory**. In recent years, there has been extensive merger activity amongst unions in Germany, the UK, and the USA, which has led to the emergence of larger, **general unions** with members in a broad range of occupations and industries.

Union of Industrial and Employers' Confederations of Europe

(UNICE) The **confederation** of private sector employers that operates at European level. It is one of the European **social partners** and is involved in **social dialogue** with the European Commission and the **European Trade Union Confederation**.

union renewal A theory of change in **trade unions** formulated to analyse recent developments in the public sector. The essence of the theory is a claim that two developments are prompting the emergence of a more vital and participative workplace unionism in public sector organizations. These are the **decentralization of bargaining**, which gives union members the opportunity to participate, and the intensification of management control, which is providing an incentive to participate. The thesis has been subject to a variety of criticisms. Researchers have questioned whether renewal is in fact taking place and studies of local industrial relations in the public sector have shown quiescent and ineffective workplace trade unionism. Others have pointed to the fact that key innovations in unions often arise above the workplace and may be resisted at local level, i.e. that renewal in at least some circumstances may be a top-down phenomenon. It has also been argued that the thesis rests on unrealistic assumptions about the potential for unions to involve and mobilize their members and that it ignores the disadvantages of a fragmented and decentralized structure of bargaining. The latter include increased earnings inequality and greater opportunity for employers to escape altogether from **collective bargaining**.

union replacement is a management strategy that seeks to maintain a non-unionized workforce by offering high wages and good conditions and providing alternative mechanisms through which employees can resolve problems at work. [See **union suppression**; **welfare capitalism**.]

union shop see **closed shop**

union structure This term has two meanings: (1) the internal organization of trade unions; (2) the principles used to allocate union members to individual trade unions. In Japan, for instance, the dominant principle of union structure is enterprise unionism, with workers largely joining unions whose membership is confined to a single employing organization. In Germany, in contrast, the dominant principle until recently was industrial unionism, with workers being allocated to unions whose membership was confined to a single industrial sector. In the UK union structure is complex and the pattern of union organization is highly variable (see **job territory**). Thus, there are enterprise, occupational, industry, and **general unions**, although most trade union members are found in the latter and these now constitute the dominant form.

union suppression is a management strategy to avoid unionization that involves the victimization of union **activists** and supporters and threats to close or relocate the company if unionization occurs. In many countries action of this kind is unlawful, though research indicates it is a common response amongst managers faced with the prospect of unionization for the first time. [See **captive audience meeting**; **union busting**.]

union voice is the use of a **trade union** by workers to articulate grievances or express their preferences to management. Research evidence indicates that union voice can be effective in influencing management in two ways. First, it is associated with redistribution of resources within the firm, such that unionized workers receive higher pay and benefits compared with non-union counterparts. Second, it is associated with perceptions of fair treatment by the employer and lower rates of **turnover**. According to some commentators, unions provide an effective mechanism for **employee voice** because they have the power to pressure management into acting in accordance with employee wishes and also monitor management behaviour to ensure compliance with agreed policy.

unitarism is a **frame of reference** that emphasizes the shared interests of all members of an organization. It assumes there are compatible goals, a common purpose, and a single (unitary) interest which means that, if managed effectively, the organization will function harmoniously. This viewpoint assumes that conflict is abnormal and is caused by troublemakers, bad communication, and poor management. Consequently, a unitarist will seek to eliminate conflict. Unitarism is the opposite of **pluralism**—both terms were coined by industrial relations theorist Alan Fox.

unity of command is the concept that nobody should receive instructions from more than one superior. It stems from early management theories that stressed the importance of producing a simple chain of command with clear lines of authority. Some contemporary management methods have broken away from the principle of unity of command through developments such as **teamworking**.

University for Industry (UFI) A UK government programme launched in 2000 that seeks to provide opportunities for continuing training and education for workers. Unlike a traditional university, the UFI is planned to operate through around 1,000 local learning centres and provides most of its services through the internet. [See **distance learning; e-learning; on-line learning.**]

unofficial strike An unofficial **strike** is one that has not been ratified by a **trade union** in accordance with its internal procedures. Unofficial action, therefore, is taken by union members acting independently of the formal union, and perhaps in open defiance of trade union leaders. Under current law unofficial action is likely to be unlawful action that has not been preceded by a properly conducted **strike ballot**. Unlawful unofficial action of this kind must be publicly repudiated by a trade union if it is not to lose its **immunity** and become liable for civil action for damages from the employer (see **vicarious liability**).

unsocial-hours payment A supplementary payment or allowance made to employees whose work requires attendance outside the normal working week. For example, employees who have to work weekends or attend work in the evening may be entitled to an unsocial-hours payment.

upsizing is the process of increasing the number of employees after having previously undertaken **downsizing**. The need for upsizing occurs when an organization has gone through a dramatic process of reducing **headcount** in order to lower costs, only to find that it has gone too far. In particular this can occur where employees are the means through which an organization can increase its revenue—for example, by getting more contracts. So upsizing can be seen as the process of reversing the negative effects of downsizing.

upskilling is an increase in skill level resulting from technical change or **job redesign**. Optimistic theories of **post-industrial society** posit a general upskilling across the workforce as the economy shifts from manufacturing to services. [See **deskilling**.]

utilitarianism is an ethical justification for action on the grounds that it promotes the 'greatest good for the greatest number'. HRM policies that are seemingly unethical, such as heavy reliance on a **contingent workforce**, may be justified, therefore, on the grounds that they allow improvements in business performance that benefit the broad mass of employees in the longer term (see **tough love**). Utilitarianism can be contrasted with a deontological position in **business ethics**, which asserts that actions (including HR policies) should be pursued because they are right in themselves and not solely because they may have beneficial consequences.

V

validity When a particular selection technique is used to decide between job applicants, it ought to be valid. There are three main sorts of validity that apply. (1) Content validity refers to whether the technique is a good measure of the quality or attribute being assessed. For example, if word processing skill were needed, getting the candidate to undertake a practical test would have greater content validity than asking them about their word processing ability in an interview. (2) Predictive validity refers to the ability of a particular technique to predict future job performance. For example, scores on a numeracy test might be a good indicator of likely future accuracy of candidates applying for the job of accounts clerk. (3) Face validity refers to whether the technique is deemed an appropriate method for assessing the applicant. For example, if an applicant for a security guard's job was given a test for telephone skills, there would be little face validity (assuming such guards rarely use a telephone in the course of their work). Where there is little face validity, the applicant is likely to underperform, seeing no relevance to the technique being used and the future requirements of the job. [See **reliability**.]

valorization see **labour process theory**

value chain A set of activities and processes that, when linked together, provide value for the end user. A value chain therefore might stretch across several organizations, each providing the linkages that create the products and services. Managing the value chain requires organizations actively involving their customers and suppliers in their business planning processes. The idea is of developing partnerships that create mutual gain across the whole value chain, although cynics argue that some parts of the chain inevitably benefit more than others. The value chain is an important part of creating **boundaryless organizations** that rely on mutually beneficial co-operation. The original concept of the value chain was developed by the business strategist Michael Porter.

values are the preferences people have for how things ought to be. They represent a person's judgment about what is right and wrong. Organizational values are designed to guide the behaviour and thinking of employees in everything they do. Values are typically embodied in slogans and symbols within the organization.

value sapping is a term used to describe an activity or function that does not add any value and is considered to be a drain upon the organization. Sometimes, the personnel/human resource function is criticized as being value sapping because it is more difficult for management accountants to assess the value that personnel activities add than to assess the costs that such activities incur.

variable pay is that proportion of **total remuneration** not consolidated into **base pay** which has to be re-earned in each pay period (week, month, or year). Examples of variable pay include **sales incentives**, an annual profit share, or a cash bonus based on estimates of employee performance. The key features are that payments vary upwards or downwards, depending on performance, and that they are discrete: after payment the slate is wiped clean and employees have to earn their commission, profit share, or bonus afresh. There has been increased interest in variable pay amongst employers and management consultants as a means of importing greater flexibility into labour costs and sharpening financial incentives for employees. Advocates of the **new pay** tend to recommend variable pay and urge that base pay and **benefits** are kept to a minimum in order to release a larger proportion of total earnings for the reward of performance. Their recommendation, essentially, is to make earnings more risky or 'variable' out of a belief that this will incentivize workers and secure higher levels of output, quality, or profit. Critics argue that variable pay increases employee insecurity and is more likely to encourage employees to look elsewhere for a more secure position with assured remuneration, especially when employees have dependants and financial commitments, such as a mortgage.

VDU regulations Under the Health and Safety (Display Screen Equipment) Regulations 1992, employers have a special responsibility to protect the **health and safety** of employees who use visual display units (VDUs). Employers whose staff use VDUs should carry out a work situation assessment and identify any special needs of the person using it, including ensuring it is suitably lit. In addition, employers must ensure employees take sufficient breaks, including movement to other types of work, and give the opportunity to have regular eye tests at the employer's expense.

verbal warning see **oral warning**

vertical loading is the technique of adding more tasks of a higher, more demanding skill level to an existing job. [See **job redesign**.]

vertical segregation is a concept that describes a workplace where different levels in the organization can be distinguished by the particular characteristics of the employees at that level. For example, if all the sewing machine operators in a clothing factory were women and all the supervisors were men, then it could be described as being vertically segregated by sex. Such a pattern of lower levels in the hierarchy dominated by women and management levels composed mainly of men is typical of vertical segregation. However, the term can also apply to other characteristics. For example, there might be age segregation in a financial consultancy where all the financial advisers were in their twenties and the managers/partners in their forties; or race segregation in an electrical retail outlet where all the sales staff were Asian and the management team white. Social class is also an important determinant of vertical segregation. [See **horizontal segregation**.]

vibration is a major workplace hazard which includes two main forms. Vibration from work with powered hand-held tools and equipment can damage the hands and arms, leading to 'hand–arm vibration syndrome'. This is an irreversible condition, which includes 'vibration white finger'. The effects include impaired blood circulation, damage to nerves and muscles, and the loss of ability to grip properly. The second form is whole body vibration, which occurs when driving or riding over rough terrain and which can lead to back problems. In the UK there are no specific regulations to minimize vibration risk, though it is covered by the Health and Safety at Work Act 1974 and the Management of Health and Safety at Work Regulations 1992. The **Health and Safety Commission** has issued advice on how to avoid vibration problems.

vicarious learning is the process of learning by watching other people, and then copying them. [See **training; sitting-with-Nellie; shadowing**.]

vicarious liability Under UK employment law a **trade union** can be held responsible ('vicariously liable') for the unauthorized actions of its officers and **shop stewards** who organize unlawful strike action. This means the union can be sued for damages unless it issues a formal repudiation and instructs its members to return to work. [See **unofficial strike**.]

video-conferencing is the technique of linking together individuals in different locations through video cameras mounted on their computer screens. The individuals are brought together in a 'virtual conference room' on their computer monitor, in which they can see real-time images of the other people. The facility is considered to be particularly useful for organizations that need to bring together managers from diverse locations around the world because it can save on time and travel. It is considered superior to telephone conferencing because it is closer to real meetings where participants pick up many non-verbal cues in the process of communicating with each other. [See **teleworking**.]

virtual organization An organization that combines temporarily with one or more other organizations in order to collaborate on a commercial project—each organization bringing its **core**

competencies to the project. Once the project has been completed, the connections between the organizations are broken and they go their separate ways. In this sense, the virtual organization is a network that exists only as long as the connections are maintained.

virtual team A group of employees who are physically dispersed but communicate through information technology. They meet in cyberspace, rather than physical space, through e-mail, **videoconferencing**, and intranet chat rooms. Like regular teams they have common, specific goals and complementary skills.

visible minority is a term used in Canada to distinguish ethnic or racial groups that differ from the majority due to physical characteristics (such as skin colour). This distinguishes them from ethnic/racial minorities within the population who are identifiable by non-visible attributes, such as language.

vocational education and training (VET) consists of those elements of the state education system plus the voluntary training activities of business and other organizations that prepare people for work. In the UK important elements of the VET system include the **Learning and Skills Councils**, **National Vocational Qualifications**, the **Modern Apprenticeship**, the **University for Industry**, and the **Welfare-to-Work** programme. The performance of the UK's VET system has been criticized repeatedly in recent years, leading to a succession of reform initiatives. It is often believed that Germany has a much more successful system of VET, based largely on apprenticeship, which supports high levels of basic competence amongst the working population.

voice see **employee voice**; **union voice**

voluntarism is the principle that government and legal intervention in employment relations should be kept to a minimum, allowing employers and trade unions maximum scope to regulate their own affairs. Voluntarism characterized the UK system of industrial relations for much of the twentieth century with **employment law** being confined to issues or groups of workers who were not easily covered by free **collective bargaining**. It was a tradition that was supported on the union side by an abiding suspicion of the judiciary and its anti-union animus; unions were concerned that legal intervention would provide greater opportunity for judges to make anti-union judgments. In recent decades the tide has turned against voluntarism and governments have become increasingly interventionist with regard to employment relations. The volume of employment law has risen, in large part through membership of the European Union, and union decline has led to calls for increased **legal regulation** of the labour market to compensate for declining **joint regulation**.

voluntary incomes policy see incomes policy

voluntary redundancy occurs when an employee volunteers to be dismissed for reasons of **redundancy**. It is often seen as a more acceptable way of dealing with redundancies, which is less demoralizing for the workforce. Voluntary redundancy can be relatively expensive, however, because longer-serving employees, entitled to larger redundancy payments, are more likely to volunteer. It may also lead to an imbalance of skills in the workforce, and for this reason **redundancy procedures** often state that management has the right to decide whether a particular employee should be allowed to leave. The use of voluntary as opposed to **compulsory redundancy** is more common in unionized establishments.

W

wage Payment for work within an **employment relationship**. The wage can consist of a number of elements including the basic wage or **salary**, supplementary payments, and **bonuses**. Payment of wages can be made at a variety of intervals, monthly in the case of most salary earners and weekly for many manual employees. Many of the latter continue to receive their wages in the form of a cash payment but increasingly wages are paid through credit transfer into a bank account and employers in the UK are entitled to make payments in this form. The wage rate is the basic level of payment for a given job, grade, or jobholder and may be expressed as an annual salary, weekly wage, or **hourly rate**. In the UK, the payment of wages is regulated through the Wages Act 1986, which provides protection for employees in cases of non- or underpayment or unauthorized **deductions from wages** by the employer. Redress can be sought through application to an **Employment Tribunal** and there has been an upward trend in the number of wages cases in recent years. European legislation also requires that employees should receive an **itemized pay statement**, giving details of the wage and its components and any deductions, including payment of tax, National Insurance, and pension contributions. [See **remuneration**.]

wage differential see wage-gap

wage drift is the tendency for earnings to rise more rapidly than collectively bargained rates of pay. Wage drift was identified as a major source of inflation in the UK in the 1960s when it became apparent that earnings were advancing much more rapidly than might be expected from the formal increases in pay agreed through multi-employer industry agreements. The source of the increase in earnings was the growth in informal **workplace bargaining** and poorly managed incentive schemes that allowed workers to raise their earnings well above the agreed rates at industry level. An element of wage drift will emerge in any system of centralized **pay determination** and is an important feature of the labour market in many different national economies. It can provide a valuable source of flexibility within centralized systems of pay determination and allow some differentiation of wage rates in the face of variable labour and product market conditions. Although multi-employer industry bargaining has declined in the UK since the 1960s the phenomenon of wage drift can still be identified, but within companies, as workers rely on supplementary and premium rates to boost their pay above the agreed basic rate. [See **degeneration; grade drift**.]

wage-gap The **trade union** wage-gap, 'mark-up', or 'differential' is the average increase in earnings received by trade union members compared with non-union workers in equivalent employment. Estimates of the wage-gap produced by labour economists based on individual and establishment cross-sectional surveys suggest that coverage by collective bargaining produces an average increase in pay of 8 per cent in the UK and 15 per cent in the USA. The wage-gap appears to be greater for manual workers and women. Not all unionized workers enjoy a wage premium, however, and it seems that for the wage-gap to appear two primary conditions have to be in place. First, union membership and organization have to be relatively high and the employer has to enjoy market power, that is relatively beneficial product market conditions which allow economic rents to be shared with trade union members. There is evidence from both the UK and the USA that the wage-gap has declined in recent years as a result of the overall decline in union bargaining power. For the UK, recent evidence from the Confederation of British Industry pay databank and the WERS series points to *lower* pay settlements on average in companies and establishments which are covered by **collective bargaining**.

wages council The wages councils were statutory tripartite boards that set minimum rates of pay and other conditions of employment in low-wage industries in the UK for much of the twentieth century. With the exception of the Agricultural Wages Board, they were abolished by the Conservative government of John Major in the early 1990s. Their function has since been restored by the Labour government, in the form of the **National Minimum Wage**, which sets a universal pay floor for all industries and occupations.

waiver clause A clause within a **fixed-term contract** through which the employee waives his or her right to a statutory redundancy payment. The fixed-term contract must be for a minimum of two years if the clause is to be inserted. Under the Employment Rights Act 1999 in the UK it is no longer possible for employees on fixed-term contracts to waive their rights to compensation for **unfair dismissal**.

walk the talk is a piece of management jargon that has become a cliché. It means putting your words into action—showing that you mean what you say by actively doing it yourself. It is a version of the everyday phrase 'practise what you preach'.

weak culture refers to an organization that either does not possess a clearly identifiable set of values and beliefs, or else possesses them but fails to get them widely shared by employees. Whilst weak cultures are often deemed inferior to **strong cultures**, they have the advantage of producing a greater diversity of views, ideas, and behaviour. This can be beneficial if an organization wants to encourage creativity and originality, or if it is faced with constant change and the need for flexibility. [See **organizational culture**.]

welfare capitalism is a description of the policies of large non-union companies in the United States that have developed internal welfare systems to foster worker loyalty and commitment. Examples of companies that have practised welfare capitalism include Kodak, Sears, and IBM. The main elements of the employment system in these and other non-union companies, until relatively recently, included permanent employment, internal labour markets, extensive security and fringe **benefits**, and sophisticated communications and **employee involvement**. This paternalistic package of measures, however, has been put under strain as a result of business restructuring and **downsizing**. Large American companies appear to be less prepared to shoulder risk on behalf of their employees than they were in the post-war decades.

Welfare-to-Work is the UK Labour government's policy for reducing long-term unemployment. The original and primary aim was to provide employment and training opportunities for under-25-year-olds who have been registered as unemployed for six months or more. The New Deal programme that gives effect to the policy offers four opportunities to the long-term unemployed. The first provides work with approved training with a private sector employer who receives a tax rebate of £60.00 for a period of six months. The second option provides work and training on an environmental task force with a wage equivalent to the young person's benefit payment. The third option is to work within the voluntary sector for six months, while the fourth is to enter a full-time vocational education and training course. The scheme is financed by a windfall tax levied on the privatized utilities. Since the New Deal's inception it has been extended to cover a broader section of the long-term unemployed.

whipsawing is a bargaining tactic used by trade unions in which there is an attempt to spread wage and other concessions from one employer to another using 'coercive comparisons'. A breakthrough in negotiations in a lead firm can thereby be generalized across an industry or occupational group. Whipsawing is an American term, the UK equivalent of which is **leapfrogging**.

whistle-blowing is the disclosure of information by an employee for the purpose of exposing organizational malpractice or criminal activity. Disclosure may be to higher management, the media, politicians, trade unions, professional associations, or regulatory bodies and is made in the public interest rather than for malice or gain. Under the Public Interest Disclosure Act 1998, an individual is protected against victimization or **dismissal** for disclosing information, provided the information disclosed appears to indicate that a criminal offence is being committed, a legal obligation is not being complied with, or a miscarriage of justice has occurred. The disclosure of information relating to health and safety and environmental protection is also covered. To obtain protection under the law, whistle-blowers must be able to demonstrate that they acted in good faith and not for personal gain. In the event of **unfair dismissal** for whistle-blowing there is no upper limit on the financial compensation that can be awarded to the applicant. Under pressure from the Act organizations increasingly are adopting information disclosure procedures that provide internal mechanisms through which employees can raise concerns in confidence and without fear of detriment.

Whitley Council see **Joint Industrial Council**

Whitleyism is the system of industrial relations that has been dominant in the public sector since the report of the Whitley Commission at the end of the First World War. Whitleyism is characterized by joint negotiation and consultative committees at national, regional, and local levels, with terms and conditions of employment being set through highly prescriptive national agreements. The system was first established for the civil service and schoolteachers and then extended subsequently to local government and the National Health Service. The restructuring of the public services since 1980 has led to substantial erosion of Whitleyism. In some cases joint negotiation has given way to pay determination through **Pay Review Bodies** (e.g. nurses, teachers) and in others there has been devolution of bargaining to individual service agencies (e.g. civil service). However, elements of the system continue to survive in local government and the health service. [See **Joint Industrial Council**.]

wildcat A strike that breaks out suddenly, and perhaps violently, without union authorization and in contravention of **disputes procedure**. Wildcats, therefore, are both **unofficial** and **unconstitutional strikes**. They can also be very dramatic events, unleashing pent-up discontent over wages, working practices, management style, and trade union failure. In the current period of labour quiescence, observers have noted not wildcat strikes but 'wildcat co-operation'; in other words, a tendency for workers to reject union attempts to resist or negotiate change and to accept management demands for pay freezes, changes in work practice, and organizational restructuring.

Winter of Discontent The wave of strike action in the winter of 1978–9 which preceded the election of Margaret Thatcher as Prime Minister and was used to legitimize the programme of Conservative trade union reform through the 1980s and 1990s. The strikes represented a rejection by many groups of workers of the Labour government's **incomes policy**, which had led to a fall in real earnings for public sector employees and many skilled workers in the private sector. For critics, the Winter of Discontent exemplified the problem of 'excessive' union power in the UK and the symbol of callous strike action, 'when the dead lay unburied', has been used repeatedly since then as a stick to beat the trade union movement.

womb to tomb is a phrase sometimes used to express the idea of a person having a career that lasts the whole of his or her working life. However, with the emergence of greater **flexibility**, less **security of employment**, and new ideas such as the **portfolio career**, the phrase is of declining relevance.

women's support group A group of wives, partners, and other family members and friends that is formed to provide support and campaign on behalf of striking workers. The formation of women's support groups has been a feature of major conflicts arising from the restructuring of traditional industries in Australia, the UK, the USA, and other countries and is indicative of community mobilization behind groups of workers engaged in conflict. The activities of women's support groups include providing food and other material support to strikers and their families, involvement in picketing and demonstrations, and rallying support for strikers in the labour movement and beyond.

workaholic An employee who spends as much time as possible working, neglects other aspects of his or her life, and ultimately can become stressed and ill from overwork. Workaholics will typically fail to take their full holiday entitlement and regularly work at weekends. [See **presenteeism**.]

work-based competencies see competency

worker commonly means a person who is employed, usually in a non-managerial role. However, there is also a more precise legal definition: a worker is someone engaged in 'dependent labour', whether they be an employee with a **contract of employment** or **self-employed** and providing their services to an employer. Much statutory employment legislation is concerned only to protect employees (i.e. just those with contracts of employment), although the growth of non-standard employment has led to pressure to broaden the scope of protective legislation so that it embraces all categories of dependent labour. The **National Minimum Wage** in the UK and the regulations implementing the EU **Working Time Directive** and the **Part-Time Workers Directive** apply to workers and not just to employees (i.e. all those involved in 'dependent labour' are covered and not just those with a contract of employment). European employment legislation generally applies to workers and not solely to employees.

worker capitalism is a term that was coined in the 1980s to describe **employee share ownership** and other forms of **financial participation**. It has the connotation that these arrangements issue in a new form of employment relations founded on co-operation and can effectively end the long conflict between capital and labour.

worker director A director on the board of a company who is elected as a representative of the workforce. In Germany, worker directors are a legal requirement on the supervisory boards of large companies. Under the Works Constitution Act 1952 one-third of the seats on supervisory boards are allocated to worker directors in companies with more than 500 employees and under the Codetermination Act 1976 larger companies with more than 2,000 employees must have an equal number of shareholder and worker representatives. The strongest system, however, operates in the coal and steel industry, where there must be parity on the supervisory board and where employee representatives have a right of veto over the appointment of the labour director to the company's **management board**. [See **codetermination**.]

worker participation see participation

workers' co-operative An enterprise that is wholly owned by its workforce, who therefore appoint (or even elect) the organization's management. Co-operatives have been advocated as means of job creation in depressed economic regions and as a way of avoiding the conflicts and inefficiencies of conventional firms. Although some co-operatives are highly successful they remain a marginal form of enterprise within the capitalist economy. Prominent examples include Tower Colliery in south Wales and the Mondragon co-operatives of the Basque region in Spain.

workforce agreement An agreement between an employer and non-union workforce representatives under the terms of the UK Working Time Regulations. Such agreements can be used to secure a more flexible implementation of the legal rules on **working time**, suited to the needs of an individual company; for example, the forty-eight-hour week can be averaged over a fifty-two-week period through a workforce agreement. Workforce agreements must be in writing and agreed by elected representatives in companies with twenty or more employees; in smaller companies they can be agreed directly with the workforce but a majority must express approval. Workforce agreements cannot override collective agreements negotiated with a **trade union**.

workgroup see group

working days lost is an official measure of **strike** activity which multiplies the number of workers involved in a strike by the strike's duration (number of days). Some commentators regard the term as misleading because lost production can often be made up after the end of a strike. For this reason the alternative term **striker days** is sometimes used.

working time is the time that workers spend in paid employment. There are three aspects of working time: time, timing, and tempo. Time refers to the duration of working time and can be measured in terms of the length of the working day, working week, or working year. Timing refers to the scheduling of work time, which may follow a standard pattern (e.g. nine-to-five, Monday to Friday) or a shift pattern. Under the latter, individuals may work on different days or at different times of the day in successive weeks. Tempo refers to the intensity with which people work during their working time and the extent to which periods of work are broken up by meal times and tea and coffee breaks. [See **annual-hours contracts; compressed working week; flexitime; overtime; porosity; work intensification; Working Time Directive**.]

Working Time Directive The European Union adopted a directive on the organization of working time in 1993, which establishes protective standards for employees in the areas of: daily and weekly rest periods, maximum weekly hours, shift work, annual holidays, and night work. The main substantive provisions are for: eleven hours' rest per day; thirty-five hours' rest at the weekend; a daily rest break if **working time** extends beyond six hours; a maximum of eight hours per shift on night work, averaged over two weeks; a forty-eight-hour working week; four weeks' paid holiday; and a general provision that working time be adapted to the needs of the worker. The directive was introduced as part of the Social Charter Action Programme and was adopted under **qualified majority voting** by the Council of Ministers as a **health and safety** measure. The directive was initially opposed by the UK Conservative government on the grounds that working time was not a health and safety issue, but, following the rejection of its case by the **European Court of Justice**, the UK has been required to accept the measure. The Working Time Regulations that give effect to the directive were issued by the UK Labour government in 1998.

work intensification is the process of raising the expected workload of an employee by increasing the amount of tasks to be undertaken or shortening the time allowed to complete those tasks.

It therefore involves a reduction in the **porosity** of the working day. Work intensification can arise because businesses are under pressure to increase their return on assets or to balance an increase in labour costs. Some commentators suggest there is a general tendency towards work intensification in contemporary organizations because of the growth of competition and the continual drive for higher profits. Many of the management techniques and organizational initiatives defined in this dictionary can result in intensifying the work process in various ways.

work–life balance is the principle that paid employment should be integrated with domestic life and community involvement in the interests of personal and social well-being. The UK government and major employers have endorsed this principle, reflecting growing concern that long hours of work may damage personal relationships and community cohesion. [See **family-friendly policies**.]

work overload means having too much work to do in the time available. [See **job stress**.]

work permit Work permits are issued by the Department for Education and Employment and provide authorization for non-European Union citizens to work in the UK.

workplace bargaining is **collective bargaining** between trade unions and managers at the level of the workplace. Workplace bargaining typically involves **shop stewards** and workplace managers and may be relatively informal, resulting in agreed understandings rather than formal, written agreements.

workplace bullying is any behaviour that intimidates an employee, leading to feelings of humiliation, lack of self-worth, or inadequacy. It can take various forms, including verbal abuse, shouting, swearing, and publicly belittling a person; ignoring or excluding someone from a group; persistent criticism; setting unrealistic targets; and blocking developmental opportunities (such as training or chances of taking responsibility). Bullying behaviour usually persists over a long period, gradually wearing down its victim, with the result that the workplace becomes a stressful environment for the employee. It can occur between different levels in the hierarchy (for example, a senior manager bullying a junior manager, secretary, etc.) or between employees on the same or similar level. In the former case, bullying is underpinned by an imbalance of formal power and status, whilst in the latter case it can stem from social differences (such as belonging to a minority group). Progressive organizations recognize the dysfunctional effects of workplace bullying, so they establish policies that identify bullying as a form of **harassment**, and set up procedures to provide victims with a channel through which they can complain and seek redress. [See also **dignity at work policy; grievances**.]

Workplace Employee Relations Survey (WERS98) A series of large-scale surveys of UK establishments have been undertaken in the last twenty years, of which WERS98 is the fourth, and most recent. The other surveys, previously called Workplace Industrial Relations Surveys (WIRS), were undertaken in 1980, 1984, and 1990. WERS98 covers 2,191 establishments (with ten or more employees) in Britain. The database is composed of responses from face-to-face structured interviews with 3,073 managers and 950 worker representatives, and 28,323 questionnaire responses from a representative sample of employees from selected establishments. The WERS98 survey and its predecessors are a source of important information about changing patterns and current practices in employment relations in Britain.

Workplace Industrial Relations Survey see Workplace Employee Relations Survey

workplace learning embraces all the formal and non-formal training, instruction, and coaching activities that are conducted, at least partly, at the workplace. [See **learning organization**.]

workplace violence includes threatening and abusive behaviour and physical violence directed at employees either by co-workers or, more usually, by members of the public. It is a major and growing problem within many service industries and particularly within public services, such as health, education, transport, and law enforcement. Public service unions have campaigned actively on the issue and have lobbied for systems of work design and arrangements for client contact that minimize the risk of violence to staff. Increasingly, violence at work is regarded as a **health and safety** issue to be addressed through health and safety policy within employing organizations. [See **workplace bullying**; **sexual harassment**.]

work portfolio A work portfolio means that a person has several part-time jobs at once. This multi-job portfolio is often necessary for the person concerned to maintain a decent standard of living—particularly where he or she has a family to support. Some commentators argue that, with the increase in numerical flexibility, work portfolios will become far more widespread. The concept can also be used in relation to self-employed professionals (for example, a **management consultant**) to describe the sale of business services to a range of clients at any given time.

work sampling is a selection technique whereby the candidate is asked to perform a particular task that will be a dominant part of the job. For example, candidates for a secretarial post might be asked to word-process a letter or input data into a spreadsheet. In other instances candidates might be asked to bring along samples of their work—for example, graphic artists would have a portfolio of previous work. Essentially, work sampling is a test of skills and has high **validity** and **reliability**.

works council A representative body of employees within a single workplace or enterprise which in most European countries has legal status and cannot be avoided or dissolved by employers. Works councils exist and constitute an important part of the **industrial relations system** in Germany, the Netherlands, France, Spain, Sweden, Italy, and other European countries. Moreover, in large, multinational companies operating in the European Union there is a requirement to establish a **European works council** under EU law. Works councils are not mandatory but must be established in companies above a certain size at the request either of the workforce or, in some cases, of trade unions. Works councillors are elected from amongst employees, following procedures laid down in national legislation, and in most systems trade unions are allowed to nominate candidates and may provide support to works councillors once they have been elected. The rights, obligations, and activities of works councils are highly variable but there are common themes. In most countries there is a duty to co-operate with the employer and works councils are generally prohibited in law from organizing **industrial action**. As an alternative, they have the right to legal redress through the courts when they believe their rights have been infringed. In return for accepting a peace obligation, works councils have rights to information, **consultation**, and, in Germany and the Netherlands, **codetermination**. Generally, the rights of works councils are stronger in the areas of employee welfare and personnel management and weaker with regard to business policy, technical change, and company finance. A key issue that arises in systems of industrial relations based on works councils is their relationship to trade unions and **collective bargaining**. In countries like Germany there has been a traditional division of labour between adversarial collective bargaining over pay and hours of work at industry level and more co-operative relations at enterprise level between works councils and single employers. In most large German companies, however, works councils are effectively 'captured' by trade unions, whose candidates are usually elected to works council positions. Moreover, with the **decentralization of bargaining** in Germany works councils have assumed responsibility for bargaining on issues such as **working time** where industry-wide **framework agreements** allow them to do so. Works councils are forbidden in law, however, to contravene the terms of collective contracts negotiated by trade unions. Works councils should not be confused with systems of **worker directors** (rather confusingly also known as codetermination in Germany), though these two systems of worker participation often function alongside one another, with senior works councillors occupying positions on the **supervisory boards** of large European companies.

work specialization is the extent to which jobs in an organization are subdivided into separate tasks. High work specialization, involving each employee undertaking a very narrow range of low-discretion tasks, is particularly associated with **scientific management** and **Fordism**.

work study is the use of industrial engineering to determine the time that should be taken to complete a given work task or set of work tasks. The main purpose of work study is to set incentive targets for employees within a system of **payment by results**. The work-study engineer typically will set the 'standard' time for completing a task, for which employees will receive a 'standard' payment. Performance above the standard rate will result in higher earnings. The tools of work study include observing and measuring work activity and analysing records of worker performance to generate synthetic work standards. Work study is part of the traditional armament of **scientific management**.

work-to-contract see work-to-rule

work-to-rule A form of **industrial action** in which workers perform their contractual duties but no more. Goodwill, informal work practices, and necessary flexibility are withdrawn and the employing organization's bureaucratic rules are turned against it as workers follow instructions and regulations to the letter.

work underload means not having enough work to do. [See **work overload**.]

written particulars are a written statement of the main elements of the **contract of employment** that is required under the Employment Rights Act 1996. The statement must include the name and address of the employer, the job title, the date employment began, the rate of pay and hours of work, holiday and other benefits, the notice period, grievance and disciplinary rules, and details of any collective agreements which directly affect terms and conditions. The UK statutory right to a written statement of employment particulars gives effect to the European Written Particulars Directive 1991.

written reasons for dismissal An employee who is dismissed is entitled in UK law to receive in writing the reasons for **dismissal**, provided that he or she has been continuously employed for one year.

written warning Under a company **disciplinary procedure** an employee can be issued a written warning that his or her behaviour is unacceptable and must improve if further and more serious disciplinary sanctions are to be avoided. It is common to issue an initial and final written warning before proceeding to **dismissal**. The practice of issuing disciplinary warnings in this way embodies the **corrective principle** within the management of workplace discipline.

wrongful dismissal occurs when an employee is dismissed without notice or with insufficient notice. It can arise in two types of circumstance: where the employee is expressly or summarily dismissed by the employer and where the employer repudiates the contract of employment so that the employee is contractually entitled to leave and does so. The usual remedy is to take a case to an **Employment Tribunal** and seek damages for breach of contract. In most cases the damages only cover the notice period, but this is not always the case and in some circumstances additional damages may be awarded. A claim for wrongful dismissal can be taken at the same time as a claim for **unfair dismissal**.

X

X see **theory X and theory Y**

X-efficiency refers to that element of a firm's output that derives not from inputs, such as labour and capital, but from factors internal to the firm, such as its system of incentives, its management structure, and its pattern of work organization.

X-inefficiency is the poor use of resources within a company so as to depress output below the level that could reasonably be expected, given the level of inputs.

Y

Y see **theory X and theory Y**

young workers are those who have left full-time education but who are in their first years of full-time labour market participation. In the UK the term can be used to refer to those between the ages of 16 and 18, 16 and 21, and even 16 and 25, depending on context. Young workers tend to be the focus of three kinds of government policy. First, they are often viewed as a particularly vulnerable group and in many countries there is legislation restricting the hours of work and types of activity in which young workers can become engaged. In the EU the Young Workers Directive provides protection of this kind. Second, and perhaps paradoxically given the first policy, they may be removed from certain kinds of labour market regulation as a stimulus to job creation. The British **National Minimum Wage**, for instance, does not apply to workers below 18 and there is a lower rate for 18–21-year-olds. Third, and also reflecting the relatively high unemployment of young workers, states have initiated job creation and training schemes in order to ease the transition from school to work. The UK government's **Welfare-to-Work** programme provides an example.

youth rate A lower rate of pay for **young workers** engaged in the same work tasks as adults. The traditional justification has been that young workers are less productive than their adult counterparts and therefore it is equitable to pay them less for similar work. This thinking has informed the UK's **National Minimum Wage**, which has a lower rate for young workers, though in fact many companies have failed to apply this rate because they regard it as discriminatory and costly to administer.

Z

Z see **theory Z**

zero-based budgeting is a technique that requires departmental managers to propose and justify their entire budget for the year. It is a planning system that assumes the starting point for each year is no budget, rather than the traditional method of using the previous year's budget as the baseline.

zero-hours contracts are contracts of employment that do not specify the amount of hours to be worked. This allows the employer the flexibility to offer employees work according to the fluctuating demands of the business—such contracts have been particularly popular in the retail sector. Some managers talk of 'flexing up' or 'flexing down' staff in line with demand. An alternative term for these zero-hours arrangements is 'reservism'.

zero-sum A social or economic exchange is zero-sum when one party benefits at the expense of the other. For example, **distributive bargaining** over wages is zero-sum because pay increases for the workforce result in higher labour costs and reduced profits for the employer. [See **positive-sum**.]

Appendix 1
Classification of Key Terms

In the following pages, key terms within the subject area of Human Resource Management have been categorized under thirteen topic areas. The purpose of this listing is to provide a classification that allows readers to identify related key terms, and then explore these in the A–Z listing.

1. Employee resourcing
2. Work organization and working time
3. Employee development
4. Employee reward
5. Employee involvement and participation
6. Conflict and control in employment
7. Discrimination and equality
8. Health, safety, and welfare
9. Management roles, techniques, and strategies
10. Employee representation
11. Collective bargaining
12. National and international regulation of employment
13. Concepts and theories used to study/analyze HRM

1. Employee resourcing

absenteeism
agency labour
application form
assessment centre
biodata
breadwinner
casualization
casual work
collective redundancy
compulsory redundancy
contingent work
contingent workforce
contract of employment
core employees

corporate anorexia
critical incident job analysis
curriculum vitae (CV)
demographics
dilution
early retirement
employability
employee
employment
employment agency
employment at will
employment status
entry shock
e-recruitment
executive search consultants
exit interviews
expatriation
express term
extended internal labour market
external labour market
Eysenck personality inventory (EPI)
fair reasons for dismissal
fixed-term contracts
freelance
garden leave
graphology
halo effect
headcount
hiring hall
host-country national (HCN)
human resource flow
human resource planning (HRP)
human resources (HR)
implied term
induction
internal labour market (ILM)
interview
in-tray exercise

involuntary part-time work
job analysis
JobCentres
job description
job for life
jobseeker
labour market intermediary
labour turnover
last-in-first-out (LIFO)
lay-off
McJob
management succession planning
milkround
Myers–Briggs type indicator
natural wastage
non-accelerating inflation rate of unemployment (NAIRU)
non-standard contract
notice period
outflow
outplacement
panel interview
parent-country national (PCN)
patterned behavioural description interview
personal contract
person specification
poaching
posted worker
precarious employment
private recruitment industry
psychological tests
psychometric test
realistic job preview
recruitment
recruitment advertising
recruitment consultants
recruitment freeze
redundancy

redundancy procedure
re-engagement
reference checks
reference letters
reliability
resignation
retention
retirement
ripple effect
rookie
security of employment
selection
self-employed
sequential interview
situational interview
16PF personality test
skill shortage

socialization
stereotyping
structured/unstructured interview
succession planning
temporary-help agency
temp-to-perm payment
third-country national (TCN)
unemployed
unemployment
validity
voluntary redundancy
waiver clause
womb to tomb
work permit
work sampling
written particulars
young workers

2. Work organization and working time

annual-hours contracts
attended time
atypical work
autonomous workgroup (AWG)
basic working time
body work
clocking on/in
compressed working week
controlled autonomy
cross-functional team
customer-facing jobs
degradation of work
dejobbing
delayering
demarcation
deskilling
disciplined worker thesis

division of labour
economies of scale
economies of scope
electronic cottages
flexibility
flexing
flexitime
functional flexibility
group
groupthink
homeworking
horizontal loading
hot-desking
human capital theory
insourcing
Japanization
Job Characteristics Model (JCM)

job redesign
job-sharing
just-in-time (JIT)
key-time working
lean production
line manager
long-hours culture
lump labour
management by stress
mass production
measured daywork (MDW)
moonlighting
multi-skilling
non-standard work
numerical flexibility
operating time
outworker
overtime
part-time
periphery workers
polyvalent
porosity
presentee
presenteeism
real working time
recession fatigue
responsible autonomy
restrictive practice
role ambiguity
role conflict
seasonal-hours contracts
second job
self-managed team (SMT)
shiftworking
social loafing
soldiering
specialization

Stakhanovite
standardization
statistical process control (SPC)
subcontracting
Sunday work
supervision
sweating
team
team leader
teamworking
telecottaging
teleworking
temp
temporal flexibility
temporary contracts
total productive maintenance (TPM)
total quality control (TQC)
twenty-four-hour society
unity of command
upskilling
vertical loading
virtual team
workforce agreement
working time
Working Time Directive
work intensification
work–life balance
work overload
work portfolio
work specialization
work study
work underload
X-efficiency
X-inefficiency
zero-hours contracts

3. Employee development

accreditation for prior learning (APL)
action learning
appraisal
appraisal portfolio
appraiser
apprenticeship
attendance record
attribution theory
behaviourally anchored rating scales (BARS)
behavioural observation scales (BOS)
behaviourism
body language
burnout
career
career anchors
career block
career ladder
career management
career plateau
career track/path
coaching
competency
computer-assisted instruction (CAI)
continuous learning
continuous professional development (CPD)
counselling
culture shock
deadwood
demotion
demotivation
distance learning
downward occupational mobility
e-learning
employability
employee development
executive coaching
540-degree feedback
grandfather appraisal
human resource development (HRD)
intranet learning
Investors in People (IiP)
jobshift
job stability
job tenure
Kolb's learning cycle
lateral career moves
leader
leadership
learning
Learning and Skills Council (LSC)
learning climate
learning curve
learning organization (LO)
lifelong learning
management development
managerial grid
mentor
mentoring
meta-competencies
Modern Apprenticeship
National Vocational Qualifications (NVQs)
no blame culture
on-line learning
open learning
organizational development (OD)
organizational learning
outward bound courses

peer appraisal
performance management
performance management cycle
personal development plan
portfolio career
probation
promotion
pupillage
redeployment
repatriation
retraining
Scottish National Vocational Qualifications (SNVQs)
self-appraisal
shadowing
sitting-with-Nellie
skill
solid citizen
survivor envy
survivor syndrome
tacit skills
technophile
technosceptic
teleconferencing
360-degree feedback
training
training levy
training needs analysis
trait rating
transferable skills
transformational leadership
University for Industry (UFI)
vicarious learning
vocational education and training (VET)
workplace learning

4. Employee reward

ability to pay
additional voluntary contributions (AVCs)
adoption leave
All-Employee Share Plan
annual leave
appraisal-related pay
at-risk pay
attendance bonus
back pay
base pay
behaviourism
benefits
bonus
broad-banding
cafeteria benefits
cash in hand
company car
company discount
company loan
Company Share Option Plan (CSOP)
comparability
compensation
competence-based pay
component wage job
consolidation
contingent pay
deductions from wages
deferred pay
degeneration
differential
distributive equity
distributive justice

earnings
efficiency wage
effort bargain
employee share ownership
Enterprise Management Incentive (EMI)
equal pay
equal pay audit
equity theory
ERG theory
executive pay
expectancy theory
extrinsic reward
factor
family wage
fat cat
final salary pension scheme
financial flexibility
financial participation
flexible benefits
gain-sharing
gender pay-gap
goal-setting theory
going rate
golden handcuff
golden handshake
golden parachutes
grade
grade drift
guarantee payment
Hay Management Consultants
Herzberg's two-factor theory
hourly rate
hygiene factors
incentive
incomes policy
incremental scale
indexation
indirect pay

instrumentalism
intrinsic reward
itemized pay statement
job analysis
job evaluation (JE)
job family
leapfrogging
leased car
London allowance
low pay
lower earnings limit (LEL)
luncheon voucher (LV)
management by objectives (MbO)
Maslow's hierarchy of needs
maternity pay
merit pay
minimum wage
minimum wage job
money purchase pension scheme
monopoly wage
monopsony wage
motivation
motivator factors
needs theory
New Earnings Survey (NES)
new pay
occupational pension
over-reward inequity
pay-as-you-earn (PAYE)
pay club
pay determination
pay dispersion
pay equity
pay flexibility
pay floor
pay-for-knowledge
paying the person
pay level
payment by results (PBR)

payment system
pay range
Pay Review Body (PRB)
payroll
pay scale
pay spine
pay structure
pension
performance-related pay (PRP)
piece-rate
piecework
pin money
plussage
points rating
premium payment
profit-related pay (PRP)
profit-sharing
quality incentive
rate for the job
red-circling
redundancy pay
reinforcement theory
relocation allowance
remuneration
remuneration committee
reward
reward management
salary
salary matrix
salary progression
salary review

salary survey
sales commission
sales incentive
Save-As-You-Earn (SAYE) share option scheme
self-actualization
self-efficacy
seniority
share option
shift pay
single status
skill-based pay
SMART
spot-rate
stakeholder pension
strategic pay
take-home pay
tax efficiency
team-based pay
time-rate
total remuneration
two-tier wages
unapproved share ownership scheme
under-reward inequity
unsocial-hours payment
variable pay
wage
wage drift
wage-gap
youth rate

5. Employee involvement and participation

adjourning
affective commitment
associate
attitude survey

autonomy at work
Belbin's team roles
beliefs
bounded rationality

Classification of Key Terms 423

brainstorming
captive audience meeting
cascade communication
ceremonies
charisma
company council
computer-mediated brainstorming
consultation
continuance commitment
corporate clan
culture change programmes
culture management
culture mapping
customer care
cycles of control
Delphi technique
direct communication
direct participation
dress code
dual commitment
emotional labour
employee involvement (EI)
employee voice
empowerment
escalator of participation
forming
gatekeeper
greedy institution
groupthink
heroes/heroines
high commitment management (HCM)
high trust
human relations theorists
indirect participation
internal customer
intrapreneur
Involvement and Participation Association (IPA)

job satisfaction
kaizen
legends
lifeboat democracy
mind-set
minimal compliance
myths
networking
nominal group technique
normative commitment
norming
norms
occupational culture
occupational language
organizational commitment
organizational culture
participation
performing
problem-solving group
pseudo-participation
quality circles (QC)
quality enhancement
rituals
shared-screen conferencing
stages of group development
stories
storming
strong culture
suggestion scheme
team briefing
thinking outside the box
Total Quality Management (TQM)
values
video-conferencing
weak culture
works council

6. Conflict and control in employment

absenteeism
action short of a strike
arbitration
autonomy at work
Battle of Seattle
blacking
blackleg
blacklisting
British disease
ca'canny
chiseller
constructive dismissal
consumer boycott
cooling-off period
corrective principle
custom and practice
cybersquatting
demarcation dispute
detriment
disciplinary interview
disciplinary procedure
discipline
dismissal
dismissal with notice
dismissal without notice
dispute
dispute resolution
disputes procedure
Employment Tribunal
exit-voice-loyalty
fair reasons for dismissal
fiddles
fired
flying pickets
frontier of control
gagging clause
general strike

go-slow
grievance procedure
grievances
gross misconduct
harassment
immunity
industrial action
industrial conflict
job regulation
lockout
Luddite
militancy
militant
negotiation of order
open door policy
oral warning
overtime ban
panopticon control
pendulum arbitration
picketing
pin-point strike
poet's day
political strike
rate-buster
reinstatement
restriction of output
restrictive practice
sabotage
sacking
scab
secondary action
selective strike
sexual harassment
sit-down strike
solidarity
stoppage
strike

strike ballot
strike-breaker
strike in detail
strike pay
strike prone
striker days
strike wave
suspension
technophobe
third-party intervention
trade dispute
trial of strength
unconstitutional strike

unfair dismissal
unilateral arbitration
unofficial strike
whistle-blowing
wildcat
Winter of Discontent
working days lost
work to contract
work-to-rule
written reasons for dismissal
written warning
wrongful dismissal

7. Discrimination and equality

affirmative action
ageism
bona fide occupational
 qualification (BFOC)
business ethics
Commission for Racial Equality
 (CRE)
comparable worth
comparator
concrete ceiling
dignity at work policy
direct discrimination
disability
Disability Rights Commission (DRC)
discrimination
dual burden
equality bargaining
Equal Opportunities Commission
 (EOC)
equal opportunity
equal opportunity monitoring

equal opportunity policy
equal opportunity statement
equal opportunity targets
equal pay
equal pay audit
equal value
ethnicity
ethnocentrism
family-friendly policies
gender pay-gap
gender reassignment
genuine occupational qualification
 (GOQ)
glass ceiling
horizontal segregation
mainstreaming
managing diversity (MD)
marriage bar
maternity leave
meritocratic organization
objective justification

old boys' network
Opportunity 2000
paternity leave
positive action
positive discrimination
prejudice
procedural equity
procedural justice
quotas
race
Race for Opportunity
racism
sexism
sex-typing of jobs
sexual harassment
sexual orientation
sword of justice
tokenism
vertical segregation
visible minority

8. Health, safety, and welfare

AIDS policy
alcohol policy
Approved Code of Practice (ACOP)
corporate killing
counselling
domestic-incident leave
duty of care
employee assistance programme (EAP)
environmental health officers
gender reassignment
harassment
hazardous substances
health and safety
Health and Safety Commission (HSC)
Health and Safety Executive (HSE)
health and safety inspector
health and safety regulations
health education
health insurance
job stress
manual handling
medical suspension
noise at work
no-smoking policies
occupational health care
parental leave
rehabilitation
repetitive strain injury (RSI)
Reporting of Injuries, Diseases and Dangerous Occurrences Regulations (RIDDOR)
risk assessment
safety and health
safety committee
safety culture
safety representatives
sick building syndrome (SBS)
sick pay
special leave
Statutory Sick Pay (SSP)
stress management
therapeutic activity
VDU regulations
vibration
workaholic
workplace bullying
workplace violence

9. Management roles, techniques, and strategies

adviser
analyser
balanced scorecard
Baldridge Award
bargained constitutional
benchmarking
boundaryless organization
brownfield site
bureaucracy
bureaucratization
business process re-engineering (BPR)
centralization
champion of change
changemaker
chargehand
Chartered Institute of Personnel and Development (CIPD)
clerk of works model
competitive advantage
competitive strategy
Confederation of British Industry (CBI)
conglomerate
constitutional
consultative
consumer reports
core competencies
corporate governance
cost minimization
decentralization
defender
delayering
derecognition
devolution
Dilbert
direct reports
distinctive competence
diversification
divestment
divisionalization
downsizing
dumb-sizing
employers' association
employment relationship
ethnocentric management
exit costs
exposed sector
extended organization
external consultant
external fit
externalization
false self-employment
firefighting
first-line manager
first-order strategy
five force framework
flat/tall structure
flexibility
foreman
formalization
functional silos
geocentric management
glocalization
greenfield site
handmaiden
hard contract
helicopter vision
high road
high trust
human resource accounting
human resource management (HRM)
human resource strategy

impression management
individualism
in-house agency
innovation strategy
interim manager
internal consultancy
internal consultant
key performance indicator (KPI)
low road
low trust
macho management
McKinsey 7-S framework
management board
management by walking about (MBWA)
Management Charter Initiative (MCI)
management consultant
management guru
management jargon
management prerogative
management style
managerialism
mass customization
mass production
merger
M-form
mission statement
modular organization
moments of truth
multinational corporation (MNC)
multi-unit manager
mushroom management
mutual gains
mutuality
mystery shopper
nepotism
objectives
opportunistic managers

paternalism
personnel manager
personnel officer
personnel record system
PEST analysis
policies
polycentric management
portfolio planning
pragmatic managers
prerogative
proactive managers
procedures
process owner
prospector
reactive managers
reactor
recognition
red tape
re-engineering tsar
regime shopping
regiocentric management
regulator
relayering
rightsizing
satisficing
scientific management
second-order strategy
shared services
small to medium-sized enterprises (SMEs)
social dumping
soft contract
sophisticated consultative
sophisticated human relations
sophisticated modern
sophisticated paternalist
staff manager
standard modern
stick to the knitting

Classification of Key Terms 429

strategic business unit (SBU)
supervisor
supervisory board
surveillance
SWOT analysis
synergy
takeover
third-order strategy
trade association
traditionalist
U-form
union busting

union exclusion
Union of Industrial and Employers' Confederations of Europe (UNICE)
union replacement
union suppression
upsizing
value chain
value sapping
virtual organization
walk the talk
zero-based budgeting

10. Employee representation

beauty contest
block vote
branch
Bridlington principles
business unionism
certification
Certification Officer (CO)
chapel
check-off
closed shop
closed union
collective agreement
combine committee
company union
confederation
convenor
craft union
derecognition
enterprise union
European Trade Union Confederation (ETUC)
European works council (EWC)
facilities agreement

freedom of association
free rider
friendly society
full-time officer
general secretary
general union
goal displacement
guild
harmonization
industrial democracy
industrial union
job territory
joint consultation
Joint Industrial Council (JIC)
joint shop stewards' committee (JSSC)
joint working party (JWP)
lay representative
managers of discontent
multi-unionism
non-union workplace
occupational community
open union

organizer
organizing model
political fund
postal balloting
professional association
professional union
proportionate representation
rank and file
rank-and-filism
recognition
representation gap
reserved seat
right to representation
self-organization
servicing model
shop steward
single-union agreement
staff association

staff forum
status divide
sweetheart deal
syndicalism
time off
Trades Union Congress (TUC)
trade union
unionateness
union bureaucracy
union democracy
union density
union government
union merger
union structure
union voice
women's support group
worker director
workers' co-operative

11. Collective bargaining

activist
all-out strike
articulation
bargaining coverage
bargaining level
bargaining scope
bargaining structure
bargaining unit
codetermination
collective bargaining
common rule
concertation
concession bargaining
contestation
co-ordinated bargaining
cost of living award (COLA)
counter-mobilization

decentralization of bargaining
disclosure of information
distributive bargaining
enterprise bargaining
equality bargaining
framework agreement
incorporation
industrial relations
industry bargaining
integrative bargaining
intraorganizational bargaining
jointism
joint regulation
labour–management partnership
leapfrogging
multi-employer bargaining
New Realism

no-strike clause
occupational union
pattern bargaining
positive-sum
productivity bargaining
productivity coalition
protective practice
redundancy agreement
redundancy consultation
shunto

single-employer bargaining
single-table bargaining
social movement unionism
solidaristic wages policy
Special Negotiating Body
   (SNB)
unilateral regulation
whipsawing
workplace bargaining
zero-sum

12. National and international regulation of employment

Advisory, Conciliation, and
   Arbitration Service (ACAS)
Article 6 agreement
Article 13 agreement
automatically unfair
Central Arbitration Committee
   (CAC)
child labour
Citizens' Advice Bureau
code of practice
codetermination
collective employment law
collective laissez-faire
compulsory competitive tendering
   (CCT)
conciliation
contract compliance
corporate code of conduct
corporate killing
corporatism
Council of Europe
counter-mobilization
data protection
Declaration of Philadelphia

deregulation
derogation
direct effect
directive
Disability Rights Commission
   (DRC)
Donovan Report
economic activity rate
Employment Appeal Tribunal
   (EAT)
employment law
Employment Tribunal
enemy within
Equal Opportunities Commission
   (EOC)
essential service
European Centre of Enterprises
   with Public Participation
   (Centre Européen de
   l'Entreprise—CEEP)
European Convention on Human
   Rights and Fundamental
   Freedoms (ECHR)
European Court of Justice (ECJ)

European Foundation for Quality Management (EFQM)
Eurosclerosis
extension procedure
Fixed-Term Contracts Directive
General Household Survey (GHS)
Ghent system
golden formula
incomes policy
income tax
individual employment law
infringement proceedings
interlocutionary injunction
International Labour Organization (ILO)
international labour standards
juridification
labour code
labour court
Labour Force Survey (LFS)
legal regulation
Low Pay Commission (LPC)
Low Pay Unit (LPU)
market failure
marketization
mediation
model employer
National Action Plan (NAP)
National Insurance Contributions (NICs)
National Minimum Wage (NMW)
negotiation track
Nordic system
objective justification
Office of Manpower Economics (OME)
Part-Time Workers Directive
pay-as-you-earn
Pay Review Body (PRB)
privatization
procedural rule
procedure
producerism
qualified majority voting (QMV)
qualifying period
race to the bottom
reasonableness
regime competition
right-to-work laws
Roman-German system
social charge
Social Charter
social clause
social dialogue
social dimension
Social Europe
social pact
social partner
social partnership
Social Protocol
state of emergency
Statutory Maternity Pay (SMP)
statutory regulation
Statutory Sick Pay (SSP)
subsidiarity
substantive rule
Supported Employment Programme
training levy
transfer of undertaking
Transfer of Undertakings (Protection of Employment) Regulations (TUPE)
transparency
tripartism
tripartite regulation

vicarious liability
wages council
Welfare-to-Work

Whitleyism
Working Time Directive
written particulars

13. Concepts and theories used to study/analyze HRM

adhocracy
architect model
batting average effect
big hat, no cattle
black hole
bleak house
bundles theorists
business case
business ethics
business lifecycle
clerk of works model
comparative industrial relations
contingency theory
contracts manager model
convergence
core competencies
deontology
determinism (1)
determinism (2)
deviant innovation
disciplined worker thesis
divergence
empirical evidence
empiricism
empiricist
employee relations
employment relations
ethnocentrism
European Industrial Relations Observatory (EIRO)
external fit
feminization

flexible firm model
flexible specialization
Fordism
4 Cs
frame of reference
gender-blind
globalization
good employer
Hawthorne effect
Hawthorne studies
high commitment management (HCM)
high performance work practices (HPWP)
HRMism
human capital theory
human relations theorists
human resource management (HRM)
hysterisis
Incomes Data Services (IDS)
individualism–collectivism
industrial relations (IR)
industrial relations system
internal fit
international industrial relations
interorganizational
intraorganizational
iron law of oligarchy
Japanization
knowledge-based companies
labour correspondent

labour power
labour process theory
learning organization
liberal collectivism
low trust
machiavellianism
managerialism
Marxism
mass consumption
mass customization
mass production
mutuality
neo-Fordism
neo-liberalism
normative approach
panopticon control
path dependent
personnel management
perverse effect
pluralism
post-Fordism
post-industrial society
postmodernism
power-distance
principal–agent
productivity
proletariat
psychological contract
Quality of Working Life (QWL)
regulation theory
relational contract
resource-based view
salariat

scientific management
sexual contract
sex work
short-termism
social movement theory
soft HRM
spot contract
stakeholder
strategic human resource management (SHRM)
strategic integration
surplus value
table stakes
theory X and theory Y
theory Z
tiger economies
tough love
transaction costs
transfiguration
trash can activity
Trotskyism
uncertainty avoidance
unfreezing, moving, and refreezing
union renewal
unitarism
utilitarianism
voluntarism
welfare capitalism
worker
worker capitalism
Workplace Employee Relations Survey (WERS98)

Appendix 2
Abbreviations and Acronyms

Note: **Bold type** denotes an entry in the main body of the dictionary.

ABI	Association of British Insurers
ABVV/FGTB	Algemeen Belgisch Vakverbond/Fédération Générale du Travail de Belgique—General Belgian Trade Union Federation
AC	assessment centre
ACAS	**Advisory, Conciliation, and Arbitration Service**
ACOP	**Approved Codes of Practice**
ACTU	Australian Council of Trade Unions
ADST	Approved Deferred Share Trust
AEEU	Amalgamated Engineering and Electrical Union
AEI	average earnings index
AEP	Association of Educational Psychologists
AFA	Association of Flight Attendants
AFL—CIO	American Federation of Labor—Congress of Industrial Organizations
AGR	Association of Graduate Recruiters
AI	annual incentive
AIDS	**acquired immune deficiency syndrome**
AIP	Associação Industrial Portuguesa—Portuguese Association of Industry
AIRC	Australian Industrial Relations Committee
ALGUS	Alliance and Leicester Group Union of Staff
AMED	Association for Management, Education, and Development
AMO	Association of Magisterial Officers
AMS	Arbetsmarknadsstyrelsen—Swedish Labour Market Board
AMT	advanced manufacturing technology
AMU	Associated Metalworkers' Union
ANSA	the independent union for Abbey National Staff (previously the Abbey National Staff Association)

APAC	Audit of Personnel Activities and Costs
APL	**accreditation for prior learning**
APS	Approved Profit Sharing
APT&C	Administrative, Professional, Technical, and Clerical grades in local government
ARD	Acquired Rights Directive 1977
ASLEF	Associated Society of Locomotive Engineers and Firemen
ASQ	*Administrative Science Quarterly*
ATL	Association of Teachers and Lecturers
AUT	Association of University Teachers
AVC	Algemene Vakcentrale—Dutch Federation of Occupational Unions
AVCs	**additional voluntary contributions**
AWG	**autonomous workgroup**
BACM—TEAM	British Association of Colliery Management—Technical, Energy, and Administrative Management
BALPA	British Air Line Pilots' Association
BAM	British Academy of Management
BARS	**behaviourally anchored rating scales**
BDA	British Dietetic Association
BDA	Bundesverband der Deutschen Arbeitgeberverbände—Confederation of German Employers' Associations
BDI	Bundesvereinigung der Deutschen Industrie—Federation of German Industries
BEC	Building Employers' Confederation
BECTU	Broadcasting, Entertainment, Cinematograph, and Theatre Union
BFAWU	Bakers, Food, and Allied Workers' Union
BFOC	**bona fide occupational qualification**
BIFU	Bank, Insurance, and Finance Union
BIM	British Institute of Management
BJIR	*British Journal of Industrial Relations*
BMA	British Medical Association
BMT	behaviour-modelling training
BOS	**behavioural observation scales**
BOS	British Orthoptic Society
BPIF	British Printing Industries' Federation
BPR	**business process re-engineering**
BPS	British Psychological Society

BSU	Britannia Staff Union
BUIRA	British Universities Industrial Relations Association
CAB	**Citizens' Advice Bureau**
CAC	**Central Arbitration Committee**
CAD	computer-aided design
CAI	**computer-assisted instruction**
CAJE	computer-aided job evaluation
CAM	computer-aided manufacture
CAPI	computer-assisted personal interviewing
CAPM	computer-aided production management
CATU	Ceramic and Allied Trades Union
CAW	Canadian Autoworkers
CBI	Confederation of British Industry
CBO	community-based organization
CCC	Criminal Conviction Certificate
CCT	**compulsory competitive tendering**
CDNA	Community and District Nursing Association
CEC	Commission of the European Communities
CEEP	**Centre Européen de l'Entreprise—European Centre for Enterprises with Public Participation**
CEO	chief executive officer
CEOE	Confederación Española de Organizaciones Empresariales—Spanish Confederation of Employers' Organizations
CFDT	Confédération Française Démocratique du Travail—French Democratic Confederation of Labour
CFTC	Confédération Française de Travailleurs Chrétiens—French Confederation of Christian Workers
CGB	Christlicher Gewerkschaftsbund—German Christian Federation of Trade Unions
CGIL	Confederazione Generale Italiana del Lavoro—Italian General Confederation of Labour
CGT	Confédération Générale du Travail—French General Confederation of Labour
CGTP (CGTP-IN)	Confederação Geral dos Trabalhadores Portugueses—General Confederation of Portuguese Workers, usually known as Intersindical
CIA	Chemical Industries Association Limited
CIB	computer-integrated business
CII	Confederation of Irish Industry

CIP	Confederação de Indústria Portuguesa—Confederation of Portuguese Industry
CIPD	**Chartered Institute of Personnel and Development**
CIR	Commission on Industrial Relations
CISL	Confederazione Italiana Sindacati dei Lavoratori—Italian Confederation of Workers' Unions
CIU	Congress of Irish Unions
CLC	Central Labor Council
CLIRS	Company Level Industrial Relations Survey
CNC	computer numerical control
CNPF	Conseil National du Patronat Français—National Council of French Employers
CNT	Confederación Nacional del Trabajo—Spanish National Confederation of Labour
CNV	Christelijk Nationaal Vakverbond—Dutch Confederation of Christian Trade Unions
CO	**Certification Officer**
cobas	comitati di base—Italian rank-and-file committees
COHSE	Confederation of Health Service Employees
COLA	**cost of living adjustment/award**
COMP	Contracted Out Money Purchase Pension
Confindustria	Confederazione Generale dell'Industria Italiana—General Confederation of Italian Industry
COSHH	Control of Substances Hazardous to Health
CPD	**continuing/continuous professional development**
CPI	consumer price index
CRC	Criminal Record Certificate
CRE	**Commission for Racial Equality**
CROTUM	Commissioner for the Rights of Trade Union Members
CSCW	computer-supported co-operative working
CSEU	Confederation of Shipbuilding and Engineering Unions
CSOP	**Company Share Option Plan**
CSP	Chartered Society of Physiotherapy
CSQ	customer service questionnaire
CTUC	Commonwealth Trade Union Council
CUPE	Canadian Union of Public Employees
CV	**curriculum vitae**
CWA	Communication Workers of America
CWU	Communication Workers' Union

CYWU	Community and Youth Workers' Union
DA	Dansk Arbejdsgiverforening—Danish Employers' Federation
DAG	Deutsche Angestelltengewerkschaft—German Salaried Employees' Union
DBA	Diploma of Business Administration
DBB	Deutscher Beamtenbund—German Civil Servants' Federation
DDA	Disability Discrimination Act 1995
DfEE	Department for Education and Employment
DGB	Deutscher Gewerkschaftsbund—German Trade Union Federation
DRC	**Disability Rights Commission**
DTI	Department of Trade and Industry
EAP	**employee assistance programme**
EAT	**Employment Appeal Tribunal**
EC	European Commission
EC	European Community
ECA	Electrical Contractors' Association
ECHR	**European Convention on Human Rights and Fundamental Freedoms**
ECHR	European Court of Human Rights
ECJ	**European Court of Justice**
ECOSOC	EC Economic and Social Committee
EDAP	Employee Development and Assistance Programme
EEC	European Economic Community
EEF	Engineering Employers' Federation
EFQM	**European Foundation for Quality Management**
EFTU	Engineering and Fastener Trade Union
EI	**employee involvement**
EIRO	**European Industrial Relations Observatory**
EIRR	*European Industrial Relations Review*
EIS	Educational Institute of Scotland
EJIR	*European Journal of Industrial Relations*
ELFS	European Labour Force Survey
EMA	Engineers and Managers' Association
EMI	**Enterprise Management Incentive**
EMSPS	Employers' Manpower and Skills Practices Survey
EMU	Economic and Monetary Union
EOC	**Equal Opportunities Commission**
EOP	**equal opportunity policy**

EPA	Employment Protection Act 1975
EPI	Employment Policy Institute
EPI	**Eysenck personality inventory**
EqPA	Equal Pay Act 1970
EQUITY	British Actors' Equity Association
ERA	Employment Relations Act 1999
ERA	Employment Rights Act 1996
ERM	Exchange Rate Mechanism
ESOP	employee share/stock ownership plan
ESRC	Economic and Social Research Council
ET	employment training
ETUC	**European Trade Union Confederation**
ETUCO	European Trade Union College
ETUI	European Trade Union Institute
EU	European Union
EURO-FIET	European Regional Organization of the International Federation of Commercial Employees
EWC	**European works council**
FatW	*Fairness at Work*
FBU	Fire Brigades' Union
FDA	Association of First Division Civil Servants
FDI	foreign direct investment
FEN	Fédération de l'Éducation Nationale—French Federation of National Education
FKTU	Federation of Korean Trade Unions
FMS	flexible manufacturing system
FNV	Federatie Nederlandse Vakbeweging—Confederation of Dutch Trade Unions
FO	Force Ouvrière—Workers' Strength (French trade union)
FSAVCs	free-standing additional voluntary contributions
FSB	Federation of Small Businesses
FT	*Financial Times*
FTC	fixed-term contract
FWR	Fair Wages Resolution
GATT	General Agreement on Tariffs and Trade
GDP	gross domestic product
GFTU	General Federation of Trade Unions
GHS	**General Household Survey**
GNP	gross national product

GNS	growth need strength
GNVQ	General National Vocational Qualifications
GOQ	**genuine occupational qualification**
GPMU	Graphical, Paper, and Media Union
GSA	Guinness Staff Association
HASAWA	Health and Safety at Work Act 1974
HCM	**high commitment management**
HCN	**host-country national**
HCP	high commitment practice
HCSA	Hospital Consultants and Specialists' Association
HIM	high involvement management
HMSO	Her Majesty's Stationery Office
HPWP	**high performance work practices**
HPWS	high performance work system
HR	**human resources**
HRA	Human Rights Act 1998
HRD	**human resource development**
HRM	**human resource management**
HRMJ	*Human Resource Management Journal*
HRP	**human resource planning**
HSC	**Health and Safety Commission**
HSE	**Health and Safety Executive**
HSWA	Health and Safety at Work Act 1974
HVCA	Heating and Ventilating Contractors' Association
IAM	International Association of Machinists
IBEW	International Brotherhood of Electrical Workers
IBT	International Brotherhood of Teamsters
ICFTU	International Confederation of Free Trade Unions
ICT	information and communications technology
ICTU	Irish Congress of Trade Unions
IDS	**Incomes Data Services**
IER	Institute of Employment Rights
IES	Institute of Employment Studies
IFRB	Industrial Fatigue Research Board
IG Metall	Industriegewerkschaft Metall (German metalworkers' union)
IiP	**Investors in People**
IJHRM	*International Journal of Human Resource Management*
ILJ	*Industrial Law Journal*
ILM	**internal labour market**

ILO	**International Labour Organization**
ILRR	*Industrial and Labor Relations Review*
IMF	International Monetary Fund
IMS	Institute for Manpower Studies
IMVP	International Motor Vehicle Program
IoD	Institute of Directors
IPA	**Involvement and Participation Association**
IPD	Institute of Personnel and Development (now CIPD)
IPM	Institute of Personnel Management (now CIPD)
IPMS	Institution of Professionals, Managers, and Specialists
IPPR	Institute for Public Policy Research
IPRP	individual performance-related pay
IR	**industrial relations**
IR	*Industrial Relations*
IRA	Industrial Relations Act 1971
IRJ	*Industrial Relations Journal*
IRLR	*Industrial Relations Law Reports*
IRRR	*Industrial Relations Review and Report*
IRRU	Industrial Relations Research Unit
IRS	Industrial Relations Services
ISCO	International Standard Classification of Occupations
ISTC	Iron and Steel Trades' Confederation
IT	information technology
ITB	Industrial Training Board
ITN	identification of training needs
ITO	Industrial Training Organization
ITUC	Irish Trades Union Congress
ITWF	International Transport Workers' Federation
IUHS	Independent Union of Halifax Staff
IWP	Institute of Work Psychology
JCC	**joint consultative/consultation committee**
JCM	Job Characteristics Model
JDI	Job Description Index
JE	**job evaluation**
JfJ	Justice for Janitors
JIC	**Joint Industrial Council**
JIT	**just-in-time**
JMS	*Journal of Management Studies*
JNC	joint negotiating committee

JPAC	Joint Production and Advisory Committee
JSS	Job Satisfaction Scales
JSSC	**joint shop stewards' committee**
JWP	**joint working party**
KFAT	National Union of Knitwear, Footwear, and Apparel Trades
Kommunal	Svenska Kommunalarbetareförbundet (SKAF)—Swedish Municipal Workers' Union
KPI	**key performance indicator**
KTK	Kommunaltjänstemannakartellen—Swedish Federation of Salaried Local Government Employees
LEC	Local Enterprise Company
LEL	**lower earnings limit**
LFS	**Labour Force Survey**
LGIU	Local Government Information Unit
LGMB	Local Government Management Board
LIFO	**last-in-first-out**
LO	Landsorganisasjonen i Norge—Norwegian Confederation of Trade Unions
LO	Landsorganisationen—Swedish Federation of Trade Unions
LO	Landsorganisationen i Danmark—Danish Federation of Trade Unions
LO	**learning organization**
LPC	**Low Pay Commission**
LPU	**Low Pay Unit**
LRD	Labour Research Department
LSC	**Learning and Skills Council**
LTI	long-term incentive
LV	**luncheon voucher**
MBA	Master of Business Administration
MbO	**management by objectives**
MBWA	**management by walking about**
MCI	**Management Charter Initiative**
MD	managing director
MD	**managing diversity**
MDW	**measured daywork**
MEL	Maximum Exposure Limit
Metall	Svenska Metallindustriarbetareförbundet—Swedish Metalworkers' Union
MLQ	Multifactor Leadership Questionnaire

MMC	Monopolies and Mergers Commission
MNC	**multinational corporation**
MNE	multinational enterprise
MPO	Managerial and Professional Officers
MSC	Manpower Services Commission
MSF	Manufacturing Science Finance
MU	Musicians' Union
NACAB	National Association of Citizens' Advice Bureaux
NACETTS	National Advisory Council for Education and Training Targets
NACO	National Association of Co-operative Officials
NACODS	National Association of Colliery Overmen, Deputies, and Shotfirers
NACRO	National Association for the Care and Resettlement of Offenders
NAFTA	North American Free Trade Agreement
NAHT	National Association of Head Teachers
NAIRU	**non-accelerating inflation rate of unemployment**
NALGO	National and Local Government Officers' Association
NAP	**National Action Plan**
NAPO	National Association of Probation Officers
NASUWT	National Association of Schoolmasters Union of Women Teachers
NATFHE	University & College Lecturers' Union
NBPI	National Board for Prices and Incomes
NCVQ	National Council for Vocational Qualifications
NEC	national executive committee/council
NEDO	National Economic Development Office
NES	**New Earnings Survey**
NFU	National Farmers' Union
NGA	National Graphical Association
NGSU	Nationwide Group Staff Union
NHO	Næringslivets Hovedorganisasjon—Confederation of Norwegian Business and Industry
NHS	National Health Service
NICs	**National Insurance Contributions**
NIESR	National Institute for Economic and Social Research
NJC	national joint committee/council
NLBD	National League of the Blind and Disabled
NLRA	National Labor Relations Act

NLRB	National Labor Relations Board
NMW	**National Minimum Wage**
NOS	National Occupational Standards
NOS	National Organizations Survey
NUDAGO	National Union of Domestic Appliances and General Operatives
NUJ	National Union of Journalists
NULMW	National Union of Lock and Metal Workers
NUM	National Union of Mineworkers
NUMAST	National Union of Marine, Aviation, and Shipping Transport Officers
NUMMI	New United Motor Manufacturing Incorporated
NUPE	National Union of Public Employees
NUT	National Union of Teachers
NVQ	**National Vocational Qualification**
OBES	Greek Federation of Industrial Unions
OCQ	Organizational Commitment Questionnaire
OD	**organizational development**
OECD	Organization for Economic Co-operation and Development
ÖGB	Österreichischer Gewerkschaftsbund—Austrian Trade Union Federation
OJT	on-the-job training
OMD	outdoor management development
OME	**Office of Manpower Economics**
ONS	Office of National Statistics
OPCS	Office for Population and Census Surveys
OPQ	Occupational Personality Questionnaire
OPRA	Occupational Pensions Regulatory Authority
OS&H	occupational safety and health
OSHA	Occupational Safety and Health Administration
OSI	occupational stress indicator
ÖTV	Gewerkschaft Öffentliche Dienste, Transport und Verkehr—German Union for Public Services, Transport, and Communication
P&D	personnel and development
PACT	Producers' Alliance for Cinema and Television
PAT	Professional Association of Teachers
PATCO	Professional Air Traffic Controllers' Organization
PAYE	**pay-as-you-earn**

PBR	**payment by results**
PCN	**parent-country national**
PCS	Public and Commercial Services Union
PCW	Programme for Competitiveness and Work
PESP	Programme for Economic and Social Progress
PEST	**political, economic, social, and technological factors**
PFA	Professional Footballers' Association
PMS	performance management system
PNR	Programme for National Recovery
POA	Prison Officers' Association
PRB	**Pay Review Body**
PRP	**performance-related pay**
PRP	**profit-related pay**
PSI	Policy Studies Institute
PSLB	Personnel Standards Lead Body
PTK	Privattjänstemannakartellen—Swedish Federation of Salaried Employees in Industry and Services
QC	**quality circle**
QCA	Qualifications and Curriculum Authority
QMV	**qualified majority voting**
QWL	**Quality of Working Life**
R&D	research and development
RCM	Royal College of Midwives
RCN	Royal College of Nursing
RENGO	Japanese trade union confederation
RIDDOR	**Reporting of Injuries, Diseases, and Dangerous Occurrences Regulations 1995**
RMT	National Union of Rail, Maritime, and Transport Workers
RPI	Retail Price Index
RRA	Race Relations Act 1976
RSI	**repetitive strain injury**
SA	Schweizerische Arbeitgeberverband—Swiss Employers' Association
SACO	Sveriges Akademikers Centralorganisation—Swedish Confederation of Professional Associations
SAF	Svenska Arbetsgivareföreningen—Swedish Employers' Confederation
SAK	Suomen Ammattiliittojen Keskusjärjestö—Central Organization of Finnish Trade Unions

Abbreviations and Acronyms 447

SAWG	semi-autonomous workgroup
SAYE	**Save-As-You-Earn**
SBS	**sick building syndrome**
SBU	**strategic business unit**
SCP	Society of Chiropodists and Podiatrists
SCT	social cognitive theory
SDA	Sex Discrimination Act 1975
SEA	Single European Act 1986
SEB	Federation of Greek Industries
SEIU	Service Employees' International Union
SEM	Single European Market
SERPS	State Earnings Related Pension Scheme
SGB	Schweizerischer Gewerkschaftsbund—Swiss Trade Union Confederation
SHA	Secondary Heads' Association
SHRM	**strategic human resource management**
SIPTU	Services, Industrial, Professional, and Technical Union
SLT	social learning theory
SMA	Statutory Maternity Allowance
SMART	**specific, measurable, agreed, realistic, timed**
SME	**small to medium-sized enterprise**
SMIC	salaire minimum interprofessionnel de croissance—French national minimum wage
SMP	**Statutory Maternity Pay**
SMT	**self-managed team**
SNB	**Special Negotiating Body**
SNVQ	**Scottish National Vocational Qualifications**
SOCPO	Society of Chief Personnel Officers
SOLT	Society of London Theatres
SOP	standardized operational procedure
SoR	Society of Radiographers
SOSR	some other substantial reason
SPC	**statistical process control**
SPOA	Scottish Prison Officers' Association
SRB	Special Review Body
SRSC	Safety Representatives and Safety Committee
SRSCR	Safety Representatives and Safety Committee Regulations 1997
SSP	**Statutory Sick Pay**
STQ	success through quality

SUPLO	Scottish Union of Power-Loom Overlookers
SWOT	**strengths, weaknesses, opportunities, and threats**
T&G	Transport and General Workers' Union
TCN	**third-country national**
TCO	Tjänstemännens Centralorganisation—Swedish Confederation of Professional Employees
TDLB	Training and Development Lead Body
TEC	Training and Enterprise Council
TGWU	Transport and General Workers' Union
TINALEA	this is not a legally enforceable agreement
TMT	top management team
TNA	**training needs analysis**
TPM	**total productive maintenance**
TQC	**total quality control**
TQM	**Total Quality Management**
TSSA	Transport Salaried Staffs' Association
TT	Teollisuus ja Työnantajat—the Finnish Confederation of Industry and Employers
TUAC	Trade Union Advisory Committee to the Organization for Economic Co-operation and Development
TUC	**Trades Union Congress**
TULRA	Trade Union and Labour Relations Act 1974
TUPE	**Transfer of Undertakings (Protection of Employment) Regulations 1981**
TURER/ TURERA	Trade Union Reform and Employment Rights Act 1993
TUTB	European Trade Union Technical Bureau for Health and Safety
TVEI	Technical and Vocational Education Initiative
UAW	United Automobile Workers
UBBS	Union for Bradford and Bingley Staff
UCAC	Undeb Cenedlaethol Athrawon Cymru—Welsh Language Teachers' Union
UCATT	Union of Construction, Allied Trades, and Technicians
UDM	Union of Democratic Mineworkers
UE	United Electrical, Radio, and Machine Workers
UFCW	United Food and Commercial Workers' Union
UFI	**University for Industry**
UGT	União Geral de Trabalhadores—Portuguese General Workers' Union

UGT	Unión General de Trabajadores—Spanish General Workers' Confederation
UIL	Unione Italiana del Lavoro—Italian Union of Labour
UKASS	UK Association of Suggestion Schemes
UMA	union membership agreement
UNICE	**Union of Industrial and Employers' Confederations of Europe**
UNITE	Union of Needletrades, Industrial, and Textile Employees
USDAW	Union of Shop, Distributive, and Allied Workers
USO	Unión Sindical Obrera—Spanish Workers' Trade Union Confederation
USWA	United Steelworkers of America
UTW	Union of Textile Workers
VBO/FEB	Verbond van Belgische Ondernemingen/Fédération des Entreprises de Belgique—Federation of Belgian Enterprises
VDU	visual display unit
VET	vocational education and training
VF/VI	Verkstadsföreningen (Sveriges Verkstadsindustrier)—Swedish Engineering Employers' Association (Association of Swedish Engineering Industries)
VIE theory	valence, instrumentality, expectancy theory
VNO/NCW	Vereniging van Nederlandse Ondernemers—Nederlands Christelijke Werkgeversverbond—Confederation of Dutch Business and Employers' Associations
WEA	Workers' Educational Association
WERS	**Workplace Employee Relations Survey**
WES	*Work, Employment, and Society*
WFTU	World Federation of Trade Unions
WGGB	Writers' Guild of Great Britain
WHO	World Health Organization
WIRS	Workplace Industrial Relations Survey
WISA	Woolwich Independent Staff Association
WRU	Work Research Unit
WTD	**Working Time Directive**
WTO	World Trade Organization
WWA	Welfare Workers' Association
YOP	Youth Opportunities Programme
YT	youth training
YTS	Youth Training Scheme